P9-CKE-247

iPod® & iTunes®

FOR

DUMMIES®

6TH EDITION

iPod® & iTunes® FOR DUMMIES®
6TH EDITION

by Tony Bove

WILEY

Wiley Publishing, Inc.

iPod® & iTunes® For Dummies, 6th Edition

Published by
Wiley Publishing, Inc.
111 River Street
Hoboken, NJ 07030-5774

www.wiley.com

Copyright © 2008 by Wiley Publishing, Inc., Indianapolis, Indiana

Published by Wiley Publishing, Inc., Indianapolis, Indiana

Published simultaneously in Canada

No part of this publication may be reproduced, stored in a retrieval system or transmitted in any form or by any means, electronic, mechanical, photocopying, recording, scanning or otherwise, except as permitted under Sections 107 or 108 of the 1976 United States Copyright Act, without either the prior written permission of the Publisher, or authorization through payment of the appropriate per-copy fee to the Copyright Clearance Center, 222 Rosewood Drive, Danvers, MA 01923, (978) 750-8400, fax (978) 646-8600. Requests to the Publisher for permission should be addressed to the Legal Department, Wiley Publishing, Inc., 10475 Crosspoint Blvd., Indianapolis, IN 46256, (317) 572-3447, fax (317) 572-4355, or online at http://www.wiley.com/go/permissions.

Trademarks: Wiley, the Wiley Publishing logo, For Dummies, the Dummies Man logo, A Reference for the Rest of Us!, The Dummies Way, Dummies Daily, The Fun and Easy Way, Dummies.com, Making Everything Easier, and related trade dress are trademarks or registered trademarks of John Wiley & Sons, Inc. and/or its affiliates in the United States and other countries, and may not be used without written permission. iPod and iTunes are registered trademarks of Apple, Inc. All other trademarks are the property of their respective owners. Wiley Publishing, Inc., is not associated with any product or vendor mentioned in this book.

LIMIT OF LIABILITY/DISCLAIMER OF WARRANTY: THE PUBLISHER AND THE AUTHOR MAKE NO REPRESENTATIONS OR WARRANTIES WITH RESPECT TO THE ACCURACY OR COMPLETENESS OF THE CONTENTS OF THIS WORK AND SPECIFICALLY DISCLAIM ALL WARRANTIES, INCLUDING WITHOUT LIMITATION WARRANTIES OF FITNESS FOR A PARTICULAR PURPOSE. NO WARRANTY MAY BE CREATED OR EXTENDED BY SALES OR PROMOTIONAL MATERIALS. THE ADVICE AND STRATEGIES CONTAINED HEREIN MAY NOT BE SUITABLE FOR EVERY SITUATION. THIS WORK IS SOLD WITH THE UNDERSTANDING THAT THE PUBLISHER IS NOT ENGAGED IN RENDERING LEGAL, ACCOUNTING, OR OTHER PROFESSIONAL SERVICES. IF PROFESSIONAL ASSISTANCE IS REQUIRED, THE SERVICES OF A COMPETENT PROFESSIONAL PERSON SHOULD BE SOUGHT. NEITHER THE PUBLISHER NOR THE AUTHOR SHALL BE LIABLE FOR DAMAGES ARISING HEREFROM. THE FACT THAT AN ORGANIZATION OR WEBSITE IS REFERRED TO IN THIS WORK AS A CITATION AND/OR A POTENTIAL SOURCE OF FURTHER INFORMATION DOES NOT MEAN THAT THE AUTHOR OR THE PUBLISHER ENDORSES THE INFORMATION THE ORGANIZATION OR WEBSITE MAY PROVIDE OR RECOMMENDATIONS IT MAY MAKE. FURTHER, READERS SHOULD BE AWARE THAT INTERNET WEBSITES LISTED IN THIS WORK MAY HAVE CHANGED OR DISAPPEARED BETWEEN WHEN THIS WORK WAS WRITTEN AND WHEN IT IS READ.

For general information on our other products and services, please contact our Customer Care Department within the U.S. at 800-762-2974, outside the U.S. at 317-572-3993, or fax 317-572-4002.

For technical support, please visit www.wiley.com/techsupport.

Wiley also publishes its books in a variety of electronic formats. Some content that appears in print may not be available in electronic books.

Library of Congress Control Number: 2008935269

ISBN: 978-0-470-39062-7

Manufactured in the United States of America

10 9 8 7 6 5 4 3 2

WILEY

About the Author

Tony Bove has written more than two dozen books on computing, desktop publishing, and multimedia, including iLife '04 All-In-One Desk Reference For Dummies (Wiley), *The* GarageBand Book (Wiley), The Art of Desktop Publishing (Bantam), and a series of books about Macromedia Director, Adobe Illustrator, and PageMaker. Tony also founded Desktop Publishing/ *Publish* magazine and the Inside Report on New Media newsletter, and he wrote the weekly Macintosh column for Computer Currents for a decade, as well as articles for NeXTWORLD, the Chicago Tribune Sunday Technology Section, and NewMedia. Tracing the personal computer revolution back to the 1960s counterculture, Tony produced a CD-ROM interactive documentary in 1996, Haight-Ashbury in the Sixties (featuring music from the Grateful Dead, Janis Joplin, and Jefferson Airplane). He also developed the Rockument music site, www.rockument.com, with commentary and podcasts focused on rock music history. As a founding member of the Flying Other Brothers (www.flyingotherbros.com), which toured professionally and released three commercial CDs (52-Week High, San Francisco Sounds, *and* Estimated Charges), Tony performed with Hall of Fame rock musicians. Tony has also worked as a director of enterprise marketing for leading-edge software companies, and as a communications director and technical publications manager. Tony offers iPod, iPhone, and iTunes tips and techniques on his Web site (www.tonybove.com).

Dedication

This book is dedicated to my siblings and cousins, and my sons and their cousins and children . . . the iPod generation.

Author's Acknowledgments

I want to thank John Paul Bove and Jimi Eric Bove for providing technical expertise and performing valuable testing. I also want to thank Rich Tennant for his wonderful cartoons, and Geoff Coryell and Dennis Cohen for technical expertise. And let me not forget my Wiley editors Paul Levesque and Virginia Sanders for ongoing assistance that made my job so much easier. A book this timely places a considerable burden on a publisherís production team, and I thank the production crew at Wiley for diligence beyond the call of reason.

I owe thanks and a happy hour or three to Carole McLendon at Waterside, my agent. And finally, I have Executive Editor Bob Woerner at Wiley to thank for coming up with the idea for this book and helping me to become a professional dummy — that is, a Dummies author.

Publisher's Acknowledgments

We're proud of this book; please send us your comments through our online registration form located at www.dummies.com/register/.

Some of the people who helped bring this book to market include the following:

Acquisitions, Editorial, and Media Development

Senior Project Editor: Paul Levesque

Executive Editor: Bob Woerner

Copy Editor: Virginia Sanders

Technical Editor: Geoff Coryell, Dennis Cohen

Editorial Manager: Leah Cameron

Media Development Project Manager: Laura Moss-Hollister

Media Development Assistant Project Manager: Jenny Swisher

Media Development Assistant Producers: Angela Denny, Josh Frank, Kit Malone, and Shawn Patrick,

Editorial Assistant: Amanda Foxworth

Sr. Editorial Assistant: Cherie Case

Cartoons: Rich Tennant
(www.the5thwave.com)

Composition Services

Project Coordinator: Patrick Redmond

Layout and Graphics: Stacie Brooks, Carrie A. Cesavice, Reuben W. Davis, Melissa K. Jester, Kathie Rickard, Ronald Terry, Erin Zeltner

Proofreaders: Context Editorial Services, Melissa Bronnenberg, and Amanda Steiner

Indexer: Broccoli Information Management

Special Help: Heidi Unger

Publishing and Editorial for Technology Dummies

Richard Swadley, Vice President and Executive Group Publisher

Andy Cummings, Vice President and Publisher

Mary Bednarek, Executive Acquisitions Director

Mary C. Corder, Editorial Director

Publishing for Consumer Dummies

Diane Graves Steele, Vice President and Publisher

Composition Services

Gerry Fahey, Vice President of Production Services

Debbie Stailey, Director of Composition Services

Contents at a Glance

Table of Contents

Introduction

*Y*ou don't need much imagination to see why so many people are so happy with their iPods and iPhones, or why hundreds of millions of iPods and millions of iPhones have been sold as of this writing. Imagine no longer needing to take CDs or DVDs with you when you travel — your favorite music and videos fit right in your pocket, and you can leave your precious content library at home.

What's more, this library is stored in electronic form (and easily backed up to other media), so it never deteriorates — unlike CDs, DVDs, and other physical media that may last only a few decades.

When I first encountered the iPod, it came very close to fulfilling my dream as a road warrior — in particular, the dream of filling up a car with music as easily as filling it up with fuel. For example, I use a fully loaded iPod with my car using a custom in-vehicle interface adapter that offers an iPod connector; or I use a cassette adapter, or even FM radio transmitter, in a rental car or boat (see Chapter 17). Whether you want to be *On the Road* with Jack Kerouac (in audio book form) or "Drivin' South" with Jimi Hendrix, just fill up your iPod or iPhone and go!

But first, learn about the iTunes application, which is the center of my media universe and the software that manages content on my iPods, my iPhone, and my Apple TV. I bring all my content into iTunes — from CDs, the online iTunes Store, and other sources — and then parcel it out to various iPods, iPhones, and Apple TV for playback. Even though I occasionally use Apple TV rather than my computer running iTunes to enter the iTunes Store to rent or buy movies or buy other content, that content is automatically synchronized with my main iTunes library. All my content is stored in my main iTunes library on my computer, and backed up to another hard drive and to DVD discs. You can manage all these activities with iTunes.

iTunes was originally developed by Jeff Robbin and Bill Kincaid as an MP3 player called SoundJam MP, and released by Casady & Greene in 1999. It was purchased by Apple in 2000 and redesigned and released as iTunes. Since then, Apple has released numerous updates to support new iPods and iPhones and fix bugs, and to add and tweak features such as the online store, gapless playback, support for Apple TV, the Cover Flow cover browser, improved sorting and browsing options, the Genius button, and support for purchasing higher-quality audio tracks without the Digital Rights Management (DRM) copy protection.

Do we need a Genius button, or gapless playback? The Genius button, which generates a playlist of songs from your library that go well with other songs you selected, is software at its best — suggesting new things to help you explore your library. And the gapless playback feature is truly innovative because it helps you bridge the gap between your physical and digital music collections without losing audio quality.

These are just two of many overlooked features of iTunes that can improve your music library and your iPod or iPhone experience. All the important new features are covered in this book. iTunes is getting better all the time, and this book gets you started.

About This Book

The publishers are wise about things like this, and they helped me design *iPod & iTunes For Dummies,* 6th Edition, as a reference. You can easily find the information you need when you need it. I wrote it so that you can read from beginning to end to find out how to use iTunes and your iPod, iPhone, and Apple TV from scratch. But this book is also organized so that you can dive in anywhere and begin reading the info you need to know for each task.

I don't have enough pages to cover every detail of every function of the software, and I intentionally leave out some detail so that you're not befuddled with technospeak when it's not necessary. (Really, engineers can sometimes provide too many obscure choices that no one ever uses; on the other hand, I did need gapless playback.) I write brief but comprehensive descriptions and include lots of cool tips on how to get the best results from using iTunes and your iPod, iPhone, and Apple TV.

At the time I wrote this book, I covered every iPod, iPhone, and Apple TV model available and the latest version of iTunes. Although I did my best to keep up for this print edition, Apple occasionally slips in a new model or new version of iTunes between book editions. If you've bought a new iPod, iPhone, or Apple TV that's not covered in the book, or if your version of iTunes looks a little different, be sure to check out the companion Web site for updates on the latest releases from Apple.

Conventions Used in This Book

Like any book that covers computers and information technology, this book uses certain conventions:

✔ **Choosing from a menu:** When I write "Choose iTunes⇨Preferences in iTunes," you click iTunes on the toolbar and then choose Preferences from the iTunes menu.

With the iPod, when you see "Choose Settings⇨Brightness from the iPod main menu," you highlight Settings in the main menu with the scroll wheel and press the Select button to choose Settings, and then highlight and choose Brightness from the Settings menu. With an iPod touch or iPhone, touch Settings on the Home menu and then touch Brightness.

✔ **Clicking and dragging:** When you see "Drag the song over the name of the playlist," I mean you need to click the song name, hold the mouse button down, and then drag the song with the mouse over to the name of the playlist before lifting your finger off the mouse button.

✔ **Keyboard shortcuts:** When you see ⌘-I, press the ⌘ key on a Mac keyboard along with the appropriate shortcut key. (In this case, press I, which opens the Song Information window in iTunes.) In Windows, the same keyboard shortcut is Ctrl-I (which means press the Ctrl key along with the I key).

✔ **Step lists:** When you come across steps that you need to do in iTunes or on the iPod or iPhone, the action is in bold, and the explanatory part follows. If you know what to do, read the action and skip the explanation. But if you need a little help along the way, check out the explanation.

✔ **Pop-up menus:** I use the term pop-up menu for menus on the Mac that literally pop up from dialogs and windows; in Windows, the same type of menu actually drops down and is called a drop-down menu. I use the term pop-up menu for both.

And Just Who Are You?

You don't need to know anything about music or audio technology to discover how to make the most of your iPod, iPhone, Apple TV, and iTunes. Although a course in music appreciation can't hurt, these devices and iTunes are designed to be useful even for air-guitar players who barely know the difference between downloadable music and System of a Down. You don't need any specialized knowledge to have a lot of fun while building up your digital music library.

However, I do make some honest assumptions about your computer skills:

- ✔ **You know how to use Mac Finder or Windows Explorer.** I assume that you already know how to locate files and folders and that you can copy files and folders from one hard drive to another on the computer of your choice: a Mac or a Windows PC.

- ✔ **You know how to select menus and applications on a Mac or a Windows PC.** I assume that you already know how to choose an option from a menu; how to find the Dock on a Mac to launch a Dock application (or use the Start menu in Windows to launch an application); and how to launch an application directly by double-clicking its icon.

For more information on these topics, see these excellent books, all by Wiley: *Mac OS X Leopard All-in-One Desk Reference For Dummies* (Mark L. Chambers), *Windows Vista All-in-One Desk Reference For Dummies* (Woody Leonhard), or *Windows XP GigaBook For Dummies* (Peter Weverka).

A Quick Peek Ahead

This book is organized into six parts, and each part covers a different aspect of using your iPod or iPhone and iTunes. Here's a quick preview of what you can find in each part.

Part I: Setting Up and Acquiring Media Content

This part gets you started with your iPod or iPhone: powering it up, recharging its battery, using its menus, and connecting it to your computer. You install and set up iTunes on your Mac or your Windows PC. I then show you what you can do with iTunes. To acquire music, you can buy music from the iTunes Store or rip audio CDs. You can also find podcasts, audio books, movies, TV shows, and music videos in the iTunes Store or import them into iTunes from other sources.

Part II: Managing Your Media

This part shows you how to sort the content in your iTunes library by artist, album, duration, date, and other items. You find out how to add and edit iTunes song information, and even fine-tune the sound of each song with a built-in equalizer. You also discover how to arrange songs and albums into iTunes playlists that you can transfer to your iPod, iPhone, or Apple TV and burn onto audio CDs.

Part III: Playing Your iPod or iPhone

I show you how to locate and play all types of content — music, audio books, podcasts, movies, TV shows, and videos — on your iPod, and on the iPod section of your iPhone. I also describe how to use your iPod touch or iPhone to connect wirelessly to the Internet and surf the Web, play YouTube videos, check and send e-mail, and even check your stocks and the weather in your city. With an iPod touch or iPhone you can also add personal contacts and calendar information, display maps and driving directions, and run thousands of applications.

Part IV: The Traveling iPod and iPhone

This part covers how to use your iPod or iPhone on the road with car stereos and portable speakers. You find out all the techniques of an iPod road warrior: setting your alarm clock, keeping time with your stopwatch, changing your display settings, and synchronizing your iPod or iPhone with all your personal information. I also provide initial troubleshooting steps and details about updating and restoring your iPod, iPhone, or Apple TV.

Part V: The Part of Tens

In this book's Part of Tens chapters, I outline common problems and solutions for most iPods, iPhones, and Apple TV models, and I provide tips about the iTunes and iPod equalizer settings. I also list some Web resources for even more information on iPod and iPhone products and services.

Bonus Chapters

This book includes a number of bonus chapters on the companion Web site at www.dummies.com/go/ipod6e. Scattered through those chapters you'll find even more great informational nuggets. Topics include:

- Earlier iPod models and the cables for connecting them to your computer
- Choosing audio encoders and quality settings for importing music
- Preparing photo libraries, videos, address books, and calendars for your iPod or iPhone
- Managing multiple iTunes libraries and copying your library to other hard drives or computers
- Getting wired for playback and using iPod and iPhone accessories

Icons Used in This Book

The icons in this book are important visual cues for information you need.

Remember icons highlight important things you need to remember.

Technical Stuff icons highlight technical details you can skip unless you want to bring out the technical geek in you.

Tip icons highlight tips and techniques that save you time and energy — and maybe even money.

Warning icons save your butt by preventing disasters. Don't bypass a Warning without reading it. This is your only warning!

On the Web icons let you know when a topic is covered further online at www. dummies.com/go/ipod6e, this book's companion Web site.

Part I
Setting Up and Acquiring Media Content

The 5th Wave   By Rich Tennant

"I could tell you more about myself, but I think
the playlist on my iPod says more about me
than mere words can."

In this part . . .

Part I shows you how to do all the essential tasks with your iPod or iPhone and iTunes.

- ✔ Chapter 1 gets you started with your iPod or iPhone. Here you find out how to get the most from your battery, how to use the menus and buttons, and how to connect your iPod or iPhone to your Mac or Windows PC.

- ✔ Chapter 2 describes how to install iTunes, including the iPod and iPhone software, on a Mac or Windows PC.

- ✔ Chapter 3 gets you started with iTunes on a Mac or Windows PC.

- ✔ Chapter 4 covers purchasing content online from the iTunes Store from your computer and purchasing songs directly from your iPod touch or iPhone.

- ✔ Chapter 5 describes how to get music, audio books, videos, and podcasts into your iTunes library.

- ✔ Chapter 6 describes how to play music, audio books, videos, and podcasts in your iTunes library.

- ✔ Chapter 7 shows how you can share content (legally) with other iTunes users on your network, use iTunes libraries with Apple TV over a network, and copy items to other computers (even songs, audio books, and videos you purchased online).

Chapter 1

Firing Up Your iPod and iPhone

The B-52's sing, "Roam if you want to, roam around the world" through your headphones as you take off. The flight is just long enough to watch Tom Cruise in the movie *Vanilla Sky* and the "Mr. Monk and the Airplane" episode from the first season of the *Monk* TV show, as well as catch up on the latest episodes of *The Daily Show with Jon Stewart* and *The Colbert Report*. It's so easy to hold and watch your iPod or iPhone that you don't have to put it away when your flight dinner arrives. You even have time to listen to the *NFL Rants and Raves* podcast to catch up on American football.

As the plane lands, you momentarily forget where you're going, so you read your destination information on your iPod or iPhone without even pausing the podcast and you queue up a playlist of songs to get you through the terminal. If Chicago is your kind of town, you might choose Frank Sinatra. If you're in San Francisco, you might choose anything from Tony Bennett to the Grateful Dead. You have so much content on your iPod or iPhone (that you can select and play so easily) that you probably could land anywhere in the world with appropriate music in your ear and convenient eye candy in your hand.

iPods changed the way people play music on-the-run. Now, they're changing the way people play TV shows and videos. An iPod or iPhone holds so much music that no matter how large your music collection is, you'll seriously consider putting all your music into digital format on your computer, transferring portions of it to an iPod (*and* an iPhone, if you're like me), and playing music from both your computer at home and on your iPod or iPhone on the road. And there's no need to wait for the best episodes of your favorite TV shows to be broadcast, because you can download the shows anytime you want and play them on an iPod classic, iPod nano, iPod touch, or iPhone anywhere you want. Albums, music videos, TV shows, and movies — you might never stop buying CDs and DVDs, but you won't have to buy *all* your content that way. And you'll never again need to replace the content that you already own.

As an iPod or iPhone owner, you're on the cutting edge of entertainment technology. This chapter introduces iPods and iPhones and tells you what to expect when you open the box. I describe how to power up your iPod or iPhone and connect it to your computer, both of which are essential tasks that you need to know how to do — your iPod or iPhone needs power, and it needs audio and video, which it gets from your computer.

Introducing the iPod and iPhone

An iPod is, essentially, a hard drive or flash memory drive as well as a digital music and video player in one device. An iPod is such a thing of beauty and style — and so highly recognizable by now — that all Apple needs to do in an advertisement is show one all by itself. The iPhone is everything an iPod is, plus a cell phone!

The convenience of carrying music on an iPod or iPhone is phenomenal. For example, the 120GB iPod classic can hold around 30,000 songs. That's more than six weeks of nonstop music played around the clock — or about two new songs per day for the next 41 years. And with built-in skip protection in every model, you won't miss a beat as you jog through the park or when your car hits a pothole.

A common misconception is that your iPod or iPhone becomes your music and video library. Actually, your iPod or iPhone is simply another *player* for your content library, which is safely stored on your computer. One considerable benefit of using your computer to organize your content is that you can make perfect-quality copies of music, videos, movies, podcasts, and audio books. You can then copy as much of the content as you want, in a more compressed format, onto your iPod or iPhone and take it on the road. Meanwhile, your perfect copies are stored safely on your computer. Your favorite albums, audio books, TV shows, movies, and podcast episodes can be copied over and over forever, just like the rest of your information, and they never lose their quality. If you save your content in digital format, you'll never see your songs or videos degrade, and you'll never have to buy the content again.

The iPod and iPhone experience includes *iTunes* (for Mac or Windows), which lets you synchronize content with your iPod and other devices, such as the Apple TV player for your home TV and stereo. You also use iTunes to organize your content, make copies, burn CDs, and play disc jockey without discs. I introduce iTunes in Chapter 2.

An iPod is also a *data player,* and in the case of the iPod touch and iPhone, a complete *personal digital assistant* that lets you enter data as well as play it. With an iPod touch or iPhone you can check and send e-mail, visit your favorite Web sites, get maps, obtain driving directions, check the current weather, and even check your stock portfolio, to name a just a few things. You can transfer your calendar and address book to an iPod or iPhone, and you can keep your calendar and address book automatically synchronized to your computer, no matter which device you use to add and edit information (as I describe in Chapter 19).

Comparing iPod Models

Introduced way back in the Stone Age of digital music (2001), the iPod family has grown by six generations as of this writing, with custom versions for the band U2 and offshoots such as the popular iPod nano as well as the tiny iPod shuffle that lets you wear up to 500 songs on your sleeve. Even from the beginning, iPod models were truly innovative for their times. With the MP3 music players of 2001, you could carry about 20 typical songs (or a single live Phish set) with you, but the first iPods could hold more than 1,000 typical songs (or a 50-hour Phish concert).

Earlier-generation iPods

Today's iPod models and iPhone work with iTunes on either Windows computers or Macs, but that wasn't always the case. The first-generation iPods worked only with Macs. In 2002, Apple introduced the second generation — one version for Windows and another for the Mac, using the same design for both. For the third generation (2003), Apple changed the design once again.

Third-, fourth-, fifth-, and sixth-generation iPods @md as well as offshoots, such as iPod mini, iPod nano, and iPod shuffle — work with either Windows or Mac and come in a variety of hard drive or flash memory sizes. By design, you can hold an iPod in your hand while you thumb the *scroll wheel* (my generic term for scroll wheel, scroll pad, touch wheel, or click wheel). The LCD screen on full-size models offers backlighting so that you can see it in the dark. The iPhone and iPod touch let you tap the sensitive display with your finger to select items and functions, and flick with your finger to scroll or move the display.

To find out more about previous generations of iPods, including detailed information about cables and connections, visit this book's companion Web site. For a nifty chart that shows the differences between iPod models, see the Identifying Different iPod Models page on the Apple iPod Web site (`http://support.apple.com/kb/HT1353`).

Sixth-generation iPods

Apple shook the world once again in late 2007 by introducing a new generation of iPod models with attractive enclosures and easier-to-use controls and then revised these models in 2008. (See Figure 1-1.)

Figure 1-1: Sixth-generation iPods include (left to right) the iPod touch, iPod classic, iPod nano, and iPod shuffle.

The sixth-generation iPod models include

- ✔ **The iPod touch:** The new, slimmer iPod touch shares the design characteristics and many of the features of the iPhone and now has a built-in speaker and volume controls on the left side. It offers a touch-sensitive display and Wi-Fi Internet connectivity so that you can purchase music and applications wirelessly from your iPod and surf the Web. (Wi-Fi, which is short for *wi*reless *fi*delity, is a popular connection method for local area networks; you can set up your home or office with Wi-Fi using an inexpensive Wi-Fi hub, such as Apple's AirPort Extreme.)

- ✔ **The iPod classic:** The original iPod design is slimmer and offers higher capacity (120GB) than other current models.

- ✔ **The iPod nano:** The new slimmer iPod nano now comes in a variety of colors and includes the same motion sensor as the iPhone and iPod touch; you can shake the iPod nano to shuffle your songs!

- ✔ **The iPod shuffle:** The tiniest iPod comes in a variety of colors.

You can put audio books, podcasts, and videos on your iPhone, iPod touch, iPod classic, or iPod nano models using iTunes. You can even get some of your favorite TV shows, plus music videos and full-length movies, directly from the iTunes Store.

Like third-, fourth-, and fifth-generation iPods, the sixth generation also uses a dock adapter cable to connect the iPod or iPhone to a computer or power supply. You can also use an Apple or third-party dock with your iPod or iPhone, and use the dock adapter cable to connect the dock to your computer or power supply. The dock keeps your iPod or iPhone in an upright position while connected and lets you connect a home stereo or headphones. This makes the dock convenient as a base station when you're not traveling with your iPod or iPhone, because you can slip it into the dock without connecting cables. You can pick one up at an Apple Store or order one online, or take advantage of third-party dock offerings.

Fingering the iPod touch

The iPod touch, like the iPhone, lets you access the Web over a Wi-Fi Internet connection. You can use the built-in Safari Web browser to interact with Web services and applications, and the YouTube application to play YouTube videos on the Web. The iPod touch offers an on-screen keyboard for typing login entries, passwords, and text of any kind, including numbers and punctuation symbols. The innovative touch-sensitive display provides a rich set of navigation controls and menus controlled by software. You can use the cover browser with your finger to browse your music and video collection. You can even access Apple's iTunes Store and App Store directly from your iPod touch and purchase content, as I describe in Chapter 4.

Less than a third of an inch thick and weighing only 4 ounces, the iPod touch is slightly smaller than an iPhone and offers the same single menu button on the front. Apple offers 8GB, 16GB, and 32GB models as of this writing. The 8GB model holds about 1,750 songs, 10,000 photos, or about 10 hours of video. The 16GB model holds about 3,500 songs, 20,000 photos, or about 20 hours of video. The 32GB model holds about 7,000 songs, 25,000 photos, or about 40 hours of video. All three models use the same battery that offers up to 36 hours of music playback, or 6 hours of video playback.

Twirling the iPod classic

The sixth-generation iPod classic model uses the same click wheel and buttons as the fifth-generation models, combining the scroll wheel with pressure-sensitive buttons underneath the top, bottom, left, and right areas of the circular pad of the wheel. As of this writing, Apple provides a slim, 4.9-ounce 120GB model.

The 120GB model holds about 30,000 songs, 25,000 photos, or about 150 hours of video, and its battery offers up to 36 hours of music playback, or 6 hours of video playback.

Mano a mano with iPod nano

The new iPod nano, pencil thin and only one-and-a-half inches wide by three-and-a-half inches high, weighs only 1.3 ounces but packs a punch: video. This mini marvel (see Figure 1-2) offers a 2-inch color LCD display that crisply displays video, iPod menus, and album artwork. Apple offers an 8GB model that holds about 2,000 songs or up to 8 hours of video (or 7,000 photos), and a 16GB model that holds about 4,000 songs or up to 16 hours of video (or 14,000 photos).

Each model offers a battery that can play up to 24 hours of music — all day and all night — or 4 hours of video.

The iPod nano is the smallest iPod that can serve up videos, podcasts, photos, and musical slide shows as well as your personal calendar and contacts. Unlike the smaller iPod shuffle, iPod nano is a full-featured iPod with loads of accessories tailored specifically for it.

iPod nano uses the same style of click wheel and buttons as the sixth-generation iPod classic models. Like other sixth-generation iPods, iPod nano uses a dock adapter cable to connect to a computer or power supply. A variety of docks for the iPod nano are available from Apple and other companies.

Figure 1-2: iPod nano is the smallest iPod that can display video.

Doing the iPod shuffle

If the regular iPod models aren't small enough to fit into your lifestyle, try iPod shuffle — either the 1GB or 2GB model. The 0.55-ounce iPod shuffle, as shown in Figure 1-3, is shaped like a money clip and is about the same size — 1.07 x 1.62 inches with a depth of 0.41 inch. In several different flashy colors and convenient for clipping to just about anything, the iPod shuffle is fast becoming a fashion statement.

iPod shuffle models have no display, but that's actually a good thing because this design keeps the size and weight down to a minimum, and you don't need a display to play a couple hundred songs in random or sequential order. You can also use your iPod shuffle to hold data files, just like an external flash memory drive.

The 1GB iPod shuffle holds about 240 songs, and the 2GB shuffle holds about 500 songs, assuming an average of 4 minutes per song, using the AAC format at the High Quality setting for adding music (as described in Chapter 5). Remember, iPod shuffle is not meant to store music permanently. Instead, you use it just to play selections from your iTunes library on your computer.

Figure 1-3:
An iPod shuffle weighs less than an ounce and offers skip-free playback.

With skip-free playback, lightweight design, and no need for a display, you can easily use it while skiing, snowboarding, or even skydiving. That's because it uses flash memory rather than a hard drive: You can shake it as hard as you want without a glitch. An iPod shuffle battery offers up to 12 hours of power between charges.

Unlike other iPods, iPod shuffle can't play tunes in the highest-quality Audio Interchange File Format (AIFF) or Apple Lossless formats, which consume a lot of storage space. See Chapter 5 for details on adding music to your iTunes library.

To find out more about audio encoding formats, and about converting music from one format to another, visit this book's companion Web site.

The current iPod shuffle models built to resemble a money clip connect to power and to your computer by using a special mini-dock supplied in the box. The mini-dock includes a cable that links your iPod shuffle to a computer or to an optional power supply and supplies power for recharging its battery. You don't need a separate cable. iPod shuffle charges its battery from your computer, so you don't need the optional power supply. You can also get the optional $29 iPod shuffle External Battery Pack, which provides 20 additional hours of playtime with two AAA batteries.

The Innovative iPhone

When Apple made the first iPhone available on June 29, 2007, lines formed around the block at the Apple stores as eager early adopters bought out all inventories. The iPhone was the first device to incorporate Apple's innovative touch-sensitive display, and formed the basis for the design of the iPod touch. The touch-sensitive display provides a rich set of navigation controls and menus controlled by software — including a full on-screen keyboard for entering text, numbers, and special symbols. (See Figure 1-4.) The iPhone, which includes all the features of an iPod touch, can not only phone home but also monitor all your e-mail and browse the Internet with full page display, using a Wi-Fi network when it senses one.

The iPhone 3G, introduced in July of 2008, is slimmer and more powerful than the original iPhone, adding fast 3G wireless technology, GPS mapping, and the capability for enterprises to push virtual private network (VPN) and Wi-Fi configurations out to all their iPhones in the field. It comes in 8GB ($199) or 16GB ($299) models and incorporates flash memory just like an iPod touch, iPod shuffle or iPod nano. Its 3.5-inch, widescreen, multi-touch display offers 480-x-320–pixel resolution at 160 dots per inch for crisp video pictures, and it can display multiple languages and characters simultaneously.

Figure 1-4:
The iPhone
3G offers a
touch-sensi-
tive display
with rich
menus and
navigational
controls.

The iPhone's built-in rechargeable lithium-ion battery offers up to 10 hours of talk time using 2G or 5 hours using 3G (with 300 hours on standby), up to 6 hours browsing the Internet on Wi-Fi or 5 hours using 3G, and up to 7 hours playing video, and up to 24 hours playing music. It also offers Bluetooth for using wireless headphones and microphones. And the iPhone is no slouch when it comes to acting like an iPod: It can play music, audio books, videos (such as TV shows, music videos, and even feature-length movies), and even podcasts. You can also display photos and slide shows set to music.

Thinking Inside the Box

Don't destroy the elegantly designed box while opening it; you might want to place it prominently in your collection of Technology That Ushered in the 21st Century. Before going any further, check the box and make sure that all the correct parts came with your iPod or iPhone. Keep the box in case, heaven forbid, you need to return the iPod or iPhone to Apple — the box ensures that you can safely return it for a new battery or replacement.

The iPod touch, iPod classic, iPod nano, and iPhone are each supplied with a stereo headset (earphones), a cable to connect your iPod or iPhone or its dock to a computer for power supply, and a dock adapter fitted for that use with Apple's Universal Dock. The iPod shuffle comes with earphones and a special smaller dock to connect to a power adapter or your computer.

The iPhone also comes with a power adapter for recharging the battery. You will want to get a power adapter for your iPod (not in the box but available from the Apple Store) if you want to use AC power, rather than your computer, to supply power to recharge your iPod.

You can get accessories, including Apple's Universal Dock and an AC power adapter, separately, from the Apple Store (physical or online). For example, the iPod AV Connection Kit offers the adapter, AV cables, Apple Remote, and the Universal Dock with adapters for all models.

The accessories don't stop there. Docks of various sizes, shapes, and functions are available from vendors, such as Belkin, Monster, and Griffin. Some docks are combined with home speaker systems. You might also want a carrying case and some other goodies, many of which are described in this book. They're available at the online Apple Store (www.apple.com/store) or the physical Apple Store or other consumer electronics stores.

You also need a few things that don't come with the iPod or iPhone:

✔ **A PC or Mac to run iTunes:** On a PC, iTunes version 8 requires Windows XP (with Service Pack 2), or either 32-bit or 64-bit editions of Windows Vista, running on a 1GHz Intel or AMD processor with a QuickTime-compatible audio card, and a minimum of 512MB of RAM; 1GB is required to play HD-quality videos. You need a DirectX 9.0-compatible video card with 32MB of video RAM (64MB recommended) to watch video, and you need a 2GHz Intel Core Duo or faster processor to play HD-quality videos from the iTunes Store.

With a Mac, iTunes version 8 runs on all versions of Mac OS X (Leopard) and on the older Mac OS X (Tiger) version 10.4.9. (Version 10.4.10 or newer is required for the iPhone.) You need a 500 MHz processor or better (Intel or PowerPC) and at least 512MB of RAM; 1GB of RAM is required to play HD-quality videos. You also need an Intel, Power PC G5 or 1GHz Power PC or faster processor; you need 16MB of video RAM, to watch video, and a 2GHz Intel Core 2 Duo or faster processor to play HD-quality videos from the iTunes Store.

✔ **USB connection:** You need support for USB 2.0 (also called a *high-powered USB*) for iPod classic, iPod nano, iPod shuffle, and fifth-generation iPods. However, you can use FireWire (IEEE 1394) with older iPod models. All current-model Macs and many PCs provide USB 2.0, and many Macs provide FireWire.

For details about using USB or FireWire cables, visit this book's companion Web site.

✔ **Internet connection:** Apple recommends a broadband Internet connection to buy content and stream previews from the iTunes Store, although it is possible with a dialup connection. At a minimum, you need some kind of Internet connection to download iTunes itself.

✔ **CD-R or DVD-R drive:** Without a disc burner, you can't burn your own discs. On a PC, you need a CD-R or DVD-R drive. On a Mac, you need a Combo or Super Drive to burn your own discs.

✔ **iTunes:** Make sure you have the current version of iTunes — use the automatic update feature, which I describe in Chapter 2, to keep your iTunes software up to date. You can also download iTunes for Windows or the Mac from the Apple site (`www.apple.com/itunes/download`); it's free. See Chapter 2 for instructions.

Older iPod models, still available in stores and online, might include versions of iTunes on CD-ROM as old as version 4.5, which is fine because version 4.5 works. (It just doesn't have all the features of the current version.) You can download a newer version at any time to replace it.

✔ **QuickTime:** QuickTime (required for video) comes with iTunes. The iTunes installer for the PC installs the newest version of QuickTime for Windows (version 7.5.5 as of this writing), replacing any older version you might have. Macs have QuickTime preinstalled (version 7.5.5 as of this writing), and Mac OS X automatically updates QuickTime if you use the Software Update feature of System Preferences in the Apple menu.

Powering Up Your iPod and iPhone

All iPod and iPhone models come with essentially the same requirement: power. Fortunately, each iPod and iPhone model also comes with a battery and a way of charging it, either directly from your computer or by using a cable and an AC power adapter that works with voltages in North America and many parts of Europe and Asia. (See Chapter 17 for information about plugging into power in other countries.)

Current models (iPod classic, iPod nano, iPod touch, iPod shuffle, and iPhone) — as well as the older iPod mini and third-, fourth-, and fifth-generation iPods — offer a dock connection. You can connect these models to a dock that offers USB 2.0 connections for power and synchronizing (or FireWire for third-generation models). Docks for full-size iPods can also connect to your home stereo through a line-out connection.

To find out more about previous generations of iPods, including detailed information about power cables and connections, visit this book's companion Web site.

The supplied USB-dock cable has a USB connector on one end and a flat dock connector on the other end to connect to a dock or directly to an iPod or iPhone. You can connect the USB end to either the Apple (or third-party USB) power supply or the computer's USB 2.0 port.

The connection on the iPod or iPhone is the same as the connection on the back of the dock. To connect your iPod or iPhone to your computer, plug the flat connector of the cable into the device or dock and then plug the USB connector on the other end into the USB port on your computer. (Press the same buttons on both sides of the flat connector to disconnect it.)

Most PCs and all current Macs already have USB 2.0, which is all you need to provide power and synchronize an iPod or iPhone with your computer. A USB 2.0 connection to a Mac provides power to an iPod or iPhone and recharges the battery as long as the Mac isn't in sleep mode.

Although you can use a low-powered USB 1.0 or 1.1 connection, it doesn't supply power to most iPod or iPhone models. iPod classic and older models can use FireWire connections to charge their batteries but not for synchronizing with a computer.

The iPod shuffle is supplied with a mini-dock with a USB cable attached and draws power from the USB port on the computer or from a USB power adapter.

An older USB 1.0 or 1.1 port works for synchronizing an iPod nano or iPod classic or some older iPod models but it doesn't provide power. If all you have is an older USB port, you can use it to synchronize an iPod and then use a FireWire cable (available from the Apple Store) to provide power by connecting it to a FireWire–compatible AC power adapter.

Don't use another USB device in a chain and don't use a USB 2.0 hub to connect your iPod or iPhone unless the hub is a powered hub. Note that a USB keyboard typically acts like a USB 1.1 hub, but it's not powered, so it can't provide power to the iPod or iPhone and might slow down performance.

If your iPod shows a display but doesn't respond to your touch, don't panic. Just check the Hold switch on top or bottom of the unit and make sure that it's set to one side so that the orange bar disappears (the normal position). You use the Hold switch for locking the buttons, which prevents accidental activation.

You might notice that an iPod classic or iPod nano display turns iridescent when it gets too hot or too cold, but this effect disappears when its temperature returns to normal. iPods can function in temperatures as cold as 50 degrees and as warm as 95° F (Fahrenheit), but they work best at room temperature (closer to 68° F).

If you leave your iPod or iPhone out in the cold all night, it might have trouble waking from sleep mode, and it might even display a low-battery message. Plug the iPod or iPhone into a power source, wait until it warms up, and try it again. If it still doesn't wake up or respond properly, try resetting the iPod or iPhone as I describe in Chapter 20.

Facing Charges of Battery

You can take a six-hour flight from New York City to California and listen to your iPod the entire time — and with some models, listen all the way back on the return flight — without recharging. All iPod models use the same type of built-in, rechargeable lithium-ion (Li-Ion) battery with the following power specs:

- The first-, second-, and third-generation iPod models offer up to 8 hours of battery power.
- The fourth-generation models and the iPod shuffle offer up to 12 hours.
- The iPod mini offers up to 18 hours.
- The color-display fourth-generation models offer 15 hours of music playing time or 5 hours of photo display with music.
- The fifth-generation iPod models offer between 14 and 20 hours of music playing time, between 3 and 6 hours of video playing time, or between 4 and 6 hours of photo display with music.
- The iPod nano offers 24 hours of music playing time or 4 hours of video or photo display with music.
- The sixth-generation iPod classic 120GB model offers 36 hours of music playback or 6 hours of video or photo display with music.
- The iPod touch offers 36 hours of music playing time or 6 hours of video, browsing the Internet, or displaying photo slideshows with music.

✔ The iPhone models offer up to 24 hours of music playing time, 7 hours of video playing time, or between 4 and 6 hours of photo display with music. They offer up to 10 hours of talk time using 2G or 5 hours using 3G (with 300 hours on standby) and up to 6 hours browsing the Internet on Wi-Fi or 5 hours using 3G.

However, keep in mind that playback battery time varies with the type of encoder you use when you add music to your iTunes library, as I describe in Chapter 5. It also varies depending on how you use your iPod or iPhone controls and settings.

The iPod or iPhone battery recharges automatically when you connect it to a power source. For example, it starts charging immediately when you insert it into a dock that's connected to a power source (or to a computer with a powered USB connection). It takes only four hours to recharge the battery fully for all models, and only three hours for an iPod nano.

Need power when you're on the run? Look for a power outlet in the airport terminal or hotel lobby and plug in your iPod with your AC power adapter — the battery fast-charges to 80 percent capacity in 1.5 hours. After the first hour and a half, the battery receives a trickle charge for the next hour and a half, until fully charged.

Don't fry your iPod or iPhone with some generic power adapter. Use *only* the power adapter from Apple or a certified iPod adapter, such as the power accessories from Belkin, Griffin, Monster, XtremeMac, and other vendors.

A battery icon with a progress bar in the top-right corner of the iPod or iPhone display indicates how much power is left. When you charge the battery, the battery icon displays a lightning bolt. If the icon doesn't animate, the battery is fully charged. You can also use your iPod or iPhone while the battery is charging, or you can disconnect it and use it before the battery is fully charged.

To check the battery status of an iPod shuffle, slide the Off switch to the on position. If the battery status light is

✔ **Green:** The iPod shuffle is fully charged.

✔ **Yellow:** The charge is low.

✔ **Red:** Very little charge is left, and you need to recharge it.

If no light is visible, the iPod shuffle is completely out of power, and you need to recharge it to use it.

Maintaining battery life

The iPod or iPhone built-in, rechargeable battery is, essentially, a life-or-death proposition. After it's dead, it can be replaced, but Apple charges a replacement fee plus shipping. If your warranty is still active, you should have Apple replace it under the warranty program (which may cost nothing except perhaps shipping). Don't try to replace it yourself because opening your iPod or iPhone invalidates the warranty. If your warranty is no longer active, compare Apple's prices and service to others. Some services may charge less than Apple, especially for older iPod models. For what it's worth, I've had very good (if more expensive) experiences with Apple's services.

Fortunately, the battery is easy to maintain. I recommend *calibrating* the battery once soon after you get your iPod or iPhone; that is, run it all the way down (a full discharge) and then charge it all the way up (which takes four hours). Although this doesn't actually change battery performance, it does improve the battery gauge so that the gauge displays a more accurate reading.

Unlike nickel-based batteries that require you to fully discharge and then recharge in order to get a fuller capacity, an iPod or iPhone battery prefers a partial rather than a full discharge, so avoid frequent full discharges after the initial calibration. (Frequent full discharges can lower battery life.)

Lithium-ion batteries typically last three years or more and are vulnerable to high temperatures, which decrease their life spans considerably. Don't leave your iPod or iPhone in a hot place, such as on a sunny car dashboard, for very long.

For a complete description of how Apple's batteries work, see the Apple Lithium-ion Batteries page at `www.apple.com/batteries`.

The bottom of an iPod warms up when it's powered on. The bottom functions as a cooling surface that transfers heat from inside the unit to the cooler air outside. A carrying case acts as an insulator, so be sure to remove the iPod or iPhone from a carrying case before you recharge it.

Keeping an iPod or iPhone in a snug carrying case when charging is tempting but also potentially disastrous. An iPod or iPhone needs to dissipate its heat, and you could damage the unit by overheating it and frying its circuits, rendering it as useful as a paperweight. To get around this problem, you can purchase one of the heat-dissipating carrying cases available in the Apple Store. Alternatively, MARWARE (`www.marware.com`) offers a variety of sporty cases for about $30 to $40. See Chapter 17 for more on accessories.

Even when not in use, your iPod or iPhone drinks the juice. If your iPod or iPhone is inactive for 14 days, you must recharge its battery. Perhaps it gets depressed from being left alone too long; not even an iPhone can phone home by itself.

If your iPod or iPhone isn't responding after a reset, follow the troubleshooting steps in Chapter 20. If these steps don't restore your iPod or iPhone to working condition, you might have a battery problem. Go to the Apple support page for the iPod (www.apple.com/support/ipod) or the iPhone (www.apple.com/support/iphone) and click the Service FAQ link to read frequently asked questions and answers about support. Then click the Battery Service Request Form link on the support page and follow the instructions to request service and return your iPod or iPhone for a replacement.

Saving power

The iPod classic and older models include a hard drive, and whatever causes the hard drive to spin causes a drain on power. iPod nano, iPod shuffle, iPod touch, and iPhone models use a flash drive, which uses less power but still uses power when playing content. The iPod touch and iPhone also use power accessing the Internet, running applications, and in the case of the iPhone, making and receiving calls and using Bluetooth devices. Keeping these activities to a minimum can help you save power. One particularly power-hungry activity is restarting your iPod touch or iPhone from a power-off condition — it is better to use sleep mode to turn it on and off.

If you use the AIFF or WAV formats for adding music to your iTunes library, don't use them with your iPod or iPhone. AIFF and WAV take up way too much space on the iPod or iPhone and fill up the cache too quickly, causing skips when you play them and using too much battery power because the hard drive or flash drive is accessed more often. (See Chapter 5 for details on adding music.)

To find out more about audio encoding formats and about converting music from one format to another, visit this book's companion Web site.

The following are tips on saving power while using your iPod or iPhone:

- ✔ **Pause.** Pause playback when you're not listening. Pausing (stopping) playback is the easiest way to conserve power.

- ✔ **Lock it.** Press the Sleep/Wake button on top of the iPod touch or iPhone to immediately put it to sleep and lock its controls to save battery power. You can set your iPod touch or iPhone to automatically go to sleep by choosing Settings➪General➪Auto-Lock from the Home menu, and choosing 1 Minute, 2 Minutes, 3 Minutes, 4 Minutes, or 5 Minutes (or Never, to prevent automatic sleep).

- ✔ **Back away from the light.** Turn down the brightness on an iPod touch or iPhone by choosing Settings➪Brightness and dragging the brightness slider to the left. Use the backlight sparingly in iPod classic and iPod nano models. Select Backlight Timer from the iPod Settings menu to limit backlighting to a number of seconds, or to Off, in the iPod's Settings menu. (Choose Settings from the main menu.) Don't use the backlight in daylight if you don't need it.

✔ **Stop communicating (with the iPhone or iPod touch).** Turn off Wi-Fi (choose Settings⇨Wi-Fi and touch the On button to turn it off) when not browsing the Internet. Check e-mail less frequently. (See Chapter 16 for details.) On an iPhone, turn off Bluetooth (choose Settings⇨General⇨Bluetooth and touch the On button to turn it off) if you're not using a Bluetooth device.

✔ **Hold it (with the iPod classic or iPod nano).** Flip the Hold switch on iPod classic and iPod nano models to the locked position (with the orange bar showing) to make sure that controls aren't accidentally activated. You don't want your iPod playing music in your pocket and draining the battery when you're not listening.

✔ **You may continue.** Play songs continuously without using the iPod or iPhone controls. Selecting songs and using Previous/Rewind and Next/Fast-Forward require more energy. Not only that, but the hard drive has to spin more often when searching for songs, using more power than during continuous playback.

Always use the latest iPod and iPhone software and update your software when updates come out. Apple constantly tries to improve how your iPod and iPhone models work, and many of these advancements relate to power usage.

Thumbing Through the iPod and iPhone Menus

After you bring content into iTunes and synchronize your iPod or iPhone, you're ready to play. The design of the iPod classic and iPod nano lets you hold the iPod in one hand and perform simple operations by thumb. Even if you're all thumbs when pressing small buttons on tiny devices, you can still thumb your way to iPod heaven.

The iPod touch, like the iPhone, offers a multi-touch interface that lets you tap your way into iPod heaven even faster. With an iPod touch, your fingers do the walking. You can make gestures, such as flicking a finger to scroll a list quickly, sliding your finger to scroll slowly or drag a slider (such as the volume slider), pinching with two fingers to zoom out of a Web page in Safari, or pulling apart with two fingers (also known as *un-pinching*) to zoom in to the page to see it more clearly.

Touching iPod touch and iPhone displays

The first message you see on an iPod touch or iPhone display (besides the time of day and the date) is "Slide to unlock" — slide your finger across this message to unlock your iPod touch or iPhone.

Your content is now immediately available at the touch of a finger. On an iPhone (refer to Figure 1-4),

✔ Use the iPod button in the lower-right corner of the Home menu to play your music and videos.

✔ Use the Photos button in the top row to view your photos.

✔ Use the iTunes button in the fourth row on the left side to access the iTunes store.

On an iPod touch (refer to Figure 1-5),

✔ Use the Music button on the far-left side of the bottom row of the Home menu to play your music.

✔ Use the Videos button next to the Music button in the bottom row to play your videos.

✔ Use the Photos button on the right side of the bottom row to view your photos.

✔ Use the iTunes button on the far-right side of the bottom row to access the iTunes store.

After touching a button on the iPod touch or iPhone display, a new page appears with more selections you can touch. In fact, you can touch every menu or button you see on the display. The iPod touch and iPhone run applications (Safari, Contacts, Calendar, YouTube, and so on), and the multi-touch interface changes for each application.

For example, touch the Music button on an iPod touch to view a list of artists. After touching Music, buttons appear along the bottom of the display that you can touch to view a list of playlists, artists, songs, albums, and more. With a flick of your finger, you can scroll the list and touch selections to view the albums of an artist or the contents of an album or playlist. Touch any song to start playing it, and control buttons appear to control playback: Previous/Rewind, Play/Pause, Next/Fast-Forward, and a volume slider. The physical button on the front of the iPod touch or iPhone returns you to the Home menu.

The iPod touch and iPhone applications respond to gestures you make with your fingers. For example, you make the following gestures to perform the following functions:

✔ Drag with finger: Scroll up or down lists slowly.

✔ Flick: Quickly scroll up or down lists.

✔ Touch and hold: While scrolling, touch and hold to stop the moving list.

✔ Flick from left to right or right to left (swipe): Change screens or application panes on the iPhone or iPod touch (Home menu, Weather, iPod Cover Flow view).

✔ Single tap: Select an item.

✔ Double tap: Zoom in or out with Safari, Maps, and other applications.

✔ Two-finger single tap: Zoom out.

✔ Pinch: Zoom out.

✔ Un-pinch: Zoom in.

Figure 1-5:
Touch buttons on the iPod touch main menu.

The iPod touch menu (refer to Figure 1-5) offers the following selections:

- **Safari:** Use the Safari Web browser.
- **Calendar:** View your calendar.
- **Mail:** Check and send e-mail.
- **Contacts:** View your contacts.
- **YouTube:** List and select videos from YouTube.
- **Stocks:** Check the prices for financial stocks, bonds, and funds.
- **Maps:** View maps and get driving directions.
- **Weather:** View the weather in multiple cities.
- **Clock:** View multiple clocks and use the alarm clock, timer, and stopwatch.
- **Calculator:** A simple calculator for adding, subtracting, multiplying, dividing, and so on.
- **Notes:** Add text notes.
- **Settings:** Adjust settings for Wi-Fi, sounds, brightness, and Safari usage, as well as other settings for the device.
- **App Store:** Go to Apple's online App Store to download other Apple and third-party applications for your iPod touch or iPhone.
- **Music:** Select music playlists, artists, songs, albums, and more (including podcasts, genres, composers, audio books, and compilations). The Music button also offers Cover Flow browsing, as I describe in Chapter 14.
- **Videos:** Select videos by type (movies, music videos, TV shows, or video podcasts).
- **Photos:** Select photos by photo album or select individual photos in the Photo Library.
- **iTunes:** Go to the iTunes online store to purchase content.

Tapping keys on the iPod touch or iPhone on-screen keyboard

One sure feature to amaze your friends is the ability to whip out your iPod touch or iPhone and type notes, contact information, calendar entries, map locations, stock symbols, and even the addresses for Web sites, and make selections for pop-up menus. You can do all this with your iPod touch or iPhone on-screen keyboard, shown in Figure 1-6.

Figure 1-6:
The on-screen keyboard for entering information.

You may want to start with just one finger, and as you get used to it, try also using your thumb. Touch a text entry field, such as the URL field for a Web page in Safari (as I describe in Chapter 15), or a new contact or calendar entry or e-mail message (as I describe in Chapter 16), and the on-screen keyboard appears. Tap the keys, and as you type, each letter appears above your thumb or finger. If you touch the wrong key, slide your finger to the correct key. The letter is not entered until you release your finger from the key.

To type an uppercase letter, touch the Shift key first. To quickly type a period and a space, double-tap the spacebar. To enter numbers, symbols, or punctuation, touch the Number key, and touch the Symbol key for additional symbols.

To enable caps lock, choose Settings⇨General ⇨Keyboards, and touch the Off button next to Enable Caps Lock to turn it on (touch it again to turn it off). You can then double-tap the Shift key to turn on lock caps (uppercase letters). The Shift key turns blue, and all letters you type are uppercase. Tap the Shift key again to turn caps lock off.

To edit text in an entry field, touch and hold to see a magnified view; then drag to position the insertion point. You can then tap keys to insert text, or use the backspace key to remove text.

The intelligent keyboard automatically suggests corrections as you type (some languages only). You don't need to accept the suggested word — just continue typing if you don't, but if you do want to accept it, tap the spacebar, a punctuation mark, or the Return key. To reject the suggested word, finish typing the word as you want it; then tap the *x* to dismiss the suggestion before typing anything else. Each time you reject a suggestion for the same word, your iPod touch or iPhone keeps track and eventually adds your word to its dictionary. The iPod touch and iPhone include dictionaries for English, English (UK), French, French (Canada), German, Japanese, Spanish, Italian, and Dutch. The appropriate dictionary is activated automatically when you select an international keyboard.

The keyboard supports multiple languages, and you can even change the standard U.S. key arrangement of QWERTY to QWERTZ, AZERTY, QZERTY, or Japanese IME — choose Settings⇨General ⇨Keyboards ⇨International Keyboards, and turn on the keyboards you need. You can then switch keyboards while typing information by tapping the globe icon that appears to the right of the ".?123" button when more than one international keyboard is turned on.

Scrolling iPod classic and nano wheels

The circular scroll wheel on iPod classic and iPod nano models makes scrolling through an entire music collection quick and easy. With your finger or thumb, scroll clockwise on the wheel to scroll down a list or counterclockwise to scroll up. As you scroll, options on the menu are highlighted. Use the Select button at the center of the scroll wheel to select whatever is highlighted in the menu display.

In full-size, third-generation models, the touch-sensitive buttons above the scroll wheel perform simple functions when you touch them. (First- and second-generation models aren't touch sensitive, so you need to press them.)

Fifth-generation iPods and sixth-generation iPod classic models, iPod nano, iPod mini, and fourth-generation iPods (including color-display models) provide a click wheel that offers the same functions as the scroll wheel *and* the clickable buttons. The click wheel has pressure-sensitive buttons underneath the top, bottom, left, and right areas of the circular pad of the wheel. These areas tilt as you press them, activating the buttons.

The iPod main menu for sixth-generation iPod classic and iPod nano models offers the following selections:

✔ **Music:** Select music playlists, artists, albums, songs, genres, or composers; or select an audio book. You can also select Cover Flow to browse by cover art, or Search to search for a song or album title or artist (as I describe in Chapter 14).

✔ **Videos:** Select videos by video playlist or by type (movies, music videos, or TV shows).

✔ **Photos:** Select photos by photo album or select all photos in the photo library.

- **Podcasts:** Select podcasts by title and then select podcast episodes.

- **Extras:** View the clock, set clocks for time zones, set alarms and the sleep timer, use the stopwatch, view contacts, view your calendar, view notes, and play games.

- **Settings:** Adjust menu settings, the backlight timer, the clicker, the iPod's EQ, the date and time, and so on.

- **Shuffle Songs:** Play songs from your music library in random order.

- **Now Playing:** This selection appears only when a song is playing — it takes you to the Now Playing display.

The iPod main menu for fifth-generation models offers the following selections:

- **Music:** Select music playlists, artists, albums, songs, podcasts, genres, or composers; or select an audio book.

- **Photos:** Select photos by photo album or select individual photos in the photo library. This selection appears only on color-display models.

- **Videos:** Select videos by playlist or by type (movies, music videos, TV shows, or video podcasts). This selection appears only on fifth-generation models.

- **Extras:** View and set the clock and alarm clock, view contacts, view your calendar, view notes, and play games.

- **Settings:** Adjust display settings, menu settings, the backlight timer, the clicker, and the date and time.

- **Shuffle Songs:** Play songs from your music library in random order.

- **Now Playing:** This selection appears only when a song is playing — it takes you to the Now Playing display.

The iPod main menu for fourth-generation models and iPod nano is the same as fifth-generation models but without the Videos selection.

Activating iPod Playback Functions

The touch buttons on iPod touch and iPhone models do various tasks for playing content items such as songs, audio books, podcasts, and videos:

- **Previous/Rewind:** Tap once to start an item over. Tap twice to skip to the previous item (such as the previous song in an album). Touch and hold to rewind.

- **Play/Pause:** Tap to play the selected item. Tap Play/Pause when an item is playing to pause the playback.

✔ **Next/Fast-Forward:** Tap once to skip to the next item (such as the next song in an album). Touch and hold Next/Fast-Forward to fast-forward play.

✔ **Left-arrow button:** Tap to go back to the previous menu.

✔ **Bullet-list button (playing music):** Tap to view the contents of the album containing the song.

✔ **Menu button on front:** Press once to go back to the main menu.

The buttons on full-size iPod models do various tasks for song, podcast, audio book, and video playback:

✔ **Previous/Rewind:** Press once to start an item over. Press twice to skip to the previous item (such as a song in an album). Press and hold to rewind.

✔ **Menu:** Press once to go back to the previous menu. Each time you press, you go back to a previous menu until you reach the main menu.

✔ **Play/Pause:** Press to play the selected item. Press Play/Pause when the item is playing to pause the playback.

✔ **Next/Fast-Forward:** Press once to skip to the next item. Press and hold Next/Fast-Forward to fast-forward.

The buttons and scroll wheel on full-size iPods can do more complex functions when used in combination:

✔ **Turn on the iPod.** Press any button.

✔ **Turn off the iPod.** Press and hold the Play/Pause button.

✔ **Disable the iPod buttons.** To keep from accidentally pressing the buttons, push the Hold switch to the other side so that an orange bar appears (the locked position). To reactivate the iPod buttons, push the Hold switch back to the other side so that the orange bar disappears (the normal position).

✔ **Reset the iPod.** You can reset the iPod if it gets hung up for some reason. (For example, it might get confused if you press the buttons too quickly.) See Chapter 20 for instructions on how to reset your iPod.

✔ **Change the volume.** While playing a song (the display reads `Now Playing`), adjust the volume with the scroll wheel. Clockwise turns the volume up; counterclockwise turns the volume down. A volume slider appears on the iPod display, indicating the volume level as you scroll.

✔ **Skip to any point in a song, video, audio book or podcast.** While playing an item (the display reads `Now Playing`), press and hold the Select button until the progress bar appears to indicate where you are, and then use the scroll wheel to scroll to any point in the song. Scroll clockwise to move forward and counterclockwise to move backward.

Setting the Language

Wiedergabelisten? Übersicht? (Playlists? Browse?) If your iPod classic or iPod nano is speaking in a foreign tongue, don't panic — you're not in the wrong country. You might have purchased one that's set to a foreign language. More likely, someone set it to a different language accidentally or on purpose (as a practical joke). Fortunately, you can change the setting without having to know the language that it's set to.

To set the language, no matter what language the menu is using, follow these steps:

1. **Press the Menu button repeatedly until pressing it doesn't change the words on the display or until you see the word *iPod* at the top.**

   If pressing the Menu button no longer changes the display, you're at the main menu. With fourth-, fifth-, and sixth-generation models and iPod nano, the menu displays the word *iPod* no matter what language is selected — and you know you're at the main menu.

2. **Choose the sixth option from the top on sixth-generation iPods and the iPod nano, or the fifth option on fifth-generation iPods, or the fourth option on fourth-generation iPods, iPod mini, and the older iPod nano. Choose the third option from the top on third-, second-, and first-generation models. (In English, this is the Settings option.)**

   Scroll clockwise until the item is highlighted, and then press the Select button. The Settings menu appears.

3. **Choose the third option from the bottom of the Settings menu (which, in English, is the Language option).**

   The Language menu appears.

4. **Choose the language that you want to use. (English is at the top of the list.)**

If these steps don't do the trick, the menu may have been customized. Someone could have customized it previously, or perhaps you accidentally pressed buttons that customized the menu.

To learn about advanced iPod and iPhone techniques such as customizing your menus, visit this book's companion Web site.

To get around this problem, you can *reset all the iPod settings* back to the defaults (which is not the same as simply resetting your iPod, as described in Chapter 20). Unfortunately, resetting your iPod's *settings* wipes out any customizations that you've made. You have to redo any repeat/shuffle settings, alarms, backlight timer settings, and so on.

Follow these steps to reset all your settings, no matter what language displays:

1. **Press the Menu button repeatedly until pressing it doesn't change the words on the display or until you see the word _iPod_ at the top.**

   If pressing the Menu button no longer changes the display, you're at the main menu. With fourth-, fifth-, and sixth-generation models and iPod nano, the menu displays the word _iPod_ no matter what language is selected — and you know you're at the main menu.

2. **Choose the sixth option from the top on sixth-generation iPods and the iPod nano, or the fifth option on fifth-generation iPods, or the fourth option on fourth-generation iPods, iPod mini, and the older iPod nano. Choose the third option from the top on third-, second-, and first-generation models. (In English, this is the Settings option.)**

3. **Choose the option at the bottom of the menu (in English, the Reset All Settings option).**

   The Reset All Settings menu appears.

4. **Choose the second menu option (in English, the Reset option; the first menu option is Cancel).**

   The Language menu appears after choosing to reset all settings (because language is one of the settings). The first choice you have to make after resetting all settings is to choose a language, so you're back in business.

5. **Choose the language you want to use. (English is at the top of the list.)**

The language you choose now applies to all the iPod menus. But don't pull that practical joke on someone else!

Chapter 2

Setting Up iTunes and Your iPod and iPhone

An iPod or iPhone without iTunes is like a CD player without CDs. Sure, you can use utility programs from sources other than Apple to put music, podcasts, and videos on an iPod. But iTunes gives you access to the vast online iTunes Store and App Store, and it's excellent for managing content on your computer and synchronizing your content library and personal information with your iPod or iPhone.

This chapter explains how to set up your iPod or iPhone with iTunes on a Mac or for Windows. iTunes includes the iPod and iPhone software, which provides the intelligence inside the device. iTunes is no slouch in the intelligence department either, since it immediately recognizes the type of iPod or iPhone you have and installs the correct software.

Installing iTunes on a Windows PC

Setting up iTunes is a quick and easy process. The most up-to-date version of iTunes as of this writing is version 8. However, software updates occur very rapidly. If you really want the latest version, go directly to the Apple Web site (www.apple.com/itunes) to get it. You can download iTunes for free.

The CD-ROMs supplied with older iPods offer older versions of iTunes and iPod software. You should visit the Apple Web site to download the most up-to-date version of iTunes, which recognizes all iPod and iPhone models.

Before installing iTunes, make sure that you're logged on as a Windows administrator user. Quit all other applications before installing and be sure to disable any antivirus software.

The iTunes installer also installs the newest version of QuickTime, replacing any older version you might have. *QuickTime* is the Apple multimedia development, storage, and playback technology. Although Windows users aren't required to use QuickTime beyond its use by iTunes, QuickTime is a bonus for Windows users because it offers digital video playback.

To install iTunes for Windows, follow these steps:

1. **Download the iTunes installer from the Apple site.**

   Browse the Apple Web site (`www.apple.com/itunes`) and click the Download iTunes Free button, as shown in Figure 2-1. Follow the instructions to download the installer to your hard drive. (A crucial step here is picking a location on your hard drive to save the installer and *remembering* that location.)

2. **Run the iTunes installer.**

   Double-click the `iTunesSetup.exe` file to install iTunes. At the Welcome screen, click Next. Apple's License Agreement appears in the installer window. Feel free to scroll down to read the agreement if that's something you tend to do. You must click the option to accept the agreement, or the installer goes no further.

Figure 2-1: Download the newest version of iTunes from the Internet.

3. **Click the option to accept the terms of the License Agreement and then click Next.**

   After clicking Next (which is active only if you accept), the installer displays the iTunes installation options, as shown in Figure 2-2.

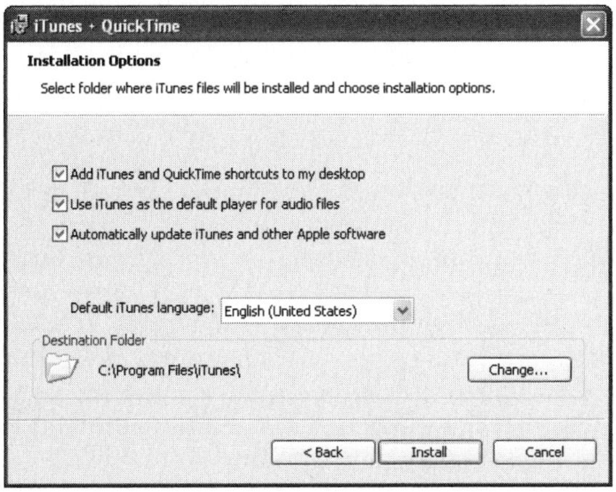

Figure 2-2:
Choose
iTunes
installation
options.

4. **Choose iTunes installation options.**

   You can turn the following options on or off (as shown in Figure 2-2):

   - *Add iTunes and QuickTime shortcuts to my desktop:* You can install shortcuts for your Windows desktop for iTunes and the QuickTime player.

   - *Use iTunes as the default player for audio files:* I suggest turning this option on, allowing iTunes to be the default audio content player for all audio files it recognizes. If you're happy with your audio player, you can deselect this option, leaving your default player setting unaffected.

   - *Automatically update iTunes and other Apple software:* I suggest turning this option on, enabling iTunes to check for its own updates automatically over the Internet. You then have a choice to install the update.

5. **Choose the destination language for iTunes.**

   By default, the installer assumes that you want English (U.S.). If you want to use a different language, select one from the drop-down menu.

6. **Choose the destination folder for iTunes.**

   By default, the installer assumes that you want to store the program in the Program Files folder of your C: drive. If you want to use a different folder, click Change to use Windows Explorer to locate the desired folder.

7. **Click Install to finish.**

   After you click Install, the installer finishes the installation and displays the Complete dialog.

8. **Click Finish.**

   Restarting your Windows PC after installing software is always a good idea.

iTunes and QuickTime are now installed on your PC. To start using iTunes, double-click the iTunes desktop shortcut, or use your Start menu to locate iTunes and launch it.

The first time you launch iTunes, yet another Apple License Agreement appears. You must click Agree to continue (or cancel). After clicking Agree, iTunes displays the iTunes Setup Assistant — to get started, click Next.

The Setup Assistant displays two options: Add MP3 and AAC Files, and Add WMA Files. Select either or both options to copy music files into the iTunes library (without changing their current locations); WMA file copies are converted to AAC (see Chapter 5 for descriptions of these formats). After selecting (or not selecting) these options, click Next to continue.

The Setup Assistant then asks if you want to keep your music folder organized. Choose Yes to keep the iTunes Music Folder organized, and click Next to continue. (For more information on how the iTunes Music Folder works,, see Chapter 12.) The Setup Assistant then displays a screen explaining how album artwork is downloaded (you need an iTunes Store account — see Chapter 4) — click Next to continue. Finally the Setup Assistant asks if you want to go directly to the iTunes Store. Choose Yes to go directly to the store, or No to go directly to your iTunes library, and click Finish.

Installing iTunes on a Mac

As a Mac user, you should already have iTunes installed because all Macs sold since 2003 come preinstalled with iTunes and Mac OS X. The most up-to-date version of iTunes as of this writing is version 8.

The version of iTunes that's provided with the Mac might be the newest version; then again, it might not be. If iTunes displays a dialog with the message that a new version of iTunes is available and asks whether you would like to download it now, click Yes to download the new version. Mac OS X not only downloads iTunes but installs it automatically.

You can set your Mac to automatically download the latest version of iTunes when it becomes available. Choose Preferences from the iTunes menu, click the General tab, and click the Check for Updates Automatically check box at the bottom of the General preferences to turn it on.

You can also set your Mac to check for all system software and Apple applications (including iTunes). Choose System Preferences from the Apple menu, and then choose Software Update from the System Preferences window. Click the Check for Updates check box to turn it on, and select Daily, Weekly, or Monthly from the pop-up menu. You can also click the Check Now button to check for a new version immediately. If one exists, it appears in a window for you to select. Click the check mark to select it and then click Install to download and install it.

If you want to manually install iTunes on your Mac or manually upgrade the version you have, browse the Apple Web site (`www.apple.com/itunes`) to get it. You can download iTunes for free. Follow these steps:

1. **Download the iTunes installer from the Apple site.**

   Browse the Apple Web site (`www.apple.com/itunes`), select the Mac OS X version you have installed on your computer, and then click the Download iTunes button. (Refer to Figure 2-1.) Your browser downloads the iTunes installer disk image file `iTunes.dmg` to your hard drive. After your browser downloads the file, locate the file in the Finder.

2. **Open the iTunes installer drive image.**

   Double-click the `iTunes.dmg` file to mount the iTunes installation drive.

3. **Double-click the `iTunes.mpkg` file to unpack the installer package.**

   The `iTunes.mpkg` file is a package containing all the elements of the iTunes software and the installation program. After double-clicking this package file, a dialog appears that asks whether the installer can run a special program to check your computer.

4. **Click Continue to run the special program.**

   The installer needs to run a program to check your computer and make sure it's capable of running iTunes. After it runs the program, the installer displays the Introduction page.

5. **Click Continue, read the Read Me page, and click Continue again.**

   The installer displays important Read Me information about the latest iTunes features. If you like, click Save to save the page as a document or click Print to print it. Click Continue to continue to the License Agreement.

6. **Read the License Agreement and click Continue to go to the second page. Click the Agree button and then click Continue again.**

   To read the entire agreement, you'll need to scroll down. You must choose to accept the agreement by clicking the Agree button, or the installer goes no further. After clicking Agree, the installer displays the Select a Destination page.

7. **(Optional) Before you click the Agree button, you can click Save to save the license agreement as a document or click Print to print it.**

8. **Select the Mac OS X startup drive as the destination volume and then click Continue.**

   The installer asks for the *destination* volume (hard drive), which must be a Mac OS X startup drive. Any other drive is marked by a red exclamation point, indicating that you can't install the software there. iTunes is installed in the Applications folder on the Mac OS X startup drive, and the iPod Software Updater is installed in the Utilities folder inside the Applications folder.

9. **Click Install (or Upgrade) to proceed with the installation.**

   After clicking Install, Mac OS X asks for the system administrator password. Supply your password, and click OK.

10. **Click Close when the installer finishes.**

You can now launch iTunes by double-clicking the iTunes application or clicking the iTunes icon on the Dock.

The first time you launch iTunes, yet another Apple License Agreement appears. You must click Agree to continue (or cancel). After clicking Agree, iTunes displays the iTunes Setup Assistant — to get started, click Next.

The Setup Assistant displays the option to Add MP3 and AAC Files; select this option to copy music files (without changing their current locations) into the iTunes library (see Chapter 5 for descriptions of these formats). After selecting (or not selecting) this option, click Next to continue.

The Setup Assistant then asks if you want to keep your music folder organized. Choose Yes to keep the iTunes Music Folder organized, and click Next to continue. (For more information on how the iTunes Music Folder works,, see Chapter 12.) The Setup Assistant then displays a screen explaining how album artwork is downloaded (you need an iTunes Store account — see Chapter 4) — click Next to continue. Finally the Setup Assistant asks if you want to go directly to the iTunes Store. Choose Yes to go directly to the store, or No to go directly to your iTunes library, and click Finish.

Setting Up Your iPod or iPhone

When you connect a new iPod or iPhone for the first time, iTunes displays the Register and Set Up screen. Follow these steps to set up your iPod or iPhone:

1. **With iTunes open, connect your iPod or iPhone to the computer with a USB cable (or FireWire cable for an older iPod model).**

   iTunes recognizes your iPod or iPhone and opens the Register and Set Up screen to get you started. If your iPod or iPhone isn't recognized in five minutes, see Chapter 21.

2. Click Continue (or click Register Later to skip the registration process).

iTunes displays the iPod Software License Agreement. You can scroll down to read it if you wish. You must choose to accept the agreement, or the installer goes no further.

3. Click the option to accept the terms at the end of the License Agreement, and then click Continue.

After clicking Continue (which is active only if you accept), iTunes lets you register your iPod or iPhone with Apple online so you can take advantage of Apple support. iTunes displays a screen for entering your Apple ID; a membership ID for the MobileMe (formerly .Mac) service is also valid. If you purchased your iPod or iPhone directly from Apple or have an Apple iTunes Store account, you already have an Apple ID. Enter that ID and password and then click Continue to swiftly move through the registration process — Apple automatically recognizes your purchase. If you bought your iPod or iPhone elsewhere or you don't have an Apple ID or MobileMe ID, select the I Do Not Have an Apple ID radio button and then click Continue to get to the page for entering your iPod or iPhone serial number and your personal information. Fields marked with an asterisk (*) are required, such as your name and e-mail address.

If you don't already have an iTunes Store account, the Setup Assistant is going to ask you to set up such an account right now, as part of your iPod setup. Chapter 4 has all the details on setting up an iTunes Store account..

4. Click Continue to advance through each screen in the registration process, and then click Submit at the end to submit your information.

After clicking Submit, iTunes displays a screen that lets you enter a name for your iPod or iPhone.

5. Give your iPod or iPhone a name, set the automatic options, and then click Done (on a Mac) or Finish (on Windows).

When it comes to setting automatic options, here's the deal:

- *Automatically sync songs and videos, or automatically choose songs:* If you want to copy your entire iTunes music and video library onto your iPod or iPhone, leave the Automatically Sync Songs and Videos option selected. This option creates a mirror image of your music and video library on the iPod or iPhone, including all playlists and audio files. (You can always change this setting later; see Chapter 11.) If your iPod or iPhone can't hold your entire library, iTunes chooses songs for you, based on your ratings and how often you've played them. (To find out how to add ratings, see Chapter 9.) If you want to control which portion of your library to copy to the iPod, deselect this option, and turn to Chapter 11 for synchronization details.

- *Automatically add photos:* Select this option to copy all the photos in your Pictures folder or photo library to your iPod or iPhone. (See Chapter 11 for information about synchronizing photo libraries.) Leave it deselected if you want to transfer photos later.

- *Automatically sync applications:* Select this option (iPod touch and iPhone only) to copy all applications in your iTunes library to your iPod touch or iPhone.

- *For an iPod shuffle:* iTunes displays an option to copy songs randomly. If you leave the Automatically Choose Songs for My iPod option selected, iTunes copies a random selection of songs to your iPod shuffle. You can always choose to fill your iPod shuffle with a different selection by clicking the Autofill button, as I describe in Chapter 11.

After finishing setup, your iPod or iPhone name appears in the iTunes Source pane (the left column) under the Devices subheading, as shown in Figure 2-3.

If you chose the option to automatically synchronize your songs and videos, your iPod or iPhone quickly fills up with music and videos from your iTunes music library. Of course, if you're just starting out, you probably have no tunes in your library. Your next step is to import music from CDs, buy music and videos online, or import music and videos from other sources.

Don't want to add songs or videos now? If you deselect the automatically synchronize option, you can still add songs and videos later, along with podcasts and audiobooks — either manually or automatically, as I describe in Chapter 11.

Figure 2-3:
Your iPod
or iPhone
appears as
a device in
the Source
pane of
iTunes, with
information
about the
device filling
the main
window.

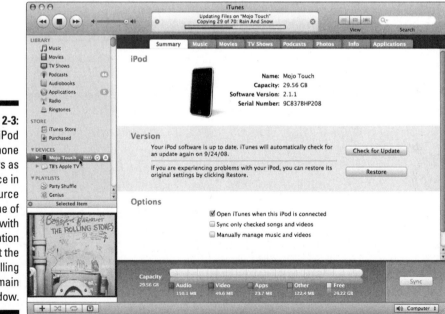

You can leave your iPod or iPhone connected to the computer, using the computer as a source of power — the iPod or iPhone appears in iTunes whenever you start iTunes. However, you might not want to leave it connected. If you have an alternative power source for your iPod or iPhone, disconnect it from iTunes and your computer by *ejecting* it. To eject your iPod or iPhone, click the eject button next to the iPod or iPhone name (refer to Figure 2-4) in the Source pane.

After ejecting the iPod or iPhone, wait for its display to show the main menu or the OK to disconnect message. You can then disconnect the iPod or iPhone from the computer. Don't ever disconnect an iPod or iPhone before ejecting it because such bad behavior might cause it to freeze up and require a reset. (If that happens, see Chapter 20 for instructions.)

Downloading and Installing Software Upgrades

Apple upgrades iTunes and the built-in iPod and iPhone software regularly to add new features and fix bugs.

The best way to stay updated with the latest version is to get in the habit of downloading and installing upgrades over the Internet. Here's how it's done:

1. **Choose Check for Updates from the iTunes Edit menu on a Windows PC, or Software Update from the iTunes menu on a Mac.**

   iTunes automatically accesses the Internet and checks for an update. If a new version is available, a dialog appears, asking whether you want to download it.

   You can set your Mac or Windows PC to automatically check for the latest version of iTunes. Choose Preferences from the iTunes menu on a Mac or from the Edit menu on a PC, click the General tab, and select the Check for Updates Automatically check box to turn on that feature.

2. **If iTunes displays a dialog with the message that a new version of iTunes is available and asks whether you want to download it now, click Yes.**

   - *On a Windows PC:* iTunes launches your Web browser and takes you right to the iTunes download page (refer to Figure 2-1). Follow the instructions in "Installing iTunes on a Windows PC" in this chapter.

   - *On a Mac:* iTunes automatically downloads and installs the upgrade. When you start iTunes after installing an upgrade, you must click the option to agree to Apple's License Agreement. iTunes then starts as usual.

3. **After installing the iTunes upgrade, connect your iPod or iPhone to your computer as you normally do.**

   iTunes automatically detects new iPod or iPhone software if it's available, and replaces the Check for Update button on the iPod or iPhone Summary page (refer to Figure 2-3) with an Update button.

4. **Click the Update button to install the software in your iPod or iPhone.**

   iTunes displays information about the new iPod or iPhone software.

5. **Click Next to continue to the Apple License Agreement, and click the option to agree with it.**

   iTunes automatically installs the update into your iPod or iPhone. After your iPod or iPhone is set up and updated with the newest version of its software, you're ready to find out what iTunes can do for you.

Chapter 3

Getting Started with iTunes

More than half a century ago, jukeboxes were the primary and most convenient way for people to select the music they wanted to hear and share with others, especially newly released music. Juke joints were hopping with the newest hits every night. You could pick any song to play at any time, but you had to insert a coin and pay for each play. Radio eventually supplanted the jukebox as the primary means of releasing new music to the public, and the music was free to hear — but you couldn't choose to play any song you wanted at any time.

Today, using iTunes, you not only have a digital jukebox *and* a radio in your computer, but you also have online access to millions of songs and thousands of podcasts, TV shows, movies, and audio books. Connect your computer to a stereo amplifier in your home (through wires or Apple TV), or connect speakers to your computer, and suddenly your computer is the best jukebox in the neighborhood. Connect your computer to a television, and you have a full multimedia environment in your home, all controlled by iTunes. And after you've organized your content in iTunes, you can put it all on your iPod to carry your jukebox with you.

This chapter gives you an overview of what you can do with iTunes, and you get started in the simplest way possible: using iTunes to play music tracks on a CD. You can use iTunes just like a jukebox, only better — you don't have to pay for each song you play, and you can play some or all of the songs on an album in any order.

The most up-to-date version of iTunes as of this writing is version 8. However, software updates occur very rapidly. If you really want the latest version, go directly to the Apple Web site to get it, as I describe in Chapter 2.

What You Can Do with iTunes

You can purchase songs or entire albums, audio books, TV shows, movies, and other videos from the iTunes Store and download them directly into your iTunes library (as I describe in Chapter 4), or you can copy these items from other sources (including audio CDs) into your iTunes library (as I describe in Chapter 5). You can also subscribe to *podcasts* that transfer audio or audio/video episodes, such as weekly broadcasts, automatically to your iTunes library from the Internet or through the iTunes Store. You can even use iTunes to listen to Web radio stations and add your favorite stations to your music library. After you store the content in your iTunes library, you can play it on your computer and transfer it to iPod, Apple TV, and iPhone models. You can also burn the audio content onto an audio CD or copy audio and video files onto other hard drives or DVD data discs as backups.

Transferring songs from a CD to your computer is referred to as *ripping* a CD (to the chagrin of the music industry old-timers who think that users intend to destroy the discs or steal the songs). Ripping an entire CD's worth of songs is quick and easy, and track information, such as artist name and title, arrives automatically over the Internet for most commercial CDs. (You can add the information yourself for rare CDs, custom-mix CDs, live CDs, and others that are unknown to the database.)

You can also add video files to your iTunes library in a couple of ways: by choosing content from the iTunes Store (such as TV shows, feature-length high-definition movies, music videos, and even free movie trailers) or by downloading standard video files in the MPEG-4 format from other sources on the Internet. You can also create your own videos with a digital camcorder (or cameras built into computers, such as the iSight camera included with MacBooks) and copy them to iTunes.

Although you can't use iTunes to transfer video content from a DVD, you can use other software to convert DVDs to digital video files, and you can transfer video content from older VHS players by using a digital video camcorder. Visit this book's companion Web site for more details.

As if that weren't enough, iTunes gives you the power to organize content into playlists. (You can even set up dynamic, smart playlists that reflect your preferences and listening habits.) It even has a built-in equalizer with preset settings for all kinds of music and listening environments, with the added bonus of being able to customize and save your own personalized settings with each item of content.

The Mac and Windows versions of iTunes are virtually identical, with the exception that dialogs and icons look a bit different between the two operating systems. There are also a few other differences, mostly related to the different operating environments. The Windows version lets you import unprotected Windows Media (WMA) songs; the Mac version, like most Mac applications, can be controlled by AppleScript programs. Nevertheless, as Apple continues to improve iTunes, the company releases upgrades to both versions at the same time, and the versions are free to download.

Opening the iTunes Window

You can run iTunes anytime (with or without an iPod, iPhone, or Apple TV) to build and manage your library of music, audio books, podcasts, Web radio stations, TV shows, and other videos. You don't have to connect your iPod or iPhone until you're ready to transfer content to it (as I describe in Chapter 11).

When you launch iTunes, your library and other sources of content appear. Figure 3-1 shows the iTunes window on a PC running Windows XP, using the List pane in Browse view to browse by artist. To see this view, click the left-most View button (refer to Figure 3-1) and choose View➪Show Browser. (To hide the top Browser, choose View➪Hide Browser.) You can then click the column headings in the List pane to sort your library by artist, album title, or any of the other view options.

The Mac and Windows versions of iTunes look nearly identical and offer the same functions and viewing options, including the *cover browser* (also known as Cover Flow). Figure 3-2 shows the iTunes window on the Mac with the cover browser open, displaying the cover art for albums. Both versions also offer the Genius sidebar (shown in Figure 3-1 but hidden in Figure 3-2) and the Speakers pop-up menu for choosing a speaker system.

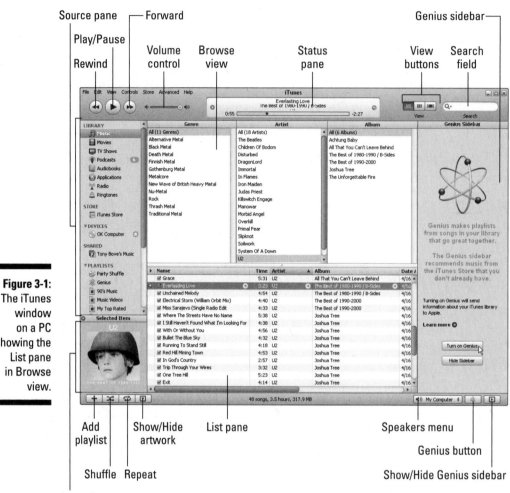

Figure 3-1:
The iTunes window on a PC showing the List pane in Browse view.

iTunes offers a view of your library and your sources for content, as well as controls for organizing, importing, and playing content, as follows:

- **Source pane:** Displays the source of content, handily divided into the following sections:

  - *Library:* Includes your music, movies, TV shows, podcasts, audio books, applications and games, ringtones, and all available radio stations

  - *Store:* Includes the iTunes Store and your Purchased list

- *Devices:* Includes audio CDs (such as the *OK Computer* CD by Radiohead in Figure 3-1), and any iPods, iPhones, and Apple TV devices (such as TB's Apple TV in Figure 3-2) that are connected to your computer

- *Playlists:* Includes Party Shuffle and your playlists

✓ **Cover browser:** Also called Cover Flow, the cover browser lets you flip through your cover art to choose songs. You can use the slider to move swiftly through your library, or you can click to the right or left of the cover in the foreground to move forward or backward in your library.

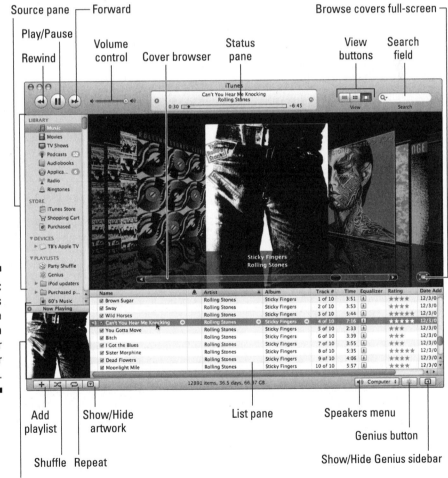

Figure 3-2: The iTunes window on a Mac with the cover browser open.

✔ **List pane:** Depending on the source that's selected in the Source pane under Library, Store, Devices, or Playlists, the List pane (refer to Figure 3-1) displays a list of the content in your library, a list of Web radio stations, the content available in the iTunes Store, the tracks of a music CD, the entire library on your iPod or iPhone, the Party Shuffle list, or any one of your playlists. (Versatile guys, aren't they?)

✔ **Genius sidebar:** The Genius sidebar (refer to Figure 3-1) makes suggestions for what to get from the iTunes Store based on what you've selected. There's no obligation to buy anything, and you can dispense with it if it bothers you — you can open or close the Genius sidebar by clicking the boxed-arrow Show/Hide Genius sidebar button in the lower-right corner of the iTunes window. (See the section, "Using the iTunes Genius Sidebar," later in this chapter.)

✔ **View buttons:** The three buttons in the upper-right corner change your view of the List pane to show items in a list, cover art thumbnail images in a grid, or the cover browser.

✔ **Genius button:** The Genius button at the lower-right corner of the iTunes window to the left of the Show/Hide Genius sidebar button, generates a playlist of songs from your library that go great with the song you selected. The Genius button appears only when selecting music or a playlist — see Chapter 10 for details.

✔ **Status pane:** When a song, audio book, radio station, podcast, or video is playing, you'll see the artist name, piece title (if known), and the elapsed time displayed in this pane.

✔ **Search field:** Type in this field to search your library. You can also use the Search field to peruse a playlist or to look within the iTunes Store.

✔ **Player buttons — Forward/Next, Play/Pause, and Previous/Rewind:** Use these buttons to control the playback of content in iTunes.

✔ **Playlist buttons — Add, Shuffle, Repeat:** Use these buttons to add playlists and shuffle or repeat playback of playlists.

✔ **Speakers pop-up menu:** Use this pop-up menu in the lower-right corner of the iTunes window to select a different speaker system than the computer's speakers (see Chapter 6). This pop-up menu appears only if you choose Preferences (from the iTunes menu on a Mac or the Edit menu in Windows), click the Devices tab, and turn on the Look for Remote Speakers Connected with AirTunes option. If iTunes locates the speakers, the pop-up menu appears.

✔ **Volume control:** You can change the volume level in iTunes by dragging the volume control slider in the upper-left section of the iTunes window to the right to increase the volume, or to the left to decrease it. The maximum volume of the iTunes volume slider is the maximum set for the computer's sound, which you set separately. See Chapter 6 for more about setting volume levels.

✓ **Show/Hide Artwork button:** Use this button to display or hide artwork (either your own or the artwork supplied with purchased songs and videos).

✓ **Show/Hide Genius sidebar:** Use this button to display or hide the Genius sidebar.

✓ **Eject button:** This button appears next to the name of an audio CD or iPod in the Source pane to eject the CD or iPod. Clicking the Eject button, um, ejects a CD or an iPod or iPhone. However, whereas a CD actually pops out of some computers, iPods and iPhones are hard drives, and ejecting them simply removes *(unmounts)* the drives from the system so that you can disconnect them.

If you don't like the width of the Source pane, you can adjust it by dragging the vertical bar between the Source and List panes. You can also adjust the horizontal bar between the song list and browser in the List pane — to show the browser, choose View⇨Show Browser; to hide it, choose View⇨Hide Browser. To resize the iTunes window on a Mac, drag diagonally from the bottom-right corner. In Windows, drag the edges of the window horizontally or vertically.

Playing CD Tracks in iTunes

iTunes needs content. You can get started right away by ripping music from CDs into your library. For more instant gratification, though, you can play music right off the CD without importing it. Maybe you don't want to put the music into your library. Maybe you just want to hear it first, as part of your Play First, Rip Later plan.

To play a CD, insert any music CD — or even a CD-R that someone burned for you — into your computer. After you insert the CD, iTunes displays a dialog that asks whether you want to import the CD into your library right now — you can click Yes to import now, or No to do nothing yet. Click No for now; I show you how to import music in Chapter 5. The iTunes Browse button changes to an Import button in anticipation of ripping the CD at any time.

If you're connected to the Internet, iTunes accesses the Gracenote CDDB for song information while you are answering the import question, so that after you click Yes or No, iTunes presents the track information for each song automatically, as shown in Figure 3-3. (*Gracenote CDDB* is a song database on the Internet that knows the track names of most commercial CDs but not those of homemade mix CDs. You can read about Gracenote CDDB and editing song information in Chapter 9.)

When you play a CD in iTunes, it's just like using a CD player. To play a CD from the first track, click the Play button. (If you clicked somewhere else after inserting the disc, you might have to click the first track to select it before clicking the Play button.) The Play button then turns into a Pause button, and the song plays.

Figure 3-3:
CD track
info appears
after iTunes
consults the
Internet.

	Name	Time	Artist	Album	Genre
1	Sgt. Pepper's Lonely Hearts Club Band	2:02	The Beatles	Sgt. Pepper's Lonely Hearts Club Band	Rock
2	With A Little Help From My Friends	2:44	The Beatles	Sgt. Pepper's Lonely Hearts Club Band	Rock
3	Lucy In The Sky With Diamonds	3:28	The Beatles	Sgt. Pepper's Lonely Hearts Club Band	Rock
4	Getting Better	2:48	The Beatles	Sgt. Pepper's Lonely Hearts Club Band	Rock
5	Fixing A Hole	2:37	The Beatles	Sgt. Pepper's Lonely Hearts Club Band	Rock
6	She's Leaving Home	3:35	The Beatles	Sgt. Pepper's Lonely Hearts Club Band	Rock
7	Being For The Benefit Of Mr. Kite!	2:37	The Beatles	Sgt. Pepper's Lonely Hearts Club Band	Rock
8	Within You Without You	5:05	The Beatles	Sgt. Pepper's Lonely Hearts Club Band	Rock
9	When I'm Sixty-Four	2:38	The Beatles	Sgt. Pepper's Lonely Hearts Club Band	Rock
10	Lovely Rita	2:42	The Beatles	Sgt. Pepper's Lonely Hearts Club Band	Rock
11	Good Morning Good Morning	2:41	The Beatles	Sgt. Pepper's Lonely Hearts Club Band	Rock
12	Sgt. Pepper's Lonely Hearts Club Band (Reprise)	1:19	The Beatles	Sgt. Pepper's Lonely Hearts Club Band	Rock
13	A Day In The Life	5:34	The Beatles	Sgt. Pepper's Lonely Hearts Club Band	Rock

13 songs, 39.7 minutes, 402.2 MB

When the song finishes, iTunes continues playing the songs in the list in sequence until you click the Pause button (which then toggles back into the Play button) or until the song list ends. You can skip to the next or previous song by using the arrow keys on your keyboard or by clicking the Forward button or the Back button (next to the Play button). You can also double-click another song in the list to start playing it.

You can press the spacebar to perform the same function as clicking the Play button; pressing it again is just like clicking the Pause button.

The Status pane above the list of songs tells you the name of the artist and the song title as well as the elapsed time of the track. When you click the artist name, the artist name is replaced by the album name. The time on the left of the slider is the elapsed time; the time on the right is the duration of the song. When you click the duration, it changes to the remaining time; click it again to return to the song's duration.

Eject a CD by clicking the Eject button or by choosing Controls⇨Eject Disc. Another way to eject the CD is to click the Eject icon next to the CD name in the Source pane. You can also right-click the CD name and choose Eject from the contextual menu that appears.

Rearranging and repeating tracks

You can rearrange the order of the tracks to automatically play them in any sequence you want, similar to programming a CD player. When you click the up arrow at the top of the first column in the List pane (refer to Figure 3-3), it changes to a down arrow, and the tracks appear in reverse order.

To change the order of tracks that you're playing in sequence, just click and hold the track number in the leftmost column for the song, and then drag it up or down in the list. You can set up the tracks to play in a completely different sequence.

Skipping tracks

To skip tracks so that they don't play in sequence, deselect the check box next to the song names. iTunes skips deselected songs when you play the entire sequence.

To remove all check marks from a list, press ⌘ on a Mac or Ctrl in Windows while clicking a check mark. Select an empty check box while pressing ⌘ or Ctrl to add check marks to the entire list.

Repeating a song list

You can repeat an entire song list by clicking the Repeat button, which you can find below the Source pane on the left side of the iTunes window (or by choosing Controls⇨Repeat All). When it's selected, the Repeat button shows blue highlighting. Click the Repeat button again to repeat the current song (or choose Controls⇨Repeat One). The button changes to include a blue-highlighted numeral 1. Click it once more to return to normal playback (or choose Controls⇨Repeat Off).

The Shuffle button, located to the left of the Repeat button, plays the songs in the list in random order, which can be fun. You can then press the arrow keys on your keyboard or click the Back and Forward buttons to jump around in random order.

Displaying visuals

The visual effects in iTunes can turn your iTunes window into a light show that's synchronized to the music in your library. You can watch a cool display of eye candy while the music plays — or leave it on like a lava lamp.

Choose View⇨Show Visualizer to display visual effects (or press ⌘-T on a Mac or Ctrl-T in Windows). An animation appears in the iTunes window and synchronizes with the music. Choose View⇨Hide Visualizer (or press ⌘-T on a Mac or Ctrl-T in Windows) to turn off the visual effects.

iTunes offers two visualizers: The iTunes Visualizer has a simulated 3D look that includes spheres, ribbons, and lights that pulsate to the beat and tempo of the song you're playing. The Classic Visualizer, with a 2D look, has been part of the application since the beginning. To switch from the iTunes Visualizer to the Classic Visualizer, choose View⇨Visualizer⇨Classic Visualizer. To switch back to the new one, choose View⇨Visualizer⇨iTunes Visualizer.

You can tweak the Classic Visualizer a bit by changing the Visualizer options. Choose View➪Visualizer➪Classic Visualizer, and then choose View➪Visualizer➪Options to open the Visualizer Options dialog, as shown in Figure 3-4.

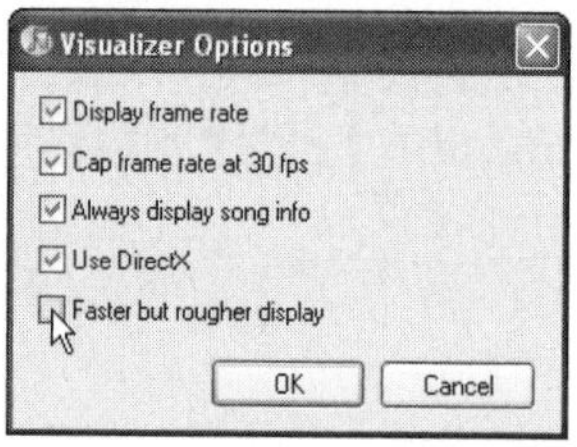

Figure 3-4:
Set options
for visual
effects.

The Visualizer Options dialog offers the following options that affect the animation (but not the performance of iTunes when it's playing music):

- ✔ **Display Frame Rate:** Choosing this option displays the frame rate of the animation along with the animation, so that you can tell whether it is going faster or slower than normal video (30 fps).

- ✔ **Cap Frame Rate at 30 fps:** Choosing this option keeps the frame rate at 30 fps (frames per second) or lower, which is roughly the speed of video, to keep animation from moving too fast.

- ✔ **Always Display Song Info:** Choosing this option displays the song name, artist, and album for the song currently playing, along with the animation.

- ✔ **Use DirectX (Windows only) or Use OpenGL (Mac only):** You can choose to use DirectX on a Windows PC or OpenGL on a Mac to display very cool animation with faster performance. These are the most widely used standards for three-dimensional graphics programming.

- ✔ **Faster but Rougher Display:** When you use this option, animation plays faster but with rougher graphics. Select this option if your animation plays too slowly.

Choosing View➪Full Screen (or pressing ⌘-F on a Mac or Ctrl-F in Windows) while showing the visualizer sets the visual effects to fill the entire screen. When displaying the full-screen visual effects, you can click the mouse button or press Escape (Esc) to stop the display and return to iTunes.

The Preferences dialog in iTunes lets you set the visualizer to always display full-screen. Choose iTunes➪Preferences on a Mac, or Edit➪Preferences in Windows, click the Advanced tab, and select the Display Visualizer Full Screen option to always display the visualizer in full-screen mode.

While the animated visual effects play, press Shift-/ (as if you're typing a question mark) to see a list of keyboard functions. Depending on the visual effect, you might see more choices of keyboard functions by pressing Shift-/ again.

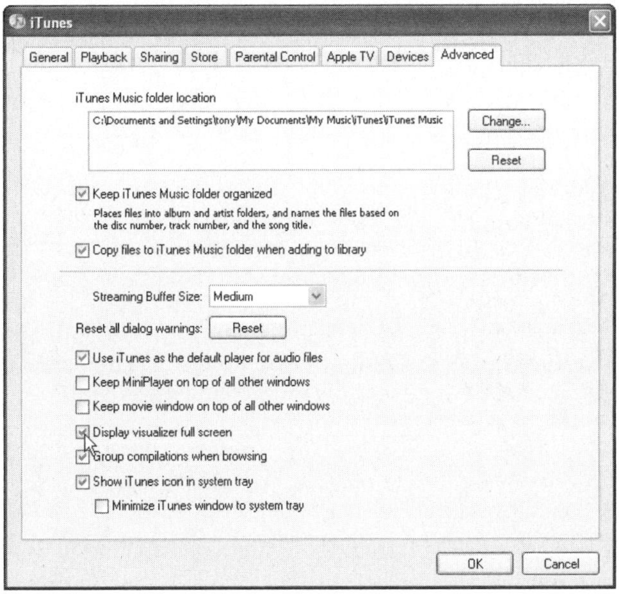

Figure 3-5:
Set the
visualizer
to always
display full-
screen.

You can enhance iTunes with plug-ins that provide even better visuals. For example, SpectroGraph from Dr. Lex displays a spectrogram of the music, and Cover Version from imagomat displays the album cover artwork. You can find them — and many other enhancements — at Apple's software download site (www.apple.com/downloads/macosx/ipod_itunes).

After installing an iTunes plug-in, you can switch from one plug-in to another by choosing View⇨Visualizer to see the submenu of plug-ins (including iTunes Visualizer and Classic Visualizer, supplied with iTunes).

Using the iTunes Genius Sidebar

If you turn on the iTunes Genius sidebar (refer to Figure 3-1), which appears next to the List pane, it makes suggestions for what to buy from the iTunes Store based on what you've selected. The Genius feature also activates the Genius button for creating the Genius playlist. (See Chapter 10 for details on using the Genius button.)

The Genius sidebar will try to skip songs that are already in your library in order to show you songs you might want to buy; but it's not perfect and sometimes doesn't recognize that you already have the song (especially if you ripped the song from CD).

The Genius informs the online store about the songs you select whenever the Genius sidebar is open. It then shows you music that other listeners purchased when they purchased the music you're playing. You can click any item in the Genius sidebar to go right to the iTunes Store page for that item. See Chapter 4 for details about using the iTunes Store.

The Genius sidebar operates only if you give it permission and if you already have an iTunes Store account. (To open an account, see Chapter 4.) When you first start iTunes, the sidebar is not yet turned on. (Refer to Figure 3-1.) To turn it on, click the Turn on Genius button, enter your Apple ID and password for your iTunes Store account, and click Continue. If you don't have an account yet, select the Create a New iTunes Store Account option and choose your country from the country pop-up menu. Then click Continue. See Chapter 4 for further instructions on creating an account.

When you have the Genius sidebar open, iTunes transmits information to the store about the selection you're playing. To hide the Genius sidebar (and stop transmitting this information), click the Show/Hide Genius sidebar button in the bottom-right corner of the iTunes window. (Refer to Figure 3-1.)

If the Genius sidebar can't find the artist for the song you're playing, it offers choices that are simply in the same genre. The Genius sidebar is available only when selecting songs in the Music portion of your library or in playlists. If you don't have an iTunes Store available for your country, you see the U.S. store, just as Chuck Berry once sang, "Anything you want, we got right here in the U.S.A."

Chapter 4

Shopping at the iTunes Store

*W*hen Apple announced its online music service, Apple chairman Steve Jobs remarked that other services put forward by the music industry tend to treat consumers like criminals. Steve had a point. Many of these services cost more and add a level of copy protection that prevents consumers from burning more than one CD or using the music (that they bought) on other computers or portable MP3 players.

Record labels dragged their feet for years, experimenting with online sales and taking legal action against online sites that allowed free downloads and music copying. Although the free music attracted millions of listeners, the free services were under legal attack in several countries, and the digital music that was distributed wasn't of the highest quality (not to mention the widespread and sometimes intentional misspellings in the song information and artist names). Consumers grew even warier when the Record Industry Association of America (RIAA), a lobbying organization looking out for the interests of record companies, began legal proceedings (illegal copyright infringement) against people who possibly thought they were downloading free music.

No one should go to jail for being a music junkie. Consumers and the industry both needed a solution. Apple did the research on how to make a service that worked better and was easier to use, and the company forged ahead with the iTunes Store. By all accounts, Apple has succeeded in offering the easiest, fastest, and most cost-effective service for buying content online.

When Apple first introduced the online store, it was called the iTunes Music Store. Although Apple has sold more than five *billion* songs as of June 2008, the company dropped *Music* from its title because the iTunes Store sells much more. You can purchase or rent movies, including HD movies, and you can purchase TV shows, music videos, applications, and games to play on your iPod or iPhone. You can buy content from the iTunes Store directly from your iPod touch or iPhone, and you can use the online App Store to download free or commercial applications — in many categories, including gaming, social networking, sports, and more — directly to your iPod touch or iPhone.

The iTunes Store offers parental controls that let you disable various sections as well as limit the purchase of various contents based on PG/TV ratings. It also offers an option to immediately burn a disc backup of the content you purchased. The iTunes Store offers gift certificates that you can e-mail to others and allows accounts that you can set up for others (such as children) with credit limits but without the need to use a credit card. In fact, Apple adds new features to the iTunes Store almost every week.

This chapter shows you how to sign in and take advantage of what the iTunes Store has to offer.

Visiting the iTunes Store

You can visit the iTunes Store by connecting to the Internet and using iTunes. You can also click an iTunes Store link on Apple's Web site, or a similar link on any other Web sites that are iTunes affiliates with songs for sale (such as www.rockument.com). The link automatically launches your installed copy of iTunes and opens the iTunes Store.

As of this writing, the iTunes Store offers millions of songs, with most songs available for download for 99 cents each and entire albums available for download at less than the CD price. You can play these copy-protected songs on up to five different computers; burn CDs; and use the songs on an unlimited number of iPods, iPhones, or Apple TVs. Apple also offers "iTunes Plus" songs and albums from some record labels with higher sound quality and *without* copy protection. You can play iTunes Plus songs on any player that supports the AAC format, and on an unlimited number of computers and burn CDs with them.

You can buy audio books and episodes and entire seasons of TV shows, and you can purchase them in advance, so you see them immediately. First-run movies are available for rent or purchase. iTunes also offers tons of free content in the form of *podcasts,* which are similar to syndicated radio and TV shows, but you can download and play them at your convenience on your computer and on your iPod, iPhone, and Apple TV. iTunes even offers free lectures, language lessons, and audio books with educational content in its iTunes U section.

Like with most online services, the music that you buy online isn't as high in audio quality as music on a commercial CD, although most people can't tell the difference when playing the music on car stereos or at low volume. The quality of the music sold in the iTunes Store is comparable with the quality you get when ripping CDs or importing songs using the MP3 or AAC formats. You also get song information (such as artist, song titles, the album title, and cover artwork), and the iTunes Store provides electronic liner notes for some albums, just like the printed notes you sometimes find on a commercial CD. Some albums are provided with the electronic equivalent of a complete jewel case booklet that you can print yourself.

To find out more about audio encoding formats, and why iTunes uses them to reduce the space the music occupies on the hard drive or flash memory of your iPod or iPhone, visit this book's companion Web site.

The iTunes Store is part of iTunes version 4 and newer, but you should be using the newest version of iTunes, and I describe how to get it in Chapter 2.

With the iTunes Store, you can preview any song for up to 30 seconds. Some movies offer one-minute previews and movie trailers you can view for free, and TV shows and audio books can offer up to 90 seconds.

If you have an account set up, you can buy and download content immediately, including movies for rent. I don't know of a faster way to purchase or rent content.

If you already have your iTunes program open, you have at least three choices when it comes to opening the iTunes Store:

- ✔ **Click iTunes Store in the Store section of the Source pane.** The iTunes Store home page opens, as shown in Figure 4-1.

- ✔ **Click any link in the Genius sidebar.** The iTunes Store home page opens and automatically switches your Source pane selection to iTunes Store. The Genius sidebar offers suggestions based on the music you select in your library; see Chapter 3 for details.

- ✔ **Follow a content link in iTunes.** Click the *content link* (the gray-circled arrow next to a song or video title, an artist name, or an album title) to go to an iTunes Store page related to the song or video, artist, or album. iTunes searches the iTunes Store based on the item you selected. If nothing closely related turns up, at least you end up in the iTunes Store, and you might even find music you like that you didn't know about.

If you need to fire up your modem and log on to your Internet service to go online, do so *before* clicking the iTunes Store option or following a content link — otherwise iTunes will wait for an Internet connection for a while and eventually give up.

Back

Forward | Home page

Sign In button

Figure 4-1:
The iTunes
Store home
page.

The iTunes Store uses the iTunes List pane to display its wares. You can check out content to your heart's content, although you can't buy content or rent movies unless you have an iTunes Store account set up. You can use the Choose Genre pop-up menu to specify music genres, or you can click links for new releases, exclusive tracks, and so on.

The iTunes Store also provides buttons on a gray bar just above the advertised content in the List pane. The left and right triangle buttons work just like the Back and Forward buttons of a Web browser, moving back a page or forward a page, respectively. The button with the Home icon takes you to the iTunes Store home page.

Setting Up an Account

You need an account to purchase content or rent movies. To create an iTunes Store account, follow these steps:

1. **In iTunes, click the iTunes Store option in the Store section of the Source pane, or click a music link or Genius sidebar link.**

   The iTunes Store home page appears (refer to Figure 4-1), replacing the iTunes List pane.

2. **Click the Sign In button in the upper-right area of the window to create an account (or sign in to an existing account).**

   When you're logged in to an iTunes account, the account name appears in place of the Sign In button.

   After you click the Sign In button, iTunes displays the account sign-in dialog, as shown in Figure 4-2.

 TIP

   If you already set up an account with the iTunes Store with the MobileMe (formerly .Mac) service or with other Apple services (such as the Apple Developer Connection), you're halfway there. Type your ID and password and then click the Sign In button. Apple remembers the personal information that you put in previously, so you don't have to re-enter it every time you visit the iTunes Store. If you forgot your password, click the Forgot Password? button, and iTunes provides a dialog to answer your test question. If you answer correctly, iTunes e-mails your password to you.

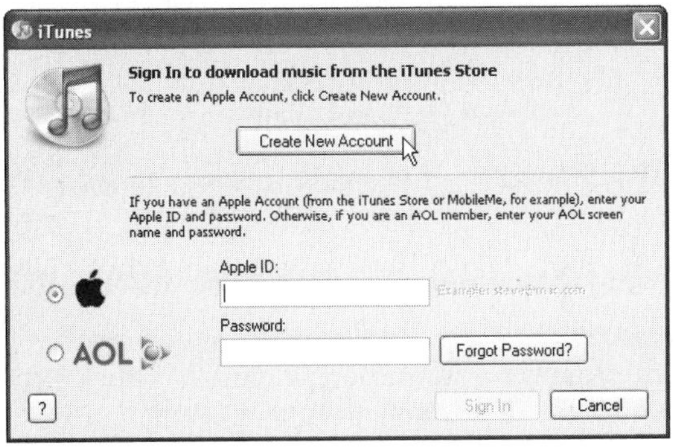

Figure 4-2:
The sign-in
dialog for
the iTunes
Store.

3. **Click the Create New Account button.**

   iTunes displays a new page, replacing the iTunes Store home page with a page welcoming you to the iTunes Store.

4. **Click Continue on the iTunes Store welcome page.**

   After you click Continue, the terms of use appear with the option at the end to agree to the terms.

5. **Select I Have Read and Agree to the iTunes Terms and Conditions and click Continue.**

   iTunes displays the next page of the setup procedure, shown in Figure 4-3.

6. **Fill in your personal account information in the new page that appears.**

   You need to enter your e-mail address, password, test question and answer (in case you forget your password), birth date, and privacy options.

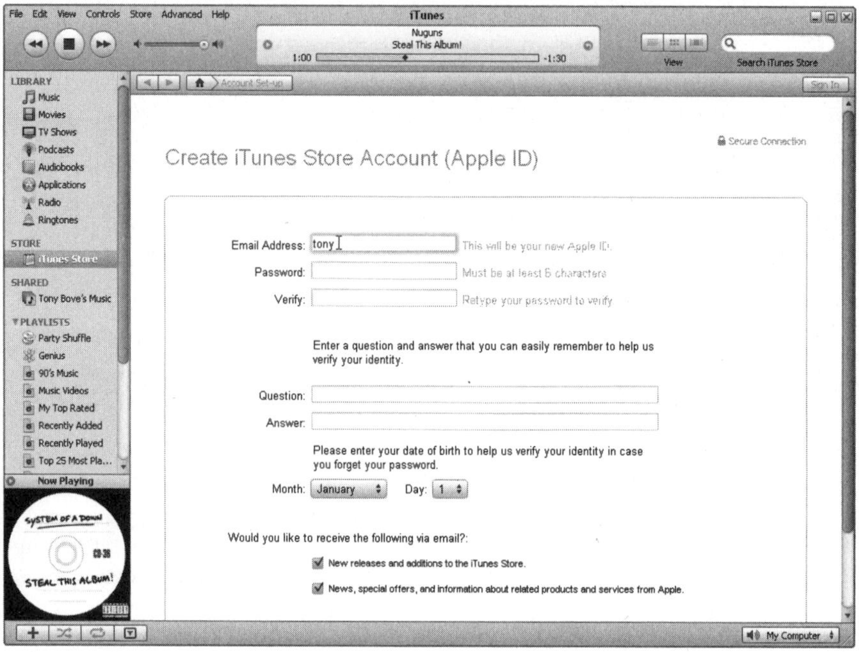

Figure 4-3:
Create
a new
account for
the iTunes
Store.

7. **Click Continue and then enter your credit card information.**

   The entire procedure is secure, so you don't have to worry. The iTunes Store keeps your personal information (including your credit card information) on file, and you don't have to type it again.

8. **Click Continue to finish the procedure.**

   The account setup finishes and returns you to the iTunes Store home page. You can now use the iTunes Store to purchase and download content to play in iTunes and use on any iPod, iPhone, or Apple TV.

Select a country from the My Store pop-up menu at the bottom of the iTunes Store page to choose online stores in other countries. For example, the iTunes Store in France displays menus in French and features hit songs and TV shows for the French market. If you've set up your account in only one country (such as the United States), you have to set an account up again for the country you're switching to, in order to purchase content in that country's store. You can set up multiple accounts in multiple countries.

Click the flag button next to the My Store pop-up menu at the bottom of the iTunes Store home page to display a page of buttons with flags of other countries; then click one to go to the home page for the iTunes Store for that country.

Browsing and Previewing Songs

The iTunes Store home page is loaded with specials and advertisements to peruse. To look at music in more depth, choose Music from the iTunes Store panel at the top left of the home page (next to the New Releases panel). iTunes displays more panels of advertisements and specials for music lovers. You can then choose a genre from the Genres pop-up menu on the iTunes Store panel to see only those specials and ads for a particular genre.

What if you're looking for particular music in a particular genre? You can browse the iTunes Store by genre and artist name in a method similar to browsing your iTunes library.

To browse the iTunes Store, choose View⇨Show Browser, or click the Browse link in the Quick Links panel on the right side of the iTunes Store home page. iTunes displays the store's offerings categorized by type of content (such as Music), and it displays music by genre and subgenre — and within each subgenre, by artist and album. Select a genre in the Genre column, then a subgenre in the Subgenre column, then an artist in the Artist column, and finally an album in the Album column, which takes you to the list of songs from that album that are available to preview or purchase, as shown in Figure 4-4.

To see more information about a song or the album that it came from, click the content link (one of the gray-circled arrow buttons in the List pane):

- ✔ Clicking the arrow in the Artist column takes you to the artist's page of albums.
- ✔ Clicking the arrow in the Album column takes you to the album page.
- ✔ Clicking the arrow in the Name column takes you to album page with the song highlighted.

My only complaint about browsing by artist is that artists are listed alphabetically by first name. For example, you have to look up Bob Dylan under *Bob* and not *Dylan.*

To preview a song, click the song title in the List pane and then click the Play button (or press the spacebar) or double-click the song.

By default, the previews play on your computer off the Internet in a stream, so you might hear a few hiccups in the playback. Each preview lasts about 30 seconds. Just when you start really getting into the song, it ends. If the song is irresistible, though, you can buy it on the spot.

Figure 4-4:
Browse the
iTunes Store
for music by
genre, artist,
and album.

If you know specifically what you're looking for, you can search instead of browse. The Search field in the top-right corner of the iTunes window lets you search the iTunes Store for just about anything. You can type part of a song title or artist name to quickly search the iTunes Store, or use the Power Search feature to narrow your search. (See the "Power searching" section later in this chapter.)

To return to the store's home menu, click the Home icon on the gray bar just above the advertised content in the List pane.

Power searching

You're serious about your content, and you truly desire the power to search for exactly what you want. I know what you want — and I have the function right here for you.

Click the Power Search link on the iTunes Store home page in the Quick Links panel to go directly to the Power Search page (or choose Store⇨Search). At the top of the Power Search page, as shown in Figure 4-5, you can choose the type of content to search through: All (search all types), Music, Movies, TV Shows, Music Videos, Audiobooks, Podcasts, or iTunes U (part of the iTunes Store that offers free lectures, language lessons, and audio books). Each content type has a particular set of entry fields for searching.

Choose Music to power-search for music. The entry fields for Artist, Composer, Song, and Album appear. You can fill in some or all of these fields (see Figure 4-5) or just fill in part of any field (such as Composer or Artist) if that's all you know. You can narrow your search by picking a genre from the Genre pop-up menu. You can also narrow your search by picking only iTunes Plus songs (which offer higher sound quality and are stripped of copy protection) — click to turn on the Search iTunes Plus option. If you want to find only songs that can be made into ringtones for your iPhone, click to turn on the Search Songs that can be Made into Ringtones option.

After you fill in as much as you know (and have perhaps narrowed your search, if that's what you wanted), click the Search button. The songs appear below in the list.

Browsing celebrity and published playlists

Do you want to be influenced? Do you want to know what influenced some of today's celebrities and buy what they have in their record collections? Choose Music from the iTunes Store panel (on the left) to go to the Music page. Scroll down the iTunes Store Music page and click a celebrity name in the Celebrity Playlists panel to go to that celebrity's page. A typical celebrity playlist offers about an album's worth of songs from different artists. You can preview or buy any song in the list or follow the music links to the artist or album page.

Figure 4-5: Use Power Search to find a song in the iTunes Store.

The Music page advertises some of the celebrity playlists, but a lot more are available (more than 480 the last time I checked). To see all the celebrity playlists, go to the More in Music panel on the left side of the Music page and click the Celebrity Playlists link. You arrive at the Celebrity Playlists page. You can use the Sort By pop-up menu in the upper-right corner to sort the list by Most Recent or by Title.

You can also be influenced by other buyers and do a little influencing your-self. Go to the Music page and click the iMix link in the More in Music panel on the left side to check out playlists that have been contributed by other consumers and published in the iTunes Store. iMixes offer 30-second pre-views of any songs in the iMix playlists. To find out how to publish your own iMix playlist, see Chapter 10.

You can also include a Web link (URL) to an iTunes Store page in an e-mail message or other document so the reader can click the link to go directly to the iTunes Store page. You can drag the last button on the gray bar just above the advertised content that displays the page name — or drag any piece of artwork from the page — to an e-mail message or document you're compos-ing, and iTunes copies the link. You can also Control-click (Mac) or right-click (Windows) the item and choose Copy iTunes Store URL from the contextual menu that appears.

Browsing and Previewing Movies, TV Shows, Videos, and Audio Books

The uncool thing about video stores — besides the weird people who hang out in them — is the lack of any ability to preview videos before you buy them. And the only way to preview TV shows is to watch TV. However, you can use the iTunes Store to preview movies, music videos, and TV shows before you buy them (and before you rent a movie) — as long as your com-puter has a broadband connection to the Internet. Most shows offer 30 sec-onds of previewing time.

To find TV shows, movies, music videos, or audio books, do one of the following:

✔ Click the TV Shows, Movies, Music Videos, or Audiobooks link in the iTunes Store panel on the left side of the iTunes Store home page. The iTunes Store displays advertisements for the most popular items, and you see a version of the cover browser that lets you drag a slider to view items.

✔ Browse the iTunes Store by clicking the Browse link in the Quick Links panel on the right side of the iTunes Store home page (or choosing View⇨ Show Browser). Select TV Shows, Movies, Music Videos, or Audiobooks from the iTunes Store column and then do one of the following:

- *For a TV show,* pick a genre in the Genre column, then a TV show in the TV Shows column, and a season of episodes in the Seasons column.

- *For a movie,* pick a genre from the Genre column.

- *For a music video,* pick a genre from the Genre column; then pick an artist from the Artist column.

- *For an audio book,* pick a genre from the Genre column, then pick an author from the Author/Narrator column.

To preview a TV show, movie, or music video, click the title in the list and then click the Play button (or press the spacebar). (Movies are actually videos on the computer, so I use the term *videos* from now on.) The video plays in the Artwork pane in the lower-left corner of the iTunes window, as shown in Figure 4-6. If the Artwork pane isn't visible, click the Show/Hide Artwork button to display it. Click the iTunes Play/Pause, Forward/Next, and Previous/Rewind buttons to control playback, and use the iTunes volume slider to control the volume, just like with songs. For more details about playing videos in iTunes, see Chapter 6.

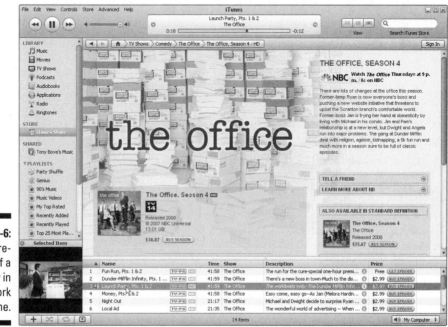

Figure 4-6: Play a preview of a TV show in the Artwork pane.

You can play the video in a larger, separate window by clicking inside the Artwork pane while the video is playing. You can then control video playback by using the separate window's controls: Click the right-facing triangle in the window to play the video and click it again to pause the video. Drag the slider to move forward or backward through the video. You can click the Rewind or Fast-Forward buttons in the window to move backward or forward through a video. You can also choose options in the View⇨Video Size submenu to show the video window half-size, actual size, double-size, fit-to-screen, or full screen. See Chapter 6 for a full description of video playing options in iTunes.

Movies are also just a click away, as shown in Figure 4-7. Although you can click the circled arrow next to the title to go to the movie page, you can also use the buttons in the far-left Price column, which include View Movie to view the movie trailer; Rent Movie to rent the movie (see "Renting Movies" later in this chapter); and Buy Movie to purchase the movie (see "Buying and Downloading Content" later in this chapter). Click the View Movie button to see the movie's page. From there, you can click the View Trailer button (see Figure 4-8) to see the theatrical trailer. The page also offers buttons to rent or buy the movie, if the movie is available for rental or purchase.

Clicking the View Trailer button does the obvious — it plays the movie trailer. At any time or after the movie trailer plays, though, you can return to the movie page by clicking Close Preview under the lower-right corner of the trailer picture.

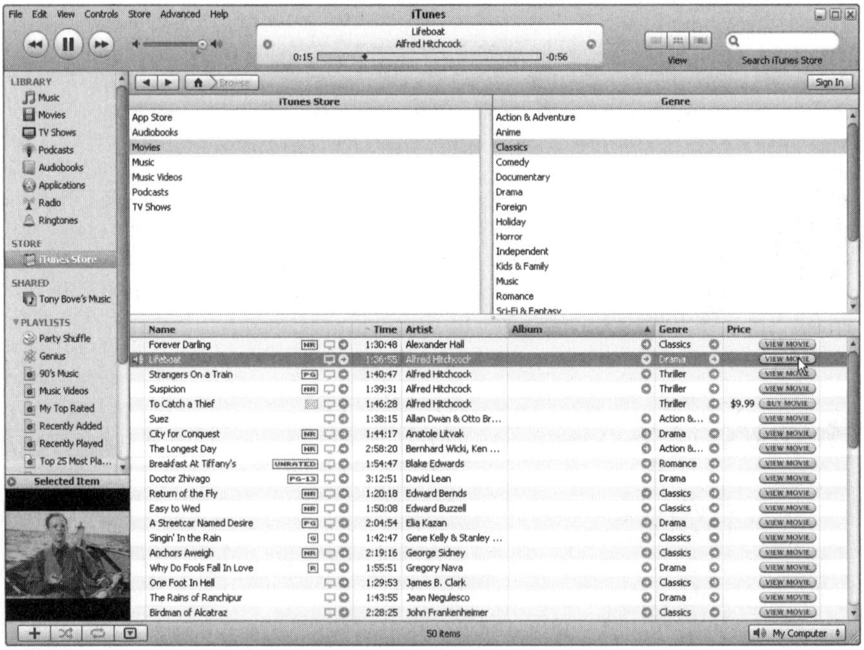

Figure 4-7:
Select
a movie
to view
a trailer
or buy or
rent it.

Figure 4-8:
Show the
movie page
to view its
trailer
or rent or
buy it.

Audio books can be even more entertaining than movies and certainly easier to consume while driving or walking. The Audiobooks link on the iTunes Store home page takes you to the Audiobooks page. Click an advertisement, thumbnail, or title, or click the circled arrow next to the title in a list of titles, to go to the specific audio book's page. Then click the Preview button to preview the audio book. Use the Play/Pause button to pause and resume playback.

You can double-click the iTunes Store option in the Store section of the Source pane to open the iTunes Store in a separate window. With two windows, you can use the first window to search for and play content in your library while using the second to browse the iTunes Store and purchase and download a video. The first window stops playing content when you use the second window to preview a song or video.

Browsing and Subscribing to Podcasts

Podcasting is a popular method of publishing audio and video shows to the Internet, enabling people to subscribe to a feed and receive the shows automatically. Similar to a tape of a radio broadcast, you can save a podcast episode and play it back at your convenience, both in iTunes on your computer and on your iPod. You can also burn a podcast episode on an audio CD or

MP3 CD. A podcast episode can be anything from a single song to a commentary-hosted radio show; a podcaster, like a broadcaster, provides a stream of episodes over time. Thousands of professional and amateur radio and video shows are offered as podcast episodes.

The iTunes Podcast page on the iTunes Store lets you browse, find, preview, and subscribe to podcasts, many of which are free. You don't need an account to browse the iTunes Store and subscribe to free podcasts.

To find podcasts in the iTunes Store, do one of the following:

- ✔ **Click the Podcasts link in the iTunes Store panel on the left side of the home page.** The iTunes Store displays the Podcast page, with advertisements for popular podcasts and a list of Top Podcasts in the far-right column. You can click the Top Podcasts link to see the most popular podcasts in specific categories.

  You can also get to the Podcast page by clicking Podcasts in the iTunes Source pane and then clicking Podcast Directory at the bottom of the List view.

- ✔ **Browse all podcasts in a particular category.** Click the Browse link in the Quick Links panel on the right side of the iTunes Store home page (or choose View➪Show Browser), and then select Podcasts in the iTunes Store column. Select options from the Category column and Subcategory column.

- ✔ **Search for a podcast by name or keyword.** You can type a search term into the Search iTunes Store field in the upper-right corner of the iTunes window to find any podcasts or other content items that match. You can also use the Power Search feature, described earlier in this chapter in the section, "Power searching."

After you select a podcast, the iTunes Store displays the podcast's specific page in the iTunes Store, as shown in Figure 4-9, with all available podcast episodes in the List pane. (There are four episodes in Figure 4-9 for the Rockument podcast.)

To select, play, and subscribe to a podcast, follow these steps:

1. **Choose a podcast in the iTunes Store.**

   The iTunes Store offers a description, a Subscribe button to receive new podcasts, and a link to the podcast's Web site for more information. The page also lists the most recent podcast. Some podcasters offer several podcasts in one feed. You can click the *i* icon on the far-right podcast listing margin to display separate information about the podcast.

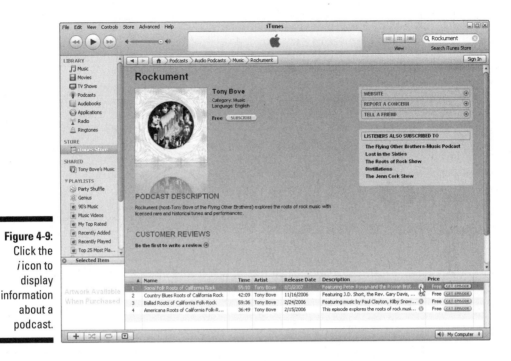

Figure 4-9:
Click the
i icon to
display
information
about a
podcast.

2. **To preview the podcast, click the Play button or press the spacebar.**

   You can play a preview of any podcast in the list. iTunes plays the podcast for about 90 seconds, just like a Web radio station streaming to your computer. To jump ahead in a podcast or play the entire podcast episode, you must first subscribe to the podcast. By subscribing, you enable downloading episodes to your computer.

3. **Click the Subscribe button to subscribe to the podcast.**

   In typical Apple fashion, iTunes first displays an alert to confirm that you want to subscribe to the podcast.

4. **Click OK to confirm.**

   iTunes downloads the podcast to your computer and switches to Podcasts in the Library section of the Source pane. iTunes displays your newly subscribed podcast in the List pane, as shown in Figure 4-10.

5. **(Optional) Get more episodes of the podcast.**

   When you subscribe to a podcast, you get the current episode. However, each podcast can contain multiple episodes. To download previously available episodes, click the triangle next to the podcast name in the List pane (refer to Figure 4-10) to see the individual episodes, and then click the Get button next to an episode to download it. For more information about adding and deleting podcasts and podcast episodes, see Chapter 5.

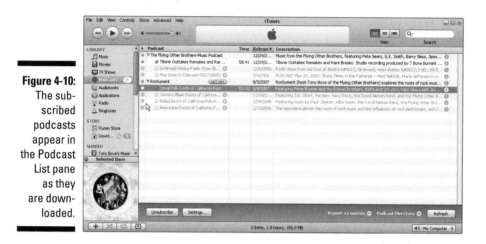

Figure 4-10:
The sub-
scribed
podcasts
appear in
the Podcast
List pane
as they
are down-
loaded.

6. To play the podcast in full, select it and click the Play button.

> A blue dot next to a podcast means you haven't yet played it. As soon as you start listening to a podcast, the dot disappears. For more information about playing podcasts, see Chapter 6.

Anyone can create a podcast and then submit it to the iTunes Store by following Apple's published guidelines. (Click the Submit a Podcast link on the Podcast page in the iTunes Store.) In fact, the Rockument and the Flying Other Brothers music podcasts, available in the iTunes Store (and from www. rockument.com), are produced by this book's author. You can find out more about creating podcasts in *Podcasting For Dummies,* 2nd Edition, by Tee Morris and Evo Terra (Wiley).

You can play the podcast, incorporate it into playlists, and make copies and burn CDs as much as you like. See Chapter 5 for details on subscribing to, deleting, and updating podcasts.

Browsing Applications and Games

Got an iPod touch or iPhone? You can get loads of free and commercial applications that run on your iPod touch or iPhone just like built-in applications like Map and Weather. To find thousands of applications and games you can download to iTunes and transfer to your iPod touch or iPhone, click App Store in the iTunes Store panel on the iTunes Store home page. Click an application's icon to go to the information page for that application, which may also contain reviews and a slideshow depicting the application in action. The information page offers the Buy App button to purchase and download a commercial application or game, or the Get App button to download a free application or game.

The iTunes Store also offers colorful "click wheel" games to play on your iPod classic or nano (or fifth-generation iPods) — all kinds of games, from Mini Golf, Monopoly, and Mahjong to the classic Tetris and Cubis 2. You can even play the wildly popular Japanese puzzle Sudoku. The games play on iPods that can play videos — not in iTunes itself. However, you can see a preview of the game while browsing the iTunes Store.

To find the iPod games, click the iPod Games link in the iTunes Store panel on the iTunes Store home page. iTunes displays the iPod Games page with thumbnail icons for each game. Click the game's icon to go to the games page. Click the Preview button on the game's page to see a preview of the game. Use the iTunes Play button, just as you would for a song, to play the game preview. At any time or after the preview plays, click the Close Preview button to return to the games page.

Buying and Downloading Content

As you select content, you can purchase the items and download them to your computer immediately. Alternatively, you can gather your selections in a virtual shopping cart first to see your choices and decide whether to purchase them before downloading them all at once.

Each time you buy content, you get an e-mail from the iTunes Store with the purchase information. It's nice to know right away what you bought.

Your decision to download each item immediately or add to a shopping cart and download later is likely based on how your computer connects to the Internet. If you have a slow connection such as a phone line, you probably want to use the shopping cart to avoid tying up the phone with each download.

Using 1-Click

Apple offers 1-Click technology in the iTunes Store so that with one click, your digital content immediately starts downloading to your computer — and the purchase is done.

With 1-Click, you click the Buy button whether the item is a song, an album, a TV show episode, or an audio book. For example, if you select a song in the List pane, click the Buy Song button in the far-right column for the song. (You might have to scroll your iTunes Store window to see the far-right column.) When you select a TV show episode, click the Buy Episode button in the far-right column. You can click the Buy Album button in an album advertisement. With 1-Click, iTunes complies immediately.

The iTunes Store may prompt you to log in to your account first after you click the Buy button (unless you just recently logged in). It then displays a warning dialog to make sure that you want to buy the item, and you can then go through with it or cancel. If you click the Buy button to purchase it, the song, album, audio book, or video download automatically shows up in your iTunes library. The iTunes Store keeps track of your purchases over a 24-hour period and charges you for a total sum rather than for each single purchase.

1-Click seems more like two clicks. If you really want to use only one click to buy an item from iTunes, select the Don't Warn Me option in the warning dialog so that you never see it again. (But then don't complain if you click a Buy button by mistake and automatically buy something.)

Using the shopping cart

You don't have to use the 1-Click technology. Instead, you can add items to the shopping cart to delay purchasing and downloading until you're ready. With the shopping cart, the iTunes Store remembers your selections, allowing you to browse the iTunes Store at different times and add to your total without making any purchases final. You can also remove items from the cart at any time. When you're ready to buy, you can purchase and download the items in your cart in one fell swoop.

If you switch to the shopping cart method (see the following section, "Changing your iTunes Store preferences"), the Buy button changes to an Add button — as in Add Song, Add Album, Add Episode, and so on. After adding items, you can view the selections in your shopping cart by selecting the Shopping Cart option underneath the iTunes Store option in the Store section of the Source pane (see Figure 4-11).

The shopping cart appears in the List view with your selections listed, and recommendations from the iTunes Store appear along the top of the window. Albums appear with a triangle next to their name, which you can click to open and see the album's songs. As you can see in Figure 4-11, albums, individual songs, music videos, TV episodes, and audio books are listed in alphabetical order by artist name (or TV show name).

When you're ready to purchase everything in your shopping cart, click the BUY NOW button in the lower-right corner of the Shopping Cart view to close the sale and download all the items at once. Alternatively, you can click the Buy (for an album) or Buy Song buttons for each item that you want to purchase.

Figure 4-11:
View your
shopping
cart before
purchas-
ing the
items from
the iTunes
Store.

Shopping Cart   Buy Now button

To delete items from your shopping cart, select them and press Delete/
Backspace. A warning appears asking whether you're sure that you want to
remove the selected items. Click Yes to go ahead and remove the selections
from your shopping cart.

You can see the list of all the items that you purchased by selecting the
Purchased playlist under the iTunes Store option in the Source pane. The List
view and Browse view change to show the items you purchased.

Changing your iTunes Store preferences

You can change your shopping method by choosing iTunes⇨Preferences on
the Mac or by choosing Edit⇨Preferences in Windows. In the Preferences
window, click the Store button. The Store Preferences window appears, as
shown in Figure 4-12.

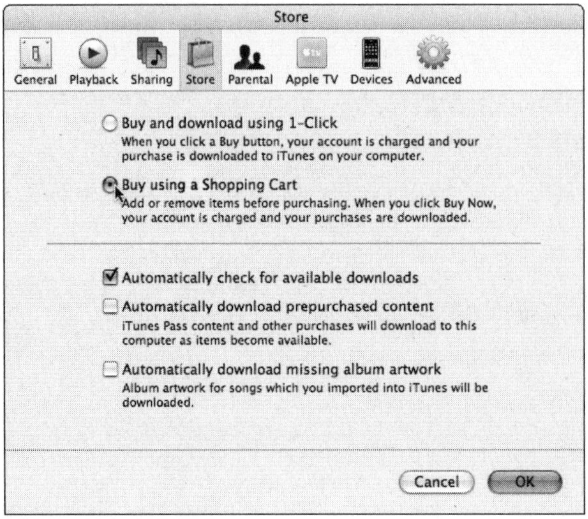

Figure 4-12:
Set your
iTunes Store
prefer-
ences.

You can set the following features:

✔ Change from 1-Click to Shopping Cart or vice versa. 1-Click is the default.

✔ Automatically check for available downloads from the iTunes Store, such as downloads that were not completed and new episodes for a podcast subscription.

✔ Automatically download prepurchased content, such as a Season Pass of TV show episodes. As the episodes become available, iTunes automatically downloads them.

✔ Automatically download missing album artwork from the iTunes Store for albums and songs you've imported from other sources (such as audio CDs).

If you use more than one computer to access your iTunes Store account, you can set the preferences for each computer differently and still use the same account. For example, your home computer might have a faster connection than your laptop on a remote connection, so you can set your iTunes prefer-ences accordingly: The home computer could be set to 1-Click, and the laptop could be set to shopping cart.

Resuming interrupted downloads

All sales are final; you can't return the digital merchandise. However, the download must be successful — you have to receive it all — before the iTunes Store charges you for the purchase. If for any reason the download is interrupted or fails to complete, your order remains active until you connect to the iTunes Store again.

iTunes remembers to continue the download when you return to iTunes and connect to the Internet. If, for some reason, the download doesn't continue, choose Store➪Check for Available Downloads to continue the interrupted download. You can also use this command to check for any purchased music that hasn't downloaded yet.

While downloading from the iTunes Store, you can select Downloads in the Store section of the Source pane, as shown in Figure 4-13, to see the progress of your downloads, and to pause and resume (or cancel) any particular download. You can also prioritize the order of downloading by dragging items into a different order.

For the impatient viewers, the iTunes Store lets you start watching a video or movie before it finishes downloading. Click Downloads in the Store section of the Source pane as you're downloading and double-click the item to watch it. The download continues as you watch from the beginning.

If your computer's hard drive crashes and you lose your information, you also lose all your digital content — you have to purchase and download that content again. However, you can mitigate this kind of disaster by backing up your iTunes library. You can also burn your songs, including purchased songs, to an audio CD, as I describe in Chapter 12.

To learn more about backing up your iTunes library, visit this book's companion Web site.

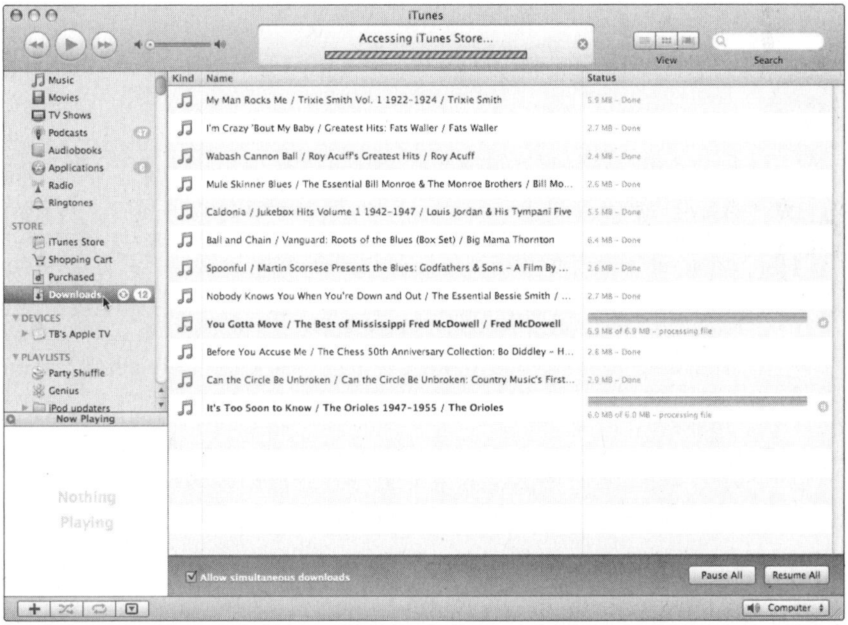

Figure 4-13:
Check the
progress of
your down-
loads.

Redeeming gift certificates and prepaid cards

If you're the fortunate recipient of an iTunes Store gift certificate, all you need to do is use iTunes to go to the iTunes Store and set up a new account — if you don't already have one. Recipients of gift certificates can set up new accounts without having to provide a credit card number. As a recipient of a gift, you can simply click None for the credit card option and use the gift certificate as the sole payment method.

You can receive gift certificates on paper (delivered by snail mail) or by e-mail. You can also receive a prepaid card with a fixed balance. To redeem a certificate, go to the Quick Links panel on the right side of the iTunes Store home page and click the Redeem link to go to the Redeem page. In the Redeem Code section of the Redeem page, type the number printed on the certificate or supplied in the e-mail and click the Redeem button to credit your account. If you haven't signed into your account yet or you have no account, iTunes displays the sign-in dialog; for information about setting up an account, see the "Setting Up an Account" section, earlier in this chapter.

If you use Apple's Mail program or access your MobileMe (formerly .Mac) e-mail through the Safari Web browser, you can redeem a gift certificate that was sent by e-mail by clicking the Redeem Now button at the bottom of the e-mail message. This button launches iTunes with the iTunes Store option selected in the Source pane and displays the Redeem page with the certificate's number automatically filled in. Click the Redeem button to credit your account.

The *balance* of your gift certificate (how much you have left to spend) appears right next to your account name in the iTunes Store window and is updated as you make purchases.

Renting Movies

First, the good news: You can rent movies from the iTunes Store and play them on your iPod classic, iPod nano, iPod touch, iPhone, or Apple TV as well as your computer. Plus, the entire experience is quick and easy, and you can even rent HD movies from your couch without your computer, just with Apple TV.

The bad news? None really, except that like other video rental stores, you have to pay a rental fee and watch the movie right away. With iTunes rentals, you have up to 29 days to start viewing the movie and up to 24 hours after starting to view it (in the U.S.; other countries vary). You don't have to return anything — expired content is automatically deleted. You need the newest version of iTunes and QuickTime (see Chapter 2), and make sure your iPod, iPhone, or Apple TV has the most recent software updates.

To rent a movie, browse the iTunes Store on your computer or Apple TV and look for movies with a Rent button. Once you select Rent, your movie begins to download immediately, and the countdown starts — you have 30 days to watch it or 24 hours after starting to watch it. (Viewing time limits vary by country.)

Renting from your computer

The iTunes Store offers a video format for movie rentals from your computer that enables the video to play on a video-enabled iPod, iPhone, or Apple TV. The video resolution is 640 x up to 480 pixels for the iPod or iPhone, and the video is encoded anamorphically to increase the quality of the movie picture. Apple TV offers rentals of movies in 720p and 1080i HD formats, and some movies also include Dolby Pro-Logic II Surround sound.

When you rent a movie using iTunes on your computer, it shows up in the Movies section of your library. Once the movie is downloaded, you can watch it on your computer or transfer the rental to an iPod, iPhone, or Apple TV by following these steps:

1. **Connect your iPod or iPhone to your computer, and select the device in the Devices section of the Source pane of iTunes.**

   If you have an Apple TV, iTunes detects it — see Chapter 7 for details on setting up your Apple TV.

2. **Click the Movies tab (for iPod) or the Videos tab (for iPhone or Apple TV).**

3. **Select the movie, and then click Move.**

You must be connected to the Internet to transfer a rented movie, and after you transfer it from your computer, iTunes removes it from your library.

If you rented the movie using iTunes on your computer, you can move the movie between an iPod, iPhone, or Apple TV as many times as you want during the rental period, but the movie can be played on only one device at a time.

If your rental doesn't show up in iTunes, choose Store⇨Check for Available Downloads. You can report problems with your movie rentals (such as accidental rentals or quality problems) directly through your Purchase History in iTunes (see "Viewing your purchase history" later in this chapter).

Renting directly on Apple TV

The iTunes Store offers the Widescreen Apple TV format, with a video resolution of 720 x up to 480 pixels (for movies you rent directly on Apple TV) and many movies are also available in high definition (HD) at 1,280 x up to 720 pixels. The Widescreen format is encoded anamorphically to increase the quality of the movie picture. Apple TV rentals offer stereo sound or Dolby Digital Surround 5.1 sound, and some offer Dolby Pro-Logic II Surround sound.

Movies rented on your Apple TV aren't transferable to any other device and can be viewed only on your Apple TV. (See Chapter 7 for instructions on how to use Apple TV menus.) To rent movies using your Apple TV, you must first use your handheld Apple Remote to navigate the Apple TV menus and sign into the online store:

1. **From the main Apple TV menu, choose Settings⮑General⮑iTunes Store.**

   The iTunes Store menu appears on your Apple TV with the Location and Sign In/Out options. If your location and iTunes account already appear next to these options, skip to the next set of steps.

2. **Choose the Location option and then scroll to highlight your country and select it.**

3. **Press Menu once to return to the previous screen, and choose Sign in (this is Sign Out if you are already signed in).**

4. **Enter your Apple ID and password.**

   If you don't have an Apple ID, create an account as described in "Setting Up an Account" in this chapter.

5. **Apple TV gives you the option to remember your password. Select Yes if you want to save the password.**

6. **Press and hold the Menu button to return to the main Apple TV menu.**

To rent movies on your Apple TV:

1. **Select Movies from the main Apple TV menu.**

2. **Choose one of the following categories to find movies: Top Movies, Genres, All HD, or Search.**

   You can search for movies with the Search option and your remote control.

3. **Find a movie and press Play/Pause for more details.**

4. **Select Rent, or Rent HD for high definition movies.**

   Rent HD may not be available for all movies, and movie rentals may not be available in all regions.

5. **Click OK to confirm and continue.**

Your movie downloads immediately into your Apple TV, and a message appears when the movie is ready watch. At this point, you can press Play to begin watching the movie, or press the Menu button to make other selections.

To see all the movies that you've rented, select Movies⇨Rented Movies from the main Apple TV menu. The Rented Movies menu also shows when your rented movie is due to expire.

If your download is interrupted, go to Setting⇨Downloads and select Check for Downloads. Apple TV will connect with the iTunes Store and will resume downloading.

Managing Your iTunes Store Account

Online stores record necessary information about you, such as your credit card number, your billing address, and so forth. You usually can change this information at any time, and the iTunes Store is no exception in this regard. You can also take advantage of special iTunes Store account features, such as sending gift certificates, setting parental controls, and setting up allowance accounts.

Viewing and changing account information

Life is unpredictable. As John Lennon sang in "Beautiful Boy (Darling Boy)," "Life is what happens to you while you're busy making other plans." So if your billing address changes, or you need to switch to another credit card, or you need to change your password for any reason, you can edit your account information at any time.

To see your account information in the iTunes Store, click the Account button that shows your account name, or click the Account link in the Quick Links panel of the iTunes Store home page. If you haven't logged in recently, iTunes displays a dialog for you to enter your account password — enter the password and then click View Account.

Your account page displays fields for your Apple ID, the last four digits of the credit card that you use for the account, your billing address, your most recent purchase, and your computer authorizations. (See "Authorizing computers to play purchased music," later in this chapter.) You can click buttons to edit your account and credit card information and also to manage *alerts* (e-mail messages sent by iTunes about new releases from artists that are listed in your purchase history). You can also manage your iMix playlists (see Chapter 10 for details on how to create and manage an iMix) and view your purchase history.

Viewing your purchase history

In the rock 'n' roll lifestyle, you might recall songs from the 1960s but not remember what you bought last week. To view your purchase history, go to your account page by clicking the Account button (top-right corner), or by clicking the Account link in the Quick Links panel of the iTunes Store home page, and then type your password to log in to your account. Click the View Account button; on your account page, click the Purchase History button.

The iTunes Store displays the items that you purchased, starting with the most recent. If you bought a lot of content, not all of the items appear on the first page. To see the details of previous purchases, click the arrow to the left of the order date. After viewing your history, click Done at the bottom of the history page to return to your account page.

Setting up allowances

Do you trust your kids with your credit card? You don't have to answer that, but you can sidestep the entire issue by gifting an *allowance account* that lets you set the amount of credit each month, from $10–$200 in increments of $10. You can change the amount of an allowance or stop it at any time. (And if these accounts are for kids, put your mind at rest by reading "Setting parental controls," later in this chapter.)

To use an allowance account, the recipient must be using iTunes version 4 or newer and live in a country where the iTunes Store is available on the Internet (such as the United States).

You can set up the allowance account yourself or define an allowance on an existing account. The recipient signs in to the account and types his or her password — no credit card required. When the recipient reaches the limit of the allowance, that account can't buy anything else until the following month. The iTunes Store saves any unused balance until the next iTunes Store purchase.

To set up an allowance account, click the Buy iTunes Gifts link in the Quick Links panel on the right side of the iTunes Store home page. Scroll the resulting Buy iTunes Gifts page to the bottom to find the Allowances section and then click the Set Up Allowance Now link. iTunes takes you to the Allowance Setup page, where you can enter your name, your recipient's name, and the monthly allowance amount (using the Monthly Allowance pop-up menu). You also enter your recipient's Apple ID and password, or choose the option to set up a new account.

Click Continue to proceed with the account setup process, and then follow the instructions to finish setting up the account.

To stop an allowance or change the amount of an allowance account, go to your account page by clicking the Account button (top-right corner), or click the Account link in the Quick Links panel of the iTunes Store home page, and then type your password to log into your account. Click the View Account button and scroll the account page until you see the Setup Allowance button; click this button to go to the Allowance page.

Sending gift certificates

A song is a gift that keeps on giving every time the recipient plays it. A gift of a music video or TV show might commemorate a special occasion. Besides, you can't go wrong giving an iTunes Store gift certificate to that special person who has everything. You can send a certificate as an e-mail message or print the certificate yourself on your own printer.

Before sending a gift certificate for some tunes, first make sure that the recipient can run iTunes 4 or newer versions. Also, he or she must be able to run iTunes 6 or newer versions for video. (You might want to subtly suggest to the future recipient in an e-mail that it's time to download the newest version of iTunes, just to find out whether he or she has the requisite system configuration; see Chapter 2.)

To buy a gift certificate to send to someone, click the Buy iTunes Gifts link in the Quick Links panel on the right side of the iTunes Store home page. Scroll the resulting Buy iTunes Gifts page to the Printable Gift Certificates or Email Gift Certificates sections. Click the Buy Now link in either section to start the process of buying a gift certificate. Follow the instructions to enter your name, the recipient's name, the recipient's e-mail or snail mail address (for printed certificates), the amount of the gift, and a personal message.

Setting parental controls

Art may imitate life, but sometimes you might not want life to imitate art — or in this case, your kids' lives to be exposed to entertainment you deem inappropriate. iTunes not only provides a Parental Advisory Label next to explicit items in the online store, but also lets you restrict explicit content from displaying in the iTunes Store. You can also disable podcasts, radio content, the iTunes Store itself, and shared music so that these items don't appear in the Source pane.

To set parental controls, choose iTunes⇨Preferences on the Mac or Edit⇨Preferences in Windows. In the Preferences window that appears, click the Parental tab to see the Parental Control preferences.

You can click options to disable podcasts, radio stations, the iTunes Store, and shared libraries. When it's disabled, the content source (podcasts, radio stations, iTunes Store, or shared libraries) doesn't appear in the iTunes Source pane and can't be selected. To restrict content itself, you can choose a rating system for a specific country in the Ratings For pop-up menu, and then click options to restrict movies, TV shows, and games using the chosen country's rating levels available in pop-up menus. You can also click the option to restrict all explicit content.

After selecting options, click the Lock icon to prevent further changes. iTunes displays a dialog requiring you to type the administrator password for your computer system. Click OK after typing the password, and then click OK again to close iTunes preferences so that the changes take effect.

To make changes later, click the Lock icon to unlock the preferences, and type the administrator password again. And, of course, don't tell your kids the administration password.

Authorizing computers to play purchased music

The computer that you use to set up your account is automatically authorized by Apple to play the content you buy from the iTunes Store. Fortunately, the content isn't locked to that computer. You can copy your purchased songs, audio books, podcasts, and videos to other computers and play them with iTunes. When you first play them on the other computers, iTunes asks for your iTunes Store account ID and password to authorize that computer. You can have up to five computers authorized at any one time. You can also authorize a computer at any time by choosing Store➪Authorize Computer.

Purchased songs, audio books, and videos need to be downloaded or copied to one of your authorized computers before you can copy them from the added computer to an iPod using iTunes.

If you want to delete one computer and add another computer, you can remove the authorization from a computer by choosing Store➪Deauthorize Computer *on that computer*. If the computer no longer works and you therefore can't deauthorize it, you can contact Apple through its iTunes Store support page (www.apple.com/support/itunes/store/authorization).

Remember to deauthorize your computer before you sell it or give it away. Also, deauthorize your computer before upgrading your RAM, hard drive, or other system components. Otherwise, the upgraded system might count as an authorized computer. If you've reached five authorizations, you can reset your authorization count by clicking Deauthorize All on the Account Information screen. You can do this only once per year. The Deauthorize All button appears only if you have five authorized computers and you haven't used the option in the last 12 months.

Accessing the Store from Your iPod touch or iPhone

The music section of iTunes Store content is available right at your fingertips if you have an iPod touch or iPhone. You can search for, browse, preview, purchase, and download songs and albums directly to iPod touch or iPhone. Whatever you buy on your iPod touch or iPhone is automatically copied to your iTunes library the next time you synchronize the device with your computer.

To use the iTunes Store on an iPod touch, join a Wi-Fi network that is connected to the Internet (see Chapter 15 for details). You can use the 3G network or Wi-Fi on an iPhone. Be sure you have an iTunes Store account set up (see "Setting Up an Account" in this chapter).

Browsing and previewing songs

To go to the iTunes Store on an iPod touch or iPhone, choose iTunes from the Home menu. The store screen appears with Featured, Top Tens, Search, and Downloads buttons along the bottom. Touch any song to hear a preview.

Touch Featured to see featured items, new releases, and store recommendations. The screen displays New Releases, What's Hot, and Genres buttons along the top. To search through genres, touch Genres and choose a genre.

Touch Top Tens to see a list of the top ten choices in different genres. Choose iTunes in the Top Tens list to see the top ten songs in all of iTunes.

Touch Search to search the store, and touch the entry field to bring up the on-screen keyboard (for details on how to use the on-screen keyboard, see Chapter 1). Type the search term and touch Search to search the store.

Touch Downloads to see the progress of your downloads from the store, or to redeem gift certificates — by touching the Redeem button.

If you happen to be in one of the select U.S. Starbucks locations that plays iTunes music, the Starbucks icon appears at the bottom of the screen next to Featured. Tap the Starbucks icon to find out what song is playing at that very moment in the Starbucks. You can also browse featured Starbucks Collections.

Purchasing songs

To purchase songs on iPod touch or iPhone, you must have been signed in to your iTunes Store account in iTunes when you last synchronized it; if not, use iTunes to sign into the iTunes Store by clicking the Account button and typing your password; then synchronize your iPod touch or iPhone. All purchases you make with your are charged to your iTunes Store account.

To buy a song, touch the price, and then touch Buy Now. Enter your password and tap OK.

Purchased songs are added to a Purchased playlist on your iPod touch or iPhone, and they're included in your Purchased playlist in iTunes as well as in a special Purchased on "your device name" playlist. iTunes automatically syncs songs and albums purchased on your iPod touch or iPhone to your iTunes library when you connect iPod touch to your computer, so that you have a backup if you delete purchases from the iPod touch or iPhone.

Some albums offer bonus content, such as liner notes, which are downloaded to your iTunes library on your computer, but not to your iPod touch or iPhone. An alert appears if you've previously purchased one or more songs from an album. Touch Buy if you want to purchase the entire album, or touch Cancel if you want to buy the remaining songs on the album individually.

To see the status of the downloading, touch Downloads in the lower-right corner of the iTunes Store screen. You can pause a download by touching the Pause icon.

If you lose your network connection or turn off your iPod touch or iPhone while downloading, the download pauses and then resumes when you reestablish an Internet connection. If you go back to your computer, iTunes can complete the download operation to your iTunes library.

To make sure you received all your downloads from purchases on your iPod touch or iPhone, use iTunes on your computer and choose Store⇨Check for Available Downloads.

Chapter 5

Bringing Content into iTunes

* *

In This Chapter

▶ Setting your music importing preferences

▶ Ripping music from CDs and adding music files

▶ Adding audio books to your library

▶ Subscribing to podcasts on Web sites

▶ Adding video files to your library

* *

Several excellent reasons to bring your music CDs into iTunes, or to download media files from the iTunes Store into iTunes, are

✔ To preserve the content forever, in digital format

✔ To play the content easily from your computer (without having to fumble with discs)

✔ To play the content with Apple TV

✔ To take the content in your iPod or iPhone with you

In this chapter, I show you how to store content in your iTunes library. A song or video in digital format can be kept in that format in a file on any number of digital media storage devices. Even if your CDs, DVDs, and hard drive fail, your backup copy (assuming that you made a backup copy on a safety CD or hard drive) is still as perfect as the original digital file. You may make any number of digital copies with no technical limitations on playing the copies except those imposed by the iTunes Store for content that you purchase.

While you add more content, your iTunes library becomes your entertainment center. With it, you can find any item you want to play faster than you can open a CD jewel case, as I show in Chapter 8. Your iTunes library also manages your content and makes it easy to transfer some, or all of it, to your iPod or iPhone (as I describe in Chapter 11).

Adding Music

Bringing music tracks from a CD into iTunes is *ripping* a CD. I'm not sure why it's called that, but Apple certainly took the term to a new level with an ad campaign for Macs that featured the slogan *Rip, Mix, Burn*. Burning a mix CD was the hip thing to do a few years ago. With iTunes, you can still rip and mix, but if you have an iPod, you may no longer need to burn CDs to play your music wherever you go — just take your iPod.

Ripping, in technical terms, is extracting the song's digital information from an audio CD. In common terms, ripping includes compressing the song's digital information and encoding it in a particular sound file format. How easy is it to rip a CD? Pop an audio CD into your CD-ROM/DVD drive, and unless you've changed your preferences (as described in the following section), you'll see the message in Figure 5-1. Click Yes to rip your CD into iTunes without further ado, or click No to set your ripping preferences and import settings first.

Figure 5-1:
Click Yes to
rip your CD
into iTunes
automati-
cally, or No
to set pref-
erences first
or edit song
information
first.

> **iTunes**
>
> Would you like to import the CD "Sgt. Pepper's Lonely Hearts Club Band" into your iTunes library?
>
> ☐ Do not ask me again
>
> [Yes]   [No]

You might want to change import settings to improve sound quality or to reduce the amount of disk space occupied by songs. The import settings affect sound quality, hard drive space on both the computer and the iPod or iPhone, and compatibility with other types of players and computers.

To find out more about import settings and how they reduce space or increase audio quality, visit this book's companion Web site.

You may also want to edit song information first, as I describe in Chapter 9. In either case, you can click No to stop the import operation and make your changes first.

Changing import preferences and settings

Although importing music from an audio CD takes a lot less time than playing the CD, it still takes time. To minimize that time, you want your import preferences and settings to be correct before starting. To do this, follow these steps:

1. **Choose iTunes⇨Preferences–>General on a Mac or Edit⇨Preferences⇨ General in Windows.**

   The iTunes Preferences dialog opens showing the General preferences, including the When You Insert a CD pop-up menu, and the Import Settings button.

2. **Choose what action iTunes should take for the When You Insert a CD option in the General preferences.**

   Choose one of the following actions in the pop-up menu for when you insert an audio CD, as shown in Figure 5-2:

   • *Show CD:* iTunes does nothing else. This setting is ideal if you regularly edit the song information first, as I describe in Chapter 9.

   • *Begin Playing:* See Chapter 3 for details on playing CDs.

   • *Ask to Import CD:* iTunes displays a dialog asking whether you want to import the CD (refer to Figure 5-1).

   • *Import CD:* iTunes uses the current import settings and automatically imports the CD. Don't use this setting unless you're sure that the import settings are already set to your liking.

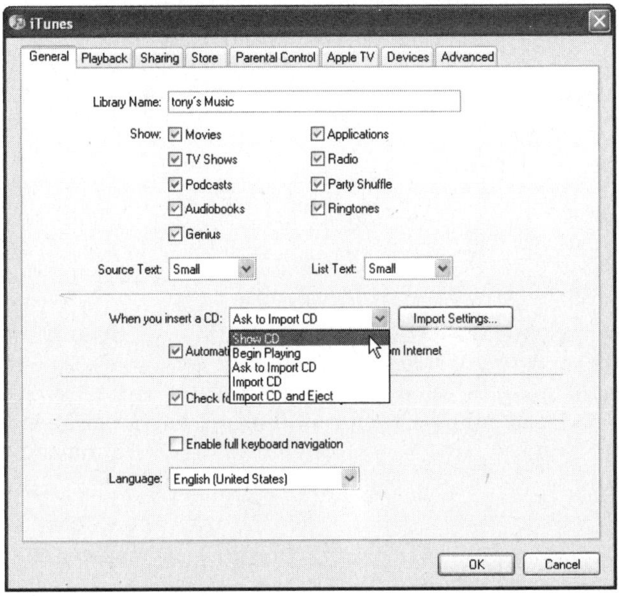

Figure 5-2:
Set the appropriate action for iTunes after a CD is inserted.

• *Import CD and Eject:* iTunes automatically imports and then ejects the CD, making way for the next one. This option is useful for importing a batch of CDs. Don't use this setting unless you're sure that the import settings are already set to your liking.

3. **Turn on the Automatically Retrieve CD Track Names from Internet option.**

   This option is turned on by default, but make sure it's on by selecting it so that a check mark appears. iTunes automatically grabs the song titles, artist names, album titles, and so forth directly from the Internet database of songs, as I describe in Chapter 9.

4. **Click the Import Settings button in the General preferences.**

   The Import Settings dialog appears, as shown in Figure 5-3.

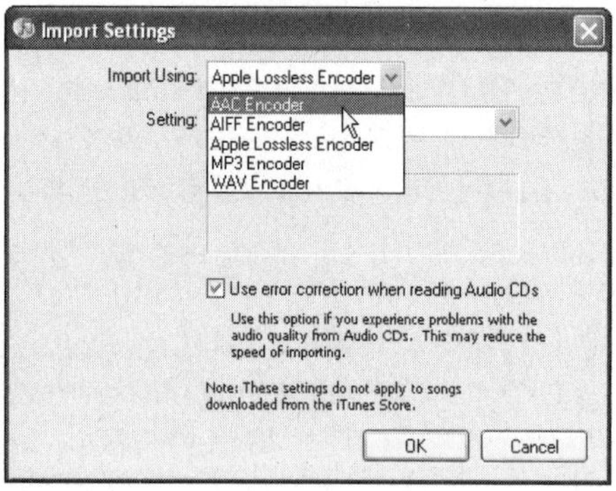

Figure 5-3:
Change
your import
settings for
ripping CDs.

The Import Settings dialog offers the following choices:

- **Import Using:** Set this pop-up menu to choose the import encoder. This choice is perhaps the most important, and I describe it in more detail later in this section.

- **Setting:** This offers different settings depending on your choice of encoder. For example, in Figure 5-4, the AAC Encoder is already selected, and I'm in the process of choosing Higher Quality. Set this pop-up menu to High Quality or better for most music.

- **Use Error Correction When Reading Audio CDs:** Although you'll reduce importing speed, select this check box to use error correction if you have problems with audio quality or if the CD skips. (Not every skipping CD can be imported even with error correction, but it might help.)

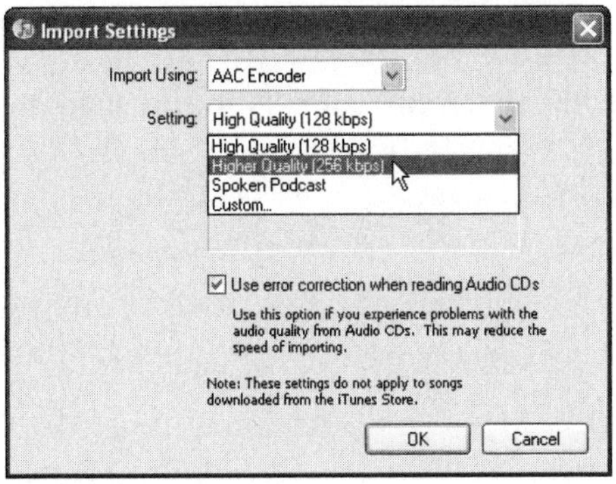

Figure 5-4:
Change the
quality set-
ting for the
encoder you
chose for
importing.

For a quick and pain-free ripping session, choose from among the following encoders in the Import Using pop-up menu based on how you plan to use the music:

- ✔ **AAC Encoder:** I recommend AAC for almost all music. (However, AIFF, Apple Lossless, or WAV is better if you plan to burn another audio CD at the highest quality with the songs you ripped.) Choose the High Quality option from the Setting pop-up menu.

  You can always convert a song that you've already ripped in AIFF, Apple Lossless, or WAV to AAC or MP3. However, ripping a CD with one encoder might be more convenient. After that, you can rip it again with a different encoder. For example, you might import *Sgt. Pepper's Lonely Hearts Club Band* with the AAC encoder for use in your Mac and iPod. You might then import it again with the higher-quality Apple Lossless or AIFF encoder under a different name (such as Sgt. Pepper-2), for burning onto an audio CD. After burning the CD, you can delete Sgt. Pepper-2 to reclaim the hard drive space.

- ✔ **AIFF Encoder:** Use AIFF if you plan to burn the song to an audio CD using a Mac (use WAV for Windows), or use it with a DVD project. AIFF offers the highest possible quality, but it takes up a lot of space (about 10MB per minute). Choose the Automatic option from the Setting pop-up menu for best results. Don't use AIFF format for songs that you intend to transfer to your iPod or to an MP3 CD; convert them first to AAC or MP3.

- ✔ **Apple Lossless Encoder:** Use the Apple Lossless encoder for songs that you intend to burn onto audio CDs as well as for playing on iPods. The files are just small enough (about 60–70 percent of the size of the AIFF versions) that they don't hiccup on playback.

✔ **MP3 Encoder:** Use the MP3 format for songs that you intend to burn on MP3 CDs or that you intend to use with MP3 players or your iPod — it's universally supported. If you use MP3, I recommend choosing the Higher Quality option from the Setting pop-up menu.

✔ **WAV Encoder:** WAV is the high-quality sound format that's used on PCs (like AIFF), but it also takes up a lot of space (about 10MB per minute). Use WAV if you plan on burning the song to an audio CD or using WAV with PCs. Choose the Automatic option from the Setting pop-up menu for best results. Don't use WAV for songs that you intend to transfer to your iPod or to an MP3 CD; use MP3 instead.

To find out more about audio encoding formats, how to adjust custom settings to reduce space and increase audio quality, and how to convert songs from one format to another (and what problems to look out for when doing so), visit this book's companion Web site.

Don't fall into the gaps

Some CDs — particularly live concert albums, classical albums, rock operas (such as The Who's *Tommy*), and theme albums (such as *Sgt. Pepper's Lonely Hearts Club Band* by The Beatles) — are meant to be played straight through, with no fading between the songs. Although you can cross-fade between songs automatically in iTunes, you can't on your iPod or iPhone.

Fortunately, you can turn on the Gapless Album option for multiple songs or for an entire album. With the Gapless Album option set in iTunes, songs play seamlessly one to the next. You can also play these songs seamlessly on fifth-generation iPods (and second-generation iPod nanos) that have the latest software update, as well as on current iPod and iPhone models.

To turn on the Gapless Album option for an entire CD before importing it, follow these steps:

1. **Click No if the import dialog appears (to postpone importing).**

2. **Select the CD title in the Source pane.**

   The CD title appears in the Source pane under Devices.

3. **Choose File⇨Get Info.**

   The CD Info dialog opens, as shown in Figure 5-5.

4. **Select the check box next to the Gapless Album option and then click OK.**

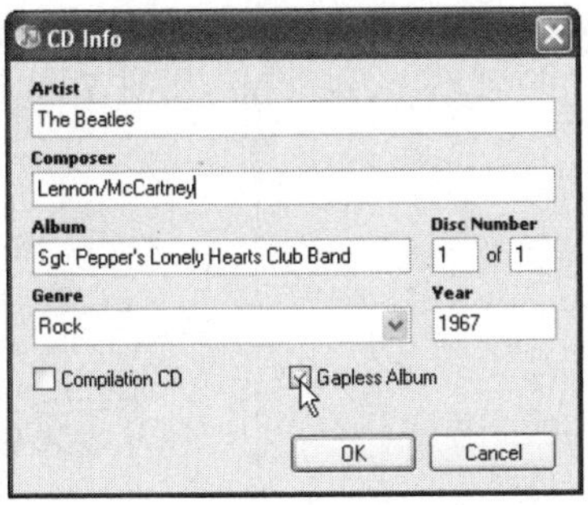

Figure 5-5:
Select the
Gapless
Album
option for
an entire
album.

To turn on the Gapless Album option for multiple songs on the CD but not the entire CD, follow these steps:

1. **Follow Steps 1 and 2 in the preceding list.**

2. **Select the songs in the list pane.**

   From the album, select the songs that you want to play continuously (such as the first two songs of *Sgt. Pepper*).

   To select multiple songs, click the first one, press ⌘ on a Mac or Ctrl in Windows, and click each subsequent song. To select consecutive songs, click the first one, hold down the Shift key, and click the last one.

3. **Choose File⇨Get Info and then click Yes in the warning dialog about editing multiple items.**

   The Multiple Item Information dialog opens.

4. **Click the Options tab to see the Options dialog, as shown in Figure 5-6.**

5. **Select Yes for the Gapless Album option pop-up menu.**

   After choosing Yes in the pop-up menu, a check mark appears next to the Gapless Album option to indicate that it has changed.

6. **Click OK to close the Multiple Item Information dialog and update the options for the selected songs.**

What happens if you turn on Crossfade Playback for playing songs in iTunes, as I describe in Chapter 6, but you *don't* want to cross-fade between specific songs on an album that has no gaps? You don't have to keep turning Crossfade Playback on and off: Simply deselect the Gapless Album option for those songs.

For older iPod models, or as an alternative to using the Gapless Album option, you can use the Join Tracks option when ripping a CD to join the tracks in your iTunes library so that they play seamlessly on an iPod. To join tracks, select the tracks and choose Advanced⇨Join CD Tracks. You can join tracks only when ripping a CD, not afterward.

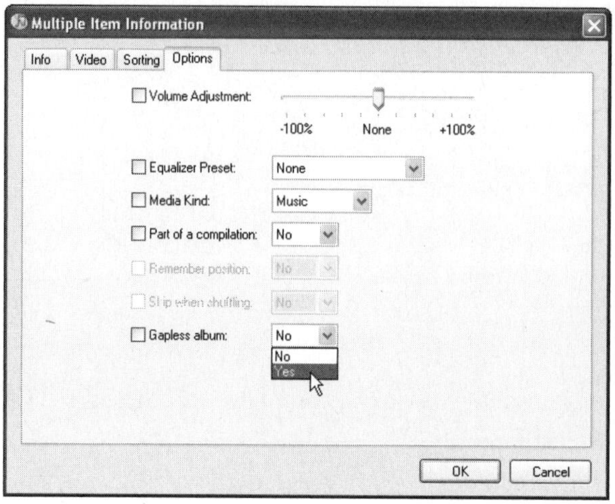

Multiple Item Information

Info | Video | Sorting | Options

☐ Volume Adjustment:

-100%   None   +100%

☐ Equalizer Preset: None

☐ Media Kind: Music

☐ Part of a compilation: No

☐ Remember position: No

☐ Skip when shuffling: No

☐ Gapless album: No
                     No
                     Yes

OK   Cancel

Figure 5-6:
Select the
Gapless
Album
option for
multiple
tracks.

Ripping music from CDs

After checking your import settings and preferences, you're ready to rip. To rip a CD, follow these steps:

1. **Insert an audio CD into your computer.**

   The songs appear in the List pane as generic, unnamed tracks at first. If your computer is connected to the Internet, if you've turned on the option to automatically retrieve song information from the Internet, and if the CD is in the Gracenote CDDB database (described in Chapter 9), iTunes automatically retrieves the track information.

   A dialog appears asking if you want to import the CD, with Yes and No buttons.

2. **Click Yes to import (and skip to Step 5), or No to set options first.**

   Click No to set preferences and import settings as described in the previous section; or to set songs to be skipped; or if you see unnamed tracks rather than the proper track, artist, and album names.

   If the first attempt at retrieving song information doesn't work and you see unnamed tracks, check your connection to the Internet first. If everything is fine with your connection, stop the importing operation and then choose Advanced⇨Get CD Track Names to try again to get the track information. If you don't want to connect to the Internet or if your CD isn't recognized by the Gracenote database, you can type the track information yourself (see Chapter 9).

3. **(Optional) Deselect the check boxes next to any songs on the CD that you don't want to import.**

iTunes imports only the songs that have check marks next to them; when you remove the check mark next to a song, iTunes skips that song.

Be sure to set your import settings and the Gapless Album option to your liking before actually ripping the CD.

4. Click the Import CD button.

The Import CD button appears at the bottom-right corner of the iTunes window after you insert a CD. The status display shows the progress of the operation. To cancel, click the small *x* next to the progress bar in the status display.

iTunes displays an orange, animated waveform icon next to the song that it's importing. When iTunes finishes importing each song, it replaces the waveform icon with a check mark, as shown in Figure 5-7. (On a color monitor, the check mark is green.) iTunes chimes when it finishes the import list.

5. When all the songs are imported, eject the CD by clicking the Eject button next to the disc name in the Devices section of the Source pane.

You can also choose Controls⇨Eject Disc to eject the disc. Mac users can press the Eject button on the upper-right corner of the Mac keyboard.

Adding music files

You can download a music file or copy it from another computer to your hard drive. After you save or copy an MP3 file — or, for that matter, an AIFF or WAV file — on your hard drive, you can simply drag it into the iTunes window to bring it into your library. If you drag a folder or disk icon, all the audio files that it contains are added to your iTunes library. You can also choose File⇨Add to Library on a Mac, or File⇨Add File to Library and File⇨Add Folder to Library on a Windows PC, as an alternative to dragging.

Figure 5-7: iTunes shows a check mark to indicate it's done ripping the song.

When you add a song to your iTunes library, a copy is placed inside the iTunes Music folder; that is, as long as you have your iTunes preferences set for Copy Files to iTunes Music Folder When Adding to Library. (This is the default setting, which you can find in the Advanced tab of the iTunes Preferences dialog.) See Chapter 12 for details on storing music in your iTunes Music folder.

If you have song files in another folder or on another hard drive, and you want to add them to the iTunes library without copying the files to the iTunes Music folder, you can copy a link to the original files without copying the files. To copy only links to song files and not copy the actual files when you add songs, you can turn off the default copy files option by doing the following:

1. **Choose iTunes⇨Preferences (Mac) or Edit⇨Preferences (Windows).**

2. **Click the Advanced tab in the iTunes Preferences dialog.**

3. **Turn off the Copy Files to iTunes Music Folder When Adding to Library setting.**

You can check out the contents of your music folder by using the Finder on a Mac or Windows Explorer on a Windows PC, as I describe in detail in Chapter 12.

When you bring a song file into iTunes, the song is copied into a new file in the iTunes library without changing or deleting the original file. You can then convert the song to another format. For example, you can convert an AIFF file to an MP3 file while leaving the original intact.

To find out more about audio encoding formats and how to convert songs from one format to another (and what problems to look out for when doing so), visit this book's companion Web site. You can also find out how to bring any sound into iTunes, even music from scratchy vinyl records or sound effects recorded through a microphone.

MP3 CDs are easy to add because they're essentially data CDs. Simply insert them into your CD-ROM drive, open the CD in the Finder, and drag and drop the MP3 song files into the iTunes window. Downloaded song files are even easier — just drag and drop the files into iTunes. If you drag a folder or CD icon, all the audio files it contains are added to your iTunes library.

Adding Audio Books

Do you like to listen to audio books and spoken magazine and newspaper articles? Not only can you bring these files into iTunes, but you can also transfer them to an iPod or iPhone and take them on the road, which is much more convenient than taking cassettes or CDs.

Audible is a leading provider of downloadable, spoken audio files. Audible lets you authorize computers to play the audio files — just like the iTunes Store; see Chapter 4. Audible does require that you purchase the files, and content from Audible is also licensed by Apple to be included in the iTunes Store. Audible content includes magazines and radio programs as well as books.

To import Audible files, follow these steps:

1. **Go to www.audible.com.**

   Set up an account if you don't already have one.

2. **Select and download an Audible audio file.**

   Files that end with .aa are Audible files.

3. **Drag the Audible file to the iTunes window.**

   If this is the first time that you've added an Audible file, iTunes asks for your Audible account information. You enter this information once for each computer that you use with your Audible account.

To disable an Audible account, open iTunes on the computer that you no longer want to use with the account, and choose Advanced⇨Deauthorize Audible Account. In the Deauthorize Audible Account dialog that appears, enter the username and password for the account, and then click OK.

You need to be online to authorize a computer or to remove the authorization from that computer.

Adding Podcasts

You can add podcasts to your iTunes library by subscribing to them in the iTunes Store (as I describe in breathtaking detail in Chapter 4) or by subscribing to them directly from Web sites that host them. Similar to a tape of a radio broadcast, you can save and play a podcast at your convenience — both in iTunes on your computer and on your iPod, iPhone, and Apple TV.

A *podcast* can be anything from a single song or video to a radio or TV show. Audio podcasts are saved in the MP3 format and may be used with any media player, device, or application that supports MP3, including your iPod. Video podcasts are saved in the QuickTime (.mov) format or the Moving Pictures Expert Group (MPEG-4) formats, including the standard .mp4 format and the Apple TV .m4v format, which can be used with iPods that play video, the iPhone, Apple TV, and many other video players.

The podcast producer uses Really Simple Syndication (RSS) technology — the same technology used to distribute blogs and news feeds across the Internet — to publish the podcast. RSS feeds are typically linked to an RSS or an eXtensible Markup Language (XML; the language of RSS) button. With a feed reader, aggregator application, or browser plug-in, you can automatically check RSS-enabled Web pages and display updated stories and podcasts. RSS version 2, the most popular version for podcasting, is supported directly by some Web browsers, including Apple's Safari for Mac OS X and Windows.

With iTunes, you can play a podcast, incorporate it into playlists, make copies, and burn it onto CD as much as you like. If you don't like the podcast, simply delete it from your iTunes library and update your iPod to delete it from your iPod.

Subscribing to podcasts

The Podcasts section of the iTunes Store offers access to many thousands of podcasts, but more than a million podcasts exist, many of which are available only on their Web sites. The iTunes Store makes it easy to subscribe to podcasts, so check there first — turn to Chapter 4 to see how to subscribe to podcasts in the iTunes Store.

By *subscribing,* I mean simply listing the podcast in your iTunes Podcasts pane so that new episodes are downloaded automatically. It's like a magazine subscription that's updated with a new issue every month or so. You don't have to register or fill out any form. You don't have to provide an e-mail address or any other information. Your copy of iTunes automatically finds new podcast episodes and downloads them to your computer.

The easiest way to subscribe to a podcast is through the iTunes Store. However, if you can't find a podcast in the store and you know how to find its Web site, open your browser and then go to that Web site. Some Web sites also offer an iTunes button to click to go directly to the iTunes Store to subscribe to the podcast.

If there is no iTunes button, you can still subscribe to a podcast directly from iTunes by grabbing information from its Web site first. Follow these steps:

1. **In your browser, Control-click (Mac) or right-click (Windows) the podcast's RSS2 link on the Web page.**

   Look for the RSS version 2 link on the Web page. Many sites use an icon, as shown in Figure 5-8.

2. **Copy the podcast's RSS2 link.**
   - *Safari:* Choose Copy Link.
   - *Firefox or Internet Explorer:* Choose Copy Link Location.

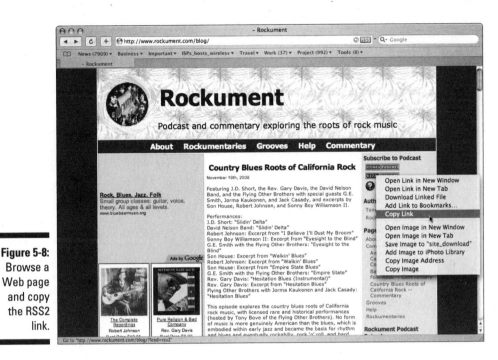

Figure 5-8:
Browse a
Web page
and copy
the RSS2
link.

3. In iTunes, choose Advanced⇨Subscribe to Podcast.

The Subscribe to Podcast dialog opens, as shown in Figure 5-9.

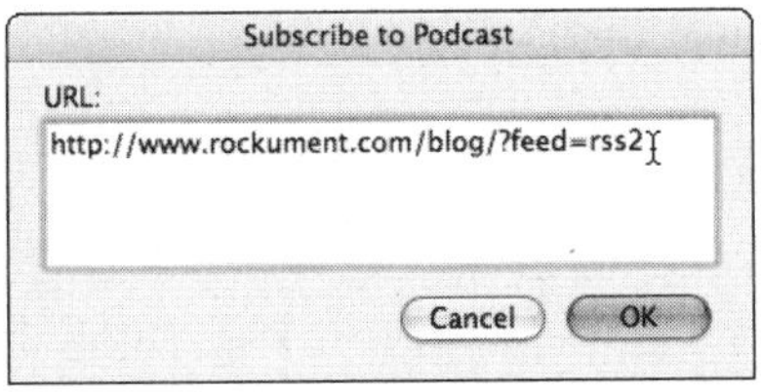

Figure 5-9:
Paste the
RSS2 link
into the
Subscribe
to Podcast
dialog.

> Subscribe to Podcast
>
> URL:
> http://www.rockument.com/blog/?feed=rss2
>
> Cancel   OK

4. Paste the RSS2 link by choosing Edit⇨Paste and then click OK.

As an alternative, you can also press ⌘-V on a Mac or Ctrl-V in Windows.

When you paste it, the link should look something like

```
http://www.rockument.com/blog/?feed=RSS2
```

iTunes downloads the podcast to your computer and switches to the
Podcasts selection in the Source pane.

5. Click the *i* icon to see information about the podcast.

You can click the *i* icon on the far-right podcast listing margin, as shown in Figure 5-10, to display separate information about the podcast's newest episode.

6. Select the podcast and then click the Play button.

You can now play the podcast just like a song or video in your iTunes library. You can use the iTunes playback controls to fast-forward, rewind, or play the podcast from any point. The blue dot next to a podcast means you haven't played it yet. As soon as you start listening to or watching a podcast, the dot disappears. You can even drag podcast episodes into a playlist, as I describe in Chapter 10, and then burn that playlist onto a CD, as I describe in Chapter 12.

Podcasts don't show up in Party Shuffle unless you drag them into the Party Shuffle playlist; see Chapter 6.

If the podcaster embedded a photo in an audio podcast file or included a link to a video from the file, the photo or video content appears in the Artwork pane.

Figure 5-10: Display information about the podcast's current episode.

Updating podcasts

Many podcast feeds provide new material on a regular schedule. iTunes can check these feeds automatically and update your library with new podcast episodes. You can, for example, schedule iTunes to check for new podcast episodes — such as news, weather, traffic reports, and morning talk shows — before you wake up and automatically update your iPod or iPhone. When you get up, you have new podcast episodes to listen to in your iPod or iPhone.

To check for updates manually, select Podcasts in the Library section of the Source pane and then click the Refresh button in the lower-right corner of the Podcasts pane, which appears if podcasts need to be updated. All subscribed podcast feeds are updated immediately when you click Refresh, and iTunes downloads the most recent (or all) episodes, depending on how you set your podcasts preferences to schedule podcast updates.

Scheduling podcast updates

To change your podcast settings so iTunes can check for new podcasts automatically, click Settings at the bottom of the Podcasts pane to display the Podcast Settings dialog, as shown in Figure 5-11.

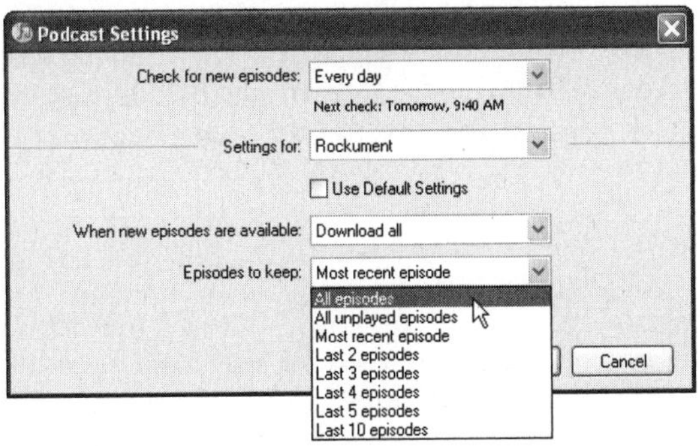

Figure 5-11:
Set iTunes to automatically check for, download, and keep podcast episodes.

You can change the settings for each podcast separately by choosing the podcast in the Settings For pop-up menu. You can also set the default settings for all podcasts by choosing Default in the Settings For pop-up menu. The settings are:

✓ **Check for New Episodes:** Choose to check for podcasts every hour, day, week, or manually — whenever you want.

✔ **When New Episodes Are Available:** You can download the most recent one (useful for news podcasts), download all episodes (useful for podcasts you might want to keep), or nothing so that you can use the Refresh button to update manually as you need.

✔ **Episodes to Keep:** Choose to keep all episodes, all unplayed episodes, the most recent episodes, or previous episodes (refer to Figure 5-11).

Keeping unplayed episodes is a useful way to organize your news podcasts. If you've played an episode (or a portion of it), you likely don't need it anymore, but you probably do want to keep the ones you haven't played yet. Set iTunes to automatically delete podcast episodes that you don't want to keep.

If you copy podcasts automatically when synchronizing your iPod or iPhone, as I describe in Chapter 11, don't set the Episodes to Keep pop-up to All Unplayed Episodes. This is why: If you listen to part of a podcast episode on your iPod or iPhone and then synchronize your iPod or iPhone, the podcast episode disappears from iTunes (because it is no longer unplayed). But don't worry; the episodes are still out there on the Internet. You can always recover them by choosing Download All for the When New Episodes Are Available option.

Adding Videos

Besides purchasing and downloading videos from the iTunes Store, as I describe in nearly orgasmic detail in Chapter 4, you can also download videos from the Internet or copy them from other computers and bring them into iTunes. You can then watch QuickTime and MPEG-4 movies (files that end in `.mov`, `.m4v`, or `.mp4`) in iTunes.

You can also use them in a video-enabled iPod or iPhone and with Apple TV. iTunes provides options for converting videos in the iTunes library into a format that looks better when you play them on an iPod or iPhone display, or into a format that looks better on televisions connected to Apple TV. To convert a video for use with an iPod or iPhone, select the video (see Chapter 8 for browsing instructions), and choose Advanced➪Create iPod or iPhone Version. To convert a video for use with Apple TV, choose Advanced➪Create Apple TV Version. The selected videos are automatically copied when you convert them, leaving the originals intact.

To find out more about converting videos in iTunes for use with iPods, iPhones, and Apple TV, visit this book's companion Web site.

QuickTime, the Apple digital video file format, is installed on every Mac. It's also downloaded and installed onto PCs along with the Windows version of iTunes. QuickTime is used extensively in the digital video production world for making videos for the Web. Music videos, movie trailers, and other videos you can buy on the iTunes Store are in the QuickTime format. MPEG-4 is a standard format for digital video that works on just about any computer that plays video.

You can drag the video into iTunes just like a song file. Drag each video file from the Mac Finder or Windows Desktop to the library, directly to a playlist in the iTunes Source pane or to the list or artwork view on the right side of the iTunes window, as shown in Figure 5-12.

The video files that you drag into iTunes, along with the movies, TV shows, and music videos you purchase from the iTunes Store, display in the Movies section of your iTunes library. Click Movies in the Library section of the Source pane to peek inside the Movies section (refer to Figure 5-12).

Video files are organized in folders and stored in the music library on your hard drive just like song files. You can find the video file's location on your hard drive and its type by selecting the video and choosing File⇨Get Info.

You can create your own QuickTime or MPEG-4 video files with a suitable video-editing application, such as iMovie for the Mac (part of the iLife software suite that includes iTunes), or Apple QuickTime Pro for Windows, available from the Apple Store.

Figure 5-12:
Bring a
video file
into iTunes.

Chapter 6

Playing Content in iTunes

*I*f you like to entertain folks by spinning tunes and playing videos at home or at parties, iTunes could easily become your media jockey console. Imagine how much music you could have at your fingertips with an iTunes library that can grow as large as your hard drive. You can fit more than 20,000 songs, or 64 days of nonstop music, in about 100GB of hard drive space. When I last checked the Apple store, you could buy a 2 terabyte (TB) external drive for either Mac or PC that would probably hold enough music to run a radio station. But that's not all: You can also manage your videos and favorite TV shows and play them in full-screen mode on your computer running iTunes.

Your computer is already a mean multimedia machine, with the capability to mix sounds, photos, and videos. You can play music through your computer's built-in speakers or through headphones, but you'll get better results with high-quality external speakers. You can even connect your home computer to an excellent stereo for high-quality sound. The same is true for video: You can use iTunes to play video on your computer's display, or you can send it to a larger television or display monitor — even a video projector — to get a bigger picture.

And if you've integrated Apple TV with your home stereo and television, you can use iTunes to feed music to Apple TV, which has its own hard drive, as I describe in this chapter. See Chapter 7 for details on setting up Apple TV.

Changing the Computer's Output Volume

You can control the volume and other characteristics of the sound coming from your computer's speakers, headphones, or external speakers. Even if you connect your computer to a stereo amplifier with its own volume and equalizer controls, it's best to get the volume correct at the source — your computer and iTunes — and then adjust the output volume as you please on your stereo or external speaker unit.

You control the volume by using your computer system's audio controls. iTunes also controls the volume, but that control is within the limits of the computer's volume setting. For example, if you set your computer's volume to half and set iTunes volume to full, you get half volume because the computer limits the volume to half. If you set your computer volume at half and also reduce the iTunes volume to half, you actually get *one-quarter* volume — half the computer's setting. After the sound leaves your computer, you can adjust it further with the volume controls of your stereo system or external speakers.

The appropriate volume depends entirely on your preferences for hearing music, audio books, or video soundtracks. In general, though, the maximum level of output from your computer is preferable when connecting to a stereo system or speakers with volume controls. After setting your computer to the maximum volume, adjust the iTunes volume or your stereo or speaker volume (or both) to get the best sound. When using the computer's speakers or headphones, the computer's volume and the iTunes volume are the only volume controls that you have, so after adjusting the volume on your computer to the maximum level (or lower if you prefer), adjust the iTunes volume.

Adjusting the sound on a Mac

The Mac was built for sound from the very start. Making and playing music has been part of the Mac culture since the day that Steve Jobs introduced an audience to the original Mac with sound coming from its small speaker. (It played synthesized speech and simple tones, but it was the first personal computer with built-in sound.)

Current Apple Mac computers come with built-in or external speakers and at least one headphone/line-out connection that you can use to connect external speakers or a stereo system. Mac OS X lets you configure output speakers and control levels for stereo speakers and multichannel audio devices.

If you use external speakers, headphones, or a stereo system, make sure that you connect these devices properly before adjusting the volume.

To adjust the volume on your Mac, follow these steps:

1. **Choose System Preferences from the Apple menu or the Dock and then click the Sound icon.**

   Otherwise, press Option and a volume control key on your keyboard simultaneously as a shortcut. You can have iTunes open and playing music while you do this.

2. **In the Sound preferences window that opens, click Output and select the sound output device.**

   If you have headphones or external speakers attached to the headphones connection on your Mac, a Headphones option appears in the list of sound output devices, as shown in Figure 6-1; if not, an External Speakers or Internal Speakers option appears for speakers connected through a line-out connection or built into the Mac.

3. **Adjust the volume.**

   You can do any of the following:

   - Drag the slider to adjust the volume while you listen to music.
   - Select the Mute check box to silence your Mac.
   - Drag the Balance slider to put more music in the left or right channels.

4. **Close the Preferences window, either by choosing System Preferences⇨Quit System Preferences, clicking the red button in the upper-left corner of the window, or pressing ⌘-Q.**

   The Sound preferences window isn't like a dialog: When you change settings, you can hear the effect immediately without having to click OK. (There isn't an OK button, anyway.)

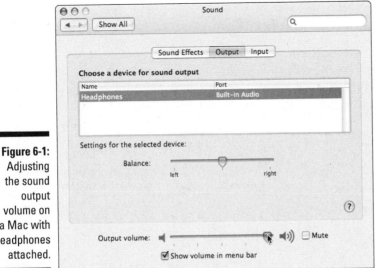

Figure 6-1:
Adjusting
the sound
output
volume on
a Mac with
headphones
attached.

Adjusting the sound in Windows

Windows XP, Windows Vista, and Windows 2000 let you configure output speakers and control levels for stereo speakers and multichannel audio devices.

Use the Sounds and Audio Devices Properties dialog to change the volume. To open this dialog, choose Start⇨Control Panel, click the Sounds and Audio Devices icon, and then click the Volume tab.

As shown in Figure 6-2, the Sounds and Audio Devices Properties dialog offers the Device Volume slider, which you drag to set the volume. You can also silence your PC by selecting the Mute check box.

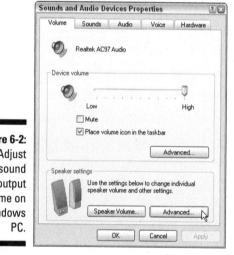

Figure 6-2:
Adjust
the sound
output
volume on
a Windows
PC.

If you select the Place Volume Icon in the Taskbar option and your sound card supports changing the volume with software, a sound icon appears in the notification area of Windows. You can then change the volume quickly without having to open the Sounds and Audio Devices Properties dialog. Simply click the speaker icon and drag the slider that pops up. For more information about adjusting sound on a PC, see *PCs For Dummies* by Dan Gookin (Wiley).

Using AirTunes or Apple TV for Wireless Stereo Playback

You want to play the music in your iTunes library, but your stereo system is across the room or in another room, and you don't want to extend wires to the stereo system. What you need is a wireless connection from your computer to your stereo system.

You can use an Apple AirPort Wi-Fi network in your home — such as AirPort Express by itself, or Apple TV with AirPort Extreme or Time Capsule. AirPort Express and Apple TV work with Apple's AirTunes technology, which lets you play your iTunes music through your stereo or powered speakers in any room of your house, without wires. The only catch is that your computer must be within range of the Wi-Fi network or connected by an Ethernet cable.

Apple's AirPort technology provides Wi-Fi networking for any AirPort-equipped Mac or wireless-capable PC that uses a Wi-Fi–certified IEEE 802.11b, 802.11g, or 802.11n wireless card or offers built-in Wi-Fi. For more about AirPort, see *Mac OS X Leopard All-in-One Desk Reference For Dummies,* by Mark L. Chambers (Wiley).

If you already have a wireless network in place, you can add AirPort Express without changing anything. The AirPort Express wirelessly links to your existing wireless network without requiring any change to the network. You can even use several AirPort Express units — one for each stereo system or set of powered speakers, in different rooms.

All by itself, AirPort Express creates a Wi-Fi network. You can attach your Internet cable modem or other Ethernet network to AirPort Express to link your ready-made Wi-Fi network to the outside world. You can also take AirPort Express on the road to use in hotel rooms to share an Internet connection among wireless computers.

To use AirTunes and AirPort Express, follow these steps:

1. **Install the software supplied with AirPort Express.**

   The CD-ROM includes support for AirTunes.

2. **Connect your stereo or a set of powered speakers to the AirPort Express audio port.**

   You can use an optical digital or analog audio cable. (Both are included in the AirPort Express Stereo Connection Kit available from the Apple Store.) Which cable you use depends on whether your stereo or set of powered speakers has an optical digital or analog connection.

3. **Plug AirPort Express into an electrical outlet.**

Use the AC plug that came with AirPort Express or the power extension cord included in the AirPort Express Stereo Connection Kit. AirPort Express turns on automatically when connected to an electrical outlet. The status light glows yellow while AirPort Express is starting up. When it is fully up and running, the light turns green.

4. **On your computer, set your iTunes preferences to look for speakers connected wirelessly with AirTunes.**

   a. *Choose iTunes⇨Preferences (Mac) or Edit⇨Preferences (Windows).*

   b. *Click the Devices button to get the Devices pane (Figure 6-3).*

   c. *Select the Look for Remote Speakers Connected with AirTunes option in the Devices pane, as shown in Figure 6-3.*

In the Devices pane, you also have some options. *To control volume from a stereo:* By default, the iTunes volume control sets the volume for the speakers. Select the Disable iTunes Volume Control for Remote Speakers option to control speakers separately (a setting you should use if connecting to a stereo with a volume control). *Allow iTunes control from remote speakers:* Select this option to allow Apple TV or other speakers controlled by Apple Remote to set the volume in iTunes when streaming music from the iTunes library.

Figure 6-3: Select the option to look for remote speakers connected to your computer using AirTunes.

After turning on the option to look for AirTunes-connected speakers, the Speakers pop-up menu appears in the lower-right corner of the iTunes window if iTunes can locate the speakers. *Note:* The menu will probably be set to Computer, the default option.

5. Choose Airtunes-Equipped Network from this new pop-up menu.

The Speakers pop-up menu includes the Computer itself and any available wireless AirTunes networks, as shown in Figure 6-4. You can select the AirTunes network to play music ("Express Buddy" in Figure 6-4). From that point, iTunes plays music through the AirTunes network rather than through the computer. To get back to playing music through speakers connected to the computer (or through the computer's built-in speakers), choose Computer from the Speakers pop-up menu.

Figure 6-4: Choosing the AirTunes network "Express Buddy" from the Speakers menu.

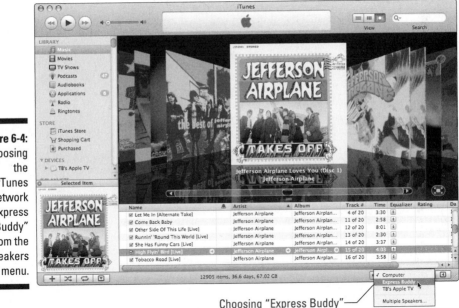

Choosing "Express Buddy"

The AirPort Express is small enough to fit in the palm of your hand, and it travels well because all it needs is a power outlet. You can take your laptop and AirPort Express to a friend's house or party, connect the AirPort Express to the stereo system and a power outlet, and then use your laptop anywhere in its vicinity to play DJ. You can even use portable powered speakers in a hotel room without wires and use a hotel room's LAN-to-Internet access with an AirPort Express to connect your wireless computer and other wireless computers in the room to the Internet.

To play music through speakers connected to your Apple TV, choose Apple TV from the Speakers pop-up menu, as shown in Figure 6-5. You can use any computer with iTunes to play its library content (audio *and* video) through Apple TV to your home entertainment system without your having to synchronize that library's content — meaning you don't have to change the content that is already synchronized with your Apple TV. That way, if you invite a friend over with her laptop, you can quickly play any tune in her laptop's library without changing the synchronized content from your computer. You can play anything in an iTunes library, even if your Apple TV is already filled with synchronized content. (To find out how to synchronize your Apple TV, see Chapter 11.)

Figure 6-5: Choosing Apple TV on a wireless network to play music and video.

Choosing "TB's Apple TV"

If you set up your Apple TV to work with an Apple AirPort-based network (as I describe in Chapter 7), you can choose the Multiple Speakers option in the Speakers pop-up menu (refer to Figure 6-5), and play your iTunes content through both the computer and Apple TV speakers at the same time.

Playing Songs

When you've found a song you want to play (see Chapter 8 for searching details), simply select it in the List pane and then click the Play button. The Play button toggles to a Pause button while the song plays. When the song finishes, iTunes continues playing the songs in the list in sequence until you click the Pause button (which then toggles back into the Play button) or until the song list ends. This setup is useful if you select an album, but not so great if you select a song at random and don't want to hear the next one. (Fortunately, you can arrange songs in playlists so that they play back in exactly the sequence you want; see Chapter 10 for details.)

You can skip to the next or previous song by pressing the right- or left-arrow keys, respectively, or by clicking the Forward or Back buttons next to the Play button. You can also double-click another song in the list to start playing it.

Press the spacebar to perform the same function as the Play button; press the spacebar again to pause.

You can choose songs to play manually, but iTunes also provides several automated features so that you can spend less time prepping your music selection and more time enjoying it.

Queuing up tunes with Party Shuffle

Playlists, as I describe in Chapter 10, are great for organizing music in the order that you want to play it, but you can have iTunes serve up songs at random by using Party Shuffle. Not a dance step or a pub game, *Party Shuffle* is a dynamic playlist that automatically generates a semirandom selection in a list that you can modify on the fly. With Party Shuffle, you might even find songs in your library you forgot about or rarely play. Party Shuffle always throws a few rarely played songs into the mix.

To use Party Shuffle, follow these steps:

1. **Select Party Shuffle in the Playlists section of the Source pane.**

   The List pane is replaced with the Party Shuffle track list and settings at the bottom, as shown in Figure 6-6.

Figure 6-6:
Adjust the
settings
for Party
Shuffle.

2. **Choose a source from the Source pop-up menu below the Party Shuffle track list.**

   You can select Music (for the entire music portion of your library) or any playlist (including a smart playlist; see Chapter 10 for details) as the source for music in Party Shuffle. If you select a playlist, Party Shuffle limits its choices to songs from that playlist.

3. **Set the following options:**

   • *Recently Played Songs:* Choose how many songs should remain in the Party Shuffle list after they're played. You can drag already-played songs (even though they're grayed out after playing) to a spot later in the list to play them again.

   • *Upcoming Songs:* Choose how many songs should be listed as *upcoming* (not yet played). By displaying upcoming songs first, you can decide whether to rearrange the list or delete songs from the Party Shuffle playlist before they're played.

   • *Play Higher Rated Songs More Often:* Select this option to have iTunes add more high-rated songs to the random list. Using this option, you weight the randomness in favor of higher-rated songs. See Chapter 9 to find out how to add ratings to songs.

4. **(Optional) If you don't like the order of songs, you can rearrange them. If you dislike any songs, you can remove them from the Party Shuffle playlist.**

   You can rearrange the order of songs in Party Shuffle by dragging songs to different positions in the Party Shuffle list. Remove songs by selecting them in the Party Shuffle playlist and pressing Delete/ Backspace (or choosing Edit⇨Delete). Don't worry — the songs aren't deleted from your library, just from the Party Shuffle playlist.

5. **Play Party Shuffle by selecting the first song and then clicking the Play button or pressing the spacebar.**

   You can start playing the first song or any song on the list. (When you pick a song in the middle to start playing, the songs before it are grayed out to show that they won't play.)

6. **Add, delete, or rearrange songs even while Party Shuffle plays.**

   While the Party Shuffle list plays, you can add songs in one of two ways:

   • *Open Party Shuffle in a separate window by double-clicking the Party Shuffle item in the Source pane.* You can then drag songs from the main iTunes window — either from the Music portion of your library (select Music in the Library section of the Source pane) or from a playlist in the Source pane — directly into position in the Party Shuffle track list.

   • *Without opening Party Shuffle in a separate window, you can switch to the music portion of your library or a playlist and drag the song to the Party Shuffle item in the Source pane.* When you add a song to Party Shuffle, it shows up at the end of the track list. You can then drag it to a new position.

You can add one or more albums to the Party Shuffle track list by dragging the albums; the songs play in album order. You can also add all the songs by an artist by dragging the artist's name. Party Shuffle acts like a dynamic playlist — you add, delete, and change the order of songs on the fly.

Cool DJs mix the Party Shuffle window with other open playlist windows. Just double-click the playlist item in the Source pane to open it in a separate window. You can then drag songs from different playlist windows to the Party Shuffle window while Party Shuffle plays, adding songs in whatever order you want in real time.

Cross-fading song playback

You can often hear a song on the radio fade out while another song immediately fades in over the first song's ending — a *cross-fade*. With iTunes, you can smoothly transition from the ending of one song to the beginning of the next one.

What's totally cool is that you can cross-fade two songs in iTunes even if they're from different sources. The songs could be in your library, in a shared library, on CD, or even on one (or more) iPods connected to your computer and playing through iTunes. You can play DJ at a party with a massive music library on a laptop and enlarge that library with one or more iPods and any number of CDs, and have the songs cross-fade.

You can change the cross-fade by choosing iTunes⇨Preferences on a Mac or Edit⇨Preferences in Windows, and then clicking the Playback button. The Playback preferences dialog appears, as shown in Figure 6-7.

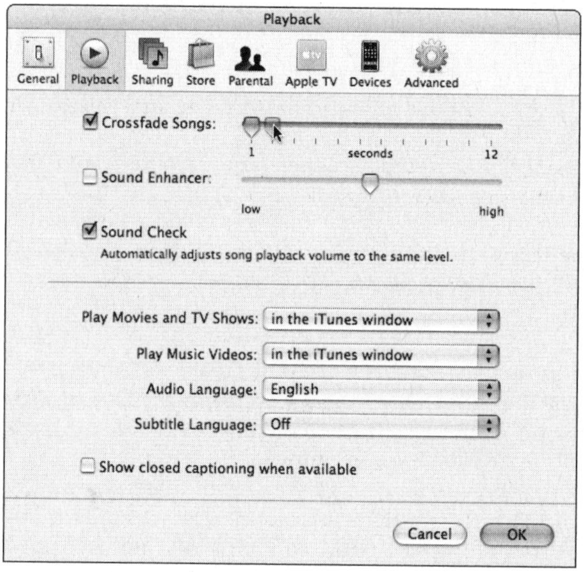

Figure 6-7:
Set the cross-fade between songs.

In the Playback preferences dialog, select the Crossfade Playback option and then increase or decrease the cross-fade by dragging the slider. Each notch in the slider represents one second. The maximum amount of cross-fade is 12 seconds. With a longer cross-fade, you get more overlap from one song to the next; that is, the second song starts before the first one ends. To turn off the cross-fade, deselect the Crossfade Playback check box.

Playing Podcasts

A podcast subscription transfers audio or audio/video episodes, such as weekly broadcasts, automatically to your iTunes library from the Internet or through the iTunes Store (as I describe in episodic detail in Chapter 5). Podcasts that you subscribe to appear in the List pane when you select the Podcasts option in the Library section of the Source pane. You can add podcast episodes to your library by subscribing to them in the iTunes Store (see Chapter 4) or on a Web site (see Chapter 5). To play a podcast episode, follow these steps:

1. **Select the Podcasts option in the Library section of the Source pane.**

   The podcasts you've subscribed to appear in the List pane.

2. **Select a podcast in the List pane and then click the triangle to see its episodes.**

   The triangle rotates, and a list of episodes appears beneath the podcast, as shown in Figure 6-8.

3. **Select the podcast and then click the Play button.**

   You can use the iTunes playback controls to fast-forward or rewind the podcast or play it from any point. The blue dot next to a podcast means you haven't yet played it. As soon as you start listening to a podcast, the dot disappears.

When you play a podcast, iTunes remembers your place when you stop listening to it, just like it remembers when you place a bookmark in an audio book or pause during a movie — even after quitting and restarting iTunes. iTunes resumes playing from that playback position when you return to the podcast to play it.

Some podcasts are enhanced to include chapter marks and photos. When you play an enhanced podcast in iTunes, a Chapters menu appears on the iTunes menu bar. Choose this menu to display the podcast's chapter marks, artwork, and chapter start times, as shown in Figure 6-9.

If the podcaster embedded a photo in an audio podcast file or included a link to a video from the file, the photo or video content appears in the Artwork pane.

While you can drag a podcast into a playlist to include it in that playlist, you can also drag a podcast to the Source pane to create a new playlist, as long as you drag it to an empty space in the Playlist section of the Source pane (and not into another playlist). The new playlist takes on the name of the podcast. You can also add other podcasts to the new playlist, and rename the playlist. For more information about playlists, see Chapter 10.

Figure 6-8:
Open a
podcast to
see its
episodes.

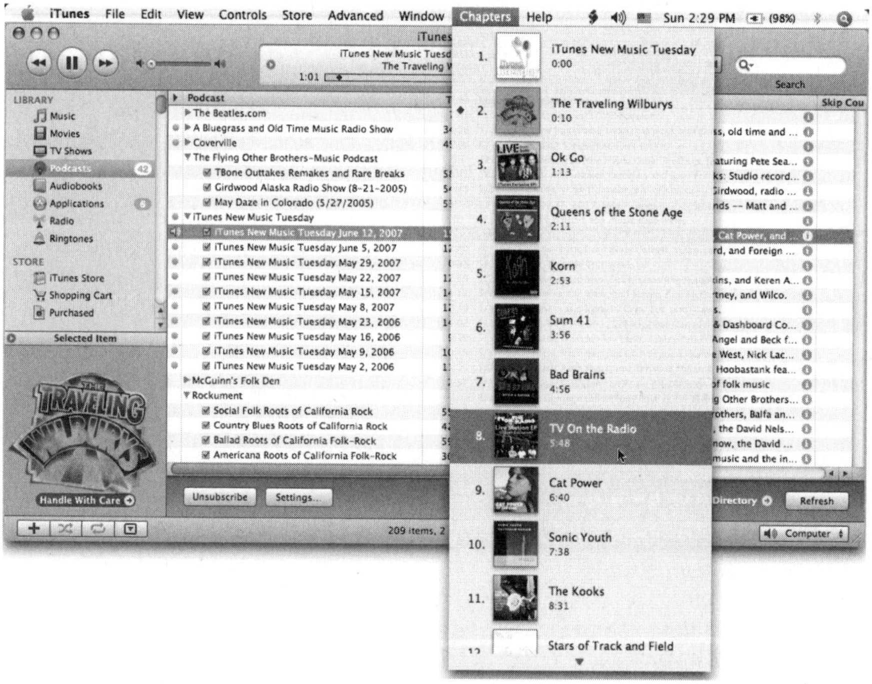

Figure 6-9:
Enhanced
podcasts
include a
Chapters
menu.

Playing Audio Books

You can store and play audio books, articles, and spoken-word titles just like songs in iTunes, and you can download titles from the iTunes Store (as I describe prolifically in Chapter 4) or from Audible (www.audible.com; as I point out in literary detail in Chapter 5).

By default, iTunes doesn't include the Audiobooks option in the Library section of the Source pane. To place Audiobooks in the Library section of the Source pane so that you can select audio books, choose iTunes⇨Preferences (Mac) or Edit⇨Preferences (Windows), click the General button at the top of the Preferences window, and select Audiobooks next to the Show option. Click OK to accept the changes. Audiobooks then appears as its own heading in the Library section of the Source pane; click the heading to see a list of your audio books.

To play an audio book, select it just like you would a song (see details on browsing and listing content in Chapter 8) and then click the Play button. You can use the iTunes playback controls to fast-forward or rewind the audio book or play it from any point.

Audio books from Audible and the iTunes Store are enhanced to include chapter marks. When you play any of these audio books in iTunes, the Chapters menu appears on the iTunes menu bar, just like it does for a podcast with chapters. Choose the Chapters menu to display and select the audio book's chapter marks (refer to Figure 6-9).

Playing Videos

iTunes is versatile when it comes to playing videos — the TV shows, movies, video podcasts, and music videos you downloaded from the iTunes Store (see Chapter 4) as well as the video files you dragged into iTunes from other sources (see Chapter 5).

To watch a video in iTunes, select it in your library (see details on browsing and listing movies, TV shows, and videos in Chapter 8), and then click the Play button. Use the iTunes Previous/Rewind, Play/Pause, and Forward/Next buttons to control playback and the iTunes volume slider to control the volume, just like with songs.

The video appears in the Artwork pane in the lower-left corner of the iTunes window, as shown in Figure 6-10. If the Artwork pane isn't visible, playing the video makes it appear. You can also make the Artwork pane appear or disappear by clicking the Show/Hide Artwork button.

Besides the Artwork pane (which is too small for normal viewing), you can view your video

   ✔ In a separate window at different sizes

   ✔ Inside the iTunes window

   ✔ Filling the entire computer display

   ✔ On a TV

In the following sections, I tell you how to get your video out of that puny Artwork pane and into larger displays.

Figure 6-10:
A video appears in the Artwork pane. Ugh, too small!

Playing a video in a separate window

To watch a video in a separate window, click the video while it plays in the Artwork pane. A separate window appears that includes a transparent QuickTime controls pane with buttons for controlling video playback, as shown in Figure 6-11. Click the Play button at the center of the pane to play or pause, and then drag the slider to move forward or backward through the video. Click the Rewind or Fast-Forward buttons on either side of the Play button in the controls pane to move backward or forward through a video. Click the red "close window" button in the top-left corner to close the window.

Figure 6-11:
Drag the QuickTime playback slider to move forward or backward through a video.

To set your iTunes preferences to always play movies and TV shows in a separate window, choose iTunes➪Preferences (Mac) or Edit➪Preferences (Windows). Next, click the Playback button and then choose the In a Separate Window option for the Play Movies and TV Shows pop-up menu, as shown in Figure 6-12. You can also choose this option for the Play Music Videos pop-up menu. From that point on, those videos in your library play in a separate window.

The transparent QuickTime controls pane disappears while the video plays, but you can make it reappear at any time by moving the cursor to the bottom center of the video window. The controls pane also offers a volume control slider to set the audio volume of the video, and the Full-Screen Video button to change the video display to full-screen. (See the section "Playing a video full-screen.")

You can resize the separate video window by dragging the lower-right corner of the window. You can also choose fixed window sizes by choosing them from the View menu. For example, choose View➪Video Size➪Half Size to display the video window at half the actual size, or View➪Video Size➪Double Size to display the window at twice the size. Choose View➪Video Size➪ Actual Size to set the window back to the actual size of the video picture.

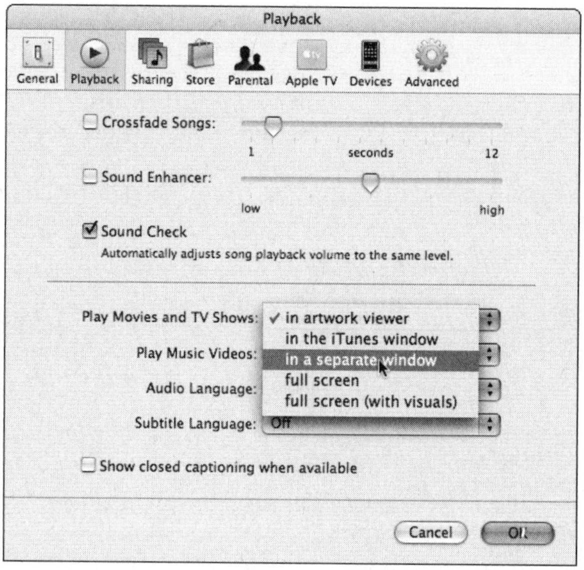

Figure 6-12:
Change
movie and
TV show
playback to
a separate
window.

Playing a video in the iTunes window

To set your iTunes preferences to play movies, TV shows, and/or music videos inside the iTunes window, choose iTunes⇨Preferences (Mac) or Edit⇨Preferences (Windows), click the Playback button, and then choose the In the iTunes Window option for the Play Movies and TV Shows and/or Play Music Videos pop-up menus (refer to Figure 6-12).

From that point on, those videos in your library play inside the iTunes window with a transparent QuickTime controls pane offering buttons for controlling video playback, as shown in Figure 6-13. Click the Play button at the center of the QuickTime controls pane to play or pause, and then drag the slider to move forward or backward through the video. Click the Rewind or Fast-Forward buttons on either side of the Play button in the controls pane to move backward or forward through a video. Click the circled X to stop playing the video and return to the normal iTunes window.

Playing a video full-screen

To set your iTunes preferences to play movies, TV shows, and/or music videos full-screen, choose iTunes⇨Preferences (Mac) or Edit⇨Preferences (Windows), click the Playback button, and then choose the Full Screen option for the Play Movies and TV Shows pop-up menu and/or the Play Music Videos pop-up menu (refer to Figure 6-12). From that point on, those videos in your library fill the screen when they play, with a transparent QuickTime controls pane offering buttons for controlling video playback.

Figure 6-13: Click the circled X to stop playing the video inside the iTunes window.

Some videos look good when displayed full-screen, but others may not. Videos purchased from the iTunes Store look fine, but video from other sources may look pixilated at full-screen resolution.

To change from watching a video in a separate window to a full-screen view, click the Full-Screen Video button in the transparent QuickTime controls pane (refer to Figure 6-11). This button doesn't appear unless you're playing a video in a separate window. You can also choose View➪Video Size➪Full Screen.

When you're playing a video in full-screen view, the following controls are available:

- ✔ **Esc (Escape):** Press to stop full-screen playback and return to the iTunes window.

- ✔ **Spacebar:** Press to pause playback. (Pressing the spacebar again resumes playback.)

- ✔ **Your mouse or pointing device:** Simply move these to display the transparent QuickTime controls pane and then click the Full-Screen Video button (now with its arrows pointing inward) to stop full-screen playback and return to the iTunes window.

A cool party trick is to seamlessly mix music videos and music with visuals. (See Chapter 3 to find out about displaying visuals.) To create a mixed playlist of music and videos (see Chapter 10 to create playlists), choose iTunes➪Preferences (Mac) or Edit➪Preferences (Windows). Then click the Playback button and choose the Full Screen (with Visuals) option from the Play Music Videos pop-up menu (or even the Play Movies and TV Shows pop-up menu, if you include these in your playlist). When you play the mixed music-video playlist, iTunes automatically shows full-screen video for your videos and full-screen visuals for your music, seamlessly moving from one to the other.

Playing videos through iTunes on your TV

For many, the computer display is just fine for viewing videos full-screen. The picture clarity on a Mac (even Mac PowerBook and iBook), for example, is better than any comparably sized television. However, if you want to connect your PC to a television, follow the instructions that came with your PC.

You can connect a Mac to a television that offers an S-video, composite video, or component video connection, and also connect the Mac to speakers or a sound system through standard RCA audio connections for sound.

You can connect an iPod or iPhone directly to a television and sound system or through a dock, and the connections are similar if not exactly the same as ones you might use to connect your computer. To learn more about connections to home video and stereo equipment, visit this book's companion Web site.

After connecting to the television and to the speakers/sound system, follow these steps:

1. **Choose System Preferences from the Apple menu.**

   The System Preferences window appears with icons for each set of preferences.

2. **Click the Displays icon in the System Preferences window.**

   The Display preferences window appears. Depending on the type of display, you might see tabs for different panes.

3. **Click the Display tab for the Display preferences pane if it isn't already selected.**

   The preferences appear with settings for your display.

4. Click the Detect Displays button.

The Mac detects the television and sets it to the appropriate resolution. For more about setting display resolutions on the Mac, see *Mac OS X Leopard All-in-One Desk Reference For Dummies,* by Mark L. Chambers (Wiley).

If you don't see a picture on your television, be sure your TV is set to the correct input source: composite video input (RCA connectors), component video input, or S-video input. You can also use other types of video equipment. For example, a video recorder, which typically accepts RCA or S-video input, can record the video, and a video projector can display it on a large screen.

Perhaps the easiest way to connect your computer (and other computers in your local network) to your television and stereo system is through Apple TV. Apple TV lets you connect wirelessly (or by wired Ethernet) to any computer running iTunes in the network and store content for playback. See Chapter 7 for details on sharing your iTunes library using Apple TV.

Chapter 7

Sharing Content Legally

. . . .

. . . .

*H*ey, it's your content after you buy it — that is, to the extent that you can make copies for yourself. You want to play your music and videos anywhere and even share them with your friends. It's only natural.

And to help, iTunes lets you share a library over a local area network (LAN) with other computers running iTunes.

If you use a Wi-Fi (wireless) network, consider getting an Apple TV, which connects wirelessly to your network and with high-quality cabling to your television and stereo system. You can then share any iTunes library on any computer on the network with Apple TV to play on your TV and stereo.

You can also copy the content files to other computers without any restrictions on copying — just keep in mind that protected content has some playback restrictions. You can easily share the music that you rip from your CDs: After the music becomes digital, you can copy it endlessly with no subsequent loss in quality. You can also share the songs, audio books, podcasts, and videos that you download. Of course, if the songs, audio books, and videos are in a protected format (such as content bought from the iTunes Store), the computers that access the shared library must be authorized to play the content. Whether the computers are connected to a LAN by cable (such as Ethernet) or by wireless technology (such as the Apple AirPort or Time Capsule), you can share your library with other computers — up to five other computers in a single 24-hour period.

In this chapter, I show you how to share your iTunes library with others. (After all, your parents taught you to share, didn't they?)

Sharing Content from the iTunes Store

To a limited extent, you can share all the content that you buy online from the iTunes Store. Some content — such as free podcasts as well as unprotected songs and albums (also known as "iTunes Plus" songs) — can be shared without any limitations. However, some songs and albums, and most commercial movies, music videos, TV shows, audio books, and paid podcasts are all limited by copy protection, also known as *digital rights management* (DRM).

You can play unprotected songs on any computer or any digital-audio player. Entire albums and individual songs are available in a higher-quality, non-DRM "iTunes Plus" format from some record labels alongside DRM-protected songs from other labels also sold through iTunes. And if you've already purchased DRM-protected songs in the past that are now available in the iTunes Plus format, you can upgrade them to iTunes Plus — for a price, typically 30 cents per song.

The Apple form of DRM is known as FairPlay, and it works with the standard AAC encoding format. Protected files are keyed to an individual purchaser's identity. Although they can be copied to and from computers, they can't be played on a given computer unless that computer has been authorized.

To find out more about audio encoding formats, visit this book's companion Web site.

Apple employs FairPlay protection for songs from many record labels, while other songs are available without FairPlay (it's the record label's choice). FairPlay-protected songs use the .m4p filename extension rather than .m4a for the unprotected AAC format. Apple also uses a protected video format for TV shows, music videos, and movies in the online store. These filenames use the .m4v or .mp4 extension for protected video rather than .mpg for the standard MPEG-4 format.

Unprotected AAC files are as freely portable and playable as MP3 files are. You can send an unprotected AAC file to anyone else with iTunes or any other software capable of reading AAC files, and the recipient can play it successfully.

To tell whether a song purchased from the iTunes Store is protected with FairPlay, select the song and choose File⇨Get Info. Next to the Kind heading you'll see "Protected AAC Audio File" for FairPlay-protected songs or "Purchased AAC Audio File" for unprotected songs purchased from the iTunes Store.

I fought the law, and the law won: Sharing and piracy

Apple CEO Steve Jobs gave personal demonstrations of the iTunes Store and the iPod to Paul McCartney and Mick Jagger before introducing the online store. According to Steven Levy at *Newsweek* (May 12, 2003), Jobs said, "They both totally get it." The former Beatle and the Stones' frontman are no slouches: Both conduct music-business affairs personally and have extensive back catalogs of music. They know all about the free music-swapping services on the Internet, but they agree with Jobs that most people are willing to pay for high-quality music rather than download free copies of questionable quality.

Digital Rights Management (DRM), also known as copy protection, is ineffective against piracy because determined pirates always circumvent it with newer technology; only consumers are inconvenienced.

The record labels are finally "getting it" as well. EMI, one of the largest, agreed in the spring of 2007 to sell unprotected "iTunes Plus" songs and albums — some at a higher price ($1.29 per song) — but without DRM getting in the way.

Many of the songs available from free sharing services are low-quality MP3 audio files, which sound only as good as an FM radio broadcast. The iTunes Store offers quite a lot of licensed music in an unprotected format that offers higher-quality sound, as well as protected songs, and I prefer the original authorized version of the song — not some knockoff that might have been copied from a radio broadcast.

As for copying songs for personal use, the law is murky at best. You can mix hit songs in with your personal videos, but don't expect to see those videos on MTV or VH1, or even YouTube for very long. (YouTube and other video sharing sites police their sites for unauthorized content.) Whether you're interested in obtaining the rights to music to use in semipublic or public presentations or even movies and documentaries for public distribution, you can contact the music publisher or a licensing agent. Music publishing organizations, such as the Music Publishers' Association (www.mpa.org), offer information and lists of music publishers as well as explanations of various rights and licenses.

The FairPlay protection used with iTunes Store content allows you to do the following:

- ✔ **Create backups.** You can download the content files and make as many copies as you want on hard drives and storage devices; you can even burn data CDs and DVDs with content files for backup purposes. (There is no limit on the number of data CDs you can make.)

- ✔ **Copy content to iTunes libraries on other computers.** Play songs and videos on up to five separate computers. See Chapter 4 to find out how to authorize your computers.

- ✔ **Copy content to iPods, iPhones, and Apple TV.** Copy the music and videos to as many iPods and iPhones as you want as well as to Apple TV. See Chapter 11 for automatic and manual device synchronization.

✔ **Burn up to seven audio CDs.** Burn seven copies of the same playlist containing protected songs to an audio CD — but no more. See Chapter 12 for tips on CD and DVD burning.

✔ **Share content over a network.** Up to five computers running iTunes on a LAN can play the content in your shared library in a 24-hour period.

You can also play music in your library over a wireless connection to a stereo amplifier or receiver by using AirTunes and AirPort Express, which I cover in Chapter 6.

You might also want to know where the songs, audio books, podcasts, and videos are stored on your hard drive so that you can copy the content to other computers and hard drives and create a backup of your entire library. You might want to move the library to another computer because computers just keep getting better year after year. To find the location of your content files, see Chapter 12.

Sharing Content on a Network

If you live like the Jetsons — with a computer in every room connected by a wireless or wired network — iTunes is made for you. You can share your iTunes library with other computers in the same network. These computers can be PCs that run Windows or Macs that run OS X — as long as they run iTunes. If they can communicate with each other over the network, iTunes can share a content library with up to five PCs in a single 24-hour period. The restriction to five in a 24-hour period is yet another one of the imposed rules of record labels and video producers.

When you share content on a network, the content is *streamed* over the network from the computer that contains the library (the *library computer*) to the computer that plays it. A stream arrives in the receiving computer bit by bit; the computer starts playing the stream as soon as the first set of bits arrive, and more sections are transferred while you listen. The result is that the recipient hears music and sees video as a continual stream. Broadcasters use this technology to continually transmit new content (just like a radio station). The content isn't copied to the receiving computer's library, and you can't burn the shared library songs onto a CD or copy the songs to an iPod without third-party software — such as WireTap Pro for the Mac (www. ambrosiasw.com/utilities/wiretap) or Blaze Media Pro for Windows (www.blazemp.com).

Sharing an iTunes library can be incredibly useful for playing content on laptops that connect to a wireless network. You can manage a very large content library on a desktop computer with a large hard drive, and then play content on the laptop or notebook computer with a smaller hard drive without having to copy files to the smaller hard drive.

Sharing your library with other computers

To share your iTunes library — turning your computer into the library computer — follow these steps:

1. **Choose iTunes⇨Preferences (Mac) or Edit⇨Preferences (Windows) and then click the Sharing tab.**

   The Sharing dialog appears, as shown in Figure 7-1, offering options for sharing music.

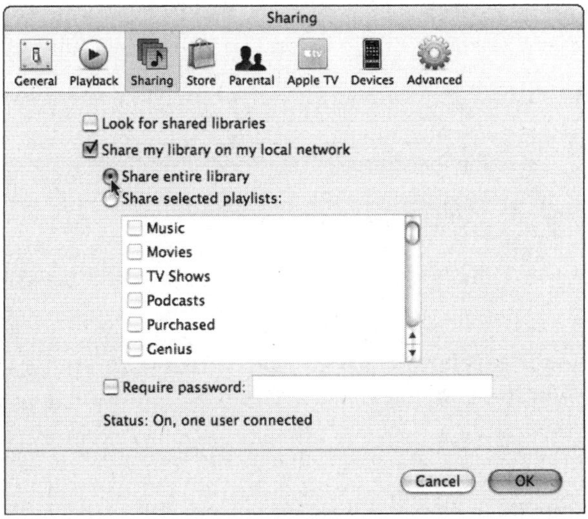

Figure 7-1: Share your iTunes library with other computers on the same network.

[Sharing dialog box showing tabs: General, Playback, Sharing, Store, Parental, Apple TV, Devices, Advanced]

- Look for shared libraries
- ☑ Share my library on my local network
  - ● Share entire library
  - ○ Share selected playlists:
    - ☐ Music
    - ☐ Movies
    - ☐ TV Shows
    - ☐ Podcasts
    - ☐ Purchased
    - ☐ Genius
- ☐ Require password:

Status: On, one user connected

[Cancel] [OK]

2. **Select the Share My Library on My Local Network option.**

3. **Select either the Share Entire Library option or the Share Selected Playlists option and then choose the playlists to share.**

4. **Add a password if you want to restrict access to the shared library or playlists.**

Pick a password that you *don't* mind sharing with others; for example, your name is a good password, because you want to share it with people you know. Your ATM PIN is *not* a good password, because you should keep that very secure. The password restricts access to only those who know it.

iTunes displays `Reminder: Sharing music is for personal use only.`

5. **Click OK.**

Shared libraries or playlists appear in the iTunes Source list in the Shared section with the computer's username. (For example, "Tony Bove's Music" is the name of the shared library on the computer where "Tony Bove" is logged in as the user.)

You can change the Library name that iTunes uses for your shared library or playlists. To change the name others see, choose iTunes⊅Preferences on a Mac or Edit⊅Preferences in Windows, click General, and then type a new name in the Library Name field. The name that you choose appears in the Shared section of the iTunes Source pane for other computers that share your library.

Before turning off sharing for your library, you must first notify anyone sharing the library to eject the shared library. Otherwise, iTunes displays a warning dialog allowing you to continue (and break off the connection to the shared library) or to leave sharing turned on for the moment.

Accessing a shared library

You can access the content from the other computers on the network by following these steps:

1. **Choose iTunes⊅Preferences on a Mac or Edit⊅Preferences in Windows and then click the Sharing tab.**

   The Sharing dialog appears and offers options for sharing content. Refer to Figure 7-1.

2. **Select the Look for Shared Libraries option.**

   The shared libraries appear in the Shared section of the Source pane, as shown in Figure 7-2 ("Tony Bove's Music" loading into iTunes).

3. **Select and play any album or song in the shared library.**

   After the shared library loads, its contents appear in the List pane, as shown in Figure 7-3, and you can browse and play its contents.

4. **(Optional) Click the triangle next to a shared library entry in the Source pane, as shown in Figure 7-3, to see playlists in the shared library. Play them as you normally would.**

5. **To unload the shared library, click the tiny Eject button that appears to the right of the shared library name in the Source pane.**

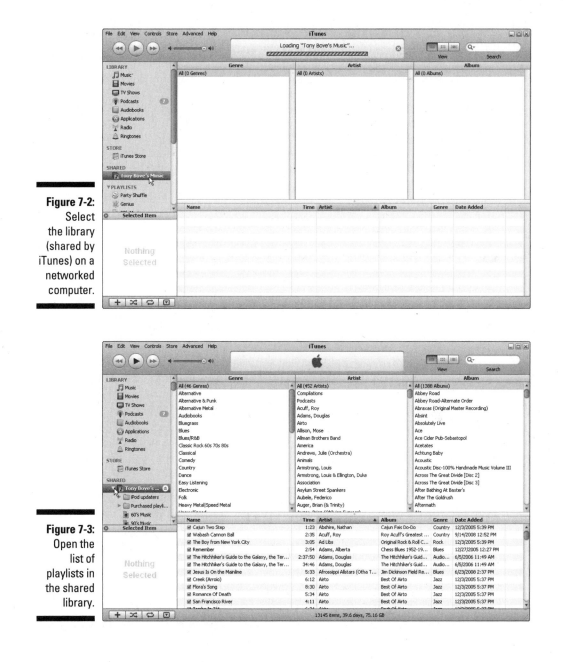

Figure 7-2:
Select
the library
(shared by
iTunes) on a
networked
computer.

Figure 7-3:
Open the
list of
playlists in
the shared
library.

Sharing Content with Your Apple TV

Wouldn't it be nice to be able to play the content in your iTunes library on your television and stereo system without having to mess with cables? You can. Just sit back on your couch and let Apple TV offer up a smorgasbord of content from your iTunes library, which can be on your computer in another room and streamed to Apple TV over the network. You can also transfer content to your Apple TV so that you don't have to use your computer to play the content or even have your computer on while playing content.

Apple TV (about $300) is like a large iPod that wirelessly synchronizes with one or more iTunes libraries on Macs and PCs and stores that content on its hard drive to play on your high-definition (HD) television and stereo system. Apple TV can also wirelessly connect to a computer's iTunes library and play it. It also supports AirTunes, as I describe in Chapter 6, so that you can play your iTunes content on your computer and redirect the sound wirelessly to Apple TV as a separate speaker system.

With Apple TV, you can rent or buy movies in high-definition (HD) format and download them directly to Apple TV's hard drive to watch on your HD television with full surround sound. You can listen to music and podcasts in your iTunes library through your home stereo and show photo slideshows with music. It's the wave of the future — couch potatoes kicking back with Apple consumer gear.

You control Apple TV with the handheld wireless Apple Remote, which is supplied with Apple TV and uses Apple TV's built-in infrared (IR) receiver. The menus for playing content and changing Apple TV settings appear on your television, so you can sit back on your couch and tune in to anything synchronized from your iTunes library. You can also play all the music in an iTunes library, streamed from the computer running iTunes, without synchronizing the entire library. Synchronizing content is useful if you want to turn off the computer and play Apple TV by itself.

Apple TV hardware isn't much different than a low-end laptop computer; it runs a slimmed version of Mac OS X. Apple TV requires a Mac or PC running iTunes version 7.6 or newer, but you should use the newest version of iTunes to take advantage of all its features. (See Chapter 2 for detailed requirements for running iTunes.) Apple TV works with widescreen, enhanced-definition, or high-definition TVs capable of 1080i, 720p, 576p, or 480p resolutions. The iTunes Store offers HD movies using the HDTV (high-definition television) format for Apple TV.

The first generation Apple TV includes a 40GB model and a 160GB model for synchronizing with iTunes. With the 40GB model, you can synchronize up to 50 hours of movies and TV shows, or you can fill it up with 9,000 songs (or about 25,000 pictures) and play them on your TV and stereo. With the 160GB model, you can synchronize up to 200 hours of video or fill it up with 36,000 songs.

Setting up Apple TV

Apple TV works transparently with a PC or Mac, taking advantage of the broadband connection to the Internet via your wireless network. It supports AirPort Extreme, Wi-Fi 802.11b, 802.11g, or 802.11n wireless networks. (Wireless video streaming requires 802.11g or 802.11n.) AirPort Extreme–enabled Macs let you create a wireless network using only your computer and Apple TV. (If you have a Mac or PC without wireless capability, though, you can connect Apple TV to a 10/100BASE-T Ethernet network using an Ethernet cable that's sold separately.)

To connect the device (only 1.1 inches thick and 7.7 inches square) to your TV or audio-video (AV) receiver, use one of the following methods, as shown in Figure 7-4:

- **For TVs with stereo or surround sound that support High-Definition Multimedia Interface (HDMI):** Use an HDMI cable, which provides video and audio to the television/audio system. The Apple Store offers HDMI-to-HDMI cables for TVs and AV receivers that support HDMI.

- **For TVs that support Digital Video Interface (DVI):** Use an HDMI-to-DVI cable or an HDMI-DVI adapter for an HDMI cable, both of which are available from the Apple Store. Then use either an optical audio cable or a standard analog audio cable pair to provide audio to your stereo or surround sound system.

- **For TVs or AV receivers that don't offer HDMI or DVI (or if these ports are used by other devices, such as your cable receiver):** Use a component video cable (with three connectors) and either an optical audio cable or a standard analog audio cable pair.

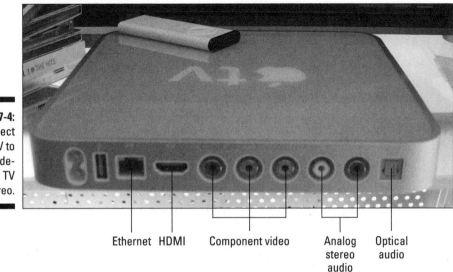

Figure 7-4: Connect Apple TV to your wide-screen TV and stereo.

Ethernet   HDMI   Component video   Analog   Optical
                                         stereo   audio
                                         audio

You should connect Apple TV to your TV and stereo first before proceeding so that when you connect Apple TV to power, you see the menu for Apple TV on your television.

Choosing an iTunes library for Apple TV

When you first connect Apple TV to a power source, it immediately starts its setup procedure, using your television as the display. Grab your Apple Remote (supplied with Apple TV) and follow these instructions — all from the comfort of your couch:

1. **Choose a language.**

   Point the Apple Remote at the Apple TV and use the remote's buttons to navigate up and down the list and select a language. The plus (+) button scrolls up, the minus (–) button scrolls down, and the Play/Pause button selects a menu choice. After you choose a language, Apple TV displays the network screen.

2. **Select a network.**

   Apple TV searches for a wireless network unless you've connected it to an Ethernet network (in which case Apple TV automatically detects it, and that's that). For wireless networks, follow the on-TV instructions to select your network by name and (if necessary) supply a password by using the Apple Remote to navigate the individual letters of the password. You can even manually configure the IP address, subnet mask, router, and DNS address if your network doesn't allow DHCP connections or you need to for other reasons. (I'm assuming here that you know what you're doing — if not, get help from the person who set up your network.)

   After setting up your network connection, Apple TV displays a five-digit passcode on your TV that identifies the device for synchronization with a computer.

3. **Remember (or write down) your five-digit passcode.**

   The next step is to get off your couch and go over to your computer — which can be in the next room, as long as it accesses the same network as Apple TV. Then follow these steps:

4. **Start iTunes.**

   Shortly (a minute or less), the Apple TV icon and name appear in the Source pane under Devices.

5. **Select Apple TV in the Devices section of the Source pane (see Figure 7-5) and enter the five-digit passcode into the digit fields.**

   This passcode appears on your TV; refer to Step 3 in this step list.

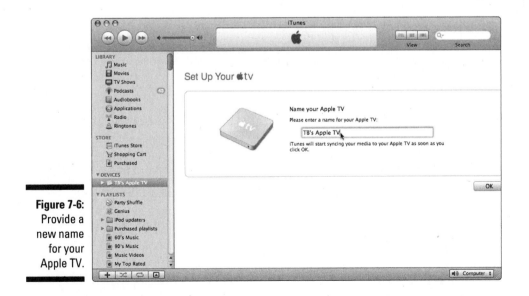

Figure 7-5:
Set up
Apple TV in
iTunes to
synchronize
with the
library.

The digit fields appear on the iTunes page, to the right of the Source pane. After entering the fifth digit, iTunes displays a page that lets you enter the name for your Apple TV, as shown in Figure 7-6.

Figure 7-6:
Provide a
new name
for your
Apple TV.

6. **Give your Apple TV a new name.**

   Enter a new name that befits the new king of the living room and then click OK. iTunes then displays the registration page for Apple TV.

7. **Register your Apple TV or skip registration if you want.**

   Click Continue (to register), Later (to register later), or Never Register (to skip registration). I recommend registering your Apple TV in order to maintain your warranty (and optionally receive e-mail notices of updates). If you choose to register, follow the instructions to enter your Apple ID and password (or select the option for no ID) and then click Continue. Fill out your personal information and then click Continue to finish the registration process. iTunes then takes you to the online store, so that you can start purchasing content or renting movies immediately.

Your new Apple TV starts synchronizing automatically with your iTunes library, copying movies, TV shows, music, podcasts, and photos (in that order) until it runs out of space. If your iTunes library is larger than the capacity of your Apple TV, you will need to manage content synchronization — see Chapter 11. You can synchronize Apple TV with an iTunes library on any Mac or PC within reach of the network. When you make any changes to your library in iTunes, Apple TV automatically synchronizes with your (updated) library.

To play content on Apple TV, use the Apple Remote to choose from the Apple TV main menu. You can select Movies, TV Shows, Music, Podcasts, Photos, and YouTube; or, choose Settings to change your Apple TV settings or change sources of content.

Copying Media Files

You can copy content freely from your iTunes window to other hard drives and computers or copy the content folders from the iTunes Music folder to other hard drives and computers. On a Mac, you can use the Finder to copy content files as well as drag stuff from the iTunes window into folders or hard drives. Windows PCs offer several methods, including using Windows Explorer to copy files.

By default, the files are organized in folders by artist name and by album title (or by book, video, or TV show title) within the iTunes Music folder — that is, unless you change options in the Advanced section of iTunes Preferences;

see Chapter 12. For example, copying an entire album, or every song by a specific artist, is easy — just drag the folder to its new home folder on another hard drive.

You can find out the location of any content item by selecting it in iTunes and choosing File⇨Get Info. Click the Summary tab in the Get Info dialog to see the Summary options. Although you can change the location of your iTunes library, most people leave the library in its default location, which is inside the iTunes Music folder in the iTunes folder on the startup hard drive, as I describe in Chapter 12.

The easiest way to copy an album from a folder on a hard drive into your iTunes library is to drag the album's folder over the iTunes window and drop it there. If you drop it into the Source pane, iTunes creates a playlist of the album's songs using the album name. To copy individual songs, you can drag the song files over the iTunes window and drop them in the List pane. When you add a piece of content (song, video, podcast, or audio book) to your iTunes library, a copy is placed inside the iTunes Music folder. An alternative, if your display is already crowded with windows, is to choose File⇨Add to Library on a Mac, or File⇨Add Folder to Library on a Windows PC, and select the album's folder.

Part II
Managing Your Media

The 5th Wave   By Rich Tennant

"Why can't you just bring your iPod like everyone else?"

In this part . . .

*V*isit this part to find out how to organize the content in your iTunes library, add song information as well as ratings, build playlists, burn CDs, make a backup of your library, and synchronize devices to keep them up to date with your library.

- ✔ Chapter 8 describes how to browse your iTunes library, change the List view options, sort your content, and search for songs, artists, albums, music videos, audio books, movies, TV shows, applications, and games.

- ✔ Chapter 9 describes how to add information, artwork, and ratings for each content item and then edit the info in iTunes.

- ✔ Chapter 10 shows you how to create playlists of songs and entire albums in iTunes, including smart playlists and Genius playlists.

- ✔ Chapter 11 describes synchronizing your iPod, iPhone, Apple TV, or iPod shuffle with your iTunes library as well as how to manually manage the contents of an iPod, iPod shuffle, or iPhone.

- ✔ Chapter 12 is a guide to burning audio CDs, MP3 CDs, and data DVDs, as well as making backup copies of your iTunes library.

- ✔ Chapter 13 describes how to set the volume and enhance the sound of your device, as well as using the iTunes and iPod equalizers for fine-tuning music playback.

Chapter 8

Searching, Browsing, and Sorting in iTunes

· ·

In This Chapter

▶ Browsing your iTunes library

▶ Changing options for viewing your content

▶ Sorting content by view options

▶ Searching for content in the library

▶ Finding pesky duplicates

▶ Deleting items from the library

· ·

*Y*ou rip a few CDs, buy some songs and movies from the iTunes Store, and you're hooked. You keep adding more and more content to your library and forget how to find items you added last month. It's time to discover how to organize your content and navigate your iTunes library.

The iTunes library is awesome, even by everyday jukebox standards. Even though previous versions were limited to a paltry (cough!) 32,000 files per library, and you had to create multiple libraries to get around that limit, the current version (actually all versions newer than version 4) can virtually hold an unlimited number of files. Of course, the limit depends entirely on how much space you have on your hard drive.

Even if you keep your iTunes library down to the size of what fits on your iPod or iPhone, you still have a formidable collection at your fingertips. If your content collection is getting large, organize it to make finding songs, audio books, podcasts, and videos easier. After all, finding U2's "I Still Haven't Found What I'm Looking For" is a challenge even in a library of "only" 32,000 songs.

This chapter shows you how to search, browse, and sort your iTunes library. You can find any media, application, game, or radio station in seconds. You can also change the viewing options to make your library's display more useful, such as displaying songs sorted by artist, album, genre, or other attributes, or sorting TV shows by season or episode.

Browsing Your Library Content

The iTunes window provides the List pane on the right side and the Source pane on the left side (refer to Figure 3-1 in Chapter 3). The List pane offers a view of your library and content, depending on which sources of content you choose in the Source pane on the left side. The choices in the Source pane are as follows:

✔ **Library section:** Select Music, Movies, TV Shows, Podcasts, Radio, or Ringtones. By default, iTunes doesn't display Audiobooks and Applications; to see these content types, or to change the options listed in the Library section, choose iTunes➪Preferences (Mac) or Edit➪Preferences (Windows), click the General tab at the top of the Preferences window, and select or deselect the Show options depending on what you want to display. Click OK to accept the changes.

   • *Music:* Lists the entire library of songs and music videos, purchased, downloaded, ripped, or copied into the library.

   • *Movies:* Lists the movies downloaded from the iTunes Store and movie files you've added to your library.

   • *TV Shows:* Lists TV shows downloaded from the iTunes Store.

   • *Podcasts:* Lists the podcasts you've subscribed to. (See Chapter 5 for details on subscribing to and browsing podcasts.)

   • *Audiobooks:* Lists the audio books downloaded from the iTunes Store or from Audible.com or other sources. (See Chapter 6 for details on playing audio books.)

   • *Applications:* Lists the iPod touch and iPhone applications downloaded from the App Store or iTunes Store, and iPod games downloaded from the iTunes Store.

   • *Radio:* Lists the Web radio stations you can play. Radio station content is streamed to your computer but not stored in your library.

   • *Ringtones:* Lists the ringtones purchased in the iTunes Store.

✔ **Store section:** The iTunes Store (see Chapter 4).

✔ **Devices section:** Your iPod, iPhone, Apple TV, and other devices appear here. When you select a device such as an iPod, iTunes displays the summary page with synchronization options. See Chapter 11 for details on navigating the library on an iPod set for managing content manually.

✔ **Playlist section:** Smart playlists and regular playlists appear in this section, along with the Genius button (see Chapter 10). Also appearing in this section is Party Shuffle, which lists the Party Shuffle playlist (see Chapter 6).

Overwhelmed by all the content in the List pane? Try browsing. iTunes offers three View buttons in the upper-right corner for browsing your content in the List pane:

- ✔ **List** (the left button, or choose View➪As List) shows items in a list. Choose View➪Show Browser to show the browser, which displays columns you can browse to easily find items, such as music albums or TV episodes. The browser appears in the top part of the List pane (peek ahead to Figure 8-3 to see it). To make the browser disappear and see your content in a full list, choose View➪Hide Browser. You can also display songs in a list with the album cover art by choosing View➪Show Artwork Column. (Turn this off by choosing View➪Hide Artwork Column.)

- ✔ **Grid** (the center button, or choose View➪As Grid) shows thumbnail cover art images in a grid, as shown in Figure 8-1. Double-click a thumbnail to display a list of albums with an artwork column.

- ✔ **Cover Flow** (the right button, or choose View➪As Cover Flow) shows the cover browser, also known as Cover Flow, as described in the upcoming section, "Browsing by cover art."

Figure 8-1: Browse music in the List pane as a grid of cover art.

Browsing by cover art with Cover Flow

Does viewing a cover whet your appetite for the music, story, or video inside? Of course it does. Covers provide a context that simply can't be put into words or conveyed by sound. One fantastic innovation of iTunes is how it integrates cover art from albums, books, podcasts, and videos with your library so that you can flip through your content to find items based on the artwork. Figure 8-2 shows the iTunes window using Cover Flow view to display the Music portion of the iTunes library.

To select Cover Flow, click the rightmost of the three View buttons in the upper-right corner of the iTunes window. You can also show the cover browser by choosing View⇨As Cover Flow.

Cover Flow lets you flip through your cover art to select music, movies, TV shows, podcasts, and audio books. (The cover browser doesn't work with ringtones, applications, or radio stations.) Just drag the slider to scroll swiftly through your library or click to the right or left of the cover art in the foreground to move forward or backward, respectively. When you scroll or click through cover art, the content items in the List pane also change. Double-click the foreground cover art to start playing the first item — whether it's an album's first song, a movie, the first chapter of an audio book, or the first episode of a TV show.

Figure 8-2:
Browse
music using
Cover Flow
view.

Browse Full-Screen button ⌐

Click the Browse Full-Screen button to display Cover Flow, um, full-screen. You can still click a cover to select an album, click within each cover to move forward and backward, and use the cover browser's slider to navigate your library. iTunes also offers a volume control slider to set the audio volume while browsing full-screen cover art. Press Esc (Escape) or click the Browse Full-Screen button (with its arrows pointing inward) in the lower-right corner of the display to stop displaying the cover browser full-screen and return to the iTunes window.

To fill your library automatically with cover art, get yourself an iTunes Store account (if you don't already have one). Log in to your account; then choose Advanced⇨Get Album Artwork. iTunes grabs the cover art not only for content downloaded from the iTunes Store — including movies, TV shows, audio books and podcasts — but also for CDs you ripped, provided that the albums are also available in the iTunes Store. Even if you downloaded or ripped only one song of an album, you get the album's cover art for that song.

You can also get your cover art from other places that sell CDs, audio books, and DVDs (including Amazon.com) or even scan them from the actual CDs, DVDs, or books. You can then add cover art from a scanned or downloaded image file to any content item in your iTunes library, as I describe in Chapter 9. The optimal size for cover art is 300 x 300 pixels.

Browsing songs by artist and album

To browse music in your library, select Music in the Source pane in the Library section. The List view shows the title of each song in the Name column, the artist or band name in the Artist column, and the title of the album in the Album column. The browser in List view organizes songs by Genre, Artist, and Album. You can switch to Grid (refer to Figure 8-1) or to Cover Flow view (refer to Figure 8-2) to show the album cover art.

Select a genre in the Genre column to see artists in that genre or select All at the top of the column to see all artists for all genres. When you select an artist in the Artist column (the middle column; see Figure 8-3), the album titles appear in the Album column (on the right). When you select an album in Browse view, iTunes displays only the songs for that album in the List pane below the browser.

To see more than one album from an artist at a time, press ⌘ (Mac) or Ctrl (Windows) and then click each album name.

When you select different albums in the Album column, the List pane below the browser displays the songs from that album. The songs are listed in proper track order, just as the artist, producer, or record label intended.

Figure 8-3:
Select an
artist to see
the list of
albums for
that artist.

If you don't get track information from the Internet for each song (as I show dramatically in Chapter 5) or add the track information yourself via the content item's information dialog (as I describe in wondrous detail in Chapter 9), iTunes displays only a blank space for the Artist and Album name along with Track 01 and so on for each track. That makes browsing for a song or artist by name difficult, to say the least.

To see all the songs in the library in the browser, select All at the top of each of the columns — Genre, Artist, and Album.

Note: iTunes version 7.1.1 and newer versions no longer consider Clash and The Clash to be different music groups, sorting them properly under the letter C. I show you how to edit the artist name and other information in Chapter 9.

Browsing audio books

If you don't see Audiobooks in the in the Library section of the Source pane, choose iTunes➪Preferences (Mac) or Edit➪Preferences (Windows), click the General tab at the top of the Preferences window, select the Audiobooks option next to the Show heading, and click OK. The Audiobooks option then appears in the Source pane in the Library section.

To browse the audio books in your library, select Audiobooks in the Source pane. The List view shows the title of each book with its part number (long books typically have multiple parts) in the Name column, and the author's name in the Artist column. If you add the Album column heading to your List view (as I describe in the section, "Changing the List view options," later in this chapter), the title of the book appears in the Album column. The browser in List view organizes audio books by Genre, Artist (the author), and Album (the book).

Browsing podcasts

To browse podcasts, select Podcasts in the Library section of the Source pane. The podcasts appear in the List pane. You can then see the episodes of a podcast by clicking the triangle next to the podcast name, and play the episode, as I describe in Chapter 6.

The List view shows the title of each podcast and its episodes in the Podcast column. The browser in List view organizes podcasts by Genre, Artist (podcast author), and Album (podcast title). The Grid and Cover Flow views show the cover art for the podcast. The mysterious blue dot next to a podcast means you haven't played one or more episodes of the podcast yet. (The same blue dot appears next to each unplayed episode.) As soon as you start listening to or watching a podcast, the dot disappears (accompanied by the theme of *The Twilight Zone*).

You can click the *i* icon on the far-right podcast listing margin to display separate information about the podcast's newest episode.

Browsing movies, videos, and TV shows

To browse movies, select Movies in the Library section of the Source pane. Any video files you add to your library from sources other than the iTunes Store are classified as movies. You can also find in the Movies listing those movies and short films you downloaded from the iTunes Store.

The List view shows the title of each movie in the Name column, and the browser in List view organizes movies by Genre, Artist, and Album. The Grid view (as shown in Figure 8-4) and the Cover Flow view show the first key frame of the movie or the box cover art for the movie.

You can browse TV shows downloaded from the iTunes Store (or any video set as TV Show with the Media Kind option, as described in Chapter 9) by selecting TV Shows in the Library section of the Source pane. The List view shows the episode title, show title, and season number. The browser in List view organizes TV shows by Genre, Show, and Season. The Grid and Cover Flow views show the promotional cover art for the TV show.

Figure 8-4:
Browse
and play
movies in
your iTunes
library in
Grid view.

Browsing applications and iPod games

Your iPod or iPhone is, in a sense, a pocket game machine as well as a tiny computer that runs applications. iPods that play video can also play games you can purchase and download from the iTunes Store, and the iPod touch and iPhone can run applications available in the App Store (see Chapter 4). And although you can't run the applications or play the games in iTunes, you can browse the list of applications and games you downloaded.

If you don't see Applications in the Library section of the Source pane, choose iTunes⇨Preferences (Mac) or Edit⇨Preferences (Windows), click the General tab at the top of the Preferences window, select the Applications option from the list of options for the Show heading, and click OK. The Applications option then appears in the Source pane in the Library section.

To browse iPod touch or iPhone applications and games, or iPod "click wheel" games, select Applications in the Source pane. A scrollable pane appears to the right of the Source pane, displaying thumbnail images of the applications and games, divided into sections for iPhone and iPod touch Apps, and iPod Games. Click a thumbnail image to see a description of the application or game.

In case you're a closet gamer, Chapter 4 shows you how to browse games and apps in the iTunes Store. Visit this book's companion Web site for details on how to use iPod and iPhone applications and play games.

Displaying Content in List View

To display your content in the List pane as a list, click the left View button (refer to Figure 8-1). Choose View⇨Show Browser to show the browser in the top part of the List pane in List view, or View⇨Hide Browser to hide it.

iTunes displays a playlist as a song list in the List pane, even if it includes other content items. The column headings for playlists have different meanings for the following types of content:

- **Songs and music videos:** The Name is the title of the song; the Artist is the band, artist, or performer. The Album is the title of the CD or vinyl record on which the song appeared. For music videos, the Name is typically the title of a song in the music video.

- **Podcasts:** The Name is the title of the podcast episode (as in "Ballad Roots of California Folk-Rock"), the Artist is the name of the podcast author (as in Tony Bove) or producer (such as Chicago Public Radio), and the Album is the name of the podcast (as in *Rockument*).

- **Audio books:** The Album is typically the book's title (as in *Fear and Loathing in Las Vegas*), and the Name is typically the title of one of the parts (as in *Fear and Loathing in Las Vegas*–Part 1 of 3).

- **TV shows:** The Name is the name of the TV show episode (as in "Mr. Monk and the Airplane"), the Artist is the name of the show (as in *Monk*), and the Album is the season (as in *Monk,* Season 1).

Understanding the content indicators

When you make choices in iTunes, it displays an action indicator next to each content item in List view — song, movie, TV show episode, music video, audio book, radio station, or podcast episode — to show you what it's doing. Here's a list of the indicators and their meanings:

- **Orange waveform:** iTunes is importing the item.

- **Green check mark:** iTunes finished importing the item.

- **Exclamation point:** iTunes can't find the item.

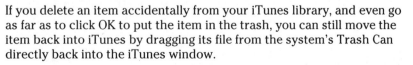

    If you delete an item accidentally from your iTunes library, and even go as far as to click OK to put the item in the trash, you can still move the item back into iTunes by dragging its file from the system's Trash Can directly back into the iTunes window.

- **Broadcast icon:** The item is on the Internet and plays as a stream.

✔ **Black check mark:** The item is marked for the next operation, such as importing from an audio CD or playing in sequence.

Click to remove the check mark.

✔ **Speaker:** The item (song, movie, episode, or whatever) is playing.

✔ **Chasing arrows:** iTunes is copying the content item from another location or downloading it from the Internet.

Changing the List view options

iTunes lets you customize the List view in the List pane for each type of content. For music, the list starts out with the Name, Artist, Album, Track, Time, Genre, My Rating, Play Count, and Last Played categories. You might have to drag the horizontal scroll bar along the bottom of the song list to see all these columns. You can display more, less, or different information in your song list.

Customize your List view in the following ways:

✔ **Make a column wider or narrower.** While you move your cursor over the divider between two columns, the cursor changes to a vertical bar with opposing arrows extending left and right; you can click and drag the divider to change the column's width.

✔ **Change the order of columns.** Click a column heading and drag the entire column to the left or right.

You can't change the position of the Name column and the narrow column to its left, which displays indicators and shows the playlist order.

✔ **Add or remove columns.** All columns except Name and the playlist order can be added or removed:

a. Select the type of content in the Source pane in the Library section (Music, Movies, TV Shows, Podcasts, Audiobooks, Radio, or Ringtones), and choose View⇨View Options.

b. Select the columns that you want to appear in the list from the View Options dialog (as shown in Figure 8-5).

You can also change the view options by Ctrl-clicking (on a Mac)or right-clicking (on Windows) any column heading in the list in either Browse view or List view.

Enabling the Kind column in the View Options dialog can help you keep track of different kinds of files, such as songs encoded as AIFF, AAC, or MP3 or videos encoded in QuickTime or MPEG.

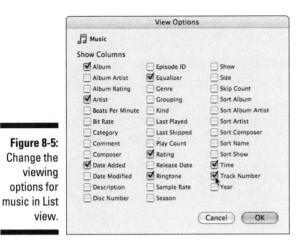

Figure 8-5:
Change the
viewing
options for
music in List
view.

Sorting Content by the List View Options

With just a little know-how, you can use the List view options to sort the listing of content items. You can sort items not only by name or album but also
by composer, the date the items were added to the library, or other information that you can add to an item (as I describe in Chapter 9).

At the very least, you can sort the content by the column headings you now
use in the List view. You can also add other column headings to your List
view (as I describe in the earlier section, "Changing the List view options")
and sort with them.

For example, clicking the Time heading reorders the items by their duration
in *ascending order,* from shortest to longest. If you click the Time heading
again, the sort is in *descending order,* which is reversed, starting with the longest item. You can sort by any column heading, such as Artist, Album, Track,
Date Added, and Ratings.

You can tell whether the sort is in ascending or descending order by the
little arrow indicator in the heading. When the arrow points up, the sort is in
ascending order; when pointing down, it's in descending order.

Alternatively, you can sort the list in alphabetical order. Click the Artist heading to sort the items in the list by artist name in alphabetical order (arrow
pointing up). Click it again to sort the list in reverse alphabetical order (arrow
pointing down).

iTunes also lets you sort the song list via the Album column. Each time you click Album, the heading cycles through each of the following options:

- ✔ **Album,** which sorts alphabetically by album title.
- ✔ **Album by Artist,** which groups albums by artist and then lists them alphabetically.
- ✔ **Album by Year,** which groups albums by artist and then lists them chronologically by year (set in the Song Information dialog).

iTunes keeps track of the songs, audio books, and podcasts you skip — not to be polite, just to be useful. You can use this feature to sort the Music and Audiobooks lists of your library in List view, thereby making it easier to select and delete the items you skip.

Searching for Content

Because your iTunes library will most likely grow, you might find the usual browsing and scrolling methods that I describe earlier in this chapter too time-consuming. Let iTunes find your content for you!

If you want to search the entire library with the browser open in List view, select All at the top of the Genre and Artist columns to browse the entire library before typing a term in the Search field. Or, if you prefer, choose View⊃Hide Browser to show the List view without the browser.

Locate the Search field — the oval field in the top-right corner — and follow these steps:

1. **Click in the Search field and enter several characters of your search term.**

   Use these tips for successful searching:

   - *Specify your search* with a specific title, artist, or album.
   - *Narrow your search* by typing more characters. Using fewer characters results in a longer list of possible songs.
   - *Case doesn't matter, nor do whole words.* The Search feature ignores case. For example, when I search for *miles*, iTunes finds a long list that includes "Eight Miles High," "Forty Miles of Bad Road," and "She Smiles like a River," as well as everything by Miles Davis.

2. **Look through the results, which display while you type.**

   The search operation works immediately, as shown in Figure 8-6, displaying any matches in the Name, Artist, and Album columns.

Figure 8-6:
Search for anything by typing any part of the name, artist, album, or title.

3. Scroll through the search results and then click an item to select it.

To back out of a search so that the full list appears again, you can either click the circled X in the Search field (which appears after you start typing characters) or delete what you typed. You then see the entire list in the List pane, just like before you began your search. All the items are still there and remain there unless you explicitly remove them. Searching manipulates only your view of the items.

Finding the Content's Media File

Getting lost in a large library is easy. While you browse your library, you might want to return quickly to view the current item playing. While your file plays, choose View➪Show Current Song (or press ⌘-L on a Mac or Ctrl-L in Windows as a shortcut). iTunes shows you the item that's playing.

You can also show the location of the media file for any content item. This trick comes in handy when you want to open the media file's folder. On a Mac, choose File➪Show in Finder (or press ⌘-R); in Windows, choose File➪ Show in Windows Explorer (or press Ctrl-R). iTunes gives control to the operating system (Mac or Windows), which displays the folder containing the media file.

You can show the file location if it's on your hard drive, but not if it's in a shared library on another computer. See Chapter 12 for more details on looking for media files.

Showing Duplicate Items

Because your library will grow, you'll probably want to check for duplications. Some songs that appear on artist CDs also appear on compilation or soundtrack CDs. If you rip them all, you could have duplicate songs that take up space on your hard drive. You might even have duplicate videos and audio books.

On the other hand, maybe you want to find different versions of the same song by the same artist. Even when the songs appear on different albums, iTunes can quickly find all the songs with the same title by the same artist.

To show duplicate items in the list, choose File⇨Show Duplicates. iTunes displays all the duplicate items in the List pane in the order of the last sort. (For example, if you last sorted by Album, the items appear in Album order.) If you're using the browser in List view, you see all the duplicate items in artist order. Click the artist to see the duplicate items specifically for that artist.

To stop showing duplicate items and return to your previous view, click the Show All button below the list of duplicates.

Deleting Content

Deleting content might seem counterproductive when you're trying to build up your iTunes library, but sometimes you just have to do it. For example, you want to delete the following:

- **Versions of songs:** You might have ripped a CD twice — say, once in AIFF format to burn the songs onto another CD and once in AAC format for your library and iPod or iPhone. You can delete the AIFF versions in your library after burning your CD (see Chapter 12 for burning instructions).

- **Songs from playlists:** You can delete songs from playlists yet keep the songs in your library. When you delete a song from a playlist, the song is simply deleted from the list — not from the library. You can delete entire playlists as well without harming the songs in the library. You have to select a media category in the Library section in the Source pane first, in order to delete songs from the library. (See Chapter 10 for more information about playlists.)

✔ **Any podcast, video, song, or audio book album, or artist from the library:**

  • *Podcasts:* Select Podcasts in the Library section of the Source pane and then select any podcast or podcast episodes. Press Delete/Backspace (or choose Edit⇨Delete) to delete them. If you delete the podcast, you remove it from your library, and you have to re-subscribe to it to get it back. If you delete an episode, you can get it back by clicking the Get button next to the episode. You can also select a single podcast episode and then choose Edit⇨Delete All to delete all episodes but keep the podcast itself.

  • *Movies or TV shows:* Select Movies or TV Shows in the Library section of the Source pane and then select any movie or TV show episodes or seasons. Press Delete/Backspace (or choose Edit⇨Delete). You can also select a single TV show episode and then choose Edit⇨Delete All to delete all episodes.

  • *Audio books:* Select Audiobooks in the Library section of the Source pane and then select any book section or all the sections of a book (books are typically divided into multiple sections). Press Delete/Backspace (or choose Edit⇨Delete).

  • *Songs (individually, or albums, or artists) or music videos:* Select Music in the Library section of the Source pane and then select the item or items — which can be on or more songs, an entire album, all the works of an artist, or a selection of albums or artists. For example, you can select an album in the browser in List view to automatically select all the songs on the album. Press Delete/Backspace (or choose Edit⇨Delete).

Deleting a content item from the iTunes library removes the item from your library, but it doesn't remove it from your hard drive until you agree.

In the first warning dialog that appears, click Remove to remove the selected items from the library, or click Cancel.

iTunes then displays a second warning about moving the files that are still in the iTunes Music folder to the Trash (Mac) or Recycle Bin (Windows). You can click Move to Trash on a Mac, or Move to Recycle Bin in Windows, to trash the item. Click Keep File to keep it in your music folder, or click Cancel to cancel the operation.

If you choose to move the album or artist folder to the Trash or Recycle Bin, the album or artist folder is deleted from your hard drive; otherwise, it remains in your iTunes Music folder.

If you leave music files and folders in your iTunes Music folder, you can add them back to your iTunes library by dragging and dropping them into the iTunes window.

You can delete multiple items in one clean sweep. Press Shift while you click a range of items. Alternatively, press ⌘ (Mac) or Ctrl (Windows) when you click individual items to add them to the selection. Then press Delete/Backspace (or choose Edit➪Delete).

Chapter 9

Adding and Editing Information in iTunes

In This Chapter

▶ Retrieving information online

▶ Editing information for each content item

▶ Adding information, cover art, comments, and ratings

*O*rganization depends on information. You expect your computer to do a lot more than just store a song with *Track 01* as the only identifier. Not only can iTunes retrieve the song's track information from the Internet, but it can also find the cover art for you.

Adding all the information for your iTunes content seems like a lot of trouble, but you can get most of the information automatically from the Internet — and without all that pesky typing. Adding track information is important because you certainly don't want to mistakenly play Frank Zappa's "My Guitar Wants to Kill Your Mama" when trying to impress your classical music teacher with the third movement of Tchaikovsky's *Pathétique Symphony,* do you? And because videos you make yourself or convert from other sources don't have this automatic information, you have to enter some description to tell them apart.

This chapter shows you how to add information to your content library in iTunes and edit it for better viewing so that you can organize your content by artist, album name, genre, composer, and ratings. You can then use this information to sort in List view by clicking the column headings. This chapter also describes how to add cover art for navigating your library with Cover Flow.

Retrieving Song Information from the Internet

Why bother entering information if someone else has already done it for you? You can easily get information about most music CDs from the Internet (that is, assuming you can connect to the Internet). The online database available for iTunes users holds information for millions of songs on commercial CDs and even some bootleg CDs.

Retrieving information automatically

When you pop a commercial music CD into your computer running iTunes, iTunes automatically looks up the track information for that CD on the Internet and fills in the information fields (name, artist, album, and so on). You don't need to do anything to make this happen. You can also edit the information after iTunes fills in the fields.

If your computer doesn't access the Internet automatically, you might want to turn off this automatic information retrieval. (You can always retrieve the information manually, as I describe later in this section.) To turn off the retrieval of track information, follow these steps:

1. **Choose iTunes⇨Preferences (Mac) or Edit⇨Preferences (Windows).**

   The iTunes Preferences dialog appears with buttons along the top.

2. **Click the General button.**

   The General preferences appear.

3. **Deselect the Automatically Retrieve CD Track Names from Internet option.**

   With this option turned on, iTunes connects to the Internet automatically and retrieves the track information. When turned off, iTunes doesn't retrieve the information, but you can retrieve it manually, as I describe in the next section.

Retrieving information manually

You can connect manually to the Internet at any time (for example, by using a modem connection) and retrieve the song information when you're ready to use it. After you connect to the Internet, choose Advanced⇨Get CD Track Names.

Using the Gracenote database

The first time I popped a commercial music CD into a computer, song information appeared like magic. iTunes automatically displayed the song names, album title, and artist names. How did it know? This information isn't stored on a standard music CD in digital form, but iTunes has to recognize the disc somehow.

The magic is that the software knows how to reach out and find the information on the Internet — in the Gracenote CDDB service. CDDB stands for (you guessed it) *CD Database.* The site (www.gracenote.com) hosts CDDB on the Web and searches for music CDs by artist, song title, and other methods. The iTunes software already knows how to use this database so you don't have to!

Gracenote recognizes an audio CD by taking into account the number, sequence, and duration of tracks. (This is how the database recognizes CD-Rs that are burned with the identical songs in the same order.) The database keeps track of information for most of the music CDs that you find on the market.

The database doesn't contain any information about personal or custom CDs unless people submit information to the database about such CDs. You can submit information about your personal or custom CDs by using iTunes: Type the information for each track while the audio CD is in your computer and then choose Advanced⇨Submit CD Track Names. The information that you enter is sent to the Gracenote CDDB site, where the good people who work tirelessly on the database check out your information before including it. In fact, if you spot a typo or something erroneous in the information that you receive from the Gracenote CDDB, you can easily correct it. Just use the Submit CD Track Names command to send the corrected version back to the Gracenote site. The good folks at Gracenote appreciate the effort.

Entering Content Information

You have to enter the information for certain media, including CDs that aren't known by the Gracenote CDDB, custom CD-Rs, and videos and audio books that you bring into iTunes from sources other than the iTunes Store. No big deal, though; just follow these steps:

1. **Click directly in the information field (such as Artist) in List view.**

2. **Click again so that the mouse pointer toggles to an editing cursor.**

3. **Type text directly into the information field.**

After grabbing the song information from the Internet or typing it, iTunes keeps track of the information for the CD even if you just play the CD without importing it. The next time you insert the CD, the song information is automatically filled in.

Editing the Information

Retrieving ready-made song information from the Internet is a great help, but you might not always like the format it comes in. Maybe you want to edit artist and band names or other information the way I do — I like to list solo artists by last name rather than by first name. (Gracenote CDDB lists artists by first name.) For example, I routinely change *Miles Davis* to *Davis, Miles*.

Other annoyances sometimes occur when bands feature *The* at the beginning of their names, such as The Who, The Band, The Beatles, and The Beach Boys. Even though these names sort correctly (in alphabetical order, under their proper names), I dislike having *The* before the band name, so I routinely remove it.

You might also want to change the information that is supplied by the iTunes Store for the movies, TV shows, music videos, audio books, and podcasts you download. And if you obtain your content from other sources, you might need to add information for the first time.

In List view, you can edit the content information by clicking directly in the specific track's field (such as the Artist field) and then clicking again so that the mouse pointer toggles to an editing cursor. You can then select the text and type over it — or use the Copy, Cut, and Paste commands on the Edit menu — to move tiny bits of text around within the field. As you can see in Figure 9-1, I changed the Artist field to *Beck, Jeff*.

Figure 9-1:
Click inside
a field to
edit the
information.

You can edit the Name, Artist, Album, Genre, and My Ratings fields in the list. However, editing this information by choosing File⇨Get Info is easier. Keep reading to find out why.

Editing multiple items at once

Editing in the content list is fine if you're editing the information for one item, but typically you need to change all the tracks of an audio CD. For example, if a CD of songs by Bob Dylan is listed with the artist as *Bob Dylan,* you might want to change all the songs at once to *Dylan, Bob.* Changing all the information in one fell swoop is fast and clean, but like most powerful shortcuts, you need to be careful because it can be dangerous.

You can change a group of items in List view. Follow these steps to change a group of items at once:

1. **Select a group of content items by clicking the first item and then pressing Shift while you click the last item.**

   All the items between the first and last are highlighted. You can extend a selection by Shift-clicking other items or add to a selection by ⌘-clicking (Mac) or Ctrl-clicking (Windows). You can also remove items already selected by ⌘-clicking (Mac) or Ctrl-clicking (Windows).

2. **Choose File⇨Get Info or press ⌘-I (Mac) or Ctrl-I (Windows).**

   A warning message displays:

   ```
   Are you sure you want to edit information for multiple
   items?
   ```

   Speed-editing the information in multiple items at once can be dangerous for your library organization. If, for example, you change an informational snippet for one item in a selected group (the song or movie title, for example), the corresponding snippet for all items in the selected group are going to change as well! Be careful about what you edit when using this method.

3. **Click Yes to edit information for multiple items.**

   The Multiple Item Information dialog appears, as shown in Figure 9-2.

4. **Edit the field(s) you want to change for all the items.**

   When you edit a field, a check mark appears automatically in the check box next to the field. iTunes assumes that you want that field changed in all the selected items. Make sure that no other check box is selected except the one for the field that you want.

5. **Click OK to make the change.**

   iTunes changes the field for the entire selection of items.

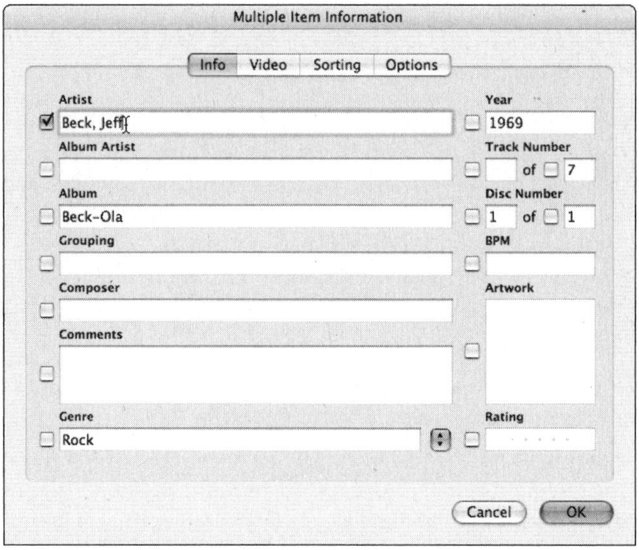

Multiple Item Information

Info Video Sorting Options

Artist
☑ Beck, Jeff

Year
☐ 1969

Album Artist
☐

Track Number
☐ of ☐ 7

Album
☐ Beck–Ola

Disc Number
☐ 1 of ☐ 1

Grouping
☐

BPM
☐

Composer
☐

Artwork
☐

Comments
☐

Genre
☐ Rock ⬍

Rating
☐ · · · · ·

Cancel OK

Figure 9-2:
Change the field info for multiple items at once.

iTunes offers both Artist and Album Artist fields for a song, so that you can include the album artist if it's different — such as the artist names for a duet album or a compilation album that features songs by different artists (such as Eric Clapton's Crossroads box set, in which the Album Artist is Clapton, but the Artist for each song might be the Yardbirds, Cream, Blind Faith, and so on). You can also use this field for Artist name formatted differently; for example, the Artist field could have the artist as "Bob Dylan" and the Album Artist as "Dylan, Bob." You can then change the list view options (as I describe in Chapter 8) to include the Album Artist field as a column for sorting the song list.

Editing fields for a single item

Although the track information grabbed from the Internet is enough for identifying a song in your iTunes library, some facts — such as composer credits — might not be included. Adding composer credits is usually worth your effort because you can then search and sort by composer and create playlists based on the composer. Videos (movies, TV shows, and music videos), podcasts, and audio books might also have information in their fields that you want to change or have blank fields that could use some helpful information.

To get all the details about an item — song, video, podcast, or audio book — select the item and then choose File⇨Get Info (or press ⌘-I on a Mac or Ctrl-I in Windows). You see the item's information dialog, as shown in Figure 9-3.

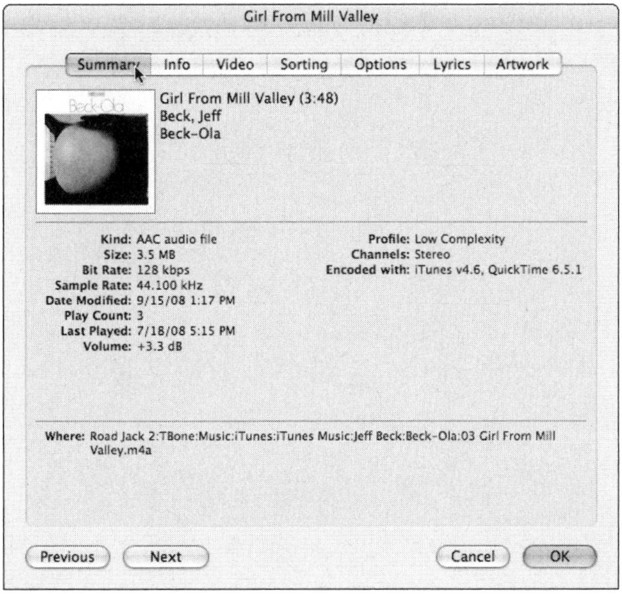

Girl From Mill Valley

Summary | Info | Video | Sorting | Options | Lyrics | Artwork

Girl From Mill Valley (3:48)
Beck, Jeff
Beck-Ola

Kind: AAC audio file
Size: 3.5 MB
Bit Rate: 128 kbps
Sample Rate: 44.100 kHz
Date Modified: 9/15/08 1:17 PM
Play Count: 3
Last Played: 7/18/08 5:15 PM
Volume: +3.3 dB

Profile: Low Complexity
Channels: Stereo
Encoded with: iTunes v4.6, QuickTime 6.5.1

Where: Road Jack 2:TBone:Music:iTunes:iTunes Music:Jeff Beck:Beck-Ola:03 Girl From Mill Valley.m4a

Previous | Next   Cancel | OK

Figure 9-3:
A content
item's
information
dialog.

When you select one item, its information dialog appears, and your edits affect only one item; when you select multiple items, the Multiple Item Information dialog appears, and your edits affect multiple items.

A selection's information dialog offers the following tabs:

- ✔ **Summary:** The Summary tab (as shown in Figure 9-3) offers useful information about the media file format and location on your hard drive, the file size, and the digital compression method (bit rate, sample rate, and so on).

- ✔ **Info:** The Info tab allows you to change the name, artist, composer, album, genre, year, and other information. You can also add comments, as shown in Figure 9-4.

- ✔ **Video:** The Video tab lets you set the type of video — movie, TV show, or music video — in the Kind pop-up menu. For TV shows, you can add show information, including the title of the show, episode number and ID, and season number.

- ✔ **Sorting:** The Sorting tab allows you to add information to fields for additional choices while sorting your library content. For example, you can add a different name for the artist in the Sort Artist field to the right of the Artist field, such as "Dylan, Bob" for "Bob Dylan." Information from the Info tab appears on the left side, and you can add an alternative sort field on the right side. You can even add a Show field for the title of a concert or some other use. Choose View➪View Options to select a sort field as a List view option, and then you can sort your content in List view by using the sort fields.

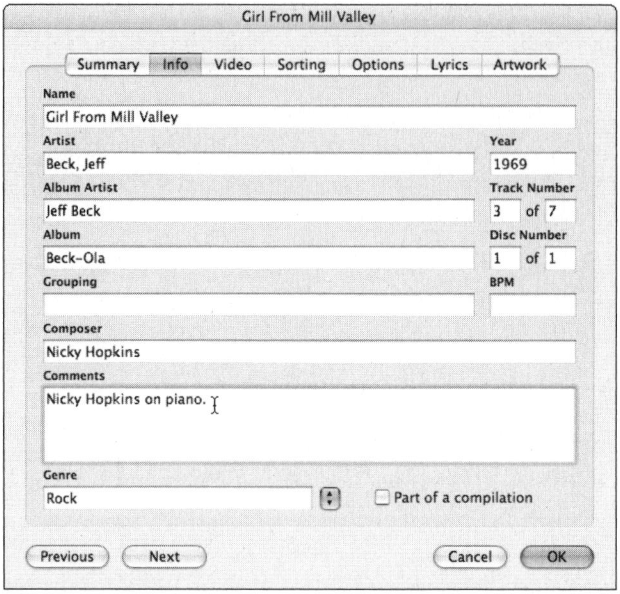

Figure 9-4:
View and
edit
information
from the
Info tab.

✔ **Options:** The Options tab, as shown in Figure 9-5, offers the following:

- *Volume Adjustment:* You can set the volume for a song, video, podcast, or audio book in advance so that it always plays at that volume (or lower, if your overall iTunes or iPod volume is set lower). Drag the slider to the right to increase the volume adjustment up to 100% (twice the usual volume); drag the slider to the left to decrease the volume adjustment down to –100% (half the usual volume). For more details on setting the volume in advance, see Chapter 13.

- *Equalizer Preset:* Choose an equalizer preset for an item. See Chapter 13 for details on how you can use this preset to control how an item sounds on your iPod as well as in iTunes.

- *Media Kind:* You can assign a different media type to the item so that it appears in a different part of your iTunes library. For example, you can assign the audiobook type to a sound file that appears as a music file.

- *Ratings:* Assign up to five stars to an item as a rating. (See how in the upcoming section, "Adding a rating.")

- *Start Time and Stop Time:* Set the start and stop times for an item. You can use these options to cut unwanted intros and outros of a song (such as announcers, audience applause, and tuning up), or to skip opening credits or commercials of movies. You can also use it to split an item (or, in the parlance of record label executives and artists, split a track) into multiple items (tracks).

Visit this book's companion Web site for details.

- *Remember Playback Position:* Set this option for an item so that when you select and play the item, iTunes resumes playing it from where you left off. This option is usually turned on for audio books, movies, and TV shows.

- *Skip When Shuffling:* Set this option for an item to be skipped from Party Shuffle.

- *Part of a Gapless Album:* Set this option for an item to be played back without a gap between songs. (See Chapter 5 to find out about the gaps between songs.)

✔ **Lyrics:** The Lyrics tab offers a text field for adding text.

You can view lyrics on iPod touch/classic/nano, older color-display models, and iPhone and by starting a song (or choosing the Now Playing option from the main menu) and then tapping the album cover on an iPod touch or iPhone, or pressing the Select button three or four times. (The first click shows the slider, the second shows the cover art if there is cover art, the third click shows ratings you've entered, and the fourth shows the lyrics.) If you press the Select button too many times, the iPod returns to the Now Playing display.

✔ **Artwork:** The Artwork tab allows you to add or delete artwork for the item. See the upcoming section, "Adding Cover Art."

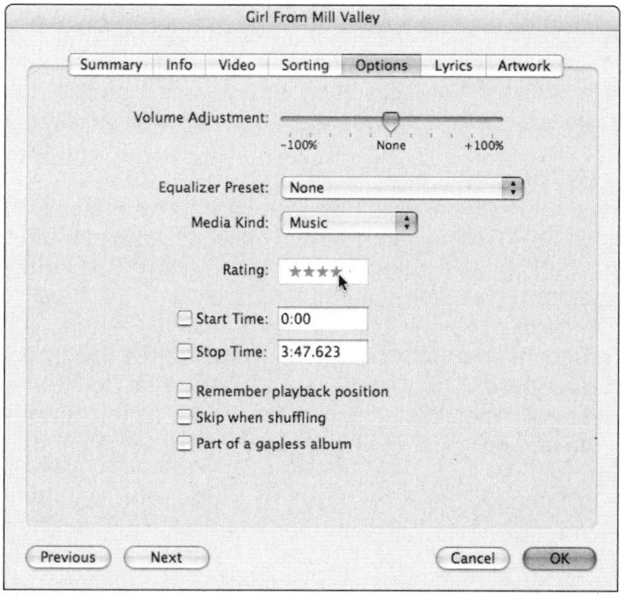

Girl From Mill Valley

| Summary | Info | Video | Sorting | Options | Lyrics | Artwork |

Volume Adjustment: ───────○───────
-100%   None   +100%

Equalizer Preset: None

Media Kind: Music

Rating: ★★★★

☐ Start Time: 0:00
☐ Stop Time: 3:47.623

☐ Remember playback position
☐ Skip when shuffling
☐ Part of a gapless album

Previous   Next   Cancel   OK

Figure 9-5:
Add a rating
to a song
from the
Options tab.

If you follow the careers of certain guitarists, vocalists, or session musicians, you can sort your music in List view by something other than the given artist for the album. First, provide a new entry for the Sort Artist or Sort Album Artist fields in the Sorting tab, and then choose that field as a view option so that you can sort on it. For example, I like to use the Sort Artist field for the leader, lead guitarist, or lead singer in a band; or a session player or special guest (such as Nicky Hopkins, who played keyboards on a variety of albums by different bands including The Who, The Rolling Stones, and The Beatles). After entering *Nicky Hopkins* into the Sort Artist field for the songs, I can choose View⇨View Options and select Sort Artist for a column heading. I can then sort the List view by clicking the new Sort Artist heading to find all recordings featuring Nicky Hopkins.

You can apply the entry of a sort field in the Sorting tab to all the tracks of the same album or to all tracks by the same artist, album artist, composer, or show. After changing the sort field for an item in the Sorting tab, select the item in List view, Control-click (right-click in Windows) the item to display the contextual menu, and then choose Apply Sort Field. Click Yes to make the change.

To move through an album one item at a time when using Get Info (without closing and reopening the information dialog), click the Previous or Next buttons in the bottom-left corner of the dialog.

Adding a rating

iTunes allows you to rate your content. The cool thing about ratings is that they're *yours*. You can use ratings to mean anything you want. For example, you can rate songs based on how much you like them, whether your mother would listen to them, or how they blend into a work environment. You can also rate videos based on your watching habits, as well as audio books and podcasts.

To add a rating to a content item, click the Options tab (refer to Figure 9-5) and drag inside the My Rating field to add stars. The upper limit is five stars (for the best). You can also select the item and choose File⇨Rating to assign a rating to an item.

You might have noticed the My Top Rated playlist in the Source pane. This playlist is an example of a *smart playlist* — a playlist that updates when ratings are changed. The My Top Rated playlist plays all the top-rated songs in your library. You can find out more about playlists in Chapter 10.

Adding Cover Art

iTunes displays the cover art for your albums, videos, movies, podcasts, audio books, and TV shows in the Cover Flow browser. (See Chapter 8 for details.) Color-display iPods, Apple TV, iPod touch, and the iPhone also display the cover art. So it makes sense to get the art, especially since it's free!

Items that you buy from the iTunes Store typically include an image of the album, book, or box cover art or a photo of the artist that serves as cover art. You can see the artwork in the artwork viewer in the lower-left corner of the iTunes window by clicking the Show/Hide Artwork button, as shown in Figure 9-6. The artwork changes for each item or album that you select or play. You can toggle between displaying the cover art of the item playing to the cover art of a selected item by clicking the right arrow (or the words "Now Playing") above the artwork viewer. Toggle back to displaying the cover art of the now-playing item by clicking the right arrow again (or the words "Selected Item").

Figure 9-6:
Show the artwork for a song's album.

Show/Hide Artwork button

To fill your library automatically with cover art for the CDs you ripped, get yourself an iTunes Store account if you don't already have one. Log in to your account and then choose Advanced⇨Get Album Artwork. iTunes grabs the cover art not only for iTunes Store purchases but also for CDs you ripped — provided that the albums are also available in the iTunes Store.

To download cover art for ripped CDs automatically after ripping them (without having to manually choose Advanced⇨Get Album Artwork each time), choose Preferences from the iTunes menu on a Mac or the Edit menu in Windows, click the Store tab, and select the Automatically Download Missing Album Artwork option.

You can also get your cover art from other places that sell CDs, such as Amazon.com, or you can even scan them from the actual CDs. The optimal size for cover art is 300 x 300 pixels. Save it in a graphics format that iTunes (and its underlying graphics technology, *QuickTime*) understands — JPEG, GIF, PNG, TIFF, or Photoshop. With a Web browser, you can visit Web pages to scout for suitable art; just Control-click (Mac) or right-click an image (Windows) to download and save the image on your hard drive.

To add artwork to one or more items, select it (or them) in your iTunes library and do one of the following:

- **Drag the artwork's image file from a folder on your hard drive into the artwork viewer (the bottom-left corner of the iTunes window).**

  To add artwork for an entire album (rather than just individual songs) or season of TV shows, first select the album or season in the browser in List view, or select all the items individually. Then drag the image file into the artwork viewer.

- **Add artwork to a single item through the information window.**

  Choose File➪Get Info and then click the Artwork tab in the Get Info dialog. Click the Add button, browse your hard drive or network for the image file, select the file, and then click OK.

- **Add artwork for multiple items in the Multiple Item Information dialog.**

  Choose File➪Get Info after selecting the items, enable the Artwork field (select its check box), and then drag a graphics file for the cover art from a Desktop folder to the Artwork well. Click Yes to the warning message to change the artwork.

  See the "Editing multiple items at once" section, earlier in this chapter, to find out more about using the Multiple Item Information dialog.

To remove the artwork from an item, view the artwork in a larger window or resize the artwork, choose File➪Get Info and then click the Artwork tab. You can add a different image (or several images) with the Add button, delete images with the Delete button, or resize images with the size slider.

Chapter 10

Organizing iTunes Content with Playlists

*T*he ability to play any set of songs in a specific order is one of the joys of using iTunes and iPods. A *playlist* is a list of the items that you want in the sequence that you want to play them. You can use playlists to organize your music playback experience. For example, you can make a playlist of love songs from different albums to play the next time you need a romantic mood, or you can compile a playlist of surf songs for a trip to the beach.

You can also organize your content for different operations — such as copying to your iPod, iPhone, or Apple TV or burning a CD — by creating playlists. I create playlists that combine songs from different albums based on themes or similarities. For example, I have a jazz playlist for cruising around with my iPhone in the city at night, a classic rock playlist for jogging with my iPod shuffle in the morning and hanging out in coffee shops with my iPod nano, a playlist of short films mixed with TV shows for a long airplane ride with my iPod touch, and a playlist of rain songs to celebrate rainy days with any of these devices, including my Apple TV.

You can create as many playlists of songs, audio books, podcast episodes, and videos as you want, in any order that you like. The items and their files don't change, nor are they copied: iTunes simply creates a list of the item names with links to the actual items and their files.

You can even create a *smart playlist,* which automatically includes items in the playlist based on the criteria you set up and also removes items that don't match the criteria. The information included in iTunes (see Chapter 9) is very useful for setting up the criteria. For example, you can define the criteria for a smart playlist to automatically include songs from a particular artist or songs that have the highest rating or fit within a particular musical genre.

Creating Playlists

You need to create a playlist to burn a CD, but playlists can also make it easier to play items you like without searching the entire library for them. You can create playlists of individual songs or entire albums. You can also include audio books, TV shows, videos, podcast episodes, and Web radio stations in playlists.

Song playlists

You can drag individual songs into a playlist and rearrange the songs to play in any sequence you want.

To create a playlist, follow these steps:

1. **Click the Add Playlist button (in the bottom-left corner of the iTunes window under the Source pane) or choose File⇨New Playlist.**

   This step creates a new, untitled playlist in the Playlists section of the Source pane named, appropriately enough, *untitled playlist,* highlighted and ready to rename.

2. **Give the playlist a new descriptive name.**

   You can begin typing a new name and press Return (or just click somewhere else) to save the name. (If the playlist name wasn't highlighted first, click once to select it, click the name again so that the text cursor appears, and the playlist name is highlighted and ready for you to type the new name.)

   After you type the new name, iTunes automatically sorts it into alphabetical order in the Playlists section of the Source pane (underneath the preset smart playlists).

3. **Select Music in the Library section of the Source pane and then drag songs from the library to the playlist.**

   Drag one song at a time or drag a group of songs, dropping them onto the playlist name in the Source pane. The initial order of songs in the playlist is based on the order in which you drag them to the list.

4. **Select the playlist in the Playlists section of the Source pane to play it.**

   After selecting a playlist, the songs in the playlist appear in the List pane. Select any song in the playlist to start playing from that song to the end of the playlist, and click the Play button.

To rearrange the list of songs in the playlist, see "Rearranging and managing playlists" later in this chapter.

To open a playlist in a new window, double-click the icon next to the playlist name in the Source pane. You can then select Music in the Source pane to browse your music library, and drag items from your music library to the separate playlist window.

To create a playlist quickly, select the group of songs in the List pane that you want to make into a playlist. Choose File➪New Playlist from Selection, or drag the selection to an area between playlists in the Source pane. You can then type a name for the new playlist that appears.

Album playlists

Making a playlist of an album is simple. Select the Music option in the Library section of the Source pane, select List view by choosing View➪As List and then show the browser by choosing View➪Show Browser, and finally drag an album from the Album list to an area between playlists in the Playlists section of the Source pane. Or, select the album and then choose File➪New Playlist from Selection. iTunes automatically creates a new playlist named after the album.

You might want to play several albums back to back without having to select each album to play it. For example, you might want to use an iPod on that long drive from London to Liverpool to play The Beatles' albums in the order they were released (or perhaps in the reverse order, following The Beatles' career from London back to Liverpool).

To create a playlist of entire albums in a particular order, follow these steps:

1. **Create a new playlist.**

   Create a playlist by clicking the Add Playlist button under the Source pane or by choosing File➪New Playlist.

   A new, untitled playlist appears in the Playlists section of the Source pane, highlighted and ready to rename.

2. **In the Playlists section of the Source pane, give the playlist a new, descriptive name.**

3. **Select the Music option in the Library section of the Source pane, and click the leftmost View button in the upper-right corner of the iTunes window to view as list (or choose View⇨As List).**

   The List pane displays a list of all the songs.

4. **Choose View⇨Show Browser, then find and click the name of the artist who created the album you're seeking.**

   After clicking the artist name, the Album list for that artist appears in the right panel.

5. **Drag an album name from the right panel over to the playlist name in the Source pane.**

6. **Select and drag each subsequent album over the playlist name.**

   Each time you drag an album, iTunes automatically lists the songs in the proper track sequence for each album. The albums are listed in the playlist in the order that you dragged them.

Podcast playlists

You can add one or more podcast episodes to your playlists, or add all the episodes of a podcast at once. You can even create a playlist consisting entirely of episodes from different podcasts.

To add one or more podcast episodes to a playlist, follow these steps:

1. **Click the Add Playlist button or choose File⇨New Playlist.**

   The Add Playlist button is in the bottom-left corner of the iTunes window under the Source pane.

   A new, untitled playlist appears in the Playlists section of the Source pane.

2. **In the Playlists section of the Source pane, click the untitled playlist twice and give it a new descriptive name.**

   After you type a new name, iTunes automatically sorts it into alphabetical order in the Playlists section of the Source pane, underneath the preset smart playlists.

3. **Select the Podcasts option in the Source pane and then open a podcast by clicking the triangle next to its name.**

   The podcast opens to reveal its episodes. (See Chapter 6 for details on opening podcasts and playing podcast episodes.)

4. **Drag episodes from the Podcasts list to the playlist.**

   You can drag one episode at a time, or drag a selection of episodes, and then drop them onto the playlist name in the Playlists section of the Source pane. The initial order of episodes in the playlist is based on the order in which you drag the episodes to the list.

Of course, you can rearrange the episodes in any order after dragging them, as I show you in "Rearranging and managing playlists" later in this chapter.

You can also add all of the podcast episodes to a playlist. Follow these steps:

1. **Create a new playlist by following Steps 1 and 2 of the preceding list.**

   You know, you might as well memorize those two steps so that you can do them in your sleep.

2. **Select the Podcasts option in the Source pane and then select a podcast by name.**

3. **Drag the podcast name over the playlist name.**

   iTunes adds all of the podcast episodes to the playlist. The initial order of episodes in the playlist is based on the podcast order. Of course, you can rearrange the episodes in the playlist in any order after dragging them.

 To create a playlist with all of a podcast's episodes quickly, choose Podcasts in the Source pane and select the podcast that you want to make into a playlist. Then choose File⇨New Playlist from Selection or drag the selection to an area between playlists in the Playlists section of the Source pane. You can then type a name for the new playlist that appears.

Video playlists

You can drag individual videos and TV shows into a playlist and rearrange them to play in any sequence you want.

To create a video playlist, follow these steps:

1. **Click the Add Playlist button or choose File⇨New Playlist.**

   Clicking the Add Playlist button, in the bottom-left corner of the iTunes window under the Source pane, creates a new, untitled playlist in the Playlists section of the Source pane.

2. **In the Playlists section of the Source pane, click the untitled playlist twice and give it a new descriptive name.**

   After you type a new name, iTunes automatically sorts it into alphabetical order in the Playlists section of the Source pane, underneath the preset smart playlists.

3. **Select the Movies or TV Shows option in the Source pane and then drag videos from the library to the playlist.**

   Drag one video at a time or drag a selection of items, dropping them onto the playlist name in the Playlists section of the Source pane. The initial order of videos (movies, TV show episodes, or music videos) in the playlist is based on the order in which you drag them to the list.

Of course, you can rearrange these videos in any order after dragging them, as I show you in "Rearranging and managing playlists" later in this chapter.

You can mix videos with songs and other items in a playlist. For example, mixing songs and music videos; songs and a video documentary; or just a selection of TV shows, music, podcasts, movies, and audio books for an entire day's worth of entertainment. However, if you transfer the playlist to an iPod that doesn't play video, the iPod skips the videos.

Rearranging and managing playlists

To rearrange the items in a playlist, follow these steps:

1. **Select the playlist in the Playlists section of the Source pane.**

   After selecting a playlist, the songs in the playlist appear in the List pane.

2. **Drag items in the List pane to rearrange the list.**

   - *To move an item (such as a song) up the list and scroll at the same time,* drag it over the up arrow in the first column.

   - *To move an item down the list and scroll,* drag it to the bottom of the list.

   - *To move a group of items at once,* press Shift and select a range of items (or press ⌘ on a Mac or Ctrl in Windows while clicking to select specific songs) and then drag them into a new position.

   Besides dragging items, you can also rearrange a playlist by sorting it: Just click one of the column headings, such as Name, Time, or Artist.

You can drag items from one playlist to another. Only links are copied, not the actual files.

You can rename a playlist at any time by clicking its name twice and typing a new one. Also, in case you forget which songs are in which playlists, you can see all the playlists that include a particular song. In List view, press Control on a Mac and click the song; in Windows, right-click the song and choose Show in Playlist from the contextual menu. The playlists that include the song are listed in the submenu.

You can organize playlists into folders in the Source pane. Choose File⇨New Playlist Folder to create a folder in the Playlists section. Then drag playlist names and drop them over the new folder — just like how you treat files and folders in your operating system. Folders are useful for grouping playlists that are similar in content or function. For example, I created a different folder corresponding to each of my iPods to organize the playlists I use to synchronize with those iPods. (See Chapter 11 to read about iPod synchronization.) You can include smart playlists in folders as well as regular playlists.

Deleting items from a playlist

You can delete items from playlists while keeping the items in your library. When you delete an item from a playlist, the item is simply deleted from the list — not from the library. You can also delete entire playlists without harming the content in the library. *Note:* You'll need to switch to the Library section of the Source pane (Music, Movies, TV Shows, and so on) if you want to delete items permanently from your library.

To delete an item from a playlist, select the playlist in the Playlists section of the Source pane and then select the item. Press Delete/Backspace or choose Edit⇨Delete. In the warning dialog that appears, click Remove to remove the selected item from the list.

The one way you can completely delete an item from your library from within a playlist is by selecting the item and pressing ⌘-Option-Delete (Mac) or Ctrl-Alt-Backspace (Windows).

To delete a whole playlist, select the playlist in the Playlists section of the Source pane and then press Delete/Backspace or choose Edit⇨Delete.

Using Smart Playlists

Under Party Shuffle (near the top of the Playlists section of the Source pane), you can find *smart playlists,* which are indicated by a gear-in-a-document icon. iTunes comes with a few sample smart playlists, such as My Top Rated and Recently Added, and you can create your own. Smart playlists add items to themselves based on prearranged criteria, or *rules.* For example, when you rate your content items, My Top Rated changes to reflect your new ratings. You don't have to set up anything because My Top Rated and Recently Added are already defined for you.

Of course, smart playlists are ignorant of your taste in music or video. You have to program them with rules by using the information in iTunes (see Chapter 9). For example, you can create a smart playlist that uses the Year field to grab all the songs from 1966. This list, in no particular order, might include The Beatles ("Eleanor Rigby"), Frank Sinatra ("Strangers in the Night"), The Yardbirds ("Over Under Sideways Down"), and Ike and Tina Turner ("River Deep, Mountain High") — a far-out playlist, no doubt, but not necessarily what you want. You can use other fields of information that you entered (such as ratings, artist name, or composer) to fine-tune your criteria. You can also use built-in functions, such as *Play Count* (the number of times the item was played) or *Date Added* (the date the item was added to the library).

A smart playlist for recent additions

Setting up rules gives you the opportunity to create playlists that are smarter than the ones supplied with iTunes. For example, I created a smart playlist with criteria (as shown in Figure 10-2) that does the following:

✔ Includes any item added to the library in the past week that also has a rating greater than three stars.

✔ Limits the playlist to 72 minutes to be sure it fits on a 74-minute audio CD, even with gaps between the songs. It also refines the selection to the most recently added if the entire selection becomes greater than 72 minutes.

✔ Matches only selected items.

✔ Performs live updating.

Creating a smart playlist

To create a new smart playlist, choose File⇨New Smart Playlist. The Smart Playlist dialog appears (as shown in Figure 10-1), offering the following choices for setting criteria:

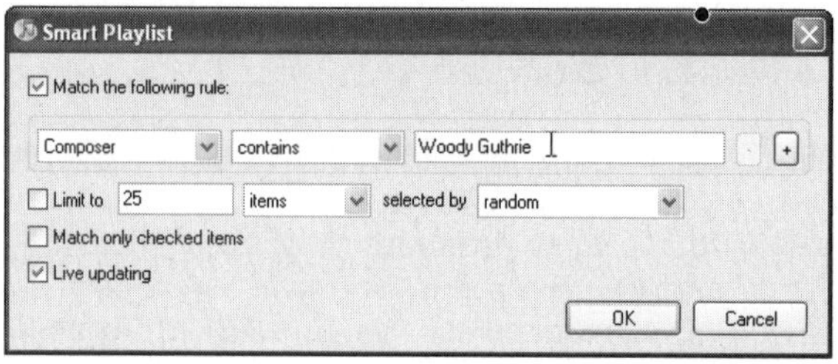

Figure 10-1:
Set the first match rule for a smart playlist.

✔ **Match the Following Rule:** From the first pop-up menu (refer to Figure 10-1), you can choose any of the categories used for information, such as Artist, Composer, or Last Played. From the second pop-up menu, you can choose an operator, such as the greater-than or less-than operator. The selections that you make in these two pop-up menus combine to create a rule, such as `Year is greater than 1966` or, as in Figure 10-1, `Composer contains` (the words) `Woody Guthrie`.

You can also add multiple conditions by clicking the + button (on the right) as shown in Figure 10-2. You then decide whether to match all or any of these conditions. The Match *xx* of the Following Rules option is enabled by default when you set one or more rules.

✔ **Limit To:** You can limit the smart playlist to a specific *duration*, measured by the number of songs (items), time, or size in megabytes or gigabytes, as shown in Figure 10-2. You can have items selected by various methods, such as random, most recently played, and so on.

✔ **Match Only Checked Items:** This option selects only those songs or other items in the library that have a check mark beside them, along with the rest of the criteria. Selecting and deselecting items is an easy way to fine-tune your selection for a smart playlist.

✔ **Live Updating:** This allows iTunes to continually update the playlist while you play items, add or remove items from the library, change their ratings, and so on.

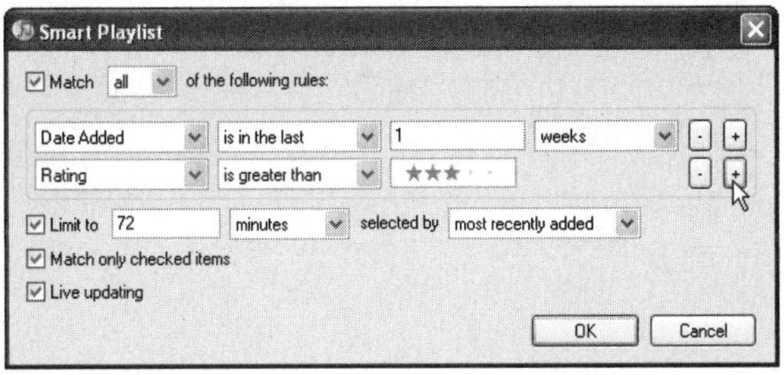

Figure 10-2:
Use multiple conditions and a time limit for a smart playlist.

> **Smart Playlist**
>
> ☑ Match [all ▾] of the following rules:
>
> [Date Added ▾] [is in the last ▾] [1] [weeks ▾] [−] [+]
> [Rating ▾] [is greater than ▾] [★★★ · ·] [−] [+]
>
> ☑ Limit to [72] [minutes ▾] selected by [most recently added ▾]
> ☑ Match only checked items
> ☑ Live updating
>
> [OK] [Cancel]

After setting up the rules, click OK. iTunes creates the playlist, noted by a gear-in-a-document icon and the name *untitled playlist* (or whatever phrase you used for the first condition, such as the album or artist name). You can click in the playlist field and then type a new name for it.

Editing a smart playlist

To edit a smart playlist, select it from the Playlists section of the Source pane and choose File⇨Edit Smart Playlist. Or, you can Control-click (Mac) or right-click (Windows) the playlist and then choose Edit Smart Playlist from the pop-up menu. Either way, the Smart Playlist window appears with the criteria for the smart playlist.

For example, to modify the smart playlist so that items with a higher rating are picked, simply add another star or two to the My Rating criteria.

You can also choose to limit the playlist to a certain number of items selected by various methods, such as random, most recently played, and so on.

Using the Genius Button

If you select a song and click the Genius button, iTunes takes a look at your selection and creates a playlist of songs that go along with it. That's genius!

The Genius button and the Genius sidebar (which I describe in glorious detail in Chapter 3) work with Apple's iTunes Store content to match up your tastes to other iTunes users using a technique called *collaborative filtering*. The Genius feature analyzes the music in other people's iTunes libraries — people who also have the same song you selected (if they use the Genius feature). All of this information is shared anonymously. The only music Genius knows, however, is the music available in the iTunes Store.

For the Genius feature to work, you need an iTunes Store account (see Chapter 4), and you must turn on Genius to enable iTunes to scan your music library and catalog your iTunes collection. The scanning process may take a few minutes or (for very large collections) a few hours, but you can continue using iTunes while it scans your music.

To turn on Genius, click the Turn on Genius button in the Genius sidebar enter your Apple ID and password for your iTunes Store account, and click Continue.

You can also turn on the Genius feature by choosing Store⇨Turn On Genius, and turn if off by choosing Store⇨Turn Off Genius. If you add new music, you can tell iTunes to immediately update the Genius feature with new information by choosing Store⇨Update Genius.

To create a genius playlist, select a song in the List pane and click the Genius button (the button with the atom icon) at the bottom right corner of the iTunes window. iTunes displays the genius playlist based on the selected song. You can set the limit of the number of songs for the genius playlist by clicking the Limit To pop-up menu in the top row of buttons on the right side of the List pane, as shown in Figure 10-3.

You can refresh the genius playlist with a new batch of songs based on the selected song by clicking the Refresh button in the top row of buttons (refer to Figure 10-3). When you refresh a genius playlist, you lose the previous version of that playlist.

To save a genius playlist, click Save Playlist in the right corner of the top row of buttons. The playlist is saved with the genius icon using the name of the selected song and listed in the Playlists section of the Source pane at the top, above smart playlists. You can revisit this genius playlist and refresh it, or change its song limit. You can also rearrange the songs in the genius playlist by dragging them. To sort the songs, click the column headers in the List pane — just like other playlists.

You can synchronize your saved genius playlists with your iPod or iPhone (see Chapter 11 for details). Synchronized genius playlists on the iPod or iPhone contain the same songs that appeared in the iTunes version of the playlist. See Chapter 14 for details on using genius playlists with iPods and iPhones.

Figure 10-3:
Limit the
number of
songs for
the Genius
playlist.

Genius button

Creating an iMix

Amateur disk jockeys, rejoice! The iTunes Store offers the iMix section for sharing your iTunes playlists with other iTunes users. Anyone can find your iMix playlist by selecting the iTunes Store in the Source pane, choosing Music from the iTunes Store menu on the left panel at the top of the home page next to the new releases panel, and then clicking iMix in the More in Music menu on the left panel of the Music page.

Although you can submit a playlist of any items to be published in the iMix section of the store, only items available from the store are actually published. Unavailable items are skipped.

Browsers in the iTunes Store can enter the iMix section and click any playlist to view it. See Chapter 4 for information about navigating the iTunes Store, playing short preview clips, and buying content.

To create an iMix, follow these steps:

1. **Select the playlist in the Playlists section of the Source pane and choose Store⇨Create an iMix.**

   iTunes displays a warning dialog before accessing the iTunes Store to publish your playlist.

2. **Click the Create button in the warning dialog.**

   iTunes displays the iTunes Store sign-in dialog.

3. **Enter your ID and password and then click Publish.**

   iTunes selects the iTunes Store option in the Source pane and displays the iMix page. You see the iMix playlist that will be published, which includes only those items that are available from the store.

4. **Edit the title and description for the iMix playlist and then click the Publish button.**

iTunes publishes the playlist in the iMix section of the store. Others can browse the playlist and buy any items.

Chapter 11

Synchronizing Devices with iTunes

*i*Tunes is the all-knowing, all-powerful synchronizer, the software you use to put content on your iPod, iPhone, and Apple TV. Synchronizing your iPod, iPhone, or Apple TV with iTunes means keeping it up-to-date with your iTunes library. Your iPod, iPhone, or Apple TV mirrors as much of the content of your iTunes library as will fit, making assumptions if the entire library won't fit. With iTunes, you can fill these devices very quickly and keep them synchronized every time you connect them. (iTunes can also keep your iPod or iPhone synchronized with contacts, calendars, and other personal info; see Chapter 19 for more info on that aspect of synchronization.)

iTunes lets you decide whether to copy only a portion of your content library or *all* your songs and audio books, photos, movies, TV shows, music videos, and podcasts. The choice is easy if your iTunes library and photo library together are small enough to fit in their entirety on your iPod, iPhone, or Apple TV. For example, if your iTunes and photo libraries combined are less than 148GB and you have a 160GB iPod classic, simply copy everything. (You can see the size of your iTunes library in GB, or *gigabytes,* at the bottom of the iTunes window in the center.) Copying your entire library is just as fast as copying individual items (if not faster) because you don't have to select among albums and movies, create special playlists to keep your devices filled, or do anything except connect the devices to your computer. iTunes does the rest.

iTunes is flexible in that you can use separate options to synchronize music, TV shows, movies, and so on. For example, you can copy to your iPod or iPhone all your songs and audio books, but only some of your TV shows, none of your movies, and only the podcasts you haven't heard yet. Or you can automatically copy TV shows, movies, music videos, and podcasts, and then manually copy music and audio books to your iPod to fill up the rest of the space, or delete music and audio books directly from your iPod if you need to make more room.

You have the option to set your iPod, iPhone, or Apple TV to automatically synchronize with your entire iTunes library when you set it up the first time. (See Chapter 2 for details on setting up your iPod, and Chapter 7 for details on setting up Apple TV.) You can also set these devices to sync automatically with specific content types — music, TV shows, movies, and so on — at any time. This chapter shows you how to synchronize your iPod, iPhone, and Apple TV with portions or all of your library, as well as how to copy content to these devices selectively. You can also copy music, audio books, and podcasts to your iPod or iPhone manually, and copy music to your iPod shuffle automatically or manually. (Apple TV synchronizes only by playlist.)

Synchronizing Your iPod or iPhone

When you set up your iPod or iPhone, you can choose the option to copy your entire iTunes library (or part of your library) automatically, matching it exactly, item for item, playlist for playlist. From that point on, your iPod or iPhone synchronizes with your library automatically, right after you connect it to your computer.

If you make changes in iTunes after synchronizing a device, those changes are automatically made in the device when you synchronize again. If you add or delete content in your iTunes library, that content is added or deleted in the iPod or iPhone when you sync again.

If you store photos in an iPhoto library (on a Mac) or in a program (such as Adobe Photoshop Album in Windows), you can set up your iPod or iPhone with the option to copy your entire photo library. Your iPod or iPhone is then synchronized automatically so that any changes you make to the photo library are copied to the device.

Content items stored *remotely* (such as songs shared from other iTunes libraries on a network) aren't synchronized because the files aren't physically on your computer. (See Chapter 7 for more info on how to share iTunes files over a network with iTunes as well as how to copy files to different computers and their iTunes libraries.)

If you set your iPod or iPhone to synchronize automatically during the setup process (see Chapter 2), it starts synchronizing automatically after you connect it. Even so, you can choose content types to sync or not sync, as described in "Synchronizing Content Selectively" later in this chapter. Even so, you can then synchronize the device again after making changes to your sync options.

Follow these steps to start synchronizing your iPod or iPhone (for an iPod shuffle, see "Synchronizing an iPod shuffle" later is this chapter):

1. **With iTunes running, connect the iPod or iPhone, and select its name when it appears in the Devices section of the Source pane.**

   iTunes displays the device's Summary page (under the Summary tab of the device's synchronization pages) to the right of the Source pane, including how much space on the device is occupied by content and how much is still free. (Figure 11-1 shows an iPod touch Summary page, while Figure 11-2 shows an iPhone Summary page.)

2. **If the iPod or iPhone isn't automatically synchronizing, click the Sync button in the bottom-right corner to synchronize it.**

   The iTunes Status pane tells you that iTunes is syncing the device.

3. **Wait for the synchronization to finish and then click the Eject button next to the iPod or iPhone name in the Source pane.**

   You should always wait until the iTunes Status pane (at the top) displays that the synchronization is complete (refer to Figure 11-2).

4. **Disconnect your iPod or iPhone from your computer.**

   Don't disconnect your iPod or iPhone until its menu appears in its display.

   That's it. Your iPod or iPhone is now synchronized.

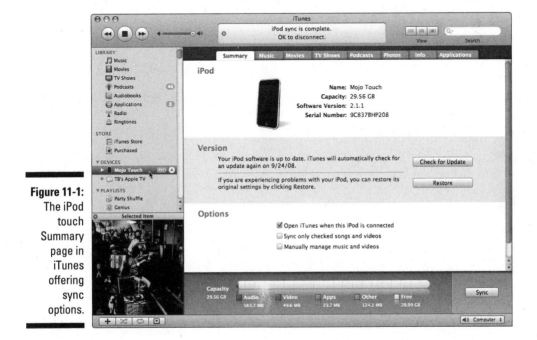

Figure 11-1: The iPod touch Summary page in iTunes offering sync options.

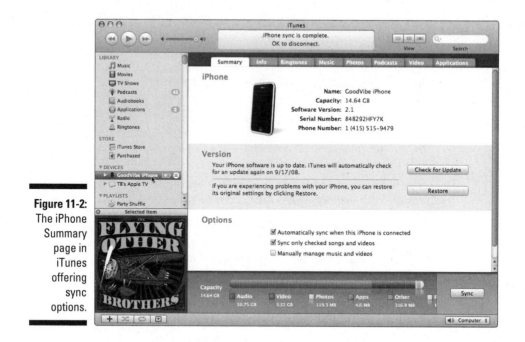

Figure 11-2:
The iPhone
Summary
page in
iTunes
offering
sync
options.

You probably don't need to know anything else in this chapter about synchronizing your iPod unless your iTunes library and additional photo library are too large to fit (see the upcoming section, "If Your Library Won't Fit"). Or, if you want to be more selective about the content while synchronizing, see the later section, "Synchronizing Content Selectively."

iTunes backs up your synchronization settings for each iPod or iPhone that you connect from the last time when you synchronized the device.

To prevent an iPod from automatically synchronizing, press ⌘-Option (Mac) or Ctrl-Alt (Windows) while you connect the device, and then keep pressing until the iPod name appears in the iTunes Source pane.

If you connect an iPod previously linked to another computer to *your* computer, iTunes displays a message warning you that clicking Yes replaces the device's content with the content from your computer's library. If you don't want to change the iPod's content, click No. If you click Yes, iTunes erases the iPod and synchronizes the device with your computer's library.

Synchronizing Your Apple TV

Apple TV lets you play your iTunes library content on your home TV and stereo. When you set up your Apple TV (as described in Chapter 7), you can choose to have iTunes automatically copy all or part of your library to it, matching your library exactly, item for item, playlist for playlist. From that point on, your Apple TV synchronizes with your library automatically whenever you start iTunes. If you make changes in iTunes after synchronizing Apple TV, those changes are automatically made in Apple TV when you start iTunes again.

You can also synchronize Apple TV at any time and customize the sync operation to include only the content items you choose. The content you synchronize to Apple TV is stored on the Apple TV hard drive for instant play-back. However, you can also use Apple TV to play any content in your iTunes library, without synchronizing it, as long as iTunes is running and connected (wirelessly or by Ethernet network) to the Apple TV — the content is streamed from your computer to Apple TV, as described in Chapter 7. You can also use iTunes to play content on Apple TV using AirTunes, as described in Chapter 6.

Content items stored *remotely* (such as songs shared from other iTunes libraries on a network) aren't synchronized because the files aren't physically on your computer. Apple TV can stream content from other iTunes libraries on the same network, but it synchronizes with only one library.

If you set up Apple TV to connect wirelessly or via Ethernet to your computer running iTunes (as described in Chapter 7), the name of your Apple TV automatically appears in the iTunes Source pane in the Devices section as soon as iTunes detects it on the network. You don't have to do anything — iTunes immediately begins synchronizing the Apple TV device with your library. However, you can choose sync options to customize synchronization, which is especially useful if your iTunes library is larger than the capacity of your Apple TV.

Select the name of the Apple TV in the Devices section of the Source pane, as shown in Figure 11-3. The Summary page (under the Summary tab of the device's synchronization pages) appears with synchronization options and information about how much space is occupied by content and how much is still free. You can then choose one of the following:

- ✔ **The Automatic Sync option** lets iTunes choose the audio and video to transfer over to the Apple TV with the priority on newer items.

- ✔ **The Custom Sync option** lets you choose the audio and video to synchronize. iTunes transfers movies first, then TV shows, then music, and finally podcasts. After choosing Custom Sync, select content to synchronize as described in the "Synchronizing Content Selectively" section later in this chapter.

If synchronization doesn't start automatically, click the Sync button in the bottom-right corner on the Summary page to start things rolling.

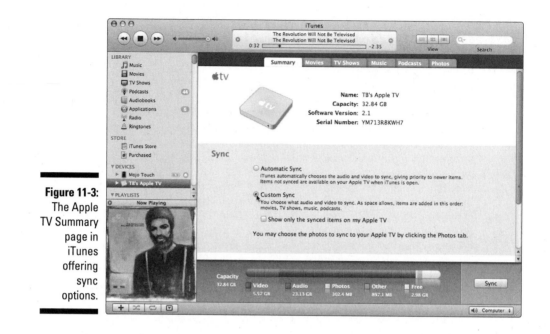

Figure 11-3:
The Apple
TV Summary
page in
iTunes
offering
sync
options.

When Apple TV and iTunes get together, not only can you smile on your brother and love one another, but

✔ **You can start playing while synchronizing.** You can start watching video content (or listen to audio content) that has been synchronized and stored on Apple TV, even while Apple TV is still synchronizing the rest of it.

✔ **You can play your library without synchronizing.** You can use Apple TV to play content on your computer wirelessly over the network, without synchronizing and saving the content on Apple TV, as long as iTunes is running — choose Music⇨My Music from the Apple TV main menu.

If your playlists don't appear, iTunes isn't connected to your Apple TV. (See Chapter 7 for details on how to set up your Apple TV.)

✔ **You can play a shared library on another computer without synchronizing, and leave your synchronized Apple TV content intact.** You can use Apple TV to play content on another computer wirelessly over the network, without synchronizing and saving the content on Apple TV, as long as iTunes is running on that computer — choose Settings⇨Computers from the Apple TV main menu.

✔ **You can resynchronize with another library.** You can choose a different iTunes library on a different computer to synchronize and save content on your Apple TV. To synchronize with a different library, follow the instructions for choosing an iTunes library with Apple TV (see Chapter 7).

If Your Library Won't Fit

If your iTunes library is too large to fit on your iPod, iPhone, or Apple TV, you can still keep it automatically synchronized to a subset of your library. You have several options:

✔ **Synchronize content selectively.** You can automatically synchronize your iPod, iPhone, or Apple TV to specific music and music video playlists, TV shows and movies, podcasts, and photo albums. (See the upcoming section, "Synchronizing Content Selectively.")

✔ **Manage your content directly.** You can also copy content directly to your iPod or iPhone and delete content on your iPod or iPhone. (See the later section, "Managing Content on Your iPod or iPhone Manually.")

✔ **Let iTunes decide what goes on the device.** When you set up your iPod, iPhone, or Apple TV, iTunes tries to fill the device if you choose to synchronize your entire library. If the library doesn't entirely fit, iTunes decides which songs and albums to include by using the ratings that you set for each song, and it creates a playlist specifically for synchronizing with that device. When you sync again, iTunes again tries to fit more content, going as far as to suggest what other content to delete. I explain this method in this section.

✔ **Create multiple iTunes libraries.** You can create several subsets of your main library (sub-libraries) so that each sub-library could be small enough to fit on a certain type of device. For example, you might create a sub-library for a 32GB iPod touch, and another sub-library for an 8GB iPod nano. Before connecting a device, you could switch to its corresponding sub-library and then synchronize automatically.

To find out how to manage multiple iTunes libraries, visit this book's companion Web site.

If you've synchronized your iPod or iPhone before but your iTunes library has grown larger and now won't fit, iTunes first checks for photos on the device. If your iPod or iPhone already has photos on it, iTunes asks whether you want to delete them to gain more space. After clicking Yes or No, iTunes tries its best to fit everything. If it has to cut something, though, it skips the photos and displays the message Some photos were not copied.

If you're still short of space even after skipping photos, iTunes displays a warning about the lack of free space, and it asks whether you want to disable podcast synchronization for the device and let iTunes create a selection of songs.

✔ **If you click Yes,** iTunes creates a new playlist (titled *Your device name* Selection, as in "TBone iPod Video Selection") and displays a message telling you so. Click OK, and iTunes synchronizes your iPod or iPhone using the new playlist. iTunes also sets your iPod or iPhone to synchronize music automatically by playlist, as I describe later in "Synchronizing Content Selectively."

✔ **If you click No,** iTunes updates automatically until it fills your iPod or iPhone without creating the playlist.

Either way, iTunes decides which songs and albums to include by using the ratings that you set for each song. iTunes groups album tracks together and computes an average rating and play count for the album. It then fills the iPod or iPhone, giving higher priority to albums with play counts and ratings greater than zero. You can therefore influence the decisions that iTunes makes by adding ratings to songs or entire albums; see Chapter 9.

The 40GB Apple TV actually holds about 32 gigabytes of iTunes library content; the 160GB model holds about 144GB. (The rest of the space is occupied by the system and media files provided by Apple.) Your iTunes library could be larger than your Apple TV's capacity, so iTunes synchronizes Apple TV starting with all movies and TV shows before moving on to music videos, music, audio books, podcasts, and finally photos. See the following section to discover how to copy playlists and items selectively to your Apple TV.

Synchronizing Content Selectively

Even if your iTunes library is too large to fit on your iPod, iPhone, or Apple TV, you can still use automatic methods to synchronize them. Just be selective, choosing which content to automatically synchronize from your iTunes library.

You can automatically keep your device synchronized to a subset of your library, adding new material under your control, in the following ways:

✔ **Select content items to ignore** during synchronization with iPods and iPhones.

✔ **Create playlists of the music you want to transfer,** or create a *smart playlist* that selects content for you (as described in Chapter 10) and then synchronize by playlists.

✔ **Select which movies to transfer.** Movies take up the most space in an iPod, iPhone, or Apple TV device.

✔ **Select which TV shows to transfer.** TV shows take up considerable space in an iPod, iPhone, or Apple TV.

✔ **Select which podcasts to transfer.** Some podcasts offer daily and weekly episodes that take up a lot of space, and you may want to limit the number of episodes.

✔ **Limit the transfer and synchronization of photos** to albums or collections rather than the entire photo library.

I give you instructions for each of these options in the following sections.

By synchronizing selectively, you can still make your iPod, iPhone, or Apple TV match at least a subset your iTunes library. If you make changes to that subset in iTunes, those changes are automatically made in the device when you synchronize again. For example, if you change your settings to update by certain playlists, any changes you make to those playlists — adding or deleting songs, for example — are reflected in your iPod, iPhone, or Apple TV the next time you synchronize it to your computer.

Selecting items to ignore when synchronizing

You can decide which items you don't want to synchronize, and simply not include them with your iPod or iPhone. (This feature is not available with Apple TV.) To use this method, you must first deselect the items in your iTunes library that you don't want to transfer. If you have a large iTunes library, this may take some time — you may find it easier to synchronize by playlists, as described in the later section, "Choosing playlists to synchronize."

By default, all content items are selected — a check mark appears in the check box next to the item. To deselect an item in your iTunes library, deselect the check box next to the item. To deselect a podcast episode, open the podcast first; then deselect the check box next to the episode. (See Chapter 6 for information about opening and playing podcasts.) To reselect an item, just select the check box.

You can quickly select (or deselect) an entire album by selecting it in Browse view and pressing ⌘ (Mac) or Ctrl (Windows) while making your selections. (See Chapter 8 for more on browsing and making selections.)

After you *deselect* the items you don't want to transfer, connect your iPod or iPhone to your computer. Then follow these steps:

1. **Select the device name in the Devices section of the iTunes Source pane.**

   After selecting the name, the Summary page for that device appears, displaying the device's synchronization options. (Refer to Figure 11-1 for an iPod touch or Figure 11-2 for an iPhone.)

2. **Select the Sync Only Checked Songs and Videos option, click Apply, and then click Sync if synchronization hasn't already started automatically.**

   iTunes restarts synchronization and deletes from the device any items in the library that are deselected, to save space, before adding back in the items in the iTunes library that are selected. That means the deselected items are now *gone* from your iPod, iPhone, or Apple TV — replaced by whatever items were selected. Of course, the items are still in your iTunes library.

3. **Wait for the updating to finish and then click the Eject button next to the iPod or iPhone name in the Source pane.**

   Always wait until the iTunes Status pane tells you the sync is complete before ejecting your iPod or iPhone.

Choosing playlists to synchronize

When syncing your iPod, iPhone, or Apple TV, you can include just the items defined in playlists. You can create an infinite number of playlists of any length, including Genius playlists (see Chapter 10). The Music tab of the synchronization pages for the device gives you options for choosing music in playlists.

For example, you can create four playlists that contain all essential rock, folk, blues, and jazz albums, and then select all four, or just one, two, or three of these playlists to synchronize with your iPod, iPhone, or Apple TV. You can create sets of playlists specifically for synchronizing different devices, such as your Apple TV set containing movie-related music, or an all-jazz set for your iPod.

Synchronizing automatically by playlists is also an easy way to automatically synchronize an iPod, iPhone, or Apple TV when a large iTunes library won't fit in its entirety. You can also drag songs and albums directly to your iPod or iPhone just like you do with any other content item, as I describe in the later section, "Managing Content on Your iPod or iPhone Manually."

Before using this option, create the playlists in iTunes (see Chapter 10) that you want to copy to the device and then connect your iPod or iPhone to your computer. (If you're synchronizing an Apple TV, it should already be detected and in the Source pane.) Then follow these steps:

1. **Select the device name in the Devices section of the iTunes Source pane.**

   iTunes displays the device's Summary page (under the Summary tab of the device's synchronization pages) to the right of the Source pane.

2. **Click the Music tab of the synchronization pages.**

   The Music synchronization options page appears, as shown in Figure 11-4.

Figure 11-4:
Synchronize
your iPod
with only
selected
playlists.

3. **Select the Sync Music and the Selected Playlists options.**

4. **From the list box, select each playlist that you want to synchronize with the device.**

   You can scroll to see all your playlists. Click the check box to select a playlist. In Figure 11-4, I selected two Genius playlists and the Recently Added smart playlist. (Chapter 10 has info on creating playlists.)

5. **Click Apply to apply changes, and click the Sync button if synchronization hasn't already started automatically.**

   iTunes synchronizes the device by erasing its contents and copying only the playlists that you select in Step 4.

iTunes copies only the music and audio books in these playlists. If you also select the Include Music Videos option (as in Figure 11-4) on the Music synchronization options page, iTunes includes music videos listed in the playlists. You can also show album cover art on color-display iPods by selecting the Display Album Artwork on your iPod option. (iPod touch and iPhone models automatically display album artwork.)

If you select Sync Only Checked Items on the Summary page of the device synchronization options (refer to Figure 11-1 for an iPod touch or Figure 11-2 for an iPhone), only checked items are copied. iTunes ignores unchecked items unchecked, even if they're listed in the chosen playlists for synchronization.

To select all the music and audio books in your library, select the Sync Music option and then select the All Songs and Playlists option on the Music synchronization options page.

Choosing movies to synchronize

Movies take up a lot of space, so if you limit the movies you synchronize with your iPod, iPhone, or Apple TV you gain extra space for more content.

The movies portion of your library includes movies downloaded from the iTunes Store and video files copied into the iTunes library from other sources. Any video file that isn't a TV show or music video downloaded from the iTunes Store is categorized as a movie in your iTunes library. Music videos downloaded from the iTunes Store are included in the music section of your library; see the earlier section, "Choosing playlists to synchronize."

You can also drag movies directly to your iPod or iPhone just like you do with any other content item, as I describe in the later section, "Managing Content on Your iPod or iPhone Manually."

Follow these steps:

1. **Select the device name in the Devices section of the iTunes Source pane.**

   iTunes displays the device's Summary page (under the Summary tab of the device's synchronization pages) to the right of the Source pane.

2. **Click the Movies tab for an iPod or Apple TV, or the Video tab for an iPhone.**

   You see either the Movies synchronization options page (for an iPod touch, as shown in Figure 11-5) or the Video synchronization options page (for an iPhone).

3. **Select the movie synchronization options for the device.**

   For an iPod, select the Sync Movies option (as shown in Figure 11-5), and then select one of the following options:

   • *All Movies:* Synchronizes all movies with your iPod.

   • *Unwatched Movies:* You can choose to synchronize all unwatched movies, or choose from the pop-up menu the most recently added unwatched movie (1 most recent), or the 3, 5, or 10 most recently added unwatched movies (3, 5, or 10 most recent).

   • *Selected:* You can select specific movies or video playlists. Scroll the list box to see all your movies or video playlists. Click the check box to select a movie or video playlist to synchronize with the device.

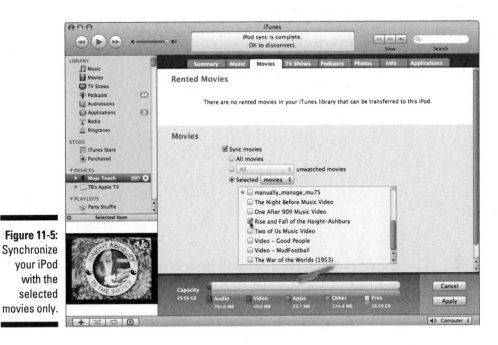

Figure 11-5:
Synchronize
your iPod
with the
selected
movies only.

For an iPhone, select the Sync Movies option and then, in the list of
movies, click each movie's check box to select that movie to transfer.

For Apple TV, select both of the following Sync options, as shown in
Figure 11-6:

- *Pop-up menu of unwatched or recent movies:* You can choose from
  the pop-up menu to synchronize all movies; all unwatched movies;
  the most recently added movie (1 most recent); or the most
  recently added 3, 5, or 10 movies (3, 5, or 10 most recent). You can
  alternatively select *unwatched* recently added movies in the same
  increments.

- *Selected:* You can select specific movies or video playlists. Scroll
  the list box to see all your movies or video playlists. Click the
  check box to select a movie or video playlist to synchronize with
  the device.

With Apple TV, you can mark both the Selected Movies option (then
selecting movies or playlists to synchronize) and the Unwatched Movies
options in the pop-up menu, to synchronize them as well.

**4. Click Apply to apply changes, and click Sync if synchronization hasn't
already started automatically.**

iTunes synchronizes the device by erasing its contents and copying only
the movies that you select in Step 3.

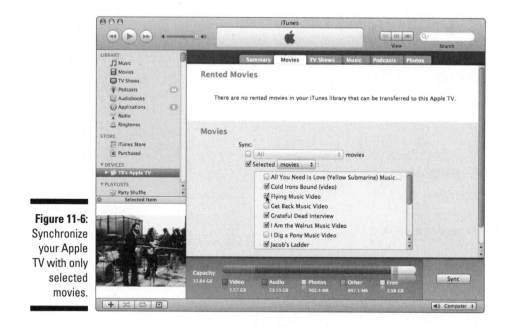

Figure 11-6:
Synchronize
your Apple
TV with only
selected
movies.

If you select the Sync Only Checked Items option on the Summary page of the device synchronization options for an iPod or iPhone (refer to Figure 11-1 for an iPod touch or Figure 11-2 for an iPhone), only checked items are copied. iTunes ignores items that are unchecked.

Choosing TV shows to synchronize

TV shows also take up a lot of space, but you can limit the number of episodes you synchronize with your iPod, iPhone, or Apple TV to gain extra space for more content.

You can also drag TV show episodes directly to your iPod or iPhone just like you do with any other content item, as I describe in the upcoming section, "Managing Content on Your iPod or iPhone Manually."

Follow these steps:

1. **Select the device name in the Devices section of the iTunes Source pane.**

   iTunes displays the device's Summary page (under the Summary tab of the device's synchronization pages) to the right of the Source pane.

2. **Click the TV Shows tab for an iPod or Apple TV, or the Video tab for an iPhone.**

   The TV Shows synchronization options page appears, as shown in Figure 11-7 for an iPod touch; for an iPhone, the Video synchronization page appears with separate sections for TV Shows and Movies.

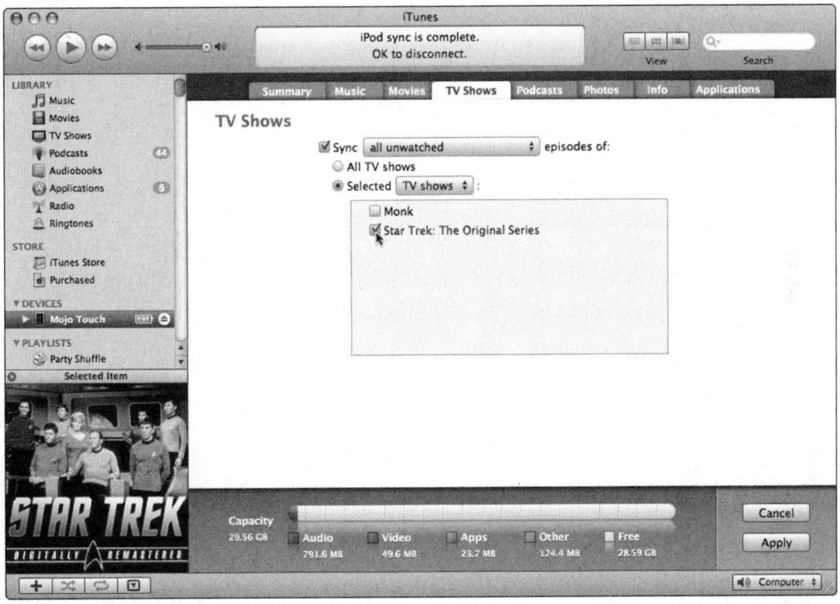

Figure 11-7:
Synchronize
your iPod
with only
selected TV
show
episodes.

3. **Select the Sync Episodes Of option and choose a modifier from the pop-up menu.**

   You can choose from the pop-up menu to synchronize all unwatched episodes; the most recently added episode (1 most recent); or the 3, 5, or 10 most recently added episodes (3, 5, or 10 most recent). You can also select unwatched recently added episodes in the same increments.

4. **Select one of the following options below the Sync Episodes Of option:**

   - *All TV Shows:* Synchronizes the episodes selected in Step 3 for all shows with your iPod, iPhone, or Apple TV.

   - *Selected:* Synchronizes the episodes selected in Step 3 for selected TV shows. For example, in Figure 11-7, I'm synchronizing all unwatched episodes of *Star Trek: The Original Series* but no other TV shows. You can select specific TV shows or video playlists of TV show episodes. Scroll the list box to see all your TV shows or video playlists. Mark the check box to select a TV show or video playlist to synchronize with the device.

5. **Click Apply to apply changes and click the Sync button if synchronization hasn't already started automatically.**

iTunes synchronizes the device by erasing its contents and copying only the TV show episodes that you selected in Steps 3 and 4.

Choosing podcasts to synchronize

Although you can listen to an audio podcast or watch a video podcast at any time on your computer, a podcast's real value is that you can take it with you in your iPod or iPhone, or play it on your home TV and stereo with your Apple TV. You can keep your iPod, iPhone, and Apple TV automatically synchronized with the most recent podcast episodes.

You can also drag podcast episodes directly to your iPod or iPhone just like you do with any other content item, as I describe in the upcoming section, "Managing Content on Your iPod or iPhone Manually."

The Podcasts tab of the synchronization pages for the device gives you options for choosing podcast episodes to include. Follow these steps:

1. **Select the device name in the Devices section of the iTunes Source pane.**

iTunes displays the device's Summary page (under the Summary tab of the device's synchronization pages) to the right of the Source pane.

2. **Click the Podcasts tab.**

The Podcasts synchronization options page appears. (Figure 11-8 shows the page for an iPod touch.)

3. **Select the Sync Episodes Of option and choose a modifier from the pop-up menu.**

You can choose from the pop-up menu to synchronize all unplayed episodes; the most recently added episode (1 most recent); or the 3, 5, or 10 most recently added episodes (3, 5, or 10 most recent). You can also select unplayed recently added episodes and new episodes in the same increments.

4. **Select one of the following podcast options below the Sync Episodes Of option:**

   • *All Podcasts:* Synchronizes the episodes selected in Step 3 for all podcasts with your iPod, iPhone, or Apple TV.

   • *Selected Podcasts:* Synchronizes the episodes selected in Step 3 for selected podcasts. For example, in Figure 11-8, I'm synchronizing all episodes of the selected podcasts. (Use the pop-up menu to switch from "all" to other choices, such as all unplayed episodes of the selected podcasts.) Scroll the list box to see all your podcasts. Click the check box next to each podcast to synchronize with the device.

Figure 11-8: Synchronize your iPod with all episodes of selected podcasts.

5. **Click Apply to apply changes, and click the Sync button if synchronization hasn't already started automatically.**

   iTunes synchronizes the device by erasing its contents and copying only the episodes of podcasts that you selected in Steps 3 and 4.

If you set iTunes to keep only your unplayed episodes, listen to part of a podcast episode on your iPod or iPhone, and then synchronize your iPod or iPhone, the podcast episode disappears from iTunes.

As described in Chapter 6, iTunes can keep track of the playback position so that when you play a podcast, iTunes remembers your place when you stop listening to it, just like a bookmark in an audio book. iTunes resumes playing from the bookmark when you return to the podcast to play it. You can synchronize podcasts with filenames ending with .m4b to an iPod, iPhone, or Apple TV and never lose your bookmarked place, whether you listen on your iPod, iPhone, Apple TV, or even your computer.

Choosing photo albums to synchronize

You can take your pictures with you, safely tucked into your iPod or iPhone, and you can display slide shows at home with your Apple TV. On a Mac, you can use iPhoto to import photos into your computer and organize them into albums. You can then use iTunes to transfer photos from your iPhoto library automatically.

In Windows, you can use Adobe Photoshop Album or Photoshop Elements to import photos onto your computer and to organize your photos into collections. You can then use iTunes to transfer photos from your photo library automatically.

To learn more about organizing photos into albums, visit this book's companion Web site.

If you don't have any of these programs, you can use any other photo-editing or photo-organizing software and store your photos in a folder on your hard drive, or on a CD or server volume. You can then use iTunes to transfer photos from the folder, treating the folder as a photo album. The folder could be on CD-ROM, DVD data disc, or on a server volume as long as the CD-ROM, DVD data disc, or volume is mounted.

Whether you transfer photos from a library or from a folder on your hard drive, you can keep your iPod, iPhone, and Apple TV synchronized with the photo library and its albums or with the subfolders and image files in the folder.

If you chose to copy your entire photo library when you set up your iPod, iPhone, or Apple TV, your entire photo library syncs automatically. Any changes you make to the library are consequently copied to your iPod, iPhone, or Apple TV.

To transfer only photos in specific albums in a library to your iPod and keep your iPod synchronized with these albums (not the entire library), follow these steps:

1. **Select the device name in the Devices section of the iTunes Source pane.**

   iTunes displays the device's Summary page (under the Summary tab of the device's synchronization pages) to the right of the Source pane.

2. **Click the Photos tab.**

   The Photos synchronization options page appears, as shown in Figure 11-9.

3. **Select the Sync Photos From option and then choose a photo library or a folder from the pop-up menu.**

   You can choose your photo library (such as iPhoto on a Mac, or Adobe Photoshop Album in Windows) from the pop-up menu to synchronize photo albums, or you can choose a folder from the pop-up menu. You can also choose Folder from the pop-up menu to browse files and folders on your hard drive or other storage media (such as a CD-ROM or a server volume). In Finder or Windows Explorer, browse your hard drive or other storage media for the folder containing images and then click Choose (Mac) or OK (Windows).

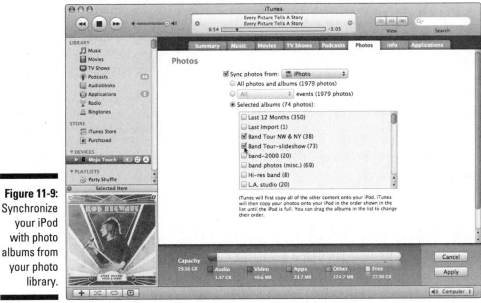

Figure 11-9:
Synchronize
your iPod
with photo
albums from
your photo
library.

If you want photos in a folder to appear in separate photo albums on
your iPod or iPhone, use the Finder on a Mac, or Windows Explorer
on Windows, to create subfolders inside the folder and organize your
photos and image files inside these subfolders. iTunes copies the sub-
folder assignments as if they were album assignments.

4. **Select one of the following photo options below the Sync Photos From
   option:**

   • *All Photos and Albums:* Synchronizes all photos and albums from
     the library or folder selected in Step 3 with your iPod, iPhone, or
     Apple TV.

   • *Selected Albums:* Synchronizes the photo albums from the library
     (or subfolders from the folder) selected in Step 3. For example,
     in Figure 11-9, I synchronize from my iPhoto library the selected
     albums "Band Tour NW & NY" and "Band Tour-slideshow." Scroll
     the list box to see all the photo albums in your photo library (or
     subfolders in your folder). Click the check box next to each photo
     album (or subfolder) to synchronize with the device.

5. **Click Apply to apply changes, and click the Sync button if
   synchronization hasn't already started automatically.**

   iTunes synchronizes the device by erasing its contents and copying only
   the photo albums that you selected in Step 4.

iTunes copies all other types of content first before even bothering to copy photos, but you can influence the order in which iTunes copies photo albums. When you select photo albums to synchronize in Step 4, you can drag the albums in the list into any order you choose — for example, you can select and drag the most important photo albums to the top of the list.

No matter what photo application you use, you can save photos as image files in a folder on your hard drive and then bring them into your iPod or iPhone whenever you want. It's rare for an iPod to meet an image file format it doesn't like. On a Mac, use JPEG (JPG), GIF, TIFF (TIF), Pict, PNG, PSD (Photoshop), PDF, jpg 2000, SGI, and BMP. In Windows, use JPEG (JPG), GIF, TIFF (TIF), PNG, and BMP.

Managing Content on Your iPod or iPhone Manually

By setting your iPod or iPhone to manually manage music and videos, you can add content to your iPod and iPhone directly via iTunes, and you can delete content as well.

You might have one or more reasons for managing content manually, but here are some obvious ones:

- ✔ Your entire library is too big for your iPod or iPhone, and you want to copy individual items directly.

- ✔ You want to share a single library with several iPods (or an iPod and an iPhone), and you have different song selections that you want to copy to each them directly.

- ✔ You share an iPod with others, and you want to copy your content to the iPod without wiping out its existing content.

- ✔ You want to copy some songs or videos from another computer's iTunes library without deleting any content from your iPod or iPhone.

- ✔ You want to edit the playlists and content information directly on your iPod or iPhone without changing anything in your computer's library.

When you set your iPod or iPhone to manually manage music and videos, all contents on your iPod or iPhone are active and available in iTunes. You can copy items directly to your iPod or iPhone, delete items on the iPod or iPhone, and edit the iPod or iPhone playlists directly.

To set your iPod or iPhone to manually manage music and videos, first connect your iPod or iPhone to your computer. Then follow these steps:

1. **Select the iPod or iPhone name in the Devices section of the iTunes Source pane.**

   iTunes displays the device's Summary page (under the Summary tab of the device's synchronization pages) to the right of the Source pane. (Refer to Figure 11-1 for an iPod touch or Figure 11-2 for an iPhone.)

2. **Select the Manually Manage Music and Videos option and then click OK to the warning.**

   iTunes displays a message warning you that disabling automatic synchronization requires manually ejecting the iPod or iPhone before each disconnect.

3. **Click Apply to apply the change.**

Don't disconnect your iPod or iPhone while managing music and videos manually. You have to eject the device and wait until it displays the message OK to disconnect (in first- and second-generation iPods) or the main menu. You risk making the device's hard drive or flash memory unreadable, forcing you to restore it to its original factory condition (see Chapter 20).

After setting your iPod or iPhone to manually manage music and videos, you can copy items directly to your iPod or iPhone (and even select the iPod or iPhone content directly to delete it, as I describe later in this section).

Copying items directly

As soon as you set your iPod or iPhone to manually manage music and videos, you can copy music and video directly from your iTunes library. Follow these steps (with your device connected to your computer):

1. **Select Music in the iTunes Source pane in the Library section (or a playlist in the library).**

   You can select music in your library using List, Grid, or Cover Flow view, or select songs in a playlist. In Figure 11-10, I'm using Cover Flow.

2. **Drag items directly from your iTunes library or playlist over the iPod or iPhone name in the Devices section of the Source pane.**

   You can drag an entire album from Cover Flow view, as I do in Figure 11-10, or from List or Grid view. When you drag an album cover or album title, all the songs in the album are copied. When you drag a playlist name, all the songs associated with the playlist copy along with the playlist itself.

Figure 11-10:
Copy an album directly from the iTunes library to an iPod ("Mojo Touch").

3. **Wait for the copying to finish and then click Eject to eject the iPod or iPhone.**

   Always wait until the iTunes Status pane (at the top) tells you that the copying is completed.

4. **Disconnect your iPod or iPhone from your computer.**

   Don't disconnect your iPod or iPhone until its menu appears in its display.

Deleting items on your iPod or iPhone

When you manually manage music and videos, you can delete content from the iPod or iPhone directly. Manual deletion is a nice feature if you just want to go in and delete a song, video, or album to make room for new content.

To delete any item in your iPod or iPhone, set the option to manually manage music and videos (if it isn't set that way already) and then follow these steps:

1. **In the Source pane, click the triangle next to the iPod or iPhone name to expand its library.**

   The library appears in the Source pane with Music, Movies, TV Shows, and other sections, followed by playlists — indented underneath the device's name.

2. **Click any content type in the library to see the items.**

   The content items appear in the iTunes List pane to the right of the Source pane.

3. Select an item and press Delete/Backspace or choose Edit⇨Delete.

iTunes displays a warning to make sure you want to do this; click OK to go ahead or Cancel to stop. If you want to delete a playlist, select the playlist underneath the iPod or iPhone name in the Source pane, and press Delete or choose Edit⇨Delete.

Like in the iTunes library, if you delete a playlist, the items listed in the playlist aren't deleted. They're still on your iPod or iPhone unless you delete the items directly from the iPod or iPhone library.

Synchronizing an iPod shuffle

The iPod shuffle is designed for quick and convenient music synchronizing. Just plug it into your computer and then click the Autofill button in iTunes. It also offers automatic compression to fit more songs (or audio books, which are treated as songs) into your iPod shuffle space.

Although Apple proudly advertises its ability to shuffle songs randomly, the key to its success isn't that you can shuffle the songs already there but that you can copy random songs to it every time you connect it to your computer. Eventually, you can shuffle through everything in your library if you so wish, by randomly filling your iPod shuffle every time. On the other hand, you can fine-tune your random selection and even reorder the iPod shuffle's playlist to play back in a specific order.

Although you can add songs to your iPod shuffle manually by dragging a playlist or song, you can also automatically fill it without having to set options for automatic updating. Autofill automatically picks songs from your entire iTunes library or from a playlist you select in the Source pane. You can also manage the playlist for your iPod shuffle directly, after using Autofill, to fine-tune your selection.

Using Autofill

To use Autofill to copy songs to your iPod shuffle, follow these steps:

1. Connect the iPod shuffle to your computer.

When you connect an iPod shuffle to your computer, its name shows up in the Devices section of the Source pane.

2. Select the iPod shuffle in the Devices section of the iTunes Source pane.

The Autofill pane appears below the List pane, as shown in Figure 11-11. The songs on the iPod shuffle appear in List view, replacing the view of your library.

Figure 11-11:
Autofill
your iPod
shuffle from
an iTunes
playlist.

3. **Choose your source of music in the Autofill From pop-up menu.**

   Choose either a playlist or Music (for the entire music library). If you choose a playlist, Autofill uses only the playlist as the source of music. After choosing your source of music, iTunes creates a playlist and displays it in the List pane.

4. **(Optional) To pick random songs, select the Choose Items Randomly option.**

5. **(Optional) To pick only the best songs (if you're choosing them randomly), select the Choose Higher Rated Items More Often option.**

6. **(Optional) To replace songs already on the iPod shuffle, select the Replace All Items When Autofilling option.**

   If you don't select this option, iTunes adds the songs without replacing existing songs.

7. **Click the Autofill button to start copying songs.**

   iTunes copies the contents of the playlist to your iPod shuffle.

8. **Wait for the copy operation to finish and then click the Eject button.**

   Always wait until the iTunes Status pane (at the top) tells you that the copying is finished.

You can click the Autofill button over and over to create different random playlists. When you get one you like, select all its contents and choose File➪New Playlist From Selection to create a new playlist that contains the songs generated by Autofill. The next time you connect your iPod shuffle, select this new playlist from the Autofill From pop-up menu and then click the Autofill button to load the music from the playlist to your shuffle.

iPod shuffle can play audio books sold by the iTunes Store and by Audible.com. Unfortunately, iTunes won't automatically add them to the iPod shuffle — you have to add them manually. Be sure to play audio book sections on your iPod shuffle in sequential order rather than in random (shuffle) order, or you may hear chapters in the wrong order — see Chapter 14 for details on playing content on an iPod shuffle.

Copying and deleting items manually

iPod shuffle is always set for manual management. When you connect an iPod shuffle to your computer, you can copy music (or audio books) directly to it, delete items on it, and edit its playlist.

To copy items to your iPod shuffle directly, connect it to your computer and follow these steps:

1. **Select Music in the iTunes Source pane in the Library section.**

   Your music library's content appears in List view.

2. **Drag and drop items directly from your iTunes library to the iPod shuffle's name in the Devices section of the Source pane.**

   When you copy a playlist, all the songs in the playlist are copied. When you copy an album, all the songs in the album are copied.

3. **Wait for the copy operation to finish and then click the iPod Eject button.**

To delete any item in your iPod shuffle, follow these steps:

1. **Select the iPod shuffle in the Devices section of the iTunes Source pane.**

   The songs on the iPod shuffle appear in List view, replacing the view of your library.

2. **Select one or more songs on the iPod shuffle and then press Delete/ Backspace or choose Edit➪Delete.**

   iTunes displays a warning to make sure you want to do this; click OK to go ahead or Cancel to stop.

Chapter 12

Gimme Shelter for My Media

. . . .

In This Chapter

▶ Choosing the format and settings for burning a disc

▶ Burning an audio CD, an MP3 CD, or a data DVD

▶ Locating and backing up files in the iTunes library

▶ Backing up your entire iTunes library

. . . .

*Y*ou might think that your digital content is safe, stored as-is, on your iPod, iPhone, Apple TV, and hard drive. However, demons in the night are working overtime to render your hard drive useless — and at the same time, someone left your iPod out in the rain, your iPhone can't phone home, and your Apple TV is on the fritz.

Copyright law and common sense prohibit you from using copyrighted content and then selling it to someone else. However, with iTunes, you're allowed to make copies of music, videos, audio books, and podcasts that you own for personal use, including copies for backup purposes.

This chapter boils down everything you need to know about burning your own discs to make copies of your content. I burn audio CDs or MP3 CDs to make safety copies of songs I buy from the iTunes Store. I also like to custom-mix songs from different artists and albums onto an audio or MP3 CD.

I burn data DVDs to back up my video files — and I also copy my entire iTunes library to another hard drive as a backup, as I describe in this chapter. This operation is very important, especially if you've purchased items that don't exist anywhere else in your collection but on your computer. That way, even if your hard drive fails, you still have your iTunes library.

To find out how to consolidate media files into one library, how to manage multiple iTunes libraries for easier synchronization with multiple devices, and how to move a library from one computer to another (such as a PC to a Mac or vice versa), visit this book's companion Web site.

You should not rely on your iPod, iPhone, or Apple TV as your sole music storage device or as a backup for your iTunes library, because you can't copy content from your iPod, iPhone, or Apple TV to your computer via iTunes. It's a one-way trip from iTunes *to* your iPod, iPhone, or Apple TV because record labels and video distributors don't want indiscriminate copying, and Apple has complied with these requests. You can, however, use *third-party utility programs* (not supported by Apple) to copy content both ways.

To learn more about third-party utility programs for managing your iPod or iPhone, visit this book's companion Web site.

The iTunes Store uses Apple FairPlay technology for many songs, which protects the rights of copyright holders while also giving you some leeway in using the copyrighted content. But you can still copy the media files freely so that backup is easy and straightforward on either a Mac or a PC.

Do not violate copyright law. You're allowed to copy content for your own use, but you cannot legally copy content for any other purpose. Consult a lawyer if you're in doubt.

Burning Your Own Discs

Once upon a time, when vinyl records were popular, rock radio disk jockeys (who didn't like disco) held disco-meltdown parties. People were encouraged to throw their disco records onto a pile to be burned or steamrolled into a vinyl glob. I admit that I shamelessly participated in one such meltdown. However, this section isn't about that (nor is it about anything involving fire or heat). Rather, *burning* a disc is the process in which the CD drive recorder's laser heats up points on an interior layer of the disc to record information.

Using recordable CDs and DVDs

If you have a CD-R, CD-RW, or DVD-R drive (such as the Apple SuperDrive for a Mac) and a blank CD-R (*R* stands for *recordable*), you can burn music, audio books, and audio podcast episodes on audio CDs that play in most CD players. You can fit up to 74 minutes of music on a high-quality audio-format CD-R; most can go as high as 80 minutes.

Blank audio CD-Rs (I'm talking discs now and not drives) are available in stores that carry consumer electronics. You can also get them online from the Apple Store (not the music store — the store that sells computers and accessories). Choose iTunes⇨Shop for iTunes Products (Mac) or Help⇨Shop for iTunes Products (Windows) to reach the Apple Store online.

TECHNICAL STUFF

The little Red Book that launched an industry

Typical audio CDs and CD-Rs use the Compact Disc-Digital Audio (CD-DA) format Mode 2 Form 2, better known as *Red Book*. This book isn't something from Chairman Mao: It's a document (published in 1980) that provides the specifications for the standard CD developed by Sony and Philips. According to legend, this document was in a binder with a red cover.

Here's another legend: In 1979, Norio Ohga, honorary chairman and former CEO of Sony (and a maestro conductor), overruled his engineers and insisted that the CD format be able to hold Beethoven's *Ninth Symphony*. This symphony is 74 minutes and 42 seconds long — now the standard length of a Red Book audio CD.

CD-DA defines audio data digitized at 44,100 samples per second (44.1 kHz) and in a range of 65,536 possible values (16 bits). The format for the audio is called *pulse code modulation* (PCM).

To import music onto the computer from an audio CD, you have to convert the music to digital sound files by a program, such as iTunes. When you burn an audio CD, iTunes converts the sound files back into the CD-DA format while it burns the disc.

You can also burn an audio CD-R of song files in the MP3 format, which is useful for backing up a music library or making discs for use in MP3 CD players. You can play MP3 files burned on a CD-R in MP3 format on any MP3 disc player, on combination CD/MP3 players, on many DVD players, and (of course) on computers that recognize MP3-formatted CDs (including computers with iTunes). An MP3-formatted CD-R can hold more than 12 hours of music. You read that right — *12 hours on one disc*. This is why *MP3 discs* are popular: because they are essentially CD-Rs with MP3 files stored on them.

If you have a DVD burner, such as an Apple SuperDrive, you can burn *data discs* in the DVD-R or DVD-RW formats to use with other computers. This approach is suitable for making backup copies of media files (or any data files). A DVD-R can hold about 4,700,000,000 bytes (more than 4GB).

Creating a disc burn playlist

To burn a CD (actually a CD-R, but most people refer to recordable CD-R discs as *CDs*), you must first define a playlist for the CD. (See Chapter 10 to find out how to create a playlist.) You can use songs encoded in any format that iTunes supports; however, you get higher-quality music with the uncompressed AIFF and WAV formats or with the Apple Lossless format. (You can back up your library to DVD without creating a playlist, as I describe in "Backing up to DVD-R or CD-R discs" later in this chapter.)

If your playlist includes music purchased from the iTunes Store in the protected AAC-encoding format, some rules might apply. For example, as of this writing, the iTunes Store allows you to burn seven copies of the same playlist containing protected songs to an audio CD, but no more.

You can get around this limitation by creating or using a new playlist, copying the protected songs to the new playlist, and then burning more CDs with the new playlist.

Calculating how much music to use

When you create an audio CD playlist, you can calculate how many songs can fit on the CD by totaling the durations of the songs. You can see the size of a playlist by selecting it; the bottom of the iTunes window shows the number of songs, the duration of the songs, and the amount in megabytes for the selected playlist. Click the duration to see a more precise total time for the playlist, as shown in Figure 12-1.

Figure 12-1:
Click the duration of the playlist below the List pane to see the total time.

In Figure 12-1, the selected playlist takes about 1.1 hours (exactly 1:08:54) to play, so it fits on a standard audio CD. (The 15 songs take up only 65.3MB of hard drive space; they were purchased from the iTunes Store and encoded in the compressed and protected AAC format.)

A one-hour playlist of AIFF-encoded music, which might occupy over 600MB of hard drive space, also fits on a standard audio CD. You calculate the amount you can fit on a standard audio CD using the duration, not the hard drive space occupied by the music files. Although a CD holds between 650MB and 700MB (depending on the disc), the music is stored in a special format known as CD-DA (or Red Book) that fills byte sectors without error-correction and checksum information. (You can read about CD-DA and Red Book in the sidebar, "The little Red Book that launched an industry.") Thus, you can fit about

90MB more — 740MB total — of AIFF-encoded music on a 650MB disc. I typically put 1.1 hours (about 66 minutes) of music on a 74-minute or an 80-minute CD-R, leaving minutes to spare.

Always use the actual duration in hours, minutes, and seconds to calculate how much music you can fit on an audio CD — either 74 or 80 minutes for blank CD-Rs. I recommend leaving at least one extra minute to account for the gaps between songs.

You do the *opposite* for an MP3 CD or a data DVD. Use the actual megabytes to calculate how many song files can fit on a disc — up to 700MB for a blank CD-R. You can fit lots more music on an MP3 CD-R because you use MP3-encoded songs rather than uncompressed AIFF songs.

If you have too many songs in the playlist to fit on a CD, iTunes gives you the option to cancel the burn operation, or to burn as many songs in the playlist as will fit on the CD (either audio or MP3). Then it asks you to insert another CD to continue burning the remaining songs in the playlist.

Importing music for an audio CD-R

Before you rip an audio CD of songs that you want to burn to an audio CD-R, as I describe in Chapter 5, you might want to change the import settings. Use the AIFF, WAV, or Apple Lossless encoders for songs from audio CDs if you want to burn your own audio CDs with music at its highest quality. You can also burn MP3-encoded songs on an audio CD, but the quality is not as good as with AIFF, WAV, or Apple Lossless.

AIFF is the standard digital format for uncompressed sound on a Mac, and you can't go wrong with it. *WAV* is basically the same thing for Windows. The Apple Lossless encoder provides CD-quality sound in a file size that's about 55 to 60 percent of the size of an AIFF- or WAV-encoded file. Both the AIFF encoder and the WAV encoder offer the same custom settings for sample rate, sample size, and channels, which you can set by choosing Custom from the Settings pop-up menu in the Importing section of the Advanced pane of iTunes Preferences. You can choose the automatic settings, and iTunes detects the proper sample rate, size, and channels from the source. Apple Lossless is always set to automatic.

Many songs you can purchase from the iTunes Store are supplied in an unprotected format encoded in AAC that carries no restrictions. (The format is also known as iTunes Plus.) However, others are sold in a protected AAC format. You can't convert the protected format to anything else, but you can still burn the songs onto CDs, and the quality of the result on CD is acceptable. Audio books also come in a protected format that can't be converted by iTunes, but you can burn them onto CDs with acceptable quality.

The AAC encoder creates an audio file that is similar in audio quality to one created by the MP3 encoder, but takes up less space; both are acceptable to most CD listeners. I think AAC offers a decent trade-off of space and quality and is suitable (although not as good as AIFF or Apple Lossless) for burning to an audio CD.

For a complete description of these encoders, visit this book's companion Web site.

Switching import encoders for MP3 CD-R

MP3 discs are essentially CD-Rs with MP3 files stored on them. Consumer MP3 CD players are readily available in consumer electronics stores, including hybrid models that play both audio CDs and MP3 CDs.

You can fit 8–12 hours of stereo music on an MP3 CD with the MP3 format — the amount varies depending on the encoding options and settings you choose. For example, you might be able to fit up to 20 hours of mono (monaural) recordings because they use only one channel and carry less information. On the other hand, if you encode stereo recordings at high bit rates (above 192 bits per second), you may fit up to 9 hours.

You can use only MP3-encoded songs to burn an MP3 CD-R. Any songs not encoded in MP3 are skipped and not burned. Audible books and commercial spoken-word titles are typically provided in an audio format that uses security technologies, including encryption, to protect purchased content; however, you can include anything that is encoded in MP3, including audio books from other sources. But you can't burn an MP3 CD-R with Audible files; any Audible files in a burn playlist are skipped when you burn an MP3 CD-R.

Burning a disc

Burning a CD is a simple process, and getting it right the first time is a good idea because when you burn a CD-R, it's done — right or wrong. You can't erase content and reuse a CD-R. Fortunately, CD-Rs are inexpensive, so you won't be out more than a few cents if you burn a bad one. (Besides, they're good as coasters for coffee tables.)

Follow these steps to burn a disc:

1. **Select the playlist and then click the Burn Disc button.**

   The Burn Disc button appears in the lower-right corner of the iTunes window whenever you select a playlist (refer to Figure 12-1). After clicking Burn Disc, the Burn Settings dialog appears, as shown in Figure 12-2.

2. **Select options in the Burn Settings dialog and click OK.**

   See the following section, "Choosing your burn settings," for instructions on selecting these important options.

3. **Insert a blank disc (label side up).**

   iTunes immediately checks the media and begins the burn process, displaying a progress bar and the names of the songs burning to the disc.

   If you chose the MP3 CD format, iTunes skips over any songs in the playlist that aren't in this format.

   When iTunes finishes burning the disc, iTunes chimes, and the disc is mounted on the Desktop.

4. **Eject the newly burned disc from your drive and then test it.**

5. **Don't delete your burn playlist yet.**

   You can read why in the later section, "Troubleshooting burns."

Burning takes several minutes. You can cancel the operation at any time by clicking the X next to the progress bar, but canceling the operation isn't like undoing the burn. If the burn has already started, you can't use that CD-R or DVD-R again.

If the playlist has more music than can fit on the disc using the chosen format, iTunes asks whether you want to create multiple audio CDs with the playlist. If you choose to create multiple audio CDs, iTunes burns as much as possible from the beginning of the playlist and then asks you to insert another disc to burn the rest. To calculate the amount of music in a playlist, see the earlier section, "Calculating how much music to use."

Spoken word fans: Audible audio books with chapter markers are burned onto a CD with each chapter as a separate track.

Choosing your burn settings

Set the following options in the Burn Settings dialog to ensure that you burn your CD right the first time:

✔ **Preferred Speed:** Choose a specific recording speed or the Maximum Possible option from the Preferred Speed pop-up menu. iTunes typically detects the rating of a blank CD-R and adjusts the recording speed to fit. However, if your blank CD-Rs are rated for a slower speed than your burner or if you have problems creating CD-Rs, you can change the recording speed setting to match the CD's rating.

✔ **Disc Format:** The disc format is perhaps the most important choice you have to make. Decide whether you're burning an audio CD (CD-R), an MP3 CD (CD-R), or a Data CD (CD-R) or DVD (DVD-R or DVD-RW). Your choice depends on what type of player you're using, or whether you're making a data backup of files rather than a disc that plays in a player. Choose one of the following:

- *Audio CD:* Burn a normal audio CD of up to 74 or 80 minutes (depending on the type of blank CD-R) using any iTunes-supported music files, including songs bought from the iTunes Store. Although connoisseurs of music might use AIFF- or WAV-encoded music to burn an audio CD, you can also use songs in the AAC and MP3 formats.

- *MP3 CD:* Burn an MP3 CD with songs encoded in MP3 format. No other formats are supported for MP3 CDs.

- *Data CD or DVD:* Burn a data CD-R, CD-RW, DVD-R, or DVD-RW with music files. You can use any encoding formats for the songs. *Important:* Data discs won't play on most consumer CD players: They're meant for use with computers. However, data discs are good choices for storing backup copies of music bought from the iTunes Store.

✔ **Gap between Songs:** You can add an appropriate gap between songs, just like commercial CDs. With this option enabled, you can set the gap time as well. You can choose from a gap of 0 to 5 seconds, or None. I recommend leaving the menu set to the default setting of 2 seconds. Albums and song selections that you set to be gapless (see Chapter 5) will likewise be gapless if you set the Gap Between Songs option to None.

✔ **Use Sound Check:** Musicians do a sound check before every performance to check the volume of microphones and instruments and their effect on the listening environment. The aptly named Use Sound Check option in the Burning preferences dialog (see Figure 12-2) turns on the Sound Check feature to balance your tunes, volume-wise.

Note: This option, for audio CDs only, works regardless of whether you're already using the Sound Check option in the Playback preferences for iTunes playback. You can select this option for burning without ever changing the preferences for iTunes playback.

✔ **Include CD Text:** Selecting this option adds the artist and track name text to the CD for certain CD players (often, in car players) that can display the artist and track name while playing a CD.

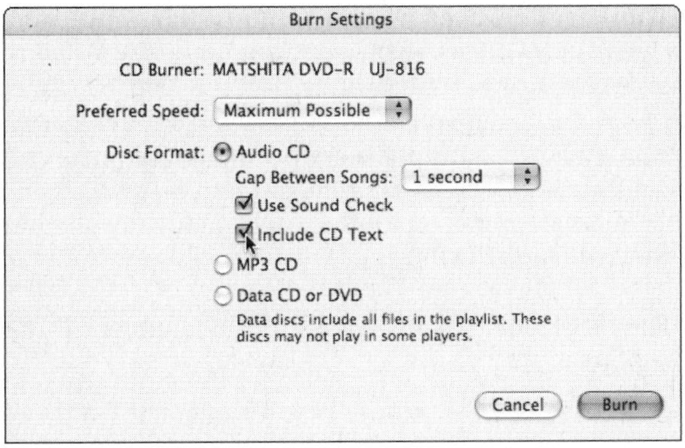

Figure 12-2:
Choose burn
settings
before burn-
ing the disc.

Troubleshooting burns

Murphy's Law applies to everything, even something as simple as burning a CD-R. Don't think for a moment that you're immune to the whims and treacheries of Murphy (no one really knows who Murphy is), who, in all his infinite wisdom, pronounced that anything that *can* go wrong *will* go wrong (and usually at the least convenient time). In this section, I cover some of the most common problems that you might encounter when burning discs.

The best way to test your newly burned disc is to pop it right back into your computer's drive — or, if it's an audio CD, try it on a consumer CD player. On most CD players, an audio CD-R plays just like any commercial audio CD. MP3 CDs play fine on consumer MP3 CD players and also work in computers with CD-ROM and DVD drives.

If the disc works on the computer but not on a commercial CD player, you might have a compatibility problem with the commercial player and CD-R. For example, I have a ten-year-old CD player that doesn't play CD-Rs very well, and car players sometimes have trouble with them.

The following list gives some typical problems, along with the solutions, that you might run into when burning a CD:

> *Problem:* The disc won't burn.

> *Solution:* Perhaps you have a bum disc. Hey, it happens. Try using another disc or burning at a slower speed.

> *Problem:* In a consumer CD player, the disc doesn't play or stutters while playing.

Solution: This happens often with older consumer players that don't play CD-Rs well, and with some players that are fussy about reading less-expensive CD-Rs or certain brands. Try the disc in your computer's CD-ROM or DVD drive. If it works there and you set the format to Audio CD, you probably have a compatibility problem with your consumer player. You may want to clean your consumer player with CD drive cleaners available in consumer electronics stores. You may also want to try a different brand of blank CD-Rs.

Problem: The disc doesn't show tracks on a consumer CD player or ejects immediately.

Solution: Be sure to use the proper disc format. The Audio CD format works in just about all consumer CD players that can play CD-Rs. MP3 CDs work in consumer MP3 CD players and computer CD-ROM and DVD drives. Data CDs or DVDs work only in computer drives.

Problem: Some songs in your playlist were skipped and not burned onto the disc.

Solution: Audio CD-Rs burn with songs encoded in any format, but you can use only MP3-encoded songs to burn an MP3 CD-R. Any songs not encoded in MP3 — including songs purchased from the iTunes Store in protected AAC format — are skipped when burning MP3 CDs. (Any Audible files are also skipped because they can't be put onto an MP3 CD.) If your playlist for an audio CD-R includes music purchased from the iTunes Store, some rules might apply — see the earlier section, "Creating a disc burn playlist."

Studying Files in an iTunes Library

If you like to keep your records properly filed, you'll love iTunes and its nice, neat file-storage methods. For all content items, iTunes creates a folder named for the artist and subfolders within the artist folder named for each album. These folders are stored in the iTunes Music folder unless you change your storage preferences.

Finding the iTunes library

The default method of storing content in the iTunes library is to store all media files — including music, videos, podcasts, and audio books — in the iTunes Music folder, which is inside the iTunes folder. With this method, media files that you drag to the iTunes window are copied into the iTunes

Music folder (without deleting the original files). The iTunes folder also has folders for mobile applications and album artwork. So that's easy — everything is inside the `iTunes` folder.

iTunes maintains a separate `iTunes` folder (with a separate `iTunes Music` folder) in each home folder (Mac) or user folder (PC). If you share your computer with other users who have home folders, each user can have a separate iTunes library on the same computer (and, of course, a separate iPod that synchronizes with it). You need only one copy of the iTunes program.

On a Mac, iTunes stores your content library in your home folder's `Music` folder. The path to this folder's default location is

```
your home folder/Music/iTunes/iTunes Music
```

On a Windows PC, iTunes stores your content library in your user folder. The path to this folder's default location is

```
your user folder/My Documents/My Music/iTunes/iTunes Music
```

Changing how files are stored in the library

The default method of organizing files in the iTunes library is to store content files in album and artist folders, naming the files according to the disc number, track number, and title.

For example, the song "Here, There and Everywhere" has the track number and song title in the filename (`05 Here, There And Everywhere.mp3`). The filename extension even tells you the type of encoding format — in this case, MP3. This song is saved in the Revolver folder (for the album), which is in The Beatles folder (for the artist).

Movies, music videos, and TV shows follow similar naming conventions. Here's an example from the TV show *Monk*. Episode 8 (season 5) is titled "Mr. Monk Goes to a Rock Concert." This information makes up the filename (`08 Mr. Monk Goes to a Rock Concert.m4v`), which is stored in the Monk folder (the *artist*) inside the TV Shows folder in the iTunes Music folder.

What about songs performed by multiple artists, such as movie soundtrack albums and compilations with multiple artists? Compilation and soundtrack albums, and songs designated as part of a compilation, are stored in album folders within the Compilations folder, rather than within individual artist folders.

Sometimes the information retrieved automatically from the Internet (as described in Chapter 9) about a song or album is not to your liking — the album might be designated a compilation when it is not, or a compilation might not be identified as such. To designate a song as part of a compilation, select the song, choose File⇨Get Info, click the Info tab in the information dialog, and then select the Part of a Compilation check box.

To designate an entire album as a compilation album, follow these steps:

1. **Select the album and choose File⇨Get Info.**

   The warning dialog appears about editing multiple items.

2. **Click Yes to the warning dialog.**

   The Multiple Item Information dialog appears.

3. **Click the Options button in the top-right corner of the Multiple Item Information dialog.**

   The Options pane for the Multiple Item Information dialog appears, with options that include the Part of a Compilation pop-up menu.

4. **Choose Yes from the Part of a Compilation pop-up menu.**

   Even if Yes is already selected for the album, choose Yes again in order to set the check mark for updating.

The filename and location within artist and album folders change when you change the information for a song (or video, audio book, or podcast episode) in the information fields. For example, if you change the song title, the file-name also changes. If you change the artist name, the folder name for the artist might change, or the file might move to a new folder by that name. iTunes organizes the files based on the song information.

You may want to change song information without changing the names of the folders and files. To make changes to song information without changing the file and folder names on your hard drive, choose iTunes⇨Preferences (Mac) or Edit⇨Preferences (Windows) and then click Advanced. Then deselect the Keep iTunes Music Folder Organized option.

Leave the Keep iTunes Music Folder Organized option selected, especially if you plan on copying the music files to an Apple TV, or to an iPod or iPhone that will then be used with a car installation. (I describe car installations in Chapter 17.) Many iPod interfaces for car stereos provide a way to navigate the iPod with the car stereo controls but don't display the proper artist, album, and song titles unless the iTunes music folder is organized by the default method.

Maybe you don't want to store copies of your media files in the library —
especially if you already have copies stored on your hard drive in another
location and need to conserve space. If you want to add content to your
iTunes library without copying the files into the iTunes Music folder, here's
what you do:

1. **Choose iTunes➪Preferences (Mac) or Edit➪Preferences (Windows).**

2. **Click the Advanced tab.**

3. **Deselect the Copy Files to iTunes Music Folder When Adding to
   Library option.**

The next time you drag a media file into the iTunes window, it stores only a
reference in your iTunes library to the file that specifies its actual location.
The file isn't copied or moved. Of course, if you move the file, iTunes may not
find it and may display an exclamation point next to its name in the List pane.

Locating a media file

No matter where you store your iTunes library or your media files, you can
find the location of any item by selecting it, choosing File➪Get Info, and then
clicking the Summary tab of the information dialog that appears. You can see
the file type next to the Kind heading of the Summary tab. The Where section
tells you where the song is, as shown in Figure 12-3.

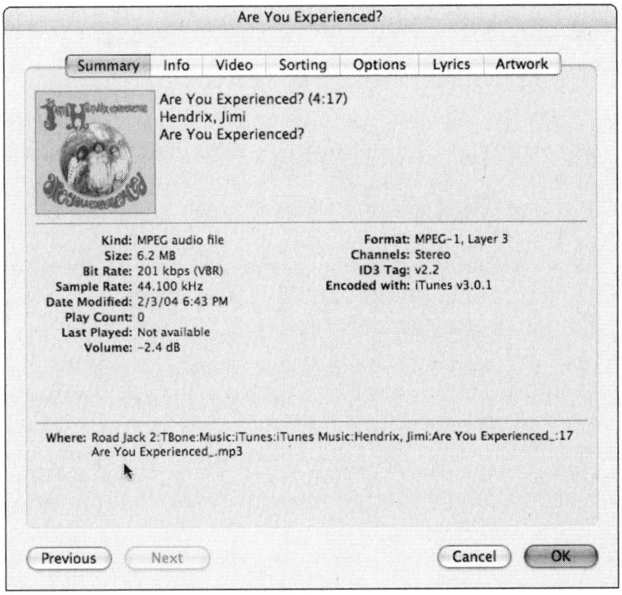

Figure 12-3:
Locate a
media file
from its
information
dialog.

If you access shared libraries on a network, you probably have content you can display in iTunes that isn't actually in your library but is part of a shared library or playlist on a network. In those situations, when you look at the Summary tab of the information dialog for an item in a shared library, the Where section doesn't appear.

You can also open the folder that contains the media file for any item. Select the item in List, Grid, or Cover Flow view. Then, on a Mac, choose File➪Show in Finder (or press ⌘-R); in Windows, choose File➪Show in Windows Explorer (or press Ctrl-R). iTunes gives control to the operating system, which displays the folder containing the media file. You can show the file if it's on your hard drive but not if it's in a shared library on another computer.

Backing Up an iTunes Library

Backups? You don't need no stinkin' backups?

Yes, you do, so think twice about not making them! I know: Backing up your files can be inconvenient and can eat up the capacity of all your external hard drives. Still, it must be done. And fortunately, it's easy to do. With iTunes, you can copy your library to another hard drive on your computer or to another computer. You can burn as many data DVDs as needed to store all the files.

Backing up to DVD-Rs or CD-Rs

Apple provides a handy wizard that walks you through backing up your iTunes library, playlists, and iTunes Store purchases to CD-Rs or DVD-Rs. You can choose to back up the entire library, perform *incremental backups* (only items added or changed since the last backup), or save only store purchases. Choose File➪Library➪Back Up to Disc and then choose one of the following:

- **Back Up Entire iTunes Library and Playlist.** This might take a stack of DVD-Rs (or a truckload of CD-Rs), but it's worth doing if you have no other way to back up your library.

- **Back Up Only iTunes Store Purchases.** This is an essential procedure because if you lose these files, you have to repurchase them. You can use CD-Rs or DVD-Rs.

- **Only Back Up Items Added or Changed Since Last Backup.** Use this method to copy only items that were added or changed since your last backup.

To restore your iTunes library from a stack of backup DVD-Rs or CD-Rs, open iTunes and insert the first disc. Then follow the instructions that appear automatically after inserting the disc.

Backing up to another hard drive

To copy your entire library to another hard drive, locate the `iTunes` folder on your computer (see "Finding the iTunes library" earlier in this chapter). Drag this folder to another hard drive or backup device, and you're all set. This action copies everything, including the playlists in your library.

The copy operation might take some time if your library is huge. Although you can interrupt the operation anytime, the newly copied library might not be complete. Finishing the copy operation is always best.

If you restore the backup copy to the same computer with the same names for its hard drive, the backup copy's playlists work fine. *Playlists* are essentially lists of songs in the XML (eXtensible Markup Language) format, with pathnames to the song files: If the hard drive name is different, the pathnames won't work. However, you can import the playlists back into iTunes by choosing File⇨Import and then browsing for and selecting the `iTunes Music Library.xml` file inside the iTunes folder, which realigns the playlist pathnames to the new hard drive.

For a complete description of how to copy your iTunes library to other computers and hard drives, including from Mac to PC or vice-versa, visit this book's companion Web site.

Chapter 13

Fine-Tuning the Sound

. . . .

. . . .

Sound is difficult to describe. Describing how to adjust sound to your liking is harder still. Maybe you want more bone-rattling bass, or treble highs that are as clear as a bell. Even if you've never mastered a stereo system beyond adjusting the bass, treble, and volume, you can use this limited knowledge to quickly fine-tune the sound in iTunes by using the equalizer settings, as you discover in this chapter.

Sound studio engineers try to make recordings for typical listening environments, so they have to simulate the sound experience in those environments. Studios typically have home stereo speakers as monitors so that the engineers can hear what the music sounds like on a home stereo. In the 1950s and early 1960s, when AM radio was king, engineers working on potential AM radio hits purposely mixed the sound with low-fidelity monaural speakers so that they could hear what the mix would sound like on the radio. (Thank goodness that those days are over and that cars offer higher-quality FM radio as well as very high-quality audio systems.)

Engineers did this because the quality of the sound is no better than the speakers you play it on. When you find out how to adjust and fine-tune the sound coming from your computer running iTunes and out of your iPod, use your everyday listening environment as a guide. If you tweak the sound specifically for your computer speakers or for your home stereo and speakers, though, remember that with an iPod you have other potential listening environments — different headphones, car stereo systems, portable boomboxes, and so on.

Fortunately, iTunes gives you the flexibility of using different equalization settings for different songs, audio books, podcasts, and videos. You can also use presets on your iPod. In this chapter, you discover how to make presets for songs in your library so that iTunes remembers them. What's more, you can use the standard iTunes presets on your iPod or use other iPod settings in tandem with the iPod's equalizer. This chapter shows you how.

Adjusting the Sound in iTunes First

Some songs are just too loud. I don't mean too loud stylistically, as in thrash metal with screeching guitars; I mean too loud for your ears when you're wearing headphones or so loud that the music sounds distorted in your speakers. And some songs are just too soft; you have to increase the volume to hear them and then lower the volume to listen to louder songs. To remedy instances like these, you can set the volume in advance in several ways.

Setting the volume in advance

With songs, audio books, podcast episodes, and videos that you already know are too loud (or too soft), consider setting the volume for those items in advance so that they always play with the desired volume adjustment. You can even set the volume for entire albums or podcasts.

To adjust the overall volume of a particular item in advance so that it always plays at that setting, perform the following steps:

1. **Click an item to select it.**

   To set the volume in iTunes for multiple songs, you can select an entire album in Browse view or you can select all the songs. To set the volume for a whole podcast, select it instead of individual episodes.

2. **Choose File⇨Get Info.**

   The information dialog appears.

3. **Click the Options tab.**

   Drag the Volume Adjustment slider left or right to adjust the volume lower or higher, as shown in Figure 13-1. You can do this while playing the file.

Enhancing the sound

Some home or car stereos offer a sound enhancer button to improve the depth of the sound. iTunes offers a similar option — *Sound Enhancer* — that enhances high and low frequencies. Audiophiles and sound purists would most likely use the equalizer to boost frequencies, but you can use this brute-force method to enhance the sound.

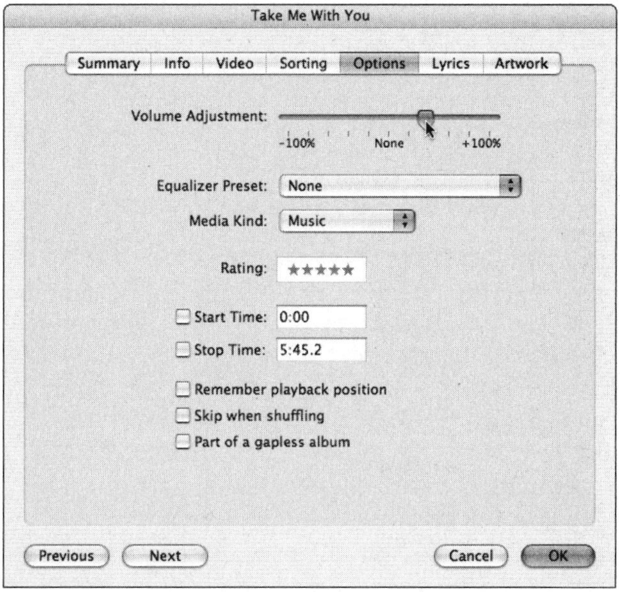

Take Me With You

| Summary | Info | Video | Sorting | Options | Lyrics | Artwork |

Volume Adjustment: ───────────○────────
-100%　　　None　　　+100%

Equalizer Preset: None

Media Kind: Music

Rating: ★★★★★

☐ Start Time: 0:00
☐ Stop Time: 5:45.2

☐ Remember playback position
☐ Skip when shuffling
☐ Part of a gapless album

Previous　Next　　　　Cancel　OK

Figure 13-1:
Adjust the volume setting in advance for a song.

To enable Sound Enhancer, follow these steps:

1. **Choose iTunes⇨Preferences (Mac) or Edit⇨Preferences (Windows).**

2. **In the iTunes Preferences dialog that appears, click the Playback tab.**

   The Playback preferences appear, as shown in Figure 13-2.

3. **Adjust the Sound Enhancer slider:**

   • *Increase the sound enhancement.* Dragging the Sound Enhancer slider to the right (toward High) is similar to pressing the loudness button on a stereo or the equivalent of boosting the treble (high) and bass (low) frequencies in the equalizer. (See the upcoming section, "Equalize It in iTunes.")

   • *Decrease the high and low frequencies.* Drag the slider to the left toward Low.

   The middle setting is neutral, adding no enhancement — the same as disabling Sound Enhancer by clearing its check box.

Sound-checking the iTunes library

Because music CDs are manufactured inconsistently, discrepancies occur in volume. Some CDs play louder than others; occasionally, even individual tracks on a CD might vary.

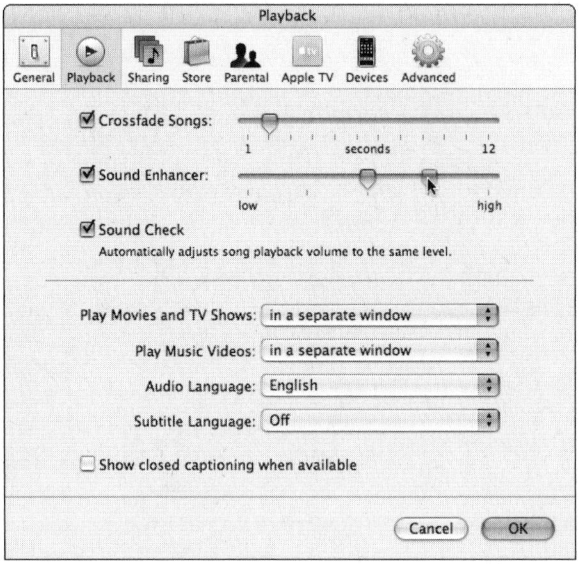

Playback

General Playback Sharing Store Parental Apple TV Devices Advanced

☑ Crossfade Songs:

1   seconds   12

☑ Sound Enhancer:

low   high

☑ Sound Check

Automatically adjusts song playback volume to the same level.

Play Movies and TV Shows: in a separate window ⬍
Play Music Videos: in a separate window ⬍
Audio Language: English ⬍
Subtitle Language: Off ⬍

☐ Show closed captioning when available

(Cancel) (OK)

Figure 13-2:
Use the
Sound
Enhancer.

You can standardize the volume level of all the songs in your iTunes library with the Sound Check option. (Think of musicians, who do sound checks to check the volume of microphones and instruments and the effect on the listening environment.) The aptly named Sound Check option in iTunes allows you to do a sound check on your tunes to bring them all into line, volume-wise. This option has the added benefit of applying the same volume adjustment when you play the songs back on your iPod, as described in the upcoming section, "Sound-checking the iPod."

 Sound Check scans the audio files, finds each track's peak volume level, and then uses this peak volume information to level the playing volume of tracks so that they have the same peak volume. The sound quality isn't affected, nor is the audio information changed: The volume is simply adjusted at the start of the track to be in line with other tracks. If you mix early Sixties music with today's much louder music, like I do, all the songs play at relatively the same volume (so I don't have to adjust the volume) without any loss in quality.

To enable Sound Check, follow these steps:

1. Drag the iTunes volume slider to set the overall volume for iTunes.

The volume slider is located in the top-left corner of the iTunes window, to the right of the Play button.

2. **Choose iTunes⇨Preferences (Mac) or Edit⇨Preferences (Windows).**

3. **In the iTunes Preferences dialog that appears, click the Playback tab.**

   The Playback preferences appear; refer to Figure 13-2.

4. **Select the Sound Check check box.**

   iTunes sets the volume level for all songs according to the level of the iTunes volume slider.

5. **Click OK.**

   The Sound Check option sets a volume adjustment based on the volume slider on all the songs so that they play at approximately the same volume.

The operation runs in the background while you do other things. If you quit iTunes and then restart it, the operation continues where it left off when you quit. You can switch Sound Check on or off at any time.

Sound-checking the iPod

You can take advantage of volume-leveling in your iTunes library with the Sound Check option and then switch Sound Check on or off on your iPod or iPhone. This feature is useful especially when using your iPod in a car or when jogging while listening to headphones because you don't want to have to reach for the volume on the iPod or on the car stereo every time it starts playing a song that's too loud.

The Sound Check option on your iPod works only if you've also set the Sound Check option in your iTunes library. If you need to enable this setting in iTunes, check out the preceding section.

With sixth-generation or older-model iPods, choose Settings⇨Sound Check⇨On from the main menu to enable Sound Check. To disable it, choose Settings⇨Sound Check⇨Off.

With the iPod touch, choose Settings from the home menu, and touch the on-off button next to Sound Check at the top of the Music section of the Settings menu so that it displays ON. To disable it, touch the on-off button so that it displays OFF.

With the iPhone, choose Settings from the home menu, and choose iPod from the Settings menu. Touch the on-off button next to Sound Check at the top of the Music section of the settings menu so that it displays ON. To disable it, touch the on-off button so that it displays OFF.

Equalize It in iTunes

To open the iTunes equalizer, choose Window➪Equalizer. The iTunes equalizer allows you to fine-tune sound spectrum frequencies in a more precise way than with the typical bass and treble controls you find on home stereos and powered speakers. (See the sidebar on equalizers, elsewhere in this chapter.) You can use the equalizer to improve or enhance the sound coming through a particular stereo system and speakers. With the equalizer settings, you can customize playback for different musical genres, listening environments, or speakers.

If you want to pick entirely different equalizer settings for car speakers, home speakers, and headphones, you can save your own settings. Learn how by visiting this book's companion Web site

Adjusting the preamp volume

The *preamp* in your stereo is the component that offers a volume control that applies to all frequencies equally.

Volume knobs generally go up to 10 — except, of course, for Spinal Tap's Marshall preamps, which go to 11.

The iTunes equalizer, as shown in Figure 13-3, offers a Preamp slider on the far-left side. You can increase or decrease the volume in 3 decibel (dB) increments up to 12 dB. *Decibels* are units of measure for the intensity (or volume) of the frequencies. Decibels are a logarithmic scale, with each additional decibel measuring a logarithmic increase. You can adjust the volume while playing the music to hear the result right away.

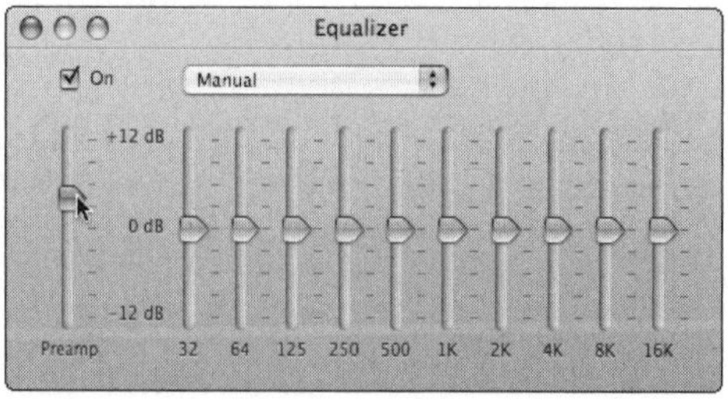

Figure 13-3:
Use the
Preamp
slider to
adjust the
volume
across all
frequencies.

Equalizer

☑ On   Manual

+12 dB

0 dB

-12 dB

Preamp 32 64 125 250 500 1K 2K 4K 8K 16K

If you want to make any adjustments to frequencies, you might need to adjust the preamp volume first if needed and then move on to the specific frequencies.

TECHNICAL STUFF

What's the frequency, Kenneth? The equalizer opportunity

The Beach Boys were right when they sang "Good Vibrations" because that's what music is — the sensation of hearing audible vibrations conveyed to the ear by a medium, such as air. Musicians measure pitch by the *frequency* of vibrations. The waves can oscillate slowly and produce low-pitched sounds, or they can oscillate rapidly and produce high-pitched sounds. *Amplitude* is a measurement of the amount of fluctuation in air pressure — therefore, amplitude is perceived as loudness.

When you increase the bass or treble on a stereo system, you're actually increasing the volume, or intensity, of certain frequencies while the music is playing. An equalizer lets you fine-tune the sound spectrum frequencies in a more precise way than with bass and treble controls. It increases or decreases specific frequencies of the sound to raise or lower highs, lows, and midrange tones. The equalizer adjusts the volume with several band-pass filters all centered at different frequencies, and each filter offers controllable *gain* (the ability to boost the volume).

On more sophisticated stereo systems, an equalizer with a bar graph display replaces the bass and treble controls. An *equalizer* (EQ in audio-speak) enables you to fine-tune the specific sound spectrum frequencies, which gives you far greater control than merely adjusting the bass or treble controls.

Adjusting frequencies

You can adjust frequencies in the iTunes equalizer by clicking and dragging sliders that look like mixing-board faders.

The horizontal values across the equalizer represent the spectrum of human hearing. The deepest frequency ("Daddy sang bass") is 32 hertz (Hz); the midrange frequencies are 250 Hz and 500 Hz; and the higher frequencies go from 1 kilohertz (kHz) to 16 kHz (treble).

The vertical values on each bar represent decibels. Increase or decrease the frequencies at 3 dB increments by clicking and dragging the sliders up and down. You can drag the sliders to adjust the frequencies while the music is playing so that you can hear the effect immediately.

Using the iTunes presets

iTunes offers presets, which are equalizer settings made in advance and saved by name. You can quickly switch settings without having to make changes to each frequency slider. iTunes comes with more than 20 presets of the most commonly used equalizer settings, including ones for specific music genres, such as classical and rock.

To choose an equalizer preset, click the Equalizer's pop-up menu, as shown in Figure 13-4, which by default is set to Manual (refer to Figure 13-3). If something is playing, you hear the effect in the sound immediately after choosing the preset.

You can assign standard iTunes presets or your own custom presets to specific items (songs, audio books, podcast episodes, and videos) in your iTunes library. You can then enable the iPod or iPhone equalizer by choosing any equalizer setting (other than Off) so that the iPod or iPhone uses the item's equalizer preset for playback. Find out how by visiting this book's companion Web site.

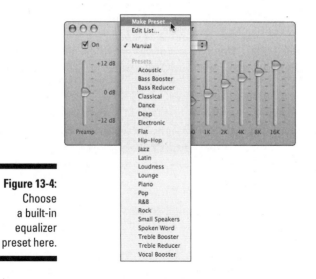

Figure 13-4:
Choose
a built-in
equalizer
preset here.

Equalize It in Your iPod

You leave the back-road bliss of the country to get on the freeway, and now the music in your car doesn't have enough bass to give you that thumping rhythm you need to dodge other cars. What can you do? Without endangering anybody, you can pull over and then select one of the iPod equalizer presets, such as Bass Booster.

Yes, your iPod and iPhone also have built-in equalizers. Similar to the iTunes equalizer, the iPod or iPhone built-in equalizer modifies the volume of the frequencies of the sound. And although you don't have sliders like the iTunes equalizer, you do get the same long list of presets (except for Loudness) to suit the type of music or environment.

The iPod or iPhone equalizer uses a bit more battery power when it's on, so you might have less playing time.

To select an iPod equalizer preset with iPod classic, iPod nano, or older-model iPods, choose Settings⇨EQ from the main menu to display a list of presets. You can scroll the list of presets and press Select to select one. The equalizer is set to Off until you select one of the presets.

With the iPod touch, choose Settings from the home menu, and choose EQ to display a list of presets. With the iPhone, choose Settings from the home menu, choose iPod from the Settings menu, and then choose EQ to display a list of presets. You can scroll the list of presets and touch a preset to select it. The equalizer is set to Off until you select one of the presets.

Each equalizer preset offers a different balance of frequencies designed to enhance the sound in certain ways. For example, Bass Booster increases the volume of the low (bass) frequencies; Treble Booster does the same to the high (treble) frequencies.

To see what a preset actually does to the frequencies, open the iTunes equalizer and then select the same preset. The faders in the equalizer show you exactly what the preset does.

The Off setting disables the iPod equalizer. You have to choose an equalizer preset to enable the iPod equalizer.

Learn how to assign standard iTunes presets or your own custom presets to specific songs, audio books, podcast episodes, and videos — and use those presets when playing these items back on your iPod or iPhone — by visiting this book's companion Web site.

Part III
Playing Your iPod or iPhone

The 5th Wave   By Rich Tennant

"It's like any other pacemaker, but it comes with an internal iPod docking accessory."

In this part . . .

Part III focuses on playing content with your iPod or iPhone, browsing Web sites with your iPod touch or iPhone, and connecting your iPod or iPhone to a stereo or TV.

✔ Chapter 14 shows you how to locate and play songs, audio books, podcasts, and videos on your iPod or iPhone, including how to play YouTube videos on your iPod touch or iPhone. You also find out how to create playlists on the fly with your iPod or iPhone, including Genius playlists and how to adjust the volume.

✔ Chapter 15 describes how to choose a Wi-Fi network, surf the Web, and browse sites with your iPod touch or iPhone by entering addresses, using bookmarks, or searching with Google or Yahoo!, as well as how to zoom into and pan around Web pages.

✔ Chapter 16 shows you how to use calendars and contacts on an iPod touch, iPhone, iPod classic, iPod nano, or older model, and how to use iPod touch or iPhone applications such as Mail to send and receive e-mail, Maps to display maps and driving directions, Stocks to check your financial portfolio, Weather to see weather conditions in various cities, and Calculator to do math, as well as how to enter information for all these applications.

Chapter 14

Playing Content on Your iPod or iPhone

. . . .

In This Chapter

▶ Locating items by artist, album, or playlist

▶ Repeating and shuffling a song list

▶ Playing podcasts, audio books, and videos

▶ Creating and saving Genius and On-The-Go playlists

▶ Playing songs in the iPod shuffle

▶ Changing the volume level and volume limit

. . . .

*F*or a music lover, nothing compares with the feeling of having a whole lot of song choices at your fingertips. Rather than sitting back and soaking up the preprogrammed sounds of radio or CDs, you can control your iPod or iPhone playback to pick any song that you want to hear at any time. Or, shuffle through songs to get an idea of how wide your music choices are or to surprise yourself or others. You may want to follow a thread of musical ideas, such as The Kingsmen's version of "Louie Louie" through "All Day and All of the Night" by The Kinks, "Dirty Water" by The Standells, "Little Bit of Soul" by The Music Explosion, The Troggs' "Wild Thing," all the way to the version of "Wild Thing" by Jimi Hendrix.

In this chapter, you discover how to locate and play content on any iPod or iPhone. *Note:* If you have an iPod shuffle, see the later section, "Playing an iPod shuffle."

With your iPhone, iPod classic, iPod touch, or iPod nano, you can locate and play music easily, browsing by artist and album — even by composer. Selecting a playlist is simple. And if you don't have playlists from iTunes (or you don't want to hear those playlists), you can create a temporary On-The-Go playlist. You can even create a Genius playlist for your iPod nano, iPod classic, iPod touch or iPhone.

Locating Songs

With so many songs on your iPod or iPhone, finding a particular one by its song title can take longer than finding it another way — like finding a needle in a haystack or even trying to find "Needle in a Haystack" by The Velvelettes in a Motown catalog. It may be faster to locate albums by cover art, or songs by searching for artist (or composer), genre, album, or playlist.

By cover art (using Cover Flow)

The iPod classic, iPod nano, iPod touch, and iPhone (as well as some earlier sixth-generation models) can display the cover art for albums. The Cover Flow browser lets you flip through your cover art to select music alphabetically by artist.

To browse music by cover art with an iPod touch or iPhone model, choose Music from the iPod touch Home menu or iPod from the iPhone Home menu, and then hold the device so that it's horizontal in order to change the display to landscape mode. The iPod touch or iPhone automatically switches to the landscape-mode display and offers the Cover Flow browser, as shown in Figure 14-1.

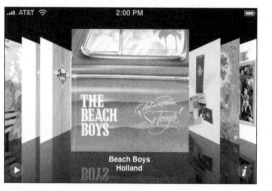

Figure 14-1: The Cover Flow browser on an iPod touch or iPhone.

Slide your finger across the album covers to scroll swiftly through the music library, or tap to the right or left of the cover art in the foreground to move forward or backward an album cover at a time. Touch the Play button in the lower-left corner to start playing the first song in the foreground album; the Play button turns to a Pause button so that you can tap it again to stop playback. Touch the *i* button in the lower-right side, or tap the foreground cover art, to list the songs in that album, and then touch a song to start playing it.

The Cover Flow browser is also available on the iPod classic and iPod nano models. Choose Music from the main menu on an iPod classic, and then choose Cover Flow from the Music menu. Rotate an iPod nano 90 degrees to the left or the right, and the Cover Flow browser appears automatically.

To browse by cover art, scroll the click wheel clockwise to move forward or counterclockwise to move backward through album covers. You can also press the Fast-Forward or Rewind buttons to step forward or backward in your library one cover at a time. Press the Select button in the middle of the click wheel to select the album in the foreground; a list of songs appears. Use the click wheel to scroll the list of songs and then press the Select button to select a highlighted song.

By artist name

Your iPod or iPhone organizes music by artist, and then within each artist by album. To browse music by artist with an iPod touch or iPhone model, choose Music from the iPod touch Home menu or iPod from the iPhone Home menu, and tap the Artists button along the bottom row. A scrollable list of artists appears with an alphabet listed vertically along the right side. Tap any letter in the alphabet to scroll the list directly to that letter. Touch an artist name to see a list of albums or songs by that artist. (You see multiple albums if more than one album is available — tap the album name to select the album.) Touch a song title to start playing the song.

Follow these steps with an iPod classic or iPod nano (or earlier models) to locate a song by artist and then by album:

1. **Choose Music from the iPod main menu.**

2. **From the Music menu that appears, choose Artists.**

   To be more selective, you can browse by genre first. Choose Genres and then choose a genre from the Genres menu to get a list of artists that have songs in that genre (in alphabetical order by artist name).

3. **Select an artist from the Artists menu.**

   The artist names are listed in alphabetical order by last name or the first word of a group. Scroll the Artists menu until the artist name is highlighted and then press the Select button. The artist's menu of albums appears.

4. **Choose All Songs or the name of an album from the artist's menu.**

   You can find All Songs at the top of the artist's menu; it should already be highlighted. Press the Select button to choose it or scroll until an album name is highlighted; then press the Select button. A song list appears after you choose either an album choice or All Songs.

5. **Select a song from the list.**

The songs in the album list are in *album order* (the order that they appear on the album); in the All Songs list, songs are listed in album order for each album.

By album title

To browse music by album title with an iPod touch, choose Music from the iPod touch Home menu, and touch the Albums button along the bottom row of the display. A scrollable list of albums appears with an alphabet listed vertically along the right side. Tap any letter in the alphabet to scroll the list directly to that letter. Touch an album title to see a list of songs in the album. Touch a song title to start playing the song.

Follow these steps with an iPod classic or iPod nano (or earlier models) to directly locate a song by album:

1. **Choose Music from the iPod main menu.**

2. **From the Music menu, choose Albums.**

   The Albums menu appears, displaying albums in alphabetical order.

3. **Choose an album from the Albums menu.**

   The albums are listed in alphabetical order (without any reference to artist, which might make identification difficult). Scroll the Albums menu until the album name is highlighted and then press the Select button. A song list appears.

4. **Select a song from the list.**

   The songs in the album list are in the order that they appear on the album. Scroll the list to highlight the song name and then press the Select button.

To browse music by album title with an iPhone, choose iPod from the iPhone Home menu and tap the More button along the bottom row of the display. A scrollable list of options appears, including Albums. Touch Albums to view a list of albums with an alphabet listed vertically along the right side. Tap any letter in the alphabet to scroll the list directly to that letter. Touch an album title to see a list of songs in the album. Touch a song title to start playing the song.

By playlist

When you automatically synchronize your iPod or iPhone with your entire iTunes library, all your playlists in iTunes are copied to the iPod or iPhone. You can choose to synchronize your iPod or iPhone with only specified playlists, as I describe in Chapter 11.

To browse music by playlist with an iPod touch or iPhone model, choose Music from the iPod touch Home menu or iPod from the iPhone Home menu, and tap the Playlists button along the bottom row of the display. A scrollable list of playlists appears. Touch a playlist title to see a list of songs in the playlist. Touch a song title to start playing the song.

Follow these steps to locate a playlist on your iPod classic or iPod nano (or earlier models):

1. **Choose Music from the iPod main menu.**

2. **From the Music menu, choose Playlists.**

3. **From the Playlists menu that appears, choose a playlist.**

   Playlists are listed in alphabetical order. Scroll the Playlists menu to highlight the playlist name and then press the Select button. A list of songs in the playlist appears.

4. **Select a song from the list.**

   The songs in the playlist are in *playlist order* (the order defined for the playlist in iTunes). Scroll up or down the list to highlight the song you want.

Playing a Song

After scrolling the song list until the song name is highlighted, press either the Select button or the Play/Pause button on an iPod classic or iPod nano (or earlier model) to play the selected song. On an iPod touch or iPhone, touch the song title to play the song. When the song finishes, the iPod or iPhone plays the next song in the song list.

Controlling playback on an iPod classic or iPod nano

While a song is playing, the artist name and song name appear on the Now Playing screen. Color-display iPods also display the album cover, and the current iPod classic and iPod nano models show a progress bar as well.

To adjust the volume on a current iPod nano or iPod classic, scroll the click wheel when you see the progress bar. On older iPod models, press the Select button once to show the progress bar. For more info, see the later section, "Adjusting and Limiting the Volume."

To pause playback, press the Play/Pause button while a song is playing. To stop playing a song, press the Play/Pause button again (the same button).

To skip to any point in a song, press the Select button to reveal the scrubber bar (on older models, press the Select button twice). Use the scroll wheel to move the playhead across the scrubber bar forward (to the right) or backward (to the left) in the song.

Press the Next/Fast-Forward button once to play the next song in sequence, and press the Previous/Rewind button once at the beginning of a song, or twice during the song, to play the previous song. You can fast-forward through a song by pressing and holding down on the Next/Fast-Forward button, and rewind a song by pressing and holding down on the Previous/Rewind button.

To start a song over from the beginning, move the playhead on the scrubber bar all the way to the left, or press the Previous/Rewind button once.

To return to the menus and make other selections when playing a song on an iPod classic or iPod nano, press the Menu button, or press and hold the Select button until a menu appears on top of the cover art.

Controlling playback on an iPod touch or iPhone

On an iPod touch or iPhone, whenever you play a song you're going to see the album cover associated with the song on the Now Playing screen, as well as the touch buttons for playback control — Previous/Rewind, Play/Pause, and Next/Fast-Forward (see Figure 14-2). Slide your finger along the volume slider at the bottom of the display to change the volume.

To skip to any point in a song, tap underneath the left-arrow button or the album title while a song is playing, and drag the playhead along the scrubber bar that appears between the Repeat and Shuffle buttons. Touch the Next/Fast-Forward button once to play the next song in sequence, and touch the Previous/Rewind button once at the beginning of a song, or twice during the song, to play the previous song. You can fast-forward through a song by touching and holding down on the Next/Fast-Forward button, and rewind a song by touching and holding down on the Previous/Rewind button. To start a song over from the beginning, drag the play head on the scrubber bar all the way to the left, or touch the Previous/Rewind button once.

The bullet-list touch button in the upper-right corner displays a list of the album's contents. You can then touch the title of another song on the album to start playing that song.

To return to menus and make other selections when playing a song on an iPhone or iPod touch, press the left-arrow button in the upper-left corner of the display.

Repeating songs

If you want to drive yourself crazy repeating the same song over and over, your iPod or iPhone is happy to oblige. (You might want to try repeating "They're Coming to Take Me Away, Ha-Haaa" by Napoleon XIV, a favorite from the old *The Dr. Demento Show* radio broadcasts — and perhaps they will come.) More than likely, you'll want to repeat a sequence of songs, which you can easily do.

You can set your iPod classic or iPod nano (or older models) to repeat a single song, or to repeat all the songs in the selected album or playlist, by following these steps:

1. **Locate and play a song.**

2. **While the song plays, press the Menu button repeatedly to return to the main menu and then choose the Settings item.**

3. **Scroll the Settings menu until Repeat is highlighted.**

   The Repeat setting displays Off, One, or All next to it.

4. **Press the Select button until the setting changes to One to repeat one song, or All to repeat all the songs in the album or playlist (or Off to turn repeat off).**

   If you press the button more than you need to, keep pressing until the setting you want reappears. The button cycles among the Off, One, and All settings.

You can also press the Previous/Rewind button to repeat a song.

The iPod touch and iPhone provide touch buttons to control repeating and shuffling. To access these touch buttons, tap underneath the left-arrow button or the album title while a song is playing. The Repeat and Shuffle touch buttons appear, along with the scrubber bar, directly below the top row of buttons, as shown in Figure 14-2.

If you're viewing another iPod menu on the iPhone or content menu on the iPod touch, touch Now Playing at the top-right corner of the display to go directly to the "now playing" display.

You can repeat an entire song list by tapping the Repeat touch button (refer to Figure 14-2). When it's selected, the Repeat button shows blue highlighting. Touch the Repeat button again to repeat only the current song — the button changes to include a blue-highlighted numeral 1. Touch it once more to return to normal playback.

Figure 14-2:
Tap under the album title to show the Repeat, Genius, and Shuffle buttons.

Shuffling song order

Maybe you want your song selections to be surprising and unpredictable, and you want your iPod or iPhone to read your mind. You can *shuffle* song playback to play in random order, just like an automated radio station without a disk jockey or program guide. See for yourself whether your iPod or iPhone knows how to pick good tunes without your help.

The shuffle algorithm is truly random, according to Apple. When an iPod or iPhone creates a shuffle, it reorders the songs (like shuffling a deck of cards), and then it plays them in the new order. By default, only songs are included in iPod or iPhone shuffling. However, you can select podcast episodes, audio books, and videos in iTunes and set an option to include them in shuffles. To do this in iTunes

1. **Select the video, podcast episode, or audio book episode.**

2. **Choose File⇨Get Info.**

3. **Click the Options tab.**

4. **Deselect the Skip When Shuffling option.**

   The next time you synchronize your iPod or iPhone, any items with this option turned off are included in shuffles.

If you want to exclude a song from shuffles, select the song in iTunes, choose File⇨Get Info, click the Options tab, and then select the Skip When Shuffling option.

You can also shuffle songs within an album or playlist, which gives you some control over random playback. For example, you could create a smart playlist for all jazz songs and then shuffle the songs within that jazz playlist. And if you want to play albums randomly, but don't like when the songs in an album aren't played in proper album order, you can shuffle all the albums but play the songs in normal album order.

On an iPod nano or iPod classic

To turn your iPod classic or iPod nano (or older model) into a random song player, choose Shuffle Songs from the main menu.

On a current iPod nano, you can shake it so that its motion detector switches to a random song. Whenever you shake it, the iPod nano shuffles again to another random song. Shaking to shuffle doesn't change your shuffle settings — it just immediately shuffles songs. Shaking to shuffle is disabled when you put the Hold switch in the hold position (so that you don't keep changing songs as you jog or exercise strenuously) , or if the iPod nano's display is off. You can also disable it by choosing Settings⇨Playback⇨Shake from the main menu, and then select Off. To turn it on, choose Settings⇨Playback⇨Shake from the main menu, and select On.

To shuffle songs in an album or a playlist with an iPod classic or iPod nano (or older model), or to shuffle albums, follow these steps:

1. **Choose Settings from the main menu, and scroll to Shuffle.**

   The Shuffle setting displays Off next to it.

2. **Press the Select button once (Off changes to Songs) to shuffle the songs in the next album or playlist you play. Press Select again (Songs changes to Albums) to shuffle the albums without shuffling the songs within each album.**

   When you set Shuffle to Songs, the iPod classic or iPod nano shuffles songs within the currently playing playlist or album, or if nothing is playing, the next album or playlist you choose to play. When you set Shuffle to Albums, it plays all the songs on the currently playing album (or the next album you play) in order, and then randomly selects another album in the list and plays through it in order.

If you press the Select button more than you need to, keep pressing until the setting you want reappears. The button cycles among the `Off`, `Songs`, or `Albums` settings.

On an iPod touch or iPhone

To turn your iPod touch or iPhone into a random song player, choose Music from the iPod touch Home menu or iPod from the iPhone Home menu, and touch the Songs button at the bottom of the display. The song list appears, with Shuffle at the top of the list. Touch Shuffle to turn on Shuffle.

You can set an iPod touch or iPhone to shuffle any album or playlist before playing it. First, select the playlist or album; and then choose Shuffle at the top of the list of songs for that playlist or album.

The iPod touch and iPhone provide touch buttons to control repeating and shuffling. To shuffle songs in an album or playlist, start playing a song in the album or playlist and then tap underneath the left-arrow button or the album title while a song is playing. The Repeat and Shuffle touch buttons appear, along with the scrubber bar, directly below the top row of buttons (refer to Figure 14-2). Touch the Shuffle button to shuffle songs within the currently playing album or playlist.

You can set your iPod or iPhone to repeat an entire album or playlist but still shuffle the playing order each time you hear it. Start playing a song in the album or playlist, and then set your iPod or iPhone to repeat all the songs in the album or playlist as described in "Repeating songs" in this section. Then set the iPod or iPhone to shuffle the songs as described above.

Playing Podcasts

Podcasts, naturally, have their own menu. Podcasts are organized by podcast name (which is like an album name), and podcast episodes are listed within each podcast in the order that they were released (by date).

To play a podcast episode, follow these steps:

1. **Display the Podcasts menu.**

   Depending on your model iPod or iPhone:

   - Choose Podcasts from the iPod classic or iPod nano main menu.

   - Choose iPod from the iPhone Home menu, touch the More button in the lower-right corner of the display, and then touch Podcasts.

   - Choose Music from the iPod touch Home menu, touch the More button in the lower-right corner of the display, and then touch Podcasts.

2. **Choose a podcast from the Podcasts menu that appears, and then choose an episode**

   A blue dot appears next to any podcast that has unplayed episodes. On an iPod classic or iPod nano, scroll the Podcasts menu until the podcast name is highlighted and then press the Select button, and then scroll and select an episode. On an iPod touch or iPhone, flick the list and touch the podcast episode.

While a podcast episode is playing, the podcast name and episode title appear. On a color-display iPod and iPhone, the podcast's graphic image — similar to an album cover — appears. To pause playback, press the Play/Pause button when a podcast episode is playing.

Podcast episodes are automatically set to remember the playback position when you pause an episode. This feature lets you pause an episode in iTunes while you synchronize your iPod or iPhone (as described in Chapter 11). After synchronization, you can continue playing the episode on your iPod or iPhone from where you paused. This feature also works in the opposite way: If you pause an episode on your iPod or iPhone, the podcast episode resumes the playback position so that you can continue playing it in iTunes (after synchronization) from where you paused.

When you synchronize your iPod or iPhone, any played episodes are deleted if you set iTunes to keep only your unplayed episodes. To make sure that a particular episode stays on your iPod or iPhone, select it in iTunes, Control-click (Mac) or right-click (Windows) the episode, and then choose Mark as New. You can also change your iPod or iPhone synchronization options for podcasts. See Chapter 11 for details.

Playing Audio Books

Audio books also have their own place of honor on the Music/iPod menu. Audio books are organized by title, with sections, or *episodes*, listed in the order that they should be read (Part 1, Part 2, and so on).

To play an audio book episode, follow these steps:

1. **Display the Audiobooks menu.**

   Depending on your model iPod or iPhone:

   - Choose Music from the iPod classic or iPod nano main menu, then Audiobooks from the Music menu.

   - Choose iPod from the iPhone Home menu, touch the More button in the lower-right corner of the display, and then touch Audiobooks.

- Choose Music from the iPod touch Home menu, touch the More button in the lower-right corner of the display, and then touch Audiobooks.

2. **Choose an audio book from the Audiobooks menu that appears, and then select a particular episode to play.**

   The audio book episodes are listed in proper order for each book. Press the Select button on an iPod classic or iPod nano (or older model) to play the highlighted episode, or touch the episode title on an iPhone or iPod touch.

While an audio book episode is playing, the book and episode titles appear. Color-display iPods and the iPhone also show the book's graphic image — similar to a book cover. To pause the playback, press the Play/Pause button when an audio book episode is playing.

Audio books are automatically set to remember the playback position when you pause an episode. This feature lets you pause an episode in iTunes while you synchronize your iPod or iPhone. After synchronization, you can continue playing the episode on your iPod or iPhone from where you paused. This feature also works the opposite way: If you start playing an episode on your iPod or iPhone and then pause, and then you sync your device with iTunes, the audio book episode resumes the playback position so that you can continue playing it in iTunes from where you paused.

Playing Movies, TV Shows, and Videos

You can play videos from your iTunes library on iPhone models, all current iPod models (except the iPod shuffle), and fifth-generation color-display iPods. You may have to use iTunes first to convert imported videos for iPod use — select the video and choose Advanced⇨Create iPod or iPhone Version. Videos you download from the iTunes Store can play without any conversion.

To learn more about preparing your own videos and converting imported videos for use with an iPod, iPhone, or Apple TV, visit this book's companion Web site.

The iTunes Store offers an amazing selection of TV shows and movies, including movie rentals (see Chapter 4). Check out the NCAA March Madness Basketball Championship while waiting in line for tickets to the next game. Watch Disney animations with your children while waiting for the bus. Get your dose of *The Daily Show with Jon Stewart* while taking the subway to work. Or watch one of my favorites, "Mr. Monk and the Airplane" from the *Monk* TV series, on your next flight.

Video is incredibly portable on an iPod classic, iPod nano, iPod touch, or iPhone. People are amazed by the crisp, clear picture quality. You watch video horizontally (also known as *landscape mode*) on the iPod touch, iPhone, and the current iPod nano — and if you rotate it to the opposite horizontal position, the video adjusts accordingly.

To play a video on an iPod touch or iPhone, follow these steps:

1. **Choose Videos from the iPod touch Home menu, or touch iPod from the iPhone Home menu and then touch the Videos button at the bottom of the display.**

2. **Touch the title of a movie, TV show, music video or podcast to play it.**

   The video titles are listed in alphabetical order divided into sections for Movies, TV Shows, Music Videos, and Podcasts.

To play a video on an iPod classic or iPod nano, follow these steps:

1. **Choose Videos from the main menu to select a movie, TV show, or imported video. Choose Music from the main menu to select a music video.**

2. **Scroll the menu until the title is highlighted and then press the Select button to play your selection.**

   Hold the current iPod nano model horizontally to view the picture. If you rotate the iPod nano to the opposite horizontal position, the video adjusts accordingly.

You can press the Play/Pause button on an iPod nano or iPod classic, or touch the Play/Pause button on an iPod touch or iPhone, while a video is playing to pause the playback. Videos are automatically set to remember the playback position when you pause. This feature lets you pause a video or TV episode in iTunes while you synchronize your iPod or iPhone. After synchronization, you can continue playing the video or episode on your iPod or iPhone from where you paused. This feature also works the opposite way: If you start playing a video on your iPod or iPhone and then pause, and then you sync the device with iTunes, the video resumes the playback position so that you can continue playing it in iTunes from where you paused.

You can delete a video directly from your iPod touch or iPhone by flicking left or right across the video selection in the Videos menu, and tapping the Delete button that appears. Your video is still in iTunes but is deleted from the device — you can sync the device again to copy the video back to the device (as described in Chapter 11). If you delete a rented movie from iPod touch or iPhone, it is deleted permanently. See Chapter 4 for more about managing iTunes Store rentals.

iPod classic and iPod nano video playback controls

The video playback controls on an iPod classic, iPod nano, or fifth-generation iPod work the same way as with songs — you use precisely the same buttons, in other words. Use the scroll wheel to adjust the volume, as described in the later section, "Adjusting and Limiting the Volume."

To pause playback, press the Play/Pause button while a video is playing. To start again, press Play/Pause again.

To skip to any point in a video, press the Select button (twice on older models) to reveal the scrubber bar. Use the scroll wheel to move the playhead across the scrubber bar forward (to the right) or backward (to the left) in the video.

Press the Next/Fast-Forward button once to play the next video in sequence (such as the next episode of a TV show), and press the Previous/Rewind button once at the beginning of a video, or twice during the video, to play the previous video in sequence. You can fast-forward through a video by pressing and holding down the Next/Fast-Forward button, and rewind a video by pressing and holding down the Previous/Rewind button. If the video contains chapters, you can skip to the previous or next chapter by pressing the Previous/ Rewind or Next/Fast-Forward button — but remember, this trick works only if the original video was set up to contain chapters. To start a video over from the beginning, move the playhead on the scrubber bar all the way to the left as described above, or press the Previous/Rewind button once.

To return to menus and make other selections on an iPod classic, iPod nano, or fifth-generation iPod, press the Menu button.

iPod touch and iPhone video playback controls

On an iPod touch or iPhone, tap the display to show video controls (as shown in Figure 14-3), and tap again to hide them.

To raise or lower the volume, drag the volume slider (refer to Figure 14-3).

To skip to any point in a video, drag the playhead along the scrubber bar. You can fast-forward through a video by touching and holding down the Next/Fast-Forward button, and rewind a video by touching and holding down the Previous/Rewind button. To start a video over from the beginning, drag the playhead on the scrubber bar all the way to the left, or touch the Previous/Rewind button if the video doesn't contain chapters.

Figure 14-3:
Tap the
iPhone or
iPod touch
video dis-
play to use
playback
controls.

If the video contains chapters, you can skip to the previous or next chapter by touching the Previous/Rewind or Next/Fast-Forward button. To start play-ing at a specific chapter, touch the bullet-list button that appears in the top-right corner — but remember, this trick works only if the original video was set up to contain chapters.

Videos are displayed on an iPhone or iPod touch in landscape mode in wide-screen format. You can also scale the video picture to fill the display or to fit within the display. Tap the Scale button (the one with two arrows facing each other), or double-tap the video picture itself, to switch from one to the other. Filling the display may crop the sides, top, and bottom to give you a larger view of the center of the picture. Fitting to the display assures that the entire picture is shown, but you may see black bars on the sides or top and bottom.

To stop watching a video before it finishes playing, touch the Done button in the upper-left corner of the display, or press the Home button.

If a video offers an alternative audio language or subtitles, a Subtitles button appears. Tap the Subtitles button and then choose a language from the Audio list, or a language from the Subtitles list, or Off to turn off subtitles.

Viewing YouTube on Your iPod touch or iPhone

YouTube is the free video-sharing Web site started in 2005 that has since exploded with video clips from all corners of the globe. You can search for and watch YouTube videos right from your iPod touch (with a Wi-Fi connec-tion) or your iPhone (with a Wi-Fi, Edge, or 3G connection). You can also bookmark videos for later playback, and share videos with others by e-mail.

Touch YouTube on the Home menu (in either your iPod touch or iPhone) to run the YouTube application. A menu appears with video selections; touch a selection to play the video. You can touch buttons along the bottom of the display to choose the Featured, Most Viewed, or Bookmarks menus; choose Search to search for videos; or choose More to see more menus. For example, touch More, and then touch Top Rated in the list of menu choices, to see the Top Rated menu (see Figure 14-4).

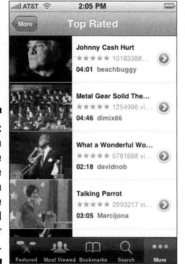

Figure 14-4:
Touch
More in the
YouTube
application
to show the
Top Rated
and other
menus.

After touching a video selection, your iPod touch or iPhone displays the video just like other videos, with the same controls (as shown in Figure 14-5). See the "iPod touch and iPhone video playback controls" section earlier in this chapter for details. YouTube streams the video to your iPod touch or iPhone so that you can start playing it immediately. The progress of the downloaded stream appears in the scrubber bar; you can wait for the entire video to download if you want to play it without any hiccups.

YouTube adds the Bookmark button (a book icon) to the left of the Previous/ Rewind button to bookmark the video, and the Share button (an envelope icon) to the right of the Next/Fast-Forward button to share the video.

You can also bookmark or share the video without playing it, and view information about the video as well as related video selections. Tap the right-arrow button on the right side of each selection (refer to Figure 14-4) to see information about the video and to use the Bookmark or Share buttons. (The Bookmark button doesn't appear if the video is already bookmarked.) Touch the Bookmark button to save a bookmark for the video — the video selection appears in the Bookmarks menu for future reference.

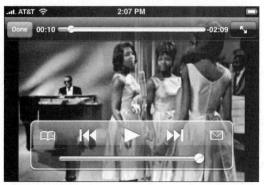

Figure 14-5:
YouTube
controls
for video
playback,
bookmark-
ing, and
sharing.

To delete entries from your Bookmarks menu, touch the Bookmarks button at the bottom of the display to show your Bookmarks menu; then touch the Edit button in the top-right corner of the iPod touch or iPhone display. The Bookmarks menu changes to circled minus (–) signs next to the video selections. To delete a bookmarked video selection, touch the circled minus sign, which rotates and displays a Delete button over the selection — tap the Delete button. To cancel deletion, tap the rotated circled minus sign again. Touch the Done button in the top-right corner of the Bookmarks menu to finish editing.

To search for videos on YouTube, touch the Search button at the bottom of the display. Touch the Search Entry field that appears at the top of the display to show the on-screen keyboard. (For instructions on using the on-screen keyboard, see Chapter 1.) If the entry field already has a search term, touch the circled _x_ in the right corner of the field to clear its contents. Then tap out the letters of the search term using the on-screen keyboard. Immediately as you start typing letters, video selections from YouTube appear below. You can scroll this list by dragging up and down. If a video selection appears that satisfies your search, touch it to play it or bookmark it without further ado. Otherwise, keep typing the search term. When finished, touch the Search button at the bottom-right corner of the on-screen keyboard to close the keyboard and display the search results.

Viewing Photos

You might remember the old days when you carried fading, wallet-sized photo prints that sported creases, rips, and tears the more you showed them around. You can now dispense with carrying prints because all you need is your color-display iPod or iPhone, which can hold up to 25,000 photos. That's a lot!

Assuming that you've already organized your photos into albums and synchronized your iPod or iPhone with photos (see Chapter 11), you can see the photos on your iPod or iPhone by following these steps:

1. **On the iPod or iPhone, choose Photos from the main or Home menu.**

   The iPod classic and iPod nano displays the Photos menu with All Photos and Settings choices at the top, followed by a list of photo albums in alphabetical order. The iPhone displays the Camera Roll choice at the top, followed by Photo Library and a list of photo albums. The iPod touch displays Photo Library and a list of photo albums. Older iPod models with color displays show a Photos menu with Photo Library and Slideshow Settings choices at the top, followed by a list of photo albums.

2. **On an iPod classic or iPod nano, choose All Photos or an album name; on an iPod touch or iPhone (or older iPod models), choose either Photo Library or the album name.**

   The All Photos or Photo Library choice displays thumbnail images of all the photos in your iPod or iPhone. Selecting an album displays thumbnail images of only the photos assigned to that album.

3. **Use the scroll wheel on an iPod classic or iPod nano (or older iPod) to highlight the photo thumbnail you want and then press the Select button to select the photo; on an iPhone or iPod touch, flick your finger to scroll the thumbnails, and tap a thumbnail to select the photo.**

   You might have several screens of thumbnails. Use the scroll wheel on an iPod classic or iPod nano (or older models) to scroll through the thumbnails or use Next/Fast-Forward and Previous/Rewind to skip to the next or previous screen. Flick your finger to scroll the thumbnails on an iPod touch or iPhone. When you select a photo thumbnail, your iPod or iPhone displays it.

To view a photo in landscape orientation on an iPod touch, current model iPod nano, or iPhone, rotate it sideways. The photo automatically changes to fit the new orientation, and expands to fit the screen if the photo is in landscape orientation.

To zoom into the photo to see more detail on an iPod touch or iPhone, double-tap the area you want to zoom into. Double-tap again to zoom out. You can also zoom into an area by unpinching with two fingers, and zoom out by pinching. To pan around a photo, drag the photo with your finger.

On an iPhone or iPod touch, tap the full-screen photo to show or hide the slide show controls. To see the next or previous photos in the album or library, flick left or right, or touch the Previous/Rewind or the Next/Fast-Forward buttons that appear when you tap the photo display.

On an iPod classic or iPod nano (or fifth-generation iPod), press the Previous/Rewind button to see the previous photo in the album or library, or the Next/Fast-Forward button to see the next photo. Press the Play/Pause button to start a slide show (see the "Setting up a slide show" section a little later). Press Menu to return to the photo thumbnails, and press Menu again to return to the Photos menu.

Setting up a slide show

Slide shows are a far more entertaining way of showing photos because you can include music as well as transitions between photos. You can display your slide show on the iPod or iPhone, or on a television. Your slide show settings work with any photo album (or with the entire photo library) on your iPod.

To find out how to connect your iPod or iPhone to televisions, stereos, video monitors, and video equipment, visit this book's companion Web site.

To set up a slide show with an iPod classic or iPod nano (or fifth-generation iPod with color display), follow these steps:

1. **Choose Photos from the main menu and then choose Settings from the Photos menu. (On fifth-generation iPods, choose Slideshow Settings.)**

2. **Choose Times per Slide from the Settings menu to set the duration of each slide.**

   You can select ranges from 2 to 20 seconds. Or, you can select Manual to set the slide show to advance to the next slide when you click the Next/Fast-Forward button

3. **Pick your music by choosing Music from the Settings menu and then choose a playlist.**

   You can choose any playlist in your iPod for your slide show, including On-The-Go or Now Playing. iPhoto lets you assign an iTunes playlist to an iPhoto album, and that assignment is saved in your iPod. If you copy the playlist to your iPod, it's automatically assigned to the slide show.

4. **Select a transition to use between photos in the slide show by choosing Transitions from the Settings menu.**

   Wipe Across is my favorite, but you can select Cross Fade, Fade To Black, Zoom Out, or Wipe Center. Choose Random if you want to use a different (and random) transition for each photo change. Choose Off for no transition. After you choose a transition, the Settings menu appears again.

5. **Set the iPod to display the slide show by choosing TV Out from the Settings menu.**

   You have three choices for TV Out:

   - *On* displays the slide show on a television. While the slide show plays on your TV, you can also see the slides as large thumbnails on your iPod, along with the photo number within the album or library, and the Next and Previous icons.

   - *Ask* displays a screen requesting that you select TV Off or TV On; you make the choice each time you play a slide show.

   - *Off* displays the slide show with full-size images on the iPod.

6. **(Optional) Select other preferences from the Settings menu:**

   - *Repeat:* Repeats the slide show.

   - *Shuffle Photos:* Shuffles photos in the slide show in a random order.

   - *TV Signal:* Changes your television signal to PAL (Phase Alternating Line) for European and other countries that use PAL as their video standard. NTSC (National TV Standards Committee, also referred to humorously as "never the same color") is the U.S. standard.

To set up a slide show with an iPod touch or iPhone, follow these steps:

1. **Choose Settings from the Home menu, and then tap Photos in the Settings menu.**

   The Photos Slideshow Settings menu appears on your iPod touch or iPhone.

2. **Touch the Play Each Slide For option to set the duration of each slide.**

   You can select ranges from 2 to 20 seconds.

3. **Touch the Transition option to pick a transition to use between photos in the slide show.**

   Wipe Across is my favorite, but you can select Cube, Dissolve, Ripple, or Wipe Down. Touch the Photos button to return to the Photos Slideshow Settings menu.

4. **Select other preferences as appropriate for your slide show:**

   - *Repeat:* Repeats the slide show.

   - *Shuffle:* Shuffles photos in the slide show in a random order.

5. **Touch the Settings button to return to the Settings menu, or press the menu button to return to the Home menu.**

To set your iPhone or iPod touch to display properly on a television, choose Settings from the Home menu and choose iPod in the Settings menu of your iPhone, or Video in the Settings menu of your iPod touch. You can then turn Widescreen format on or off (depending on your television), and change your TV signal to PAL (Phase Alternating Line) for European and other countries that use PAL as their video standard. NTSC (National TV Standards Committee) is the U.S. standard and set by default.

Playing a slide show

To play a slide show, follow these steps:

1. **On your iPod or iPhone, choose Photos from the main or Home menu.**

2. **Choose an album in the Photos menu, or choose Photo Library on an iPod touch or iPhone, or All Photos on an iPod classic or iPod nano.**

   Choosing All Photos or Photo Library includes the entire library in the slide show; choosing an album includes only the photos in that album.

3. **To start the show, press the Play/Pause button on an iPod classic or iPod nano (or older iPod), or touch the Play/Pause button at the bottom of the thumbnail display on an iPod touch or iPhone.**

   You can also start a slide show when viewing a single photo by pressing the Select button on an iPod classic or iPod nano, or by touching the Play/Pause button on an iPod touch or iPhone.

4. **If you previously set TV Out to Ask (as described in "Setting up a slide show" in this section), choose TV On or TV Off for your slide show.**

   • *TV On* displays the slide show on a television (through the video-out connection). You can also see the slides as large thumbnails on the iPod.

   TV Off displays the slide show with full-size images on the iPod.

5. **Use the playback buttons on your iPod or iPhone to navigate your slide show.**

   If you set Time per Slide to Manual, press (or touch) Next/Fast-Forward to move to the next photo and press (or touch) Previous/Rewind to return to the previous photo.

   If you set Time per Slide to a specific duration, use Play/Pause to pause and play the slide show.

6. **Press the Menu or Home button to stop the slide show.**

   On an iPod classic or iPod nano (or older iPod), pressing the Menu button returns you to the Photos menu. On an iPod touch or iPhone, the Home button returns you to the Home menu. You can also stop a slide show on an iPod touch or iPhone by touching outside the photo image.

Creating an On-The-Go Playlist

If you don't want to hear the iTunes playlists already in your iPod or iPhone (or if you haven't created playlists yet), you can create temporary — *On-The-Go* — playlists (not available in first- and second-generation iPods). You can create one or more lists of songs, entire albums, podcast episodes, audio books, and videos to play in a certain order, queuing the items right on the iPod or iPhone. This option is particularly useful for picking songs to play right before driving a car. (Hel-*lo!* You shouldn't be messing with your iPod while driving.)

Queued items that you select appear automatically in a playlist, appropriately called *On-The-Go,* on the Playlists menu. (To navigate the Playlists menu, see the earlier section, "By playlist.") This temporary playlist remains defined in your iPod or iPhone until you delete it or save it as a new playlist. If you synchronize your iPod or iPhone with new music and playlists, the On-The-Go playlist is copied to your iTunes library and cleared automatically. You can also save any new playlist you create on your iPod or iPhone in your iTunes library.

Selecting and playing items in an On-The-Go playlist

To select and then play items in your On-The-Go playlist, follow these steps for an iPod classic, iPod nano, or older iPod:

1. **Locate and highlight a song, album title, or audio book.**

2. **Press and hold the Select button until the menu appears, and choose Add To On-The-Go. On older models, press and hold Select until the title flashes.**

3. **Repeat Steps 1 and 2, adding items in the order you want them played.**

   You can continue to add items to the list of queued items in the On-The-Go playlist at any time. Your iPod keeps track of the On-The-Go playlist until you clear it, save it, or synchronize your iPod.

4. **To play the On-The-Go playlist, scroll the Music menu until Playlists is highlighted and then press the Select button.**

5. **On the Playlists menu that appears, scroll to highlight On-The-Go, and press the Select button.**

   A list of songs in the On-The-Go playlist appears.

6. **Select a song from the list and press the Select button.**

   The songs in the playlist are in *playlist order* (the order you added them). Scroll up or down the list to highlight the song you want, and press the Select button to play the playlist starting from that song.

If you happen to have an iPod touch or iPhone on you, follow these steps to select and then play items in your On-The-Go playlist:

1. **Choose Music from the iPod touch menu or iPod from the iPhone menu.**

   The Music menu appears with the Playlists and other touch buttons along the bottom of the display.

2. **Touch the Playlists button and choose On-The-Go from the Playlists list.**

   The Songs list appears with a plus (+) sign next to each song, as well as an Add All Songs option at the top. If you have only several dozen albums, this list is not too long and you can skip to Step 4, but if you have a lot more music, narrow your search with Step 3.

3. **(Optional) Touch Playlists, Artists, Songs, or More to narrow your search for songs to add to the On-The-Go playlist.**

   Touch the Playlists button to select songs from playlists; or the Artists button to browse artists to select songs; or the More button to select songs from albums or compilations, to browse by genre, or to select audio books or podcast episodes.

4. **Tap the plus (+) sign next to a song you want to add to the On-The-Go playlist, or tap the plus sign next to Add All Albums to add all the albums of an artist found in Step 3.**

   As you tap the plus sign for a song, that song is included in the On-The-Go playlist, and turns gray in the list so that you know it has already been selected. You can choose Add All Albums as an alternative if you want to add all the songs for a particular artist — first browse for that artist in Step 3.

5. **Repeat Steps 3 and 4, adding songs in the order you want them played.**

   You can continue to add songs to the list. Your iPod touch or iPhone keeps track of the On-The-Go playlist until you clear it or synchronize your iPod or iPhone.

6. **Touch the Done button when finished adding songs.**

   The Done button appears in the upper-right corner while you select songs, just waiting for you to finish. After touching Done, you return to the list of songs in the On-The-Go playlist.

7. **To play the On-The-Go playlist, touch any song to start.**

The songs in the playlist are in *playlist order* (the order you added them). Scroll up or down the list to choose a song, and touch the song title to play the playlist starting from that song. You can choose Shuffle to shuffle the songs in the playlist.

You can also add entire playlists, entire albums, or everything by an artist to the On-The-Go playlist on an iPod touch or iPhone. In Step 4, touch the the Playlists, Artists, or More button followed by the Albums selection to show one of those menus, and then select a playlist, album, or artist, and touch All Songs at the top of the list of song selections.

Deleting items from an On-The-Go playlist

To delete an item from an On-The-Go playlist in your iPod classic or iPod nano, follow these steps:

1. **Select the On-The-Go playlist.**

If you don't see the iPod main menu, repeatedly press the Menu button to return to the main menu. Choose Music from the main menu, scroll the Music menu until Playlists is highlighted, and then press the Select button. The Playlists menu appears. Scroll to On-The-Go, and press the Select button, and the list of items in the playlist appears.

2. **Locate and highlight the item you want to delete.**

3. **Press and hold the Select button until the menu appears, and choose Remove From On-The-Go. On older models, press and hold Select until the title flashes.**

4. **Repeat Steps 2 and 3 for each item you want to delete from the playlist.**

When you delete items, they disappear from the On-The-Go playlist one by one. The items are still in your iPod; only the playlist is cleared.

To delete an item from an On-The-Go playlist in your iPod touch or iPhone, follow these steps:

1. **Choose Music from the iPod touch Home menu or iPod from the iPhone Home menu.**

The Music menu appears with the Playlists and other touch buttons along the bottom of the display.

2. **Touch the Playlists button and choose On-The-Go from the Playlists list.**

The list of items in the playlist appears.

3. **Touch the Edit button in the upper-right corner of the display.**

   Circled minus (–) signs appear in front of each song title.

4. **Scroll the list to find the item you want to delete.**

5. **Touch the minus (–) sign next to the song to delete; then touch the Delete button.**

   The red Delete touch button appears after you touch the circled minus sign.

6. **Repeat Steps 4 and 5 to find and delete each item from the playlist.**

   When you delete items, they disappear from the On-The-Go playlist one by one. The items are still in your iPod; only the playlist is cleared.

Clearing an On-The-Go playlist

To clear the list of queued items in an On-The-Go playlist, follow these steps:

1. **Select the On-The-Go playlist.**

   See the earlier section, "Deleting items from an On-The-Go playlist," for instructions on how to select it.

2. **On an iPod classic or iPod nano (or older iPod), select Clear Playlist in the list of items in the playlist. On an iPod touch or iPhone, tap the Edit button in the upper-right corner of the list of items in the playlist, and then tap Clear Playlist.**

   The Clear menu appears, showing the Clear Playlist and Cancel options.

3. **Select the Clear Playlist option.**

   All the items disappear from the On-The-Go playlist. The items are still in your iPod; only the playlist is cleared. If you don't want to clear the playlist, select the Cancel option.

Saving an On-The-Go playlist in your iPod classic or nano

You might want to create more than one On-The-Go playlist in your iPod classic or iPod nano (or older iPod), and temporarily save them for transferring to your iTunes library. To temporarily save your On-The-Go playlist, follow these steps:

1. **Select the On-The-Go playlist.**

   Choose Music from the main menu, scroll the Music menu until Playlists is highlighted, and then press the Select button. The Playlists menu appears. Scroll to the On-The-Go item. Press the Select button, and the list of items in the playlist appears.

2. **Scroll to the Save Playlist item.**

   The Save menu appears, showing the Cancel and Save Playlist items.

3. **Choose Save Playlist.**

   The On-The-Go playlist is saved with the name *New Playlist 1.* (Any subsequent playlists you save are named *New Playlist 2,* and so on.) These appear at the very end of the Playlist menu, not in alphabetical order — just above the On-The-Go Playlist item. If you don't want to save the playlist, select Cancel.

On-The-Go playlists saved as *New Playlist 1, New Playlist 2,* and so on, are stored temporarily in your iPod until you synchronize the iPod with your iTunes library. The On-The-Go playlist is cleared each time you save it as a new playlist, so you can start creating another On-The-Go playlist.

The synchronization also places the newly created playlists on your iPod classic, nano, or fifth-generation iPod. ***Hint:*** They'll be in alphabetical order on the Playlist menu, named *On-The-Go 1, On-The-Go 2,* and so on. You can then rename them as you wish.

Creating a Genius Playlist in Your iPod or iPhone

Your iPod nano, iPod classic, iPod touch, or iPhone can also be a genius about songs, even when it's not connected to your computer. The Genius button in iTunes (wisely laid out for all to see in Chapter 10) has also been incorporated into these devices to create Genius playlists.

In order for Genius to work, it has to recognize the song you select and you need to have enough songs on your iPod or iPhone that are (basically) similar. As for the mechanics of it all, you do need to set up an account in the iTunes Store if you don't already have one (see Chapter 4), and then turn on the Genius feature as described in Chapter 10. Finally, you have to synchronize your iPod or iPhone as described in Chapter 11 so that the Genius is activated. (You can also add Genius playlists along with other playlists in iTunes to your iPod or iPhone while synching.)

To create a Genius playlist on an iPod touch or iPhone, choose Music from the iPod touch Home menu or iPod from the iPhone Home menu, and follow these steps:

1. **Locate and start playing a song to use as the " base" for your Genius playlist.**

   See "Locating Songs" and "Playing a Song" earlier in this chapter for details. The Now Playing screen appears when the song is playing.

2. **Tap the Now Playing screen to see the control buttons.**

   The iPod touch and iPhone provide touch buttons to control playback. To access these touch buttons, tap underneath the left-arrow button or the album title while a song is playing. The Repeat, Genius, and Shuffle buttons appear underneath the scrubber bar directly below the top row of buttons (refer to Figure 14-2). The Genius button is the atom-looking icon in the center.

3. **Touch the Genius button.**

   The Genius playlist appears, with New and Refresh buttons at the top. You can flick your finger to scroll the list. The genius playlist can be as long as 25 songs. Touch any song to start playing the playlist associated with that song.

4. **(Optional) Refresh the Genius playlist by touching Refresh.**

   Refreshing a playlist changes it to include different songs based on the same song you played (depending on how many similar songs you have in your iPod touch or iPhone).

5. **(Optional) Save the Genius playlist by touching Save in the upper right corner of the screen.**

   The playlist is saved in the playlists section of your iPod touch or iPhone using the title of the song it is based on. You can synchronize this playlist with iTunes automatically (see Chapter 11).

   If you subsequently refresh a saved Genius playlist, the saved playlist is refreshed and you lose the previous version of it.

6. **(Optional) Create a new Genius playlist by touching New, then select a new song to base it on.**

   After touching New, the song list appears for selecting a song. Choose a song, and your iPod touch or iPhone creates a new Genius playlist and starts playing the song, displaying the Now Playing screen.

7. **(Optional) After Step 6, return to the Genius playlist by touching the left-arrow button in the top left corner of the Now Playing screen.**

You can refresh any Genius playlist, whether it was created in iTunes and synced to your iPod touch or iPhone, or created directly on your iPod touch or iPhone. Select the playlist, and touch Edit in the top left corner of the playlist screen, then touch Refresh Playlist (or touch Delete Playlist to delete it, or Cancel to cancel the operation).

To create a Genius playlist on a current iPod nano or iPod classic model, follow these steps:

1. **Locate and start playing a song to use as the " base" for your Genius playlist.**

   See "Locating Songs" and "Playing a Song" earlier in this chapter for details. The Now Playing screen appears when the song is playing.

2. **Press and hold the Select button until a menu appears on top of the Now Playing screen.**

3. **Choose Start Genius and press the Select button.**

   The new Genius playlist appears, with Refresh and Save Playlist at the top of the list. Scroll the list to see all the songs, and select any song to start playing the playlist associated with that song.

4. **(Optional) Refresh the genius playlist by selecting Refresh at the top of the genius playlist.**

   Refreshing a playlist changes it to include different songs based on the same song you played (depending on how many similar songs you have in your iPod).

5. **(Optional) Save the Genius playlist by selecting Save Playlist (under Refresh at the top of the genius playlist).**

   The playlist is saved in the playlists section of your iPod using the title of the song it is based on. You can synchronize this playlist with iTunes automatically (see Chapter 11).

   If you subsequently refresh a saved Genius playlist, the saved playlist is refreshed and you lose the previous version of it.

Playing an iPod shuffle

The *iPod shuffle* is a special iPod with no display or any controls to select specific songs or albums. The idea behind an iPod shuffle is to load it with songs in the order you want them to play (like a long playlist) and then play the songs in that order or in shuffle (random) order.

The current iPod shuffle, shown in its dock in Figure 14-6, offers two switches for controlling power and playback mode as well as the familiar Play/Pause, Previous/Rewind, Next/Fast-Forward, and volume control buttons. (The older iPod shuffle offers one three-position switch on the back for playing songs in order, for shuffling songs, and for turning off the unit. On the older iPod shuffle, the Play in Order position is in the middle of the switch, and the Shuffle position is at the bottom.)

To play songs in the order they were copied, set the position switch to the Play in Order position, which is marked by an icon with arrows in a closed loop. To play songs in random order, set the position switch to the Shuffle position — marked by the crossing arrows icon.

To play songs on a shuffle, press the Play/Pause button. To stop (or pause) playback, press the Play/Pause button again. When you stop playback, the iPod shuffle status light blinks green for a minute.

To navigate through the songs in your iPod shuffle, press the Previous/ Rewind button (skip backward) or the Next/Fast-Forward button (skip forward). Press and hold these buttons to skip more than one song forward or backward (as if you were fast-forwarding or rewinding a tape). You can start a song over by pressing Previous/Rewind while the song is playing.

If you set the position switch to Play in Order, the Previous/Rewind button skips backward, and the Next/Fast-Forward button skips forward in the order the songs were copied to the iPod shuffle. However, if you set the position switch to Shuffle, the playing order is randomized first. Then the Previous/ Rewind button skips backward within the shuffle order, and the Next/Fast-Forward button skips forward within the shuffle order. For example, suppose your iPod shuffle plays the 14th song, then the 5th song, and then the 20th song. In that case, pressing the Previous/Rewind button during the 20th song takes you back to the 5th song, and pressing it again takes you back to the 14th song. From there, pressing the Next/Fast-Forward button skips through the songs in the same order again: the 14th song, the 5th song, and then the 20th song.

To go immediately to the beginning of an iPod shuffle playlist, press the Play/ Pause button three times quickly (within a second).

Power On/Off   Play songs in order/Shuffle

Figure 14-6:
The iPod
shuffle
offers two
switches:
power on/
off, and
play songs
in order/
shuffle.

Adjusting and Limiting the Volume

Because an iPod or iPhone can be quite loud when set to its highest volume, I recommend turning down the volume before using headphones.

To adjust volume for an iPod classic or iPod nano (or older iPod), follow these steps:

1. **Play something on the iPod.**

2. **While the content is playing, change the volume with the scroll wheel.**

   A volume bar appears in the iPod display to guide you. Scroll with your thumb or finger clockwise to increase the volume or counterclockwise to decrease the volume.

To adjust volume for an iPod touch or iPhone, follow these steps:

1. **Play something on the iPod touch or iPhone.**

2. **While the content is playing, touch the lower portion of the display and slide your finger on the volume slider.**

   After touching the lower portion of the display while playing something, the volume slider with a silver knob appears in the iPod touch or iPhone at the bottom of the display underneath the playback controls (refer to Figure 14-2). Slide the knob with your finger to the right to increase the volume, or to the left to decrease the volume.

To adjust the volume of an iPod shuffle, press the Volume Up (+) or Volume Down (–) buttons.

You can also limit the highest volume for your iPod or iPhone to be lower than the actual maximum. This can help protect your hearing while listening to content from sources with different volume levels.

To limit the volume to be lower than the actual maximum volume on an iPod classic or iPod nano, follow these steps:

1. **Choose Settings from the main menu.**

2. **Choose Volume Limit from the Settings menu.**

3. **Scroll the volume bar with the click wheel to limit the volume.**

   A volume bar appears in the iPod display to guide you. Scroll clockwise to increase the volume or counterclockwise to decrease the volume. While you scroll, a triangle below the volume bar indicates the new limit.

4. **Press the Select button to set the limit or press Play/Pause to optionally lock the volume limit.**

   If you press the Select button, you're basically accepting the new limit *without* locking it, which means you get to skip the next step; you're done. If you press the Play/Pause button, though, that means you want to lock this volume limit down, and to do that you need to also do Step 5. Locking the volume limit is useful if you want to prevent others from changing it (such as your children). However, it also means that you have to enter the combination to unlock the iPod (as described in Chapter 18) in order to change the volume limit.

5. **Set the combination lock for locking the volume limit.**

   If you pressed the Play/Pause button to lock the volume limit, your iPod displays the combination lock. For more details about setting your iPod combination lock, see Chapter 18.

To limit the volume to be lower than the actual maximum volume on an iPod touch or iPhone, follow these steps:

1. **Choose Settings from the Home menu.**

2. **Choose iPod from the Settings menu of an iPhone, or Music from the Settings menu of an iPod touch.**

3. **Choose Volume Limit from the iPod Settings (iPhone) or Music Settings (iPod touch) menu.**

   A volume slider appears with a silver knob.

4. **Slide your finger on the volume slider to limit the volume.**

   Slide the knob with your finger to the right to increase the volume, or to the left to decrease the volume. While you slide your finger, a triangle below the slider indicates the new limit.

5. **Touch the iPod button (iPhone) or the left-arrow button (iPod touch) in the upper-left corner of the display to set the limit and return to the previous menu, or touch the Lock Volume Limit button to optionally lock the volume limit.**

   If you accept the new limit without locking it, you get to skip the next step; you're done. The lock is useful for locking the volume limit so others can't change it (such as your children). However, it also means that you have to enter the volume limit code to unlock the iPod touch or iPhone (as I describe in Chapter 18) in order to change the volume limit.

6. **Set the Volume Limit Code for locking the volume limit.**

   If you touched the Lock Volume Limit button to lock the volume limit, your iPod touch or iPhone displays four squares for entering a code number. Touch the calculator-style number pad to type numbers for your code, and be sure to make up a code that you will remember! (If you don't want to enter a code, touch the Cancel button in the upper-left corner.) For more details about locking and unlocking, see Chapter 18.

Chapter 15

Surfin' Safari on the Web

*T*he World Wide Web makes the world go 'round a whole lot faster than ever before. I browse the Web for many different kinds of content and services. It's gotten to the point where I now make travel, restaurant, and entertainment reservations, and purchase everything from music, videos, books and clothing to electronics equipment, garden supplies, groceries, and furniture, all on the Web. I get to track my shipments and purchases, review the latest news, check up on the blogs of my friends and associates, read novels, view slide shows and movies posted on the Internet, and even scan text messages from cell phones — all thanks to the Internet.

And I do all this on my iPhone or my iPod touch, using the Safari browser. I no longer bother with a laptop when I travel, because I have access to all these services all the time — even while riding the Muni bus into downtown San Francisco. In fact, I use Safari on my iPod touch or iPhone to look up the Muni schedule and the useful NextBus Stop Selector (www.nextmuni.com) that lets me choose a bus line so I can see when the next bus is coming. I can also search using Google or Yahoo! — both services are built into Safari, and you can always browse any other search site.

To connect to the Internet, the iPhone can use the 3G and EDGE data services provided by AT&T, as well as any Wi-Fi network connected to the Internet. The iPod touch connects to the Internet through Wi-Fi networks only.

The iPhone and iPod touch can join AirPort and other Wi-Fi networks at home, at work, or at Wi-Fi hotspots around the world. When joined to a Wi-Fi network that's connected to the Internet, the iPhone or iPod touch connects to the Internet automatically whenever you use Mail, Safari, YouTube, Stocks, Maps, Weather, App Store, or iTunes Store.

Choosing a Wi-Fi Network for Your iPod touch or iPhone

An iPod touch needs a Wi-Fi network to get its Internet fix — to connect to the Web, to gather and send e-mail, to connect to the online store, and so on. An iPhone can get its Internet fix through the Edge network offered by AT&T, and an iPhone 3G can also use 3G networks, but Wi-Fi is the preferred, faster method of getting on the Internet.

You can join AirPort Wi-Fi networks or any other standard Wi-Fi networks in offices, homes, and hot spots. Although some public Wi-Fi networks are free, others require signing up with a credit card number, and still others are detected but locked — you can't use them without knowing the password.

The iPod touch and iPhone can detect and automatically acquire a Wi-Fi signal you've used before, or they can detect one or more in the area and present them in a list for you to choose. You can then tap the name of the network to choose it. You can also choose a Wi-Fi network manually by choosing Settings⇨Wi-Fi from the H4ome menu.

When connected to a Wi-Fi network, your iPod touch or iPhone displays the Wi-Fi icon in the status bar at the top of the display, which also indicates the connection strength — the more bars you see, the stronger the connection.

To turn Wi-Fi on or off, choose Settings⇨Wi-Fi from the Home menu to display the Wi-Fi Networks screen, and tap the On button for the Wi-Fi setting to turn it off (tap it again to turn it on). The list of available Wi-Fi networks appears below the Wi-Fi setting. Scroll this list quickly by flicking your finger, or scroll it slowly by dragging up or down, and choose a Wi-Fi network by touching its name.

If a Lock icon appears next to the Wi-Fi network name, it means the network is locked and you need a password. The iPod touch or iPhone displays the Enter Password screen and the on-screen keyboard. Tap out the password using the on-screen keyboard. (For details on how to use the on-screen keyboard, see Chapter 1). Touch Join to join the network or touch Cancel in the upper-right corner to cancel joining.

To join a Wi-Fi network that requires a credit-card sign-in or account log-in, select the network and then use Safari to open the network's Web page. (For more on using Safari, see "Browsing the Web" in this chapter.) The first Web page you see is typically the sign-in or log-in page for the Wi-Fi service. Follow the instructions in Chapter 16 for entering information to open Web pages manually. Your iPod touch or iPhone remembers your Wi-Fi connections and automatically uses one when it detects it within your range. If you have used multiple Wi-Fi networks in the same location, it picks the last one you used.

If your iPod touch or iPhone isn't already connected to Wi-Fi, it's set by default to look for networks and ask whether you want to join them whenever you use something that requires the network (such as Safari, Weather, YouTube, Mail, and so on). You can stop your iPod touch or iPhone from looking and asking: Scroll down to the end of the list of Wi-Fi networks in the Wi-Fi Networks screen, and touch the On button for the Ask to Join Networks option to turn it off. You can still join networks manually, but you won't be interrupted with requests to join networks.

You can also *forget* a network — such as a paid or closed Wi-Fi service that somehow got hold of your iPod touch or iPhone and won't let you move on to other Web pages without typing a password. Choose Settings⇔Wi-Fi from the Home menu and tap the circled right-arrow (>) button next to the selected network's name. The network's information screen appears. Touch the Forget This Network button at the top of the screen so that your iPod touch or iPhone doesn't join it automatically. Then touch the Wi-Fi Networks button at the top-left corner to return to the Wi-Fi Networks screen. You can always select this or other networks manually.

To join a closed network (one that is not listed in the scanned Wi-Fi networks list due to privacy or security settings), you must already know the network name, password, and security type. Choose Settings⇔Wi-Fi from the Home menu, and touch Other at the bottom of the list of networks. The Other Network screen appears, with the name entry field and the on-screen keyboard. Enter the network name using the on-screen keyboard. (For details on using the keyboard, see Chapter 1.) Touch Security to select the type of security the network uses, and then tap Other Network in the top-left corner of the display to return to the Other Network screen. Finally, touch Join to join the network.

Some Wi-Fi networks may require you to enter or adjust additional settings, such as a client ID or static IP address. To change the settings for a network, tap the circled right-arrow (>) button next to the selected network's name. You can choose the IP Address method (DHCP, BootP, or Static) and change other settings, including the IP Address, Subnet Mask, and Router address. You can also tap the Renew Lease button to renew DHCP settings, and choose an HTTP Proxy server (either automatically by URL or manually by specifying the server name and port number). Because these settings are complicated and beyond the scope of this book, ask your network administrator for help.

The iPhone also offers Virtual Private Network (VPN) settings, which allows for private data communications over public networks. Choose Settings⇨ General⇨Network from the Home menu. The Network screen appears. Touch VPN and touch the Off button for the VPN option to turn it on. The Settings screen appears. If you don't know your VPN settings for the server, the account, and the password, or the security settings, ask your network administrator for help. Then touch the Save button in the top-right corner of the display to save your settings (or Cancel in the top-left corner to cancel).

You can also turn the Data Roaming service on or off with an iPhone. This roaming service is useful for foreign access to data services, but should be left off in the U.S. (or the country of the iPhone service's origin) to avoid unnecessary roaming charges. To turn this service on or off, choose Settings⇨General⇨Network from the Home menu and touch the Off button for Data Roaming to turn it on. (Touch it again to turn it off.)

Browsing Web Sites

Safari on the iPhone or iPod touch not only lets you browse through Web sites but also lets you add bookmarks and icons to your Home screen for convenient access (and synchronize those bookmarks with your computer's Web browser, as I describe in Chapter 19).

You can rotate either the iPod touch or iPhone sideways to view Web pages in landscape orientation, and then double-tap to zoom in or out — Safari automatically fits sections of Web pages (such as columns of text) to fill the screen for easy reading. You can spread with two fingers to control the zoom.

Entering Web site addresses

If you've already synchronized your bookmarks from your computer's Web browser, as described in Chapter 19, you probably already have bookmarks you can use to go directly to your favorite pages — see the following section, "Using your bookmarks."

If you don't have any bookmarks yet, don't worry. It's a snap to browse any Web site on the Internet. Just tap out a site's address on your iPhone or iPod touch on-screen keyboard. (For instructions on using the on-screen keyboard, see Chapter 1.) For the blow-by-blow account, check out the following steps:

1. **Touch Safari on your iPod touch or iPhone Home page.**

    Your iPod touch or iPhone displays the last Web page you visited, or a blank page, with the address field at the top.

You can customize the iPod touch or iPhone Home menu screens to include your favorite Web pages. See "Adding Web Clips to Your Home Menu" later in this chapter.

2. **Touch the address field at the top of the screen. (If you don't see the address field, touch the status bar at the top.)**

   The on-screen keyboard appears. Above that is an entry field for searching (with a magnifying glass icon), and above that, an entry field for typing an address.

3. **If the entry field already has an address, touch the circled *x* in the right corner of the field to clear its contents.**

4. **Tap out the letters of the Web page name using the on-screen keyboard.**

   Immediately as you start typing letters, the search entry field disappears, and you see a list of Web addresses in your bookmarks or history list that match, as shown in Figure 15-1. (If you need instructions on how to type using the on-screen keyboard, see Chapter 1.) You can scroll the history list by dragging up and down. If the Web address you want appears, touch it to go directly to the Web page without further ado. Otherwise, keep typing the name, including the extension — the on-screen keyboard includes a ".com" button, next to the Go button, for convenience.

   The address in its full form is known as a URL (Uniform Resource Locator) and usually begins with `http://www.` followed by the name of the Web site (such as `http://www.apple.com`). However, you can leave off the `http://www.` part and just go with the Web site name.

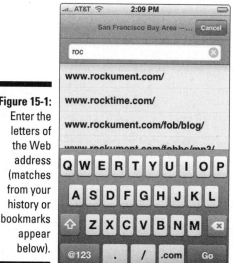

Figure 15-1:
Enter the letters of the Web address (matches from your history or bookmarks appear below).

5. Touch the Go button on the on-screen keyboard (or Cancel to cancel).

The Go button closes the on-screen keyboard, displays the message `Loading` in the status bar, and loads the Web page from the Internet, if the page exists. If you mistyped it, or the page doesn't exist, you get the message `Safari can't open the page because it can't find the server`. Touch OK and start again from Step 2.

To cancel entering a Web site address, touch the Cancel button in the top-right corner of the screen (refer to Figure 15-1).

To stop a Web page from loading if you change your mind, touch the *x* on the right side of the loading address in the iPod touch or iPhone status bar at the top of the display. To reload a Web page to refresh its contents, touch the magnifying glass icon on the left side of the address field in the iPod touch or iPhone status bar at the top of the display.

Using your bookmarks

If you've already synchronized your bookmarks from your computer's own Web browser through iTunes or MobileMe, as described in Chapter 19, or saved bookmarks of pages you already visited using your iPod touch or iPhone, as described in "Saving and Editing Bookmarks" later in this chapter, you can go directly to your favorite bookmarked pages.

Follow these steps:

1. Touch Safari on your iPod touch or iPhone Home page.

Your iPod touch or iPhone displays the last Web page you visited, or a blank page, with a navigation bar sporting various buttons along the bottom, as shown in Figure 15-2.

2. Touch the Bookmarks button — the one that looks like an open book — in the navigation bar.

The Bookmarks screen appears with History and other Bookmark folders. You can scroll this list by dragging up and down.

3. Touch a bookmarks folder to open the folder of bookmarks.

For example, touching Bookmarks Menu opens the folders and bookmarks from Safari on your Mac or from Safari or Microsoft Internet Explorer on your Windows PC. See Chapter 19 for instructions on synchronizing your computer's Web browser bookmarks with your iPhone or iPod touch.

4. Touch a bookmark to load the bookmarked Web page.

Bookmarks folders have a folder icon to the left of their names, and actual bookmarks have an open-page icon next to their Web page names. Touch a folder to reveal its contents and touch a bookmark to load a Web page.

Figure 15-2:
The Safari navigation bar at the bottom offers buttons for navigating Web pages and opening and saving bookmarks.

———— Navigation bar

Searching with Google or Yahoo!

If you've done any Web surfing at all, then you already know all there is to know about search engines. They are simply *the* tool for finding Web sites. Two of the most popular search engines out there — Google and Yahoo! — are built into Safari on your iPhone or iPod touch. Google is set up to be your default search engine, but you can quickly change that. To choose Yahoo! (or to go back to Google), touch Settings⇨Safari⇨Search Engine, and touch Yahoo! or Google. Turning one search engine on turns the other search engine off.

You can always bookmark any search site, including Google, Yahoo!, and many others, and use them by selecting from your bookmarks as described in the "Using your bookmarks" section, earlier in the chapter.

Follow these steps to search with Google or Yahoo!:

1. **Touch Safari on your iPod touch or iPhone Home page.**

   Your iPod touch or iPhone displays the last Web page you visited, or a blank page, with the address field at the top.

2. **Touch the address field at the top of the screen. (If you don't see the address field, touch the status bar at the top.)**

   The on-screen keyboard appears. Above that is the search entry field (with a magnifying glass icon), and above that is an entry field for typing a Web address.

3. **Touch inside the search entry field — the one with the magnifying glass icon next to it.**

4. Tap out the letters of the search term using the on-screen keyboard.

Immediately as you start typing letters, you see a list of bookmarks in your bookmarks folder or history list. You can scroll this list by dragging up and down. If a bookmark appears that satisfies your search, touch it to go directly to the Web page without further ado. Otherwise, keep typing the search term.

5. Touch the Google or Yahoo! button on the on-screen keyboard.

When finished, touch the Google or Yahoo! button at the bottom-right corner of the on-screen keyboard to close the keyboard and display the search results (the Google or Yahoo! button replaces the Go button on the keyboard when searching).

Opening multiple Web pages

Although you can open Web pages one at a time and switch back and forth between them (as I describe later in "Moving to the previous or next page"), you can also open several browsing pages independently of each other, and each separate page can then be the start of an entirely different browsing session.

Some links automatically open a new page instead of replacing the current one, leaving you with multiple pages open. Safari on your iPhone or iPod touch displays the number of open pages inside the Pages button in the right corner of the navigation bar at the bottom of the screen. If there is no number on the button, it means only one page is open.

To open a separate page, touch the Pages button in the navigation bar at the bottom-right corner of the screen; then touch the New Page button. Safari brushes aside the existing page to display a new one. You can then use your bookmarks, enter a Web page address, or search for a Web page. (If you change your mind and don't want to open a new page, touch the Done button to cancel.)

To close a separate page, touch the Pages button in the navigation bar at the bottom-right corner of the screen to display the page thumbnail images, and touch the red circled *x* in the top-left corner of the Web page thumbnail for the page you want to close. The page disappears.

To switch among open pages, touch the Pages button in the navigation bar at the bottom-right corner of the screen to display the page thumbnail images, as shown in Figure 15-3, and flick left or right to scroll the images. When you get to the thumbnail image of the page you want, touch it.

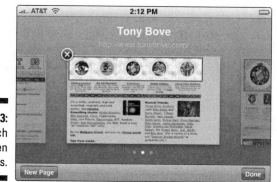

Figure 15-3:
Switch
among open
Web pages.

Sending a Web page address by e-mail

As I describe in Chapter 16, your iPod touch or iPhone can send e-mail as well as receive it. (The iPod touch requires a Wi-Fi connection to do this, while an iPhone can also use 3G or EDGE services from AT&T.) So what if you want to share a Web page you just found with your friend? Simple:

1. **Browse to the Web page and then touch the plus (+) sign in the middle of the navigation bar at the bottom of the Safari display on your iPod touch or iPhone (refer to Figure 15-2).**

   A menu magically pops up from the button with the Add Bookmark, Add to Home Screen, and Mail Link to This Page buttons, along with a Cancel button.

2. **Touch the Mail Link to this Page button.**

   Keep in mind that you must have an e-mail account set up on your iPod touch or iPhone to send e-mail, as I describe in Chapter 16.

   Your iPod touch or iPhone automatically brings up an e-mail message ready to finish composing, with the Subject field already filled out with the Web page name, and the link itself already is inserted in the body of the message. The To and Cc fields are left blank — ready for you to fill in.

3. **Touch the circled plus (+) sign on the right side of the To blank field to select a name from your Contacts list, or use the on-screen keyboard to enter the e-mail address.**

4. **Touch Send at the top-right corner of the display to send the message.**

Navigating by Touch

After you've found the Web page you want, you can navigate its links and play any media it might have to offer. You can also bounce around from previous to next pages in your browsing session, zoom into pages to see them clearly, and scroll around the page to see all of its sections while zooming.

Scrolling and zooming

To zoom into a Web page in Safari, spread two fingers apart on the screen (unpinch). To zoom back out, bring your fingers together (pinch).

You can double-tap the display to zoom into any part of the page. You can also double-tap a column to automatically zoom in so that the column fills the iPhone or iPod touch display. Double-tap again to zoom back out.

To scroll around the page, touch and drag the page. (If you happen to touch a link, drag the link so that you don't follow the link.) You can drag up, down, or sideways to see the entire Web page; or flick your finger up or down to quickly scroll the page. Use two fingers to scroll within the frame on a Web page, or one finger to scroll the entire page.

To jump to the top of a Web page, touch the status bar at the top of the iPod touch or iPhone screen.

All of these gestures work the same way in either portrait or landscape orientation. To view a Web page in landscape orientation, rotate the iPod touch or iPhone sideways. Safari automatically reorients and expands the page. To set it back to portrait, rotate the iPod touch or iPhone again.

Following links and playing media

To follow a link on a Web page, touch the link. Text links are usually underlined (sometimes in blue). Many images are also links you can touch to navigate to another page or use to play media content.

If a link leads to a sound or movie file supported by the iPhone or iPod touch, Safari plays the sound or movie. (See Chapter 14 for instructions on how to play sounds and videos on your iPod touch or iPhone.)

You can see the link's destination — without following it — by touching and holding down on the link until the destination address appears (next to your finger). You can touch and hold an image to see if it has a link.

Moving to the previous or next page

To move to the previous page in your browsing sequence, touch the left-arrow button in the navigation bar at the bottom-left corner of the screen (refer to Figure 15-2). Safari replaces the current page with the previous one. If you have just started browsing and this is the first page, the left-arrow button is grayed out.

To move to the next page, touch the right-arrow button in the navigation bar at the bottom-left corner of the screen to the right of the left-arrow button (refer to Figure 15-2). Safari replaces the current page with the next one in the browsing sequence. This button is grayed out unless you've navigated backward to some previous page.

You can always go back to any of the pages you visited by touching the Bookmarks button in the navigation bar and then touching History. To clear your history list on your iPod touch or iPhone, touch Clear.

Entering information with Web pages

Many Web pages have pop-up menus for entering information. For example, the NextBus Stop Selector site (www.nextmuni.com) offers pop-up menus for selecting the state, the transit agency, and the bus line. To enter information for a pop-up menu, touch the menu. Safari displays a list of options for that pop-up menu. Select an option by touching it; you can also flick to scroll the list of options.

After selecting an option, touch the Done button. You can also touch the Previous or Next buttons to move to the previous or next pop-up menu.

Entering text into a Web site — such as reservation information, passwords, credit card numbers, search terms, and so on — is as easy as touching inside the text field. Safari brings up the on-screen keyboard, as shown in Figure 15-4, and you can type the text.

You can move to the next or previous text field by touching the Next or Previous buttons or by touching inside another text field. To stop typing with the on-screen keyboard without submitting your information, touch the Done button.

Figure 15-4:
Type the
text for a
text field on
a Web page.

After you finish filling out the text fields on the page, touch Go on the on-screen keyboard (or touch Search, which some pages use rather than Go). If the Web page is a form, touching Go automatically submits the form. Some Web pages offer a link for submitting the form, which you must touch in order to finish entering information.

Saving and Editing Bookmarks

The best way to keep track of Web pages you've visited and want to visit again is to set bookmarks for the pages. You can then go immediately back to that page by selecting the bookmark. Your bookmarks in your iPhone or iPod touch synchronize via iTunes with your Safari bookmarks on your Mac, or your Safari or Internet Explorer bookmarks on your PC, as I describe in Chapter 19.

Follow these steps to save a bookmark:

1. **Browse to the Web page you want.**

2. **Touch the plus (+) sign in the middle of the navigation bar.**

   The Add Bookmark, Add to Home Screen, Mail Link to this Page, and Cancel buttons appear on the bottom half of the display.

3. **Touch the Add Bookmark button to add a bookmark.**

   The name of the Web site appears in the title field, ready for editing, along with the on-screen keyboard. Below that is the actual URL for the Web page, and below that, the Bookmarks folder.

4. (Optional) Edit the bookmark's title.

Before saving a bookmark, you can edit its title with the on-screen keyboard. Touch the circled *x* on the right side of the title field to clear its contents, or use the backspace key on the on-screen keyboard to erase backward from the end of the title, and type the new title.

5. (Optional) Choose a bookmark folder.

Before saving a bookmark, you can choose a bookmark folder for saving it; otherwise Safari saves the bookmark in the topmost level of bookmarks. Touch Bookmarks to see the list of bookmark folders — you can flick to scroll the list quickly, or drag it slowly. Select a bookmark folder by touching it.

6. Touch the Save button to save the bookmark, or Cancel to cancel.

The Save button appears in the upper-right corner of the display, and the Cancel button appears in the upper-left corner.

You can also edit your bookmarks and bookmark folders. Touch the Bookmarks button in the navigation bar (refer to Figure 15-2) and choose the folder to edit, or the folder that has the bookmark you want to edit. Then touch the Edit button in the bottom-left corner of the iPod touch or iPhone display. The Edit Bookmarks display appears, with circled minus (–) signs next to the bookmark folders.

You can then do any of the following:

- To make a new folder within the selected folder, touch New Folder. If you want to create a new folder at the topmost level, first touch the Bookmarks button in the upper-left corner to go back to the topmost Bookmarks list, touch the Edit button, and then touch New Folder.

- To delete a bookmark or folder, touch next to the bookmark or folder, then touch Delete.

- To reposition a bookmark or folder, drag next to the item you want to move.

- To edit the name of a bookmark or folder, touch the bookmark or folder, and use the on-screen keyboard to type the new title (touch the circled *x* in the title field to clear its contents first, if you want).

- To change where a bookmark or folder is stored, touch the Bookmark Folder field for the selected bookmark or folder and then touch a new folder to hold the folder chosen for editing.

Touch the Done button in the bottom-left corner of the Edit Bookmarks display to finish editing.

Adding Web Clips to Your Home Menu

You can add Web Clips for your favorite Web pages to the Home menu of your iPod touch or iPhone so that you can access the page with one touch. Web Clips appear as icons along with the other Home menu items.

To discover how to rearrange the buttons and add multiple screens to the Home menu for iPod or iPhone, visit this book's companion Web site.

Follow these steps to add a Web clip to your Home menu:

1. **Browse to the Web page you want.**

2. **Touch the plus (+) sign in the middle of the navigation bar.**

   The Add Bookmark, Add to Home Screen, Mail Link to this Page, and Cancel buttons appear on the bottom half of the display.

3. **Touch the Add to Home Screen button to add a Web clip to your Home menu.**

   The name of the Web site appears in the title field, ready for editing, along with the on-screen keyboard. The icon to be added appears to the left of the title field.

4. **(Optional) Edit the Web clip's title.**

   Before saving a Web clip to the Home screen, you can edit its title with the on-screen keyboard. Touch the circled x on the right side of the title field to clear its contents, or use the backspace key on the on-screen keyboard to erase backward from the end of the title, and type the new title.

5. **Touch the Add button to add the Web clip, or Cancel to cancel.**

   The Add button appears in the upper-right corner of the display, and the Cancel button appears in the upper-left corner.

Chapter 16

Using iPod and iPhone Applications

• •

In This Chapter

▶ Sending and receiving e-mail with your iPod touch or iPhone

▶ Checking your calendar and sorting your contacts

▶ Entering calendar entries, contacts, stocks, and weather locations

▶ Using the Maps program and getting directions

▶ Using the built-in calculator

• •

*L*ooking for friends or business associates? You can look up contact names, addresses, and phone numbers with your iPod or iPhone, and with the iPod touch or iPhone, use the Maps application to find their physical addresses on the map, or send e-mail to their e-mail addresses instantly.

While the iPod classic, iPod nano, and older models run "extras" (in the Extras menu) such as calendars, contacts, and "click-wheel" games, the iPod touch and iPhone can run full-blown applications and games just like a computer. This chapter shows you how to use the calendars and contacts extras on an iPod classic or nano, as well as how to use the Calendar and Contacts applications on an iPod touch or iPhone.

I also cover some iPod touch and iPhone built-in applications that work best when connected to the Internet, such as Mail for sending and receiving e-mail. (You'd use a Wi-Fi network, as described in Chapter 15, with an iPod touch, or you'd use Wi-Fi, EDGE, or 3G networks with an iPhone.) I show you how to personalize the Stocks application to check your financial stocks in real time, and the Weather application to see the temperatures for various locations. This chapter also describes how to use the Maps application to find addresses in your contacts list, or any location at all, and even obtain driving directions — without having to ask someone out on the street.

With iTunes, you can download iPod touch and iPhone applications (including games), and iPod classic and nano "click wheel" games, from the iTunes Store (as described in Chapter 4). You can also use your iPod touch or iPhone to browse the Web and play Web games such as Rubik's Cube, Hangman, Blackjack, and many others available for free on appSafari (`http://appsafari.com`). See Chapter 15 for details on surfing the Web from your iPod touch or iPhone.

To learn how to synchronize your iPod classic or nano with "click wheel" games from the iTunes Store, and to play those games, visit this book's companion Web site. I also explain how to download free and commercial applications and games directly, over a wireless Internet connection, to your iPod touch or iPhone and run them.

Checking Your E-Mail with Your iPod touch or iPhone

With an Internet connection, your e-mail is just a touch away — touch Mail on your iPod touch or iPhone Home menu. You know when you have incoming e-mail because the Mail button shows the number of unread messages in your inboxes.

The Mail application works in the background with the Internet connection, retrieving e-mail without interrupting other things you're doing with your iPod touch or iPhone. Mail can display rich HTML messages, and you can send as well as receive photos and graphics, which are displayed in your message along with the text. You can also receive Portable Document Format (PDF) files, Microsoft Word documents, and Microsoft Excel spreadsheets as attachments and view them on your iPod touch or iPhone.

Mail displays the Accounts menu listing your e-mail accounts that have been synchronized with your iPod touch or iPhone. (See Chapter 19 for details on synchronizing, setting up, deleting, and changing settings for e-mail accounts.)

Viewing e-mail

To view incoming e-mail, choose Mail from your iPod touch or iPhone Home menu, touch an account in the Accounts menu and then touch the Inbox in the account's menu of mailboxes. A list of incoming message headers appears, with the sender's name, subject, and the first sentence or two of each message, along with a blue dot if the message hasn't been read yet.

You can also check e-mail at any time by touching the circular arrow button in the bottom-left corner of the account's menu of mailboxes, the list of message headers, or the message itself.

Touch a message header to read the message. You can scroll the message by flicking or dragging your finger, and zoom into and out of the message by un-pinching and pinching with your fingers. You can also zoom directly into a column in the message by double-tapping the message, and zoom out by double-tapping it again.

To delete a message, touch the Trash Can button at the bottom center of the message display. Mail deletes the message from your iPod touch or iPhone (but *not* from your computer or mail server unless it's set up that way; see Chapter 19) and displays the next message in sequence. You can also move to the previous or next message by touching the up and down arrows in the top-left corner. You can also delete a message without opening it. In the list of message headers, drag your finger across a message header and touch the Delete button that appears.

If the e-mail includes an attachment, a down-arrow appears within the message — to attempt to download the attachment, touch the down-arrow. If the format of the attached file is one of the supported formats (which include files that have the extensions .doc, .docx, .htm, .html, .pdf, .txt, .xls, or .xlsx), Mail downloads and opens the attachment; if not, Mail displays a document icon with the name of the file — but you can't open it.

You can see all the recipients of a message (except bcc or blind carbon copy recipients) by opening the message and touching the blue word "Details" in the top-right corner of the message. Touch a name or e-mail address that appears to see the recipient's contact information. Touch Hide to hide the recipients.

You can add the recipient to your contacts list on your iPod touch or iPhone by touching the name or e-mail address and then touching Create New Contact (or Add to Existing Contact if you want to add the information to an existing contact). Touch the Email button to send an e-mail to that recipient's address. (See the "Sending e-mail" section, later in this chapter.)

You can also follow links in a message, which are usually underlined in blue, and images embedded in the message may also have links. A link can take you to a Web page in Safari, open a map in Maps, or open a new pread-dressed e-mail message in Mail. To return to your e-mail, press the Home button and touch Mail.

You can manage your e-mail messages so that they stick around in your mailbox while others are deleted the next time you synchronize. For example, you can move messages you want to keep to another mailbox by opening the message and tapping the folder icon at the bottom of the message display and then choosing a mailbox. You can also mark a message as unread so that it stays in your Inbox — open the message and touch the blue "Mark as Unread" text next to the blue dot inside the message. The message is marked as unread — a blue dot appears next to the message header in the mailbox list until you open it again.

Sending e-mail

You can use the Mail application to send e-mail to any e-mail address in the world. You can even send a message to a group of people without having to select each person's e-mail address. You can also reply to any message instantly.

To send an e-mail, follow these steps:

1. **Choose Mail from the Home menu.**

   The Accounts menu appears.

2. **(Optional) Choose an e-mail account from the the Accounts menu's accounts listing for sending the e-mail.**

   You can skip this step and use the default account for sending e-mail, or defer the decision until Step 6.

3. **Touch the pencil-document icon in the lower-right corner of the Mail screen.**

   The New Message screen appears, as shown in Figure 16-1, along with the on-screen keyboard.

4. **Enter the recipient's e-mail address in the To field.**

   If your recipient is listed in your Contacts on your iPod touch or iPhone, tap the circled plus (+) sign in the To field entry (refer to Figure 16-1) and choose a contact to add the contact's e-mail address to the To field. You can repeat this process to add multiple e-mail addresses to the To field from your contacts.

Figure 16-1:
Enter the recipient's e-mail address and the subject with the on-screen keyboard.

If your recipient isn't listed in your Contacts or if you don't know whether it is listed or not, touch the To field entry and use the on-screen keyboard to type one or more e-mail addresses (use a comma to separate each address). As you type an e-mail address, e-mail addresses that match from your Contacts list appear below. Touch one to add it to the To field.

5. **(Optional) Add more addresses to the Cc or Bcc fields.**

   You can add e-mail addresses to the Cc (carbon copy) and Bcc (blind carbon copy) fields to copy others. While Cc addresses appear on messages received by recipients indicating that they were copied on the message, Bcc addresses don't appear on messages received by recipients. Touch the Cc/Bcc letters to expand the message to include the Cc and Bcc fields; then enter addresses the same way as Step 4.

6. **(Optional) Change the From: address.**

   You can change the e-mail address for the sender to one of your e-mail accounts. The default e-mail account for sending e-mail is already selected; touch the From: letters to display a pop-up menu of e-mail accounts, and then touch an e-mail account to use as the sender's account.

7. **Enter the e-mail subject.**

   Touch the Subject entry field (refer to Figure 16-1) to type a subject with the on-screen keyboard; then touch underneath the Subject field to type a message. Press Return on the on-screen keyboard when finished.

8. **Touch Send in the upper-right corner of the display (refer to Figure 16-1) to send the message.**

To save a message as a draft so you can work on it later, start typing the message as described in the preceding steps, but before touching Send, touch Cancel in the upper-left corner of the display (refer to Figure 16-1). Then touch the Save button to save the message in your Drafts mailbox or touch Don't Save to discard the message (or Cancel to go back to typing the message). You can find the saved message in the Drafts mailbox of the same e-mail account, and touch it to add to it or change it, and then send it.

To send a photo in a message, choose Photos from the Home menu and choose a photo for viewing, as described in Chapter 14. Then touch the button that looks like a curved right arrow in a picture frame, right there in the lower-left corner of the photo display along with the other slideshow controls. (Tap the photo if the controls disappear.) You can then touch the Email Photo button to e-mail the photo.

You can also forward and reply to any message you receive. Open the message and touch the curled left-arrow button that appears in the bottom left side of the message display. Then touch Reply to reply to the sender of the message, Reply All to reply to all of the recipients as well as the sender (if there are other recipients), or Forward to forward the message to someone else (or Cancel to go back to the message). The New Message screen appears with the on-screen keyboard, so that you can type your reply or add a message to the one you are forwarding. Touch Send to send the reply or forwarded message.

When you reply to a message, files or images attached to the initial message aren't sent with the reply.

Changing e-mail message settings and sending options

To change your e-mail message settings and sending options, choose Settings⇨Mail, Contacts, Calendars from the Home menu of your iPod touch or iPhone. In the Mail, Contacts, Calendars settings screen that appears, use your finger to scroll down to the Mail section to change your e-mail message options and sending options.

In the Mail section of the Mail, Contacts, Calendars settings screen, you can change global settings for messages in all accounts. To set the number of messages you can see at once, touch Show, and then choose a setting. You can choose to see the most recent 25, 50, 75,100, or 200 messages. (To download additional messages when you're in Mail, scroll to the bottom of your inbox and tap Download More.) You can also set how many lines of each message are previewed in the message list headers. Choose Preview, and then choose to see any amount from zero to five lines of each message. To set a minimum font size for messages, touch Minimum Font Size and then choose Small, Medium, Large, Extra Large, or Giant.

You can also set whether Mail shows the To and Cc labels in message lists so that you can determine in advance whether the message was sent directly to you, or whether you were sent it as a Cc copy (which still might make it important, but at least you know). Touch the Show To/Cc Label Off button to turn it on. (Touch it again to turn it off.) If Show To/Cc Label is on, you see To or Cc in the list next to each message.

If you think you have shaky fingers and might delete a message by mistake, you can set Mail to confirm that you want to delete a message first before deleting. Touch the Off button to turn on the Ask Before Deleting option in the Mail section of the Mail, Contacts, Calendars settings screen (touch it again to turn it off). If Ask Before Deleting is on, Mail warns you first when you delete a message, and you must touch Delete to confirm the deletion.

For those of us who are obsessive about making sure e-mails are sent — and we know who we are — Mail can send a copy of every message you send. Touch the Off button to turn on the Always Bcc Myself option (touch it again to turn it off). The Bcc refers to *b*lind *c*arbon *c*opy, and it means that your message is sent and copied back to you without your e-mail address appearing in the recipient's list.

You can add a signature to your messages that can include any text — your name, title, phone number, favorite quote, or all of these — to personalize your e-mails. Touch Signature, and then type a signature with the on-screen keyboard. The signature remains in effect for all future e-mails sent from your iPod touch or iPhone.

To set the default e-mail account for sending messages, touch Default Account, and then choose an e-mail account. Your iPod touch or iPhone will use this account whenever you start the process of sending a message from another application, such as sending a photo from Photos or touching the e-mail address of a business in Maps.

For details on synchronizing e-mail accounts automatically from iTunes or MobileMe, as well as for setting up, changing account settings, and deleting accounts manually on your iPod touch or iPhone, see Chapter 19.

Using Your Calendars

Your iPod or iPhone can display calendars from calendar applications, such as iCal (Mac) or Outlook (Windows). If you haven't synchronized your iPod or iPhone with your calendar files (as I describe in Chapter 19), you see a blank calendar.

Using Calendar on an iPod touch or iPhone

Choose Calendar from the Home menu on an iPhone or iPod touch. Your iPhone or iPod touch displays the Calendars screen with a list of synchronized calendars. Touch All at the top for choosing to view all calendars merged into one, or touch a specific calendar to see only that calendar. The iPod touch or iPhone displays the calendar in a monthly view.

Touch the Today button in the lower-left corner of the display to see the calendar for today. Touch the List, Day, or Month buttons to change the calendar view to a list of events, a full day of scheduled appointments, or a month view, respectively. Touch any day to see the events on that day, and touch the plus (+) button in the upper-right corner of the display to add a new event (see "Adding Information Manually with Your iPod touch or iPhone" in this chapter).

Checking your calendars on an iPod classic or nano

Choose Extras⇨Calendars on an iPod classic, iPod nano, or older iPod. You can choose a specific calendar by name or choose All for a merged view of all your calendars. Select a calendar and then scroll the click wheel to go through the days of the calendar. Select an event to see its details. Press the Next and Previous buttons to skip to the next or previous month. To see your To-Do list, choose Extras⇨Calendars⇨To Do's.

If your calendar events use alarms, you can turn on your iPod classic or iPod nano calendar alarms. Choose Extras⇨Calendars⇨Alarms. Select Alarms once to set the alarm to Beep, select Alarms twice to set it to None (so that only the message for the alarm appears), or select it a third time to set it to Off. (The Alarms choices cycle from Beep to None to Off and then back to Beep.)

Calendars on your iPod or iPhone are far more useful if you synchronize your personal information; turn to Chapter 19 to see how.

Using Your Contacts

The bits of information that you're most likely to need on the road are phone numbers and addresses. An iPod or iPhone can store that stuff (in a Contacts format) right alongside your music. To see how to sync your personal contacts info on your computer with the info on your iPod or iPhone, check out Chapter 19.

Using Contacts on an iPod touch or iPhone

To view contacts on an iPod touch or iPhone, choose Contacts from the Home menu. If you have organized contacts into groups, touch a group or touch All Contacts, and then scroll the list of contacts with your finger, or touch a letter of the alphabet along the right side to go directly to names that begin with that letter. Then touch a contact.

You can also view contacts on an iPhone when making or receiving a call or checking voice-mail. Choose Phone and touch Contacts at the bottom of the screen.

The contact list is sorted automatically in alphabetical order by first name and then last name, or by last name followed by first name. You can change which way the contacts sort so that you don't have to look up people by their first names (which can be time-consuming with so many friends named Elvis). Choose Settings⇨Mail, Contacts, Calendars, and then scroll the Mail, Contacts, Calendars settings screen to the Contacts section. Choose Sort Order, and then touch one of these options:

- ✔ **First, Last:** Sorts the contact list by first name, followed by the last name, so that *Mick Jagger* sorts under *Mick* (after *Mick Abrahams* but before *Mick Taylor*).

- ✔ **Last, First:** Sorts the contacts by last name, followed by the first name, so that *Brian Jones* sorts under *Jones.* (*Jones, Brian* appears after *Jones, Alice* but before *Jones, Norah.*)

You can also display contacts with their first names followed by their last names, or last names followed by first names, regardless of how you sort them. Choose Settings⇨Mail, Contacts, Calendars, and then scroll the Mail, Contacts, Calendars settings screen to the Contacts section. Choose Display Order, and then touch one of these options:

- ✔ **First Last:** Displays the contacts list by first name and then last name, as in *Ringo Starr.*

- ✔ **Last, First:** Displays the contacts list by last name followed by a comma and the first name, as in *McCartney, Paul.*

Viewing and sorting your contacts on an iPod classic or nano

To view a contact on an iPod classic, iPod nano, or older iPod, choose Extras⇨ Contacts from the main menu. You can then scroll the list of contacts with the click wheel and select a contact by pressing the Select button.

The contact list is sorted automatically in alphabetical order by first name and then last name, or by last name followed by first name. You can change which way the contacts sort so that you don't have to look up people by their first names. Choose Settings⇨Sort By (or on fifth-generation and older iPods, choose Settings⇨Contacts⇨Sort), and then press the Select button in the scrolling pad for each option:

- ✔ **First (First Last on older iPods):** Sorts the contact list by first name, followed by the last name.

- ✔ **Last (Last, First on older iPods):** Sorts the contacts by last name, followed by the first name.

Adding Information Manually with Your iPod touch or iPhone

One of the major benefits of using an iPod touch or iPhone is the on-screen keyboard, which you can use to enter text, such as contact information and calendar entries. (For details on how to use the on-screen keyboard, see Chapter 1.) You can also use a combination of touch buttons and the on-screen keyboard to enter other personal information, such as your stocks for the Stocks application and your locations for the Weather application.

Entering calendar entries

While you can enter appointments and events on your computer and sync them with your iPod or iPhone, as described in Chapter 19, you can also enter appointments and events directly to the calendar in your iPod touch or iPhone, and sync them back to your computer.

To add an event, follow these steps:

1. **Choose Calendar from the Home menu on an iPhone or iPod touch.**

2. **Touch the plus (+) sign in the upper-right corner of the Calendar display.**

3. **Touch the Title and Location button and enter the event's title and location using the on-screen keyboard.**

   The Title and Location fields appear along with the on-screen keyboard.

4. **Touch Save in the upper-right corner to save the entry (or Cancel in the upper-left corner to cancel the entry).**

   The Add Event screen appears again for selecting more options.

5. **Touch the Starts Ends button and enter the starting and ending times and dates.**

   The Start & End screen appears with a slot-machine-style number wheel to select the date and time.

6. **Touch the Starts button and select the date and time or touch the Off button for All-Day to turn on the All-Day option.**

   Slide your finger up and down the slot-machine-style number wheel to select the date and time. If you turn on the All-Day option, the number wheel changes to show only dates; select a date for the all-day event and skip the next step.

7. **Touch the Ends button and select the date and time.**

8. **Touch Save in the upper-right corner to save the entry (or Cancel in the upper-left corner to cancel the entry).**

   The Add Event screen appears again for selecting more options.

9. **(Optional) Set the event to repeat by touching Repeat and selecting a repeat time, and touch Save (or Cancel).**

   You can set the event to repeat every day, every week, every two weeks, every month, or every year (or none, to not repeat). Touch Save in the upper-right corner to save the entry (or Cancel in the upper-left corner to cancel the entry). The Add Event screen appears again for selecting more options.

10. **(Optional) Set an alert for a time before the event by touching Alert and choosing an alert time, and touch Save (or Cancel).**

    You can set the alert to occur from five minutes to two days before the event. You can also set a second alert time in case you miss the first one. Touch Save in the upper-right corner to save the entry (or Cancel in the upper-left corner to cancel the entry). The Add Event screen appears again for selecting more options.

11. **(Optional) Enter notes about the event by touching Notes and using the on-screen keyboard to type notes.**

    The Notes field appears along with the on-screen keyboard. Type your notes, and then touch Save in the upper-right corner to save the notes (or Cancel in the upper-left corner to cancel the notes). The Add Event screen appears again for changing event options.

12. **Touch Done in the upper-right corner of the Add Event screen to save the event (or Cancel in the upper-left corner to cancel the event).**

To edit an event, touch the event in the calendar, and touch Edit in the upper-right corner of the Event screen. To delete an event, touch Edit, scroll down to the bottom, and then touch Delete Event.

You can set your iPod touch or iPhone to play a sound for your calendar alert. On an iPod touch, choose Settings➪General ➪Sound Effects, and then select the internal speaker, headphones, or both, for playing the sound. Select Off to turn sound effects off. If the Sound Effects option is off, your iPod touch displays a message for your calendar alerts. On an iPhone, choose Settings➪Sounds, scroll down through the Ring section of options, and touch the Off button for Calendar Alerts to turn it on (touch it again to turn it off). Your iPhone uses your set ringtone and vibrate setting for calendar alerts.

Entering contacts

You meet people all the time, so why not enter their information immediately? You can enter new contacts on your iPod touch or iPhone, edit existing contacts, and even delete contacts. If you've set iTunes to sync contacts as described in Chapter 19, iTunes automatically keeps your contacts up to date if you make changes on your iPod touch or iPhone.

To add a contact, follow these steps:

1. **Choose Contacts from the Home menu.**

2. **Touch the plus (+) sign in the upper-right corner of the Contacts display to show the New Contact screen.**

3. **Touch the First Last button and enter the contact's first and last name, as well as the company name, using the on-screen keyboard.**

   The First, Last, and Company fields appear in the Edit Name screen along with the on-screen keyboard.

4. **Touch Save in the upper-right corner of the Edit Name screen to save the name (or Cancel in the upper-left corner to cancel the name).**

   The New Contact screen appears again for selecting more options.

5. **Touch the Add New Phone button and enter the phone number and label for the number.**

   The Edit Phone screen appears with a numeric keyboard for typing the number. Touch the field under the number to select a label for the type of phone (mobile, home, work, main, home fax, etc.). To enter a pause in a phone number (sometimes required for extensions or code numbers), touch the +*# button and touch Pause, which inserts a comma representing the pause. Each pause lasts two seconds; you can enter as many as you need.

6. **Touch Save in the upper-right corner of the Edit Phone screen to save the phone number (or Cancel in the upper-left corner to cancel the entry).**

   The New Contact screen appears again for adding more information.

7. **(Optional) On an iPhone, select a ringtone for this contact by touching Ringtone and selecting a ringtone. Then touch New Contact to return to the New Contact screen.**

8. **Touch the Add New Email button to add an e-mail address using the on-screen keyboard and select a label for the type of e-mail address.**

   The Edit Email screen appears with a field to enter the information, a button to set the label describing it, and the on-screen keyboard.

9. **Touch Save in the upper-right corner to save the entry (or Cancel in the upper-left corner to cancel the entry).**

   The New Contact screen appears again for adding more information.

10. **(Optional) Repeat Steps 8 and 9 with the Add New URL button to add a new URL (Web site address) for the contact.**

11. **Touch Add New Address on the New Contact screen, and add street (or P.O. Box) information, city, state, ZIP, and country.**

   The on-screen keyboard appears with two entry fields for Street and one each for City, State, and Zip. Touch the country button to set the country, and the label button (set to home) for the type of address.

12. **Touch Save in the upper-right corner to save the address (or Cancel in the upper-left corner to cancel it).**

   The New Contact screen appears again for adding more information.

13. **(Optional) Touch Add Field to add more fields to the contact.**

   You can add a prefix, middle name, suffix, phonetic first and last names, nickname, job title, department, birthday, date, or note. Touch each field, and use the on-screen keyboard to type in the information. Then touch Save in the upper-right corner to save the field (or Cancel in the upper-left corner to cancel it).

14. **(Optional) Add a photo or change the photo by touching Add Photo or the existing photo in the upper-left corner of the New Contact screen, and choosing a photo.**

   On an iPhone, touch Choose Existing Photo (or Cancel), and then choose a photo album and photo, and touch Set Photo (or Cancel). With an iPhone you can also choose Take Photo and take the photograph using the iPhone's built-in camera.

   On an iPod touch, choose the photo album and then choose a photo, then touch Set Photo (or Cancel).

15. **Touch Save in the upper-right corner of the New Contact screen to save the contact information (or Cancel in the upper-left corner to cancel the contact information).**

To edit a contact, touch the contact to see the contact information, and touch Edit in the upper-right corner of the Info screen. You can edit or delete any information for a contact while leaving the rest of the information intact. Touch any field to edit the information in that field. Touch the circled minus (–) sign next to the information to reveal a Delete button; touch the Delete button to delete the information, or touch the circled minus sign again to leave it alone. Touch Done in the upper-right corner of the Info screen (when editing) to finish editing and return to the contact information.

To delete a contact in its entirety, touch Edit, scroll down to the bottom, and then touch Delete Contact. Remember, if you do this, the contact will also be deleted from your contact list on your computer when you sync your iPod touch or iPhone.

Entering stocks and weather locations

You can check your financial stocks in real time with your iPod touch or iPhone connected to the Internet, and with an iPhone you can call your broker immediately. With either device, you can visit your broker's Web site to make a transaction or e-mail your broker.

To see your stock portfolio on your iPod touch or iPhone, choose Stocks from the Home menu. The stock reader shows updated quotes every time you open Stocks while connected to the Internet, but quotes may be delayed by up to 20 minutes.

To add a stock, index, or fund to watch, touch the *i* button in the lower-right corner of the stock reader, and then tap the plus (+) sign in the upper-left corner of the Stocks screen. The Add Stock field appears with the on-screen keyboard. Enter the stock symbol or company name (or index or fund name) — as you type, suggestions appear below in a list. Choose one of the suggestions or continue typing the symbol or name and then touch Search.

The stock you chose appears in the list of stocks in the Stocks screen, with a circled minus (–) sign next to it on the left, and three horizontal gray I-Ching-looking bars on the right. You can add more stocks by touching the plus (+) sign in the upper-left corner again. You can reorder a list of stocks by dragging the I-Ching-looking bars next to a stock to a new place in the list. To delete a stock, touch the circled minus sign next to the stock name to show the Delete button, and touch the Delete button, or touch the circled minus sign again to leave it alone.

Touch the Done button in the top-right corner of the Stocks screen to finish adding stocks and see the stock reader.

To see your stock prices and amount (or percent) of change, scroll the list in the stock reader with your finger. To see a current graph of the stock, touch the 1d (one day), 1w (one week), 1m (one month), 3m (three months), 6m (six months), 1y (one year), or 2y (two years) buttons above the graph in the stock reader. To switch between showing percentage change and change in monetary value, touch the number showing the change (touch it again to switch back).

Your iPod touch or iPhone also offers a Weather application that looks up the current temperature and provides a six-day forecast for any city of your choice — choose Weather from the Home menu. In daytime, the weather screen is light blue, and at night it's dark purple. What makes Weather useful is your ability to add your own cities — as many as you need — so that you can look up the weather in multiple locations instantly.

To add a city, touch the *i* button in the lower-right corner of the weather display for your city, and then tap the plus (+) sign in the upper-left corner of the Weather screen. A location field appears with the on-screen keyboard. Enter the city's name or ZIP — as you type, suggestions appear below in a list. Choose one of the suggestions or continue typing the city name or ZIP and then touch Search.

The city you chose appears in the list of cities in the Weather screen, with a circled minus (–) sign next to it on the left, and three horizontal gray I-Ching-looking bars on the right. You can add more cities by touching the plus (+) sign in the upper-left corner again. You can reorder a list of cities by dragging the I-Ching-looking bars next to a city to a new place in the list. To delete a city, touch the circled minus sign next to the city name to show the Delete button, and touch the Delete button, or touch the circled minus sign again to leave it alone.

Touch the Done button in the top-right corner of the Weather screen to finish adding cities and see the weather display for your city.

To switch from one city to the next, flick your finger over the city weather display horizontally or touch the tiny white buttons at the bottom of the city weather display.

Using Maps on Your iPod touch or iPhone

I once had to find my way to a meeting on a university campus that I was already late for, and, after driving endlessly around the campus looking for the proper entrance street, I touched Maps on my iPhone and was able to immediately look up the location, see a map of it, and get directions. Yes, I pulled over to the curb first for safety.

The Maps application for the iPod touch or iPhone provides street maps, satellite photos, and hybrid street-satellite views of locations all over the world. You not only have detailed driving directions available from any location to any other location, but in some areas, you can also get up-to-the-minute traffic information.

Entering and saving locations

To find a location and see a map, choose Maps from the Home menu, and then touch the Search field at the top of the Maps screen that appears, in order to enter information with the on-screen keyboard. You can type in an address, an intersection, the name of a landmark or of a general area, the name of someone in your contacts list, or a ZIP code, and then touch Search. Or you can touch the Bookmarks button in the Search field to bring up a list of bookmarked locations, and touch a location.

You can zoom into the map by double-tapping the map or unpinching with your fingers, and zoom out by pinching or tapping with two fingers. You can also drag the map to pan around it and see more areas.

A pin marks the location you've searched for on the map, as shown in Figure 16-2 (left side), with a label showing the address. Touch the pin — or its label, or the circled right arrow in the label — to see the Info screen, as shown in Figure 16-2 (right side), with the name or description of the location. Touch Add to Bookmarks in the Info screen to save the location in your bookmarks list, which brings up the on-screen keyboard so that you can type a different name for the location. Touch Save in the upper-right corner of the Add Bookmark screen to save the bookmark (or Cancel to cancel the bookmark). Touch Map in the upper-left corner of the Info screen to go back to the map.

You can also touch the pin or its label and then touch Directions To Here or Directions From Here (refer to Figure 16-2, right side) to get directions (see the following section, "Getting directions").

Figure 16-2: Touch the pin on the map (left) to save the location as a bookmark (right).

To find your physical location on the map, touch the Compass icon in the bottom-left corner of the map screen (refer to Figure 16-2, left side). The map changes to show your general location with a compass-looking circle representing your approximate physical location. The Maps application figures out where you are by using information from some local Wi-Fi networks (if you have Wi-Fi turned on), or in the case of the iPhone 3G, by using its built-in GPS (Global Positioning System). The more accurate the available information, the smaller the circle on the map.

To show traffic information, or to change the map to show a satellite image (if available), a hybrid of street view and satellite, or a list of locations, touch the Eye icon in the bottom-right corner of the map screen (refer to Figure 16-2, left side), and then touch the Show Traffic option or touch Satellite, Hybrid, or List to change the map. If you turn on the Show Traffic option, highways are color-coded according to the flow of traffic, with green for highways moving faster than 50 miles per hour (mph), yellow for 25–50 mph, and red for less than 25 mph. If you don't see color-coded highways, you may need to zoom out to see highways and major roads.

Getting directions

To get driving directions from one location to another, you first need to search for or choose a location, as described in the previous section, and then touch Directions at the bottom of the map screen (refer to Figure 16-2, left side). You can also touch a pin on a map and then touch Directions To Here or Directions From Here to get directions (refer to Figure 16-2, right side). The Directions screen appears, with the first location selected as either the Start or End.

For example, if you want to get directions from your current location to a bookmarked location, first find your physical location on the map by touching the compass icon in the bottom-left corner of the map screen. Then tap Directions, and in the Directions screen that appears, your current location already occupies the Start field. Touch the Bookmarks icon in the End field and select a bookmarked location for the End field. You can also type entries or select bookmarks for both the Start and End fields by touching those fields and using the on-screen keyboard, as shown in Figure 16-3 (left side).

You can switch the entry for Start to End (or vice versa) by touching the looped arrow button to the left of the Start and End fields (refer to Figure 16-3, left side). Using this button you can get directions one way; then touch the button to reverse the Start and End fields to get directions for the way back.

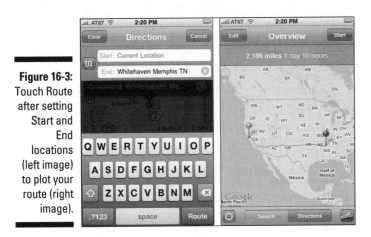

Figure 16-3:
Touch Route
after setting
Start and
End
locations
(left image)
to plot your
route (right
image).

After setting your Start and End locations, touch Route on the on-screen keyboard (bottom-right corner, refer to Figure 16-3, left side) to mark the route on the map. Alternatively you can touch Clear in the upper-left corner to re-enter your Start and End fields, or Cancel in the upper-right corner to cancel getting directions.

The route is shown on the map in the Overview screen in purple, with pins marking the start and end locations (refer to Figure 16-3, right side). The approximate driving time appears at the top of the Overview screen. If traffic data is available, the driving time is adjusted accordingly, but don't expect miracles — the information depends on data collected and services provided by third parties, not by Apple, and traffic patterns change.

To view directions one step at a time on the map, touch Start in the upper-right corner of the Overview screen (refer to Figure 16-3, right side) to see the first leg of the journey, and then touch the right-arrow button in the upper-right corner of the first leg's screen to see the next stretch. You can also touch the left-arrow button in any of the step-by-step directions to go back a step. The Maps application graciously walks you through your entire journey.

To view all the legs of your journey in a list, touch the Eye icon in the lower-right corner of the display, and touch List. Then touch any location in the list to see a map showing that leg of the trip.

To see your most recent set of directions, touch the Bookmarks icon in the search field and touch Recents at the bottom of the Bookmarks screen to change it to the Recents screen. You can also touch Contacts on the Home menu to see your contacts list, and touch a contact's address to see that person's address on your map.

Using the Calculator on Your iPod touch or iPhone

Do you need to quickly figure out your percentage of a movie deal in the Polo Lounge of the Beverly Hills Hotel? How about just figuring out the waiter's tip? You can use the calculator in your pocket iPod touch or iPhone.

Touch Calculator on the Home menu. The calculator appears looking just like a handheld calculator with numeric keys. You can add, subtract, multiply, and divide numbers by touching the numeric and function (add, subtract, multiply, divide, or equal) keys. When you touch a function key, a white ring appears around it to indicate the operation you are carrying out. The keys work as follows:

÷: Divide by.

X: Multiply by.

+: Add to a number.

–: Subtract from a number.

=: Show the result.

C: Clear the displayed number.

M+: Add the displayed number to the number in memory. If no number is in memory, store the displayed number in memory.

M–: Subtract the displayed number from the number in memory.

MR/MC: Tap once to replace the displayed number with the number in memory. Tap twice to clear the memory. If the MR/MC button has a white ring around it, there is a number stored in memory. If zero ("0") is displayed, tap once to see the number stored in memory.

Part IV
The Traveling iPod and iPhone

The 5th Wave   By Rich Tennant

"It's a fully furnished, 3-bedroom house that's designed to fit perfectly over your iPod."

In this part . . .

This part explains how you can go mobile with your iPod or iPhone using appropriate accessories, how to change your display settings, timers, clocks and alarms to adapt to traveling, and how to synchronize your contacts and calendars. It also describes how to synchronize and manage your e-mail accounts on an iPod touch or iPhone, and how to troubleshoot your iPod or iPhone.

- ✔ Chapter 17 describes the accessories you need to listen to tunes whenever you go on the road or stay at the "Heartbreak Hotel."

- ✔ Chapter 18 covers setting the time and date, waking up with the alarm clock, timing your exercises or other activities, adjusting your display settings, and setting a combination lock for your iPod or iPhone.

- ✔ Chapter 19 describes automatically synchronizing your iPod or iPhone with calendars and contacts so that you don't miss any appointments or forget someone's name, address, or phone number. It also covers managing and synchronizing e-mail accounts on your iPod touch or iPhone.

- ✔ Chapter 20 gets into the nitty-gritty of troubleshooting your iPod or iPhone, including how to use iTunes to update or restore your iPod or iPhone.

Chapter 17

Going Mobile

. . . .

. . . .

*Y*ou can truly go anywhere with an iPod or iPhone. If you can't plug your iPod or iPhone into a power source while it's playing, you can use the battery for quite a while before having to recharge. You can find all the accessories that you need to travel with an iPod or iPhone in the Apple Store at www.apple.com.

Put on "Eight Miles High" by the Byrds while cruising in a plane at 40,000 feet. Watch the "Lust for Life" music video by Iggy Pop on a bus heading out of Detroit. Ride the rails listening to "All Aboard" by Muddy Waters, followed by "Peavine" by John Lee Hooker. Or cruise on the Autobahn in Germany with Kraftwerk. The iPod or iPhone provides high-quality sound and excellent picture quality no matter how turbulent the environment.

All current iPod and iPhone models except the iPod classic use flash memory drives that play content without skipping even when jostled and thrown about. Any movement on your part doesn't affect playback (but please don't drop them). The iPod classic uses a hard drive, but it also has a *memory cache* — a nice little slice of solid-state memory, with no mechanical or moving parts. The fact that the iPod classic actually plays sound from its memory cache rather than from its hard drive means you can hop, skip, and jump as much as you want, and your listening and/or viewing experience won't be impacted. With all iPods and iPhones you essentially have skip protection, which means you don't have to worry about tremors, potholes, or strenuous exercise causing the audio to skip.

Connecting Headphones and Portable Speakers

Apple designed the iPod and iPhone to provide excellent sound through headphones. From the headphone/line-out connection, though, the iPod or iPhone can also play music through portable speaker systems. The speaker systems must be self-powered or able to work with very little power (like headphones) and allow audio to be input via a 3.5mm, stereo mini-plug connection.

Looking at specs, you'll notice that iPod and iPhone models include a small amplifier that's plenty powerful enough to deliver audio through the headphone/line-out connection. All current models, including the iPod shuffle, have a frequency response of 20 to 20,000 Hz (hertz), which provides distortion-free music at the lowest or highest pitches. (In this case, hertz has nothing to do with rental cars. A *hertz* is a unit of frequency equal to one cycle per second.) At pitches that produce frequencies of 20 cycles per second or 20,000 cycles per second, the iPod or iPhone responds with distortion-free sound.

If headphones aren't your thing, you can even wear an iPod shuffle inside a headband (and keep it relatively dry no matter how much you, um, create your own moisture). Thanko (`http://thanko.jp/voniasports`) offers the Vonia sports headband that uses *bone conduction* — a hearing aid technology that conducts "Good Vibrations" through the bones of your skull, directly into your inner ear. The sound can be surprisingly clear and crisp, although it won't be in stereo because the sound seems to come from inside your head.

Portable speaker systems typically include built-in amplifiers and a volume control, and they usually offer a stereo mini-plug that you can attach directly to the iPod or iPhone headphone/line-out connection or to a dock headphone/line-out connection. (Some portable speaker systems, such as the iBoom Travel or DLO Portable Speakers from DLO [`www.dlo.com`], or the Bose SoundDock Portable [`www.bose.com`], provide a convenient dock connection for playing audio.) To place the external speakers farther away from the iPod or iPhone, use a stereo mini-plug extension cable, which is available at most consumer electronics stores. These cables have a stereo mini-plug on one end and a stereo mini-socket on the other.

Portable speaker systems typically have volume controls. Set your iPod or iPhone volume to about half or three-quarters, and then raise or lower the volume of your speaker system.

When you travel, take an extra pair of headphones (or earbuds) and a splitter cable, which are available in any consumer electronics store. The Monster iSplitter is available in the Apple Store. That way, you can share music with someone on the road.

TIP

For a portable stereo system that offers big sound on a rechargeable battery and is perfect for environments like the beach or a boat, check out the i-Fusion or i-P23 speaker systems from Sonic Impact (www.si5.com). (See Figure 17-1.) The i-Fusion includes universal adapters for all dockable iPod models and an audio input connection for connecting your computer or an audio player. The double-duty case is a durable cover that acts as a speaker cabinet for both speakers, to give the speakers better bass response.

Figure 17-1:
The i-Fusion from Sonic Impact provides a dock and speakers for the road.

Playing Car Tunes

I always wanted to be able to fill up a car with music just as easily as filling it up with fuel, without having to carry dozens of cassettes or CDs. With an iPod or iPhone, an auto-charger to save on battery power, and a way to connect the iPod or iPhone to your car's stereo system, you're ready to pump music. (Start your engine and queue up "Getting in Tune" and then "Going Mobile" by The Who.) You can even go one step further and get a new BMW, Toyota, or similarly equipped car that offers an iPod or iPhone dock cable installed and integrated into the car's stereo system so that you can control the iPod or iPhone from your car stereo — including controls on the steering wheel.

Here are your options when it comes to linking your iPod or iPhone to a car stereo:

✔ **Use your cassette player.** Use a standard cassette adapter and an iPod power adapter for your car's lighter socket. This method works even with rental cars (as long as they're supplied with cassette players). For a semi-permanent installation, you can add a car mount to keep your iPod or iPhone secure. Cassette adapters offer medium quality that's usually better than wireless adapters.

✔ **Buy or lease a car that offers an iPod-ready stereo.** BMW, Mercedes-Benz, Toyota, Honda, and many other auto companies offer models that are iPod-ready, and you can use your iPhone with them.

✔ **Use your radio and a wireless adapter.** Use a wireless adapter that plays your iPod or iPhone as if it were a station on your FM radio dial. Some car mounts offer built-in wireless adapters. This might be your only inexpensive choice if you don't have a cassette deck. *Note:* Wireless adapters might not work well in cities where FM stations crowd the radio dial.

✔ **Install an iPod/iPhone interface.** Install an iPod or iPhone interface for your car stereo that offers high-quality, line-in audio input and power. After you install this interface, thread the iPod/iPhone dock cable into the glove box so that you can plug the cable into your iPod or iPhone, hide the iPod or iPhone in the glove box, and control the iPod or iPhone from your car stereo's head unit. This method offers the best sound quality. Toyota offers an integration kit for plugging an iPod into the car glove box and using either the steering wheel or usual audio system controls.

Unfortunately, not many car stereos offer a mini-socket for audio input. As of this writing, the few accessories that integrate directly with car stereos require custom car installations. Most connection standards are based on specific car models or stereo models. But stay iTuned, because standard car docks are on the horizon.

Using cassette and power adapters for your car

Until you get an iPod-ready car, a car stereo with a mini-socket for stereo audio input (also called *stereo-in connection*), or an iPod connection — or get one installed — you can use a cassette-player adapter to connect with your car stereo. (I describe wireless connectivity later, in the section "Connecting by Wireless Radio.") These solutions provide lower sound quality than iPod interface installations or stereo-in connections but are inexpensive and work with most cars.

Many car stereos have a cassette player, and you can buy a cassette adapter from most consumer electronics stores or from the Apple Store (such as the Sony CPA-9C Car Cassette Adapter). The cassette-player adapter looks like a tape cassette with a mini-plug cable (which sticks out through the slot when you're using the adapter). Adapters work with most front-loading and side-loading cassette decks — it's the same shape as a cassette — as long as the cable doesn't prevent its loading.

First connect the mini-plug cable directly to the iPod or iPhone. Then insert the adapter into the cassette player, being careful not to get the cable tangled up inside the player.

One inherent problem with this approach is that the cable that dangles from your cassette player looks unsightly. You also might have some trouble eject-ing the adapter if the cable gets wedged in the cassette player door. Overall, though, this method is the best for most cars because it provides better sound quality than most wireless methods.

Although some new vehicles (particularly SUVs and cars such as the Toyota Matrix mini-station wagon) offer 110-volt power outlets you can use with your Apple-supplied battery charger, most cars offer only a lighter/power socket that requires a power adapter to use with your iPod or iPhone. Be careful to pick the right type of power adapter for your car's lighter/power socket.

Belkin (www.belkin.com) offers the Auto Kit for $49.95, and it includes a car power adapter with a convenient socket for a stereo mini-plug cable (which can connect directly to a car stereo if the stereo has a mini-socket for audio input). The adapter includes a volume-adjustable amplifier to boost the sound coming from the iPod or iPhone before it goes into the cassette adapter or car stereo.

Even with a cassette adapter and power adapter, you have at best a clumsy solution that uses one cable (power) from a power adapter to the iPod or iPhone, and another cable (audio) to your car stereo cassette adapter. Attached to these wires, your iPod or iPhone needs a secure place to sit while your car moves because you don't want it bouncing around.

You can fit your iPod or iPhone securely in position in a car without getting a custom installation. The TuneDok ($30) from Belkin (www.belkin.com) holds your iPod or iPhone securely and fits into your car's cup holder. The TuneDok ratcheting neck and height-adjustment feature lets you reposition the iPod or iPhone to your liking. The cable-management clip eliminates loose and tangled cables, and the large and small rubber base and cup fits most cup holders.

MARWARE (www.marware.com) offers an inexpensive solution for both car use and personal use. The $6 Car Holder attaches to the dashboard of your car and lets you attach an iPod or iPhone that's wearing one of the MARWARE Sportsuit covering cases. (See "Dressing Up Your iPod and iPhone for Travel," later in this chapter.) The clip on the back attaches to the Car Holder.

ProClip (www.proclipusa.com) offers mounting brackets for clip-on devices. The brackets attach to the dashboard, and you can install them in seconds. After you install the bracket, you can use different custom holders for the iPod or iPhone models or for cell phones and other portable devices.

Integrating an iPod or iPhone with your car stereo

Premium car manufacturers are introducing cars that are *iPod-ready:* including an iPod interface for the car stereo system that uses the dock connector cable compatible with all iPod and iPhone models except the iPod shuffle. For example, BMW offers such a model with audio controls on the steering wheel. Mercedes-Benz, Volvo, Mini-Cooper, Nissan, Alfa Romeo, and Ferrari all also offer iPod-ready models. In addition, car stereo manufacturers (such as Alpine and Clarion) offer car audio systems with integrated iPod interfaces; see Figure 17-2.

Figure 17-2:
An iPod-
integrated
car stereo
installation.

If you can't afford an iPod-ready car, you can opt for a custom installation of an iPod interface for your existing car stereo and car power (such as using a custom cable interface for a CD changer, which a skilled car audio specialist can install in your dashboard). For example, you can order a professional installation with the Dension ICE-Link, which adds line-level audio output and recharging capability to almost any vehicle. It uses the CD-changer connections in car CD players to directly connect your iPod into the car's audio system. Dension (`www.dension.com`) assumes that the buyer is a professional installer. Although you can install it yourself (especially if you already have a CD changer unit in your trunk), most installations require taking apart the dashboard and installing the ICE-Link behind your CD stereo. ICE-Link can be combined with almost any iPod mount. Dension also offers the Gateway series of products for controlling iPod and iPhone models and auxiliary devices in a car.

If your car stereo doesn't offer a CD changer interface, you might want to have a new car stereo professionally installed that offers a CD changer interface or iPod capability — such as the Alpine CDA-9887 (`www.alpine-usa.com/driveyouripod`). With an integrated iPod setup, you can control the iPod from the car stereo's head unit or steering wheel controls. The car stereo provides power to the iPod to keep it fully charged.

Connecting by Wireless Radio

A wireless music adapter lets you play music from your iPod or iPhone on an FM radio with no connection or cable. However, the sound quality might suffer a bit from radio interference. I always take a wireless adapter with me whenever I rent a car because even if a rental car has no cassette player (ruling out the use of my cassette adapter), it probably has an FM radio.

You can use a wireless adapter in a car, on a boat, on the beach with a portable radio, or even in your home with a stereo system and tuner. I even use it in hotel rooms with a clock radio.

To use a wireless adapter, follow these steps:

1. **Set the wireless adapter to an unused FM radio frequency.**

   Some adapters offer only one frequency (typically 87.9 MHz). Others offer you a choice of several frequencies: typically 88.1, 88.3, 88.5, and 88.7 MHz. Some even let you pick any FM frequency. If given a choice, choose the frequency and set the adapter according to its instructions. Be sure to pick an unused frequency — a frequency that's being used by an FM station in range of your radio interferes with your iPod signal.

2. **Connect the wireless adapter to the iPod or iPhone headphone/line-out connector or to the line-out connector on an iPod car dock.**

   The wireless adapter acts like a miniature radio station, broadcasting to a nearby FM radio. (Sorry, you can't go much farther than a few feet, so no one else can hear your Wolfman Jack impersonation.)

3. **Tune to the appropriate frequency on the FM dial.**

   Tune any nearby radio to the same FM frequency that you chose in Step 1.

You need to set the adapter close enough to the radio's antenna to work, making it impractical for home stereos. You can get better quality sound by connecting to a home stereo with a cable.

Don't be surprised if the wireless adapter doesn't work as well in cities — other radio stations might cause too much interference.

Here are a few wireless adapters I have no trouble recommending:

- ✔ **TRAFFICJamz** ($35) from Newer Technology (www.newertech.com) is both a charger and a transmitter that works with all model iPods.

- ✔ **iTrip** ($50) from Griffin Technology (www.griffintechnology.com) offers selectable modes of broadcasting — in LX mode, the iTrip transmits in stereo with a fuller sound, whereas DX mode provides a stronger mono signal that works in areas with a lot of interference from FM radio stations. Even in large cities with lots of radio stations crowding the dial, iTrip in DX mode delivers a background noise level below that of a cassette tape adapter for higher-quality sound.

- ✔ **TuneCast 3 Mobile FM Transmitter** ($40) from Belkin (www.belkin.com) is particularly convenient in a car because it includes a 14-inch cable that delivers power when used with the Belkin Mobile Power Cord for iPod. That way, you can preserve your batteries for when you're not near an alternative source. It offers four programmable memory slots for saving the clearest radio frequency wherever you go.

- ✔ **Monster iCarPlay Wireless** ($79.95) from Monster Cable (www.monstercable.com) offers a power adapter as well as excellent quality playback for a wireless radio unit. You can select radio frequencies of 88.1, 88.3, 88.5, 88.7, 88.9, 89.1, 89.3, or 89.5 MHz. Although a bit more expensive, I prefer it for its sound quality.

- ✔ **DLO TransDock Classic** ($80) from Digital Lifestyle Outfitters (www.dlo.com) is an excellent all-in-one wireless FM transmitter, mounting system, and power adapter for using your iPod in a car. DLO also offers the new TransDock ($100) that offers all of the above plus Audio/Video Output for showing iPod or iPhone content on a mobile video system or using it with cassette adapters and car audio inputs.

Dressing Up Your iPod and iPhone for Travel

The simple protective carrying cases supplied with some iPod and iPhone models just aren't as stylin' as the myriad accessories that you can get for dressing up your iPods and iPhones for travel. You can find different types of protective gear, from leather jackets to aluminum cases, in many different styles and colors. Apple offers access to hundreds of products from other suppliers on its accessories page (`www.apple.com/ipod/accessories.html`) — click the See More in the Store button to go directly to Apple's online store to view product details and make purchases. Some are designed primarily for protecting your iPod from harm; others are designed to provide some measure of protection while also providing access to controls.

On the extreme end of the spectrum are hardened cases that are ready for battlefields in deserts or jungles — the Humvees of iPod protective gear, if you will. Matias Corporation (`http://matias.ca/armor`) offers versions of the sturdy Matias Armor case ($39.95) for each iPod and iPhone model, which offers possibly the best protection against physical trauma on the market. Your iPod or iPhone rests within a hard, resilient metal exoskeleton that can withstand the abuse of bouncing down a flight of metal stairs without letting your iPod or iPhone pop out.

Business travelers can combine personal items into one carrying case. The Leather Folio ($30) cases from Belkin (`www.belkin.com`) for iPod classic and iPod touch models are made from fine-grain leather that even Ricardo Montalban would rave about. The cases can also hold personal essentials, such as business and credit cards. The HipCase cases ($30) from DLO (`www.dlo.com`) let you stash credit cards and other essentials along with your iPod, and the HipCase includes a sturdy, leather-covered belt clip.

On the sporty side, MARWARE (`www.marware.com`) offers the Sportsuit Convertible cases ($35) for iPod and iPhone models, with a patented belt-clip system, offering interchangeable clip options for use with the MARWARE Car Holder or with an armband or belt. The neoprene case has vulcanized rubber grips on each side and bottom for a no-slip grip as well as plastic inserts for impact protection, offering full access to all of the device's controls and connections while it's in the case.

If you like to carry a backpack with everything in it, consider getting the very first backpack ever designed to control an iPod within it: The Burton Amp Pack (`http://lonelyplanet.altrec.com/shop/detail/24004`), priced at $239.95, lets you switch songs on your iPod by pressing a button on the shoulder strap. Constructed from ballistic nylon, the Amp Pack offers a secure iPod storage pocket, a headphone port located on a shoulder strap, an easy-access side entry laptop compartment, and padded ergonomic shoulder straps with a soft and flexible control pad built in to a strap. It's perfect for listening to Lou Reed while hanging on to a pole in a subway car, or the Hollies while navigating your way to the back of the bus. Other backpacks that can host iPods include the JanSport Thundervolt ($90) from Dom's Outdoor Outfitters (http://domsoutdoor.com) and the aptly named G-Tech Psycho (www.g-techworld.com).

Using Power Accessories

If you want to charge your iPod battery when you travel abroad, you can't count on finding the same voltage as in your home country. However, you still need to use your Apple power adapter, or your computer, to recharge your iPod — you need to plug something into some outlet somewhere. Fortunately, power converters for different voltages and plugs for different outlets are available in most airport gift shops, but the worldly traveler might want to consider saving time and money by getting a travel kit of power accessories from the Apple Store or from a consumer electronics store.

I found several varieties of power converter kits for world travel in my local international airport, but they were pricey — check your local Radio Shack or consumer electronics store first, or try Amazon.com. Most kits include a set of AC plugs with prongs that fit different electrical outlets around the world. You can connect your iPod power adapter to these adapters. The AC plugs typically support outlets in North America, Japan, China, the United Kingdom, Continental Europe, Korea, Australia, and Hong Kong. You should also include at least one power accessory for use with a standard car lighter, such as car chargers from Belkin (www.belkin.com), Kensington (www.kensington.com), or Newer Technology (www.newertech.com).

One way to mitigate the battery blues is to get an accessory that lets you use replaceable alkaline batteries — the kind that you can find in any convenience store — in a pinch. The TunePower Rechargeable Battery Pack for iPod ($80) from Belkin (www.belkin.com) lets you power an iPod Classic or older-model iPod with standard AA alkaline replaceable batteries even when your internal iPod battery is drained.

Another way to supply power to your iPod or iPhone on the road is to use your FireWire- or USB 2.0–equipped laptop to supply the power and then use a power adapter with your laptop. (Make sure that you use FireWire or USB 2.0 hardware that provides power; see Chapter 1.) You can use, for example, the Kensington Universal Car/Air Adapter for Apple to plug a Mac PowerBook or MacBook into any car cigarette lighter or EmPower-equipped airline seat. (The EmPower in-seat power system can provide either 110-volt AC or 15-volt DC power in an aircraft seat for passenger use.) Then connect the iPod or iPhone to the laptop with its USB 2.0 dock connector cable.

Chapter 18

Changing Your Clock, Lock, and Display Settings

*E*ven if you purchased an iPod simply to listen to music or watch videos, those thoughtful engineers at Apple crammed a lot more features into their invention. Your iPod also keeps time, as does your iPhone. You can use the iPod or iPhone time-keeper to help you keep track of your personal life by setting alarms, using the stopwatch, setting the date and time, using the sleep timer to fall asleep to music, and displaying clocks of different time zones.

And if you think your iPod or iPhone might fall into the wrong hands, consider setting a combination lock. This chapter shows you how to do all this and more: Find out how to change the timer for the backlight on iPod classic and iPod nano models, set the brightness of the display on all models, or set the contrast of the black-and-white displays of older models. You can even wallpaper the display of your iPod touch or iPhone to show a stylin' background when it's locked.

Setting the Date and Time

Your iPod or iPhone may already be set to the correct time, date, and time zone, but if not, you can set it yourself. You can also set an iPhone to set the time automatically from its cell phone network. The time and date settings apply to the time shown in the status bar at the top of the screen, to world clocks, and to your calendar.

To set the date and time with an iPod touch or iPhone, follow these steps:

1. **Choose Settings from the Home menu.**

   The Settings menu appears.

2. **Choose General from the Settings menu.**

   The General menu appears.

3. **Choose Date & Time from the General menu.**

   The Date & Time menu appears with the 24-Hour Time, Time Zone, and Set Date & Time options, and time zone support for your calendar.

4. **(Optional) Touch the Off button for the 24-Hour Time option to turn it on and show military time.**

   With 24-hour display, 11 p.m. is displayed as 23:00:00 and not 11:00:00. To turn off 24-Hour Time option, touch the On button to turn it off.

5. **iPhone only: Turn off Set Automatically in order to set the time and date manually.**

   The Set Automatically option is turned on by default for the iPhone to set the time and date automatically using its cell phone network. If this is OK with you, skip to Step 11 (you're done). If not, touch the On button to turn the Set Automatically off, so that you can set the time and date manually. After turning off the Set Automatically option, two new options appear: Time Zone and Set Date & Time.

6. **Touch the Time Zone option to set the time zone.**

   The on-screen keyboard appears; see Chapter 1 for instructions on how to use it. Type the name of the city and touch the Return button on the keyboard, and your iPod touch or iPhone looks up the time zone for you.

7. **Touch the Date & Time button in the upper-left corner of the display to finish and return to the Date & Time menu.**

8. **Touch the Set Date & Time option to set the date and time manually.**

   Touching the Date field brings up slot-machine-style Date wheel, as shown in Figure 18-1. Slide your finger over the wheel to select the month, day, and year.

   Touching the Time field brings up a Time wheel. Slide your finger over the wheel to set the hour, minutes, and AM or PM.

9. **Touch the Date & Time button in the upper-left corner of the display (refer to Figure 18-1) to finish and return to the Date & Time menu.**

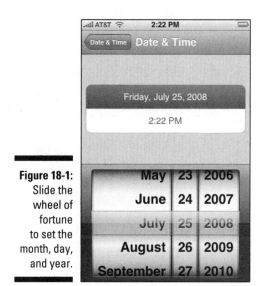

Figure 18-1:
Slide the wheel of fortune to set the month, day, and year.

10. **(Optional) Touch the On button to turn on Time Zone Support, and touch Time Zone to set the time zone for your calendar.**

    With Time Zone Support on, your calendar displays event dates and times in the time zone set for your calendars. When off, the calendar displays events in the time zone of your current location.

11. **Touch the General button in the upper-left corner to return to the General menu.**

To set the date and time with an iPod classic or iPod nano, follow these steps:

1. **Press the Menu button until you see the iPod main menu.**

2. **Choose Settings⇨Date & Time.**

    The Date & Time menu appears, with selections for setting the date, time, time zone, 24-hour clock, and the Time in Title option, which displays the time in the iPod display's menu title bar.

3. **Choose Time Zone.**

    A map appears with a red dot set to your current time zone on the map.

4. **Scroll to choose a time zone and press Select.**

    Move the red dot to another zone by scrolling the click wheel — the red dot jumps from one region of the map to another, and the time zone appears below the map. Press the Select button to choose a zone. After selecting it, the Date & Time menu appears again.

5. **Choose Date from the Date & Time menu.**

   The Date display appears with the month field highlighted.

6. **Change the field setting by scrolling the click wheel.**

   Scroll clockwise to go forward and counterclockwise to go backward.

7. **Press the Select button after scrolling to the appropriate setting.**

   The next field is now highlighted.

8. **Repeat Steps 6 and 7 for the day and year.**

   After you finish scrolling and then selecting the Year field, the Date & Time menu appears automatically.

9. **Choose Time from the Date & Time menu.**

   The Time display appears with the Hour field highlighted.

10. **Change the field setting by scrolling the click wheel.**

    Scroll clockwise to go forward and counterclockwise to go backward.

11. **Press the Select button after scrolling to the appropriate setting.**

    The next field is now highlighted.

12. **Repeat Steps 10 and 11 for minutes and AM/PM.**

    After finishing the AM/PM field, the Date & Time menu appears again.

To show military time (so that 11 p.m. is displayed as 23:00), choose the 24 Hour Clock option in the Date & Time menu and press the Select button to turn it on. The option changes from 12-hour to *24-hour*. To switch back, press the Select button again for the the 24 Hour Clock option.

To display the time in the menu title bar of an iPod classic, iPod nano, or fifth-generation iPod, scroll to the Time in Title option in the Date & Time menu and then press the Select button to turn this option On. To stop showing the time in the menu title, press the Select button again to toggle it to Off.

Using the Clock

You can always know what time it is with your iPod or iPhone — just look at the time on the Home menu, or in the main menu title of an iPod classic or iPod nano (or fifth-generation iPod) if you turn on the Time in Title option, as described in the previous section. But you can also know what time it is in other time zones — iPods and iPhones offer multiple clocks to show other time zones, and you can set alarms and a sleep timer, and use the built-in stopwatch.

To look at a clock on an iPod classic, iPod nano, or a fifth-generation or most older iPods, choose Extras⇨Clocks from the main menu. To look at the clock on an iPod touch or iPhone, select Clock from the Home menu.

Displaying multiple clocks

You can display clocks with different time zones, which is useful if you traverse time zones or simply want to keep track of time in another time zone. (Maybe you like to know the time in Paris if you're calling from New York.) The initial clock and any clocks you add sport a daytime face (white background and black hands) from 6 a.m. to 5:59 p.m. and a nighttime face (black background with white hands) from 6 p.m. to 5:59 a.m.

To create clocks on an iPod touch or iPhone, select Clock from the Home menu and touch the World Clock button. To add a clock:

1. **Touch the plus (+) button in the upper-right corner of the display.**

   The on-screen keyboard appears with a text entry field.

2. **Type a city name on the on-screen keyboard and tap Return (or tap Cancel next to the text entry field to cancel).**

   The iPod touch or iPhone looks up the city's time zone to display the clock. (For details on how to use the on-screen keyboard, see Chapter 1.)

To remove a clock, touch the Edit button in the upper-left corner of the display, and touch the circled minus (–) button next to the clock to delete.

To create more clocks; edit the clocks; or delete additional clocks with the iPod classic, iPod nano, or fifth-generation iPod, follow these steps:

1. **Choose Extras⇨Clocks from the main menu, and highlight a clock.**

   One or more clocks appear (depending on how many you have created), showing the present time and location. If you have more than one clock and you want to edit one of them, scroll the click wheel to highlight the clock you want to edit.

2. **Press the Select button on the iPod to select the clock.**

   The Add and Edit options appear, along with a Delete option if you have more than one clock.

3. **Scroll the click wheel to select Add, Edit, or Delete and press the Select button.**

   If you select Add or Edit, a list of geographical regions appears in alphabetical order, from Africa to South America. If you select Delete, the clock is deleted, and you can skip any more steps.

4. **Scroll the Region list, choose a region, and press the Select button.**

   The City menu appears with a list of cities in the region in alphabetical order.

5. **Scroll the City list, choose a city, and then press the Select button.**

   You return to the list of clocks. You now have added a new clock (or edited a clock if you selected the Edit option).

Setting alarms

Time is on your side with your iPod or iPhone. You can set *multiple* alarms to go off on different days and set a variety of tones and sounds for your alarms on an iPhone or iPod touch that play through its speaker.

To set an alarm on an iPod touch or iPhone, follow these steps:

1. **Select Clock from the Home menu and touch the Alarm button along the bottom of the display.**

2. **To add an alarm, touch the plus (+) button in the upper-right corner of the display.**

   The Add Alarm menu appears with options and a slot-machine-style wheel for setting the alarm time. Now you can set some optional features, or you can skip to Step 7 and be done with it.

3. **(Optional) Touch the Repeat option to set the alarm to repeat on other days.**

   You can set it to repeat every Monday, Tuesday, Wednesday, and so on.

4. **(Optional) Touch Sound to select a sound for the alarm.**

   A list of sounds appears; touch a sound to set it for the alarm.

5. **(Optional) Touch the On button to turn the Snooze option off, or touch it again to turn it back on.**

   With the Snooze option, the iPhone or iPod touch displays a Snooze button when the alarm goes off, and you tap Snooze to stop the alarm and repeat in 10 minutes (so that you can snooze for 10 minutes).

6. **(Optional) Touch Label to enter a text label for the alarm.**

   The label helps you identify the alarm in the Alarm list.

7. **Touch Save in the upper-right corner to save the alarm.**

When the alarm goes off, your iPod touch or iPhone displays the message You have an alarm (and the date and time), along with the Snooze button if the Snooze option is turned on (refer to Step 5). Slide your finger to unlock the iPod touch or iPhone to stop the alarm's sound, or touch the Snooze button to stop the alarm temporarily and repeat it 10 minutes later. (When it goes off again, slide the unlock slider to turn it off — don't press the Snooze button, you're late for work!)

To delete an alarm on an iPod touch or iPhone, select Clock from the Home menu and touch the Alarm button along the bottom of the display. In the Alarm list, touch the alarm you want to trash and then touch the Edit button in the upper-left corner of the display. The alarm appears with a circled minus (–) button next to it; touch this button and then touch the red Delete button that appears to delete the alarm.

Besides setting alarms to have the traditional beep sound you can hear through their tiny speakers, iPod classics, iPod nanos, and fifth-generation iPods let you set a playlist to play as your alarm — which you can hear by connecting the iPod to speakers or a stereo (or headphones, if you sleep with headphones on). To set an alarm on an iPod classic or iPod nano, follow these steps:

1. **Choose Extras⇨Alarms from the main menu.**

   The Create Alarm and Sleep Timer options appear in the Alarms main menu.

2. **Choose Create Alarm and press the Select button.**

   The Alarms submenu appears.

3. **Highlight the Alarm option and press the Select button to turn it on.**

4. **Choose Date from the Alarms submenu.**

   The Date display appears with the month field highlighted.

5. **Change the field setting by scrolling the click wheel.**

   Scroll clockwise to go forward and counterclockwise to go backward.

6. **Press the Select button after scrolling to the appropriate setting.**

   The next field is now highlighted.

7. **Repeat Steps 5 and 6 for the day and year.**

   After you finish scrolling and then selecting the Year field, the Alarms submenu appears automatically.

8. **Choose Time from the Alarms submenu.**

   The Time display appears with the Hour field highlighted.

9. **Change the field setting by scrolling the click wheel.**

   Scroll clockwise to go forward and counterclockwise to go backward.

10. **Press the Select button after scrolling to the appropriate setting.**

    The next field is now highlighted.

11. **Repeat Steps 9 and 10 for minutes and AM/PM.**

    After finishing the AM/PM field, the Alarms submenu appears again.

12. **Choose Repeat from the Alarms submenu, and choose a repeat multiple.**

    You can choose to set the alarm to go off once, every day, weekdays, weekends, every week, every month, or every year. After choosing a repeat multiple, the Alarms submenu appears again.

13. **Choose Sounds from the Alarms submenu and choose a tone or a playlist.**

    The Tones and Playlists options appear. Choose Tones to select a beep, or set Tones to none (no sound) if you want the iPod to display the alarm without making a sound. Choose Playlists to select a playlist. After choosing a tone or a playlist, the Alarms submenu appears again.

14. **Choose Label from the Alarms submenu to set a label to identify this alarm.**

    You can set labels for your alarms so that you can identify them easily in the Alarms main menu. Select a label from the prepared list, which includes labels such as Wake up, Work, Class, Appointment, and so on. After choosing a label, the Alarms submenu of settings appears again.

15. **Press Menu to return to the Alarms main menu, which now includes your new alarm with its label in a list of alarms under the Sleep Timer heading.**

You can create as many alarms, at different dates and times, as you need. To delete an alarm, select the alarm from the list in the Alarms main menu. The Alarms submenu appears with a list of options. Choose Delete.

When the alarm goes off, your iPod classic or iPod nano displays an alarm message along with the Dismiss and Snooze buttons. Choose Dismiss or Snooze by scrolling the click wheel and select it by pressing the Select button. Dismiss stops the alarm's sound, while Snooze stops the sound temporarily and repeats it 10 minutes later.

Using the timer (iPod touch and iPhone)

You can set an hour-and-minute timer for anything — baking cookies, baking CDs, or baking in the sun on the beach. The timer built into the Clock application on an iPod touch or iPhone will continue running even when playing music or videos or running other iPod touch or iPhone applications. You might want to use a timer to see if a set of activities — playing songs, playing videos, selecting from menus, and running applications — occurs within a specific time. (If you need to use seconds as well as minutes and hours, try the stopwatch — see the section "Using the stopwatch," later in this chapter.)

To use the timer, follow these steps:

1. **Select Clock from the Home menu.**

   The Clock display appears.

2. **Touch the Timer button along the bottom of the Clock display.**

   The Timer wheel for minutes and hours appears, along with the Start button.

3. **Flick the timer wheel to set the timer in hours and minutes.**

4. **Touch the When Timer Ends button and touch a sound to use when the timer is up.**

5. **Touch Set in the upper-right corner of the display to set the sound (or Cancel in the upper-left corner to cancel the sound).**

6. **Touch Start to start the timer.**

The timer runs backward. You can touch Cancel to cancel the timer or wait until it runs out. When it runs out, the iPod touch or iPhone plays the sound (if a sound is set) and presents an OK button. Touch OK to stop the sound.

Setting the sleep timer

As you can with a clock radio sleep timer, you can set your iPod or iPhone to play music or videos for a while before going to sleep.

To set the timer on the iPhone or iPod touch as a sleep timer, first follow the instructions in the "Using the timer (iPod touch or iPhone)" section, earlier in this chapter. Then touch the When Timer Ends button, and touch Sleep iPod at the top of the list to put the iPod touch or iPhone to sleep when the timer ends. Touch Set in the upper-right corner of the display to set the Sleep iPod option (or Cancel in the upper-left corner to cancel). Finally, touch Start to start the timer. You can then play music or videos until the timer ends and the iPod automatically goes to sleep.

To set the sleep timer on an iPod classic or iPod nano, choose Extras from the main menu; then choose Alarms⇨Sleep Timer. To set the sleep timer on a fifth-generation iPod, select your clock and then choose Sleep Timer from the clock's menu.

A list of intervals appears, from 0 (Off) up to 120 minutes (2 hours). You can select a time amount or the Off setting (at the top of the list) to turn off the sleep timer. After the iPod shuts itself off or you turn it off, the preference for the Sleep Timer is reset to the default status, Off.

Using the stopwatch

You can use a stopwatch with a lap timer on iPod classic, iPod nano, iPod touch, iPhone, and fifth-generation iPod models, which is useful when timing exercises, jogging, race laps, how long it takes the bus to travel across town, or how long your friend takes to recognize the song you're playing. Whatever you want to measure with accurate time to the tenth of a second, the stopwatch is ready for you.

You can use the iPod or iPhone menus and also play music, audio books, and podcasts, while running the stopwatch. When you play video, the stopwatch continues to count as usual; when you switch back to the stopwatch display, the video automatically pauses.

To use the stopwatch on an iPod touch or iPhone, follow these steps:

1. **Select Clock from the Home menu and touch the Stopwatch button along the bottom of the display.**

   A stopwatch appears with Start and Reset buttons and 00:00.00 (minutes, seconds, and fractions of seconds) as the stopwatch counter.

2. **Touch the Start button to start counting.**

   The stopwatch starts counting immediately, while the left button changes to Stop, and the right button changes to Lap.

3. **(Optional) Touch the Lap button to mark each lap.**

   Touch the Lap button to record each lap. Repeat this step for each lap.

4. **Touch the Stop button to stop counting.**

   The counter stops counting. The left button changes to Start, and the right button changes to Reset. You can resume the count from where you left off by touching Start, or you can start the count again from zero by touching Reset.

To use the stopwatch on an iPod classic or iPod nano, follow these steps:

1. **Choose Extras⇨Stopwatch from the main menu.**

   A stopwatch appears with the Play/Pause icon.

2. **Press the Select button to start counting.**

   The stopwatch starts counting immediately.

3. **(Optional) Press the Select button to mark each lap.**

   Press the Select button to record the current lap time while counting resumes accurately for the next lap. Repeat this step for each lap.

4. **Press the Play/Pause button to stop counting.**

   The counter stops counting and the Stopwatch menu appears. The menu now includes the Current Log option to show the lap timings for the stopwatch session. Also included are previous stopwatch session logs. The iPod saves the stopwatch results in a session log for convenience, so you don't have to write them down.

5. **Select Resume to resume counting, or New Timer to start a new stop-watch session.**

   You can resume the stopwatch session from where you left off, or you can start a new stopwatch session.

6. **(Optional) Read your stopwatch logs by choosing Current Log or the date of a previous log in the Stopwatch menu.**

7. **(Optional) Delete your stopwatch logs by choosing Clear Logs in the Stopwatch menu.**

Choosing Display Settings

Your future might be so bright that you gotta wear shades, but your iPod or iPhone display might not be bright enough. From the Settings menu, you can change the timer for the backlight on iPod classic and iPod nano models, and set the brightness of the display on all models, as well as set the contrast of the black-and-white displays of older models. Choose the Settings menu from the main menu of an iPod classic, nano, or older model, or from the Home menu of an iPod touch or iPhone.

Backlight timer

The iPod classic, iPod nano, and older iPods use a display backlight that turns on when you press a button or use the scroll wheel, and then turns off after a short amount of time. On third-generation iPods, the backlight also lights up the iPod buttons.

You can set the backlight on iPod classic and iPod nano models to remain on for a certain interval of time. Choose Settings➪Backlight from the main menu. A menu appears, giving you the options of 2 seconds, 5 seconds, 10 seconds, 15 seconds, 20 seconds, 30 seconds, and Always On. Select one by scrolling to highlight the selection and then press the Select button.

Using the backlight drains an iPod battery; the longer you set the interval, the more frequently you need to recharge the battery.

To set the backlight to *always* be on, choose Always On. If you want the backlight to *always* be off, choose Always Off. If you set it to always be off, the backlight doesn't turn on automatically when you press any button or use the scroll wheel.

Don't be alarmed if your backlight turns itself on at midnight for a brief flash. The iPod is just setting its internal clock. If you find this annoying, turn off the Backlight Timer.

Brightness and contrast

To adjust the brightness for an iPod touch or iPhone, choose Settings⇨ Brightness from the Home menu. The Brightness screen appears with a slider that shows the brightness setting, which ranges from low (a dim sun icon) to high (a bright sun icon). Slide the brightness slider's knob with your finger to the right to increase the brightness (toward the bright sun) and to the left to decrease the brightness (toward the dim sun).

To adjust the brightness for an iPod classic or nano, choose Settings⇨Brightness from the main menu. The Brightness screen appears with a slider that shows the brightness setting, which ranges from low (a quarter-moon icon) to high (a bright sun icon). Scroll clockwise to increase the brightness (toward the bright sun) and counterclockwise to decrease the brightness (toward the moon).

You can also set the contrast of black-and-white iPod displays to make the black characters appear sharper against the display background. (This feature isn't provided on color-display iPod models.)

To adjust the contrast, choose Settings⇨Contrast from the main menu. The Contrast screen appears with a slider that shows the contrast setting, which ranges from low contrast (a black-and-white dot) to high contrast (a full black dot). Scroll clockwise to increase the contrast (toward the black dot) and counterclockwise to decrease the contrast (toward the black-and-white dot).

You might need to adjust the contrast of a black-and-white iPod if a sharp temperature difference freezes or bakes your iPod. If you leave your iPod in your car overnight in the cold or in direct sunlight, the contrast can change so much that you can't see your iPod display. Slowly, allow the iPod to warm up (don't use the oven or microwave) or cool down. Then adjust the contrast.

If you accidentally set the contrast too dark or too light, you can reset it to the halfway point between too dark and too light by pressing and holding the Menu button for at least four seconds.

Wallpaper for your iPod touch or iPhone

Why not wallpaper the back of your display? You can make your iPod touch or iPhone display a stylish background when it is locked. You can also put up photos or other images from your photo library as your wallpaper.

It's not like you'll see it often — the iPod touch or iPhone displays the wallpaper image when you first press the Sleep/Wake button. Once you swipe with your finger to unlock your iPod touch or iPhone, the wallpaper is replaced by the Home menu or whatever application you were last running.

To set the wallpaper on an iPod touch, choose Settings⇨General⇨Wallpaper from the Home menu. On an iPhone, choose Settings⇨Wallpaper.

You can then choose from among stylish built-in wallpaper images by touching Wallpaper. You can also choose from the entire photo library on your iPod touch or iPhone by choosing Photo Library, or choose from a specific photo album in your library. On an iPhone, you can also choose the latest roll from the iPhone's built-in camera by choosing Camera Roll.

Touch a thumbnail to select the image for your wallpaper, or touch Wallpaper in the upper-left corner to return to the Wallpaper menu. After touching an image, your iPod touch or iPhone displays the Move and Scale screen, which lets you optionally pan the image by dragging your finger, and optionally zoom in or out of the image by pinching and unpinching your fingers. Touch the Set Wallpaper button to set the image as your wallpaper or touch Cancel to cancel.

Setting the Combination Lock

You can set a four-digit combination for your iPod classic, iPod nano, iPod touch, iPhone, or fifth-generation iPod that locks the navigation controls, preventing anyone else from selecting content. *Note:* The lock works only when your iPod or iPhone is not attached to a computer.

If you're playing music when you lock your iPod or iPhone, the music continues playing — and you can even use the Play/Pause button to pause and resume playback — but you can't navigate the iPod or iPhone until you provide the combination. You also can't change the volume.

To conserve power, you can force your iPod to go to sleep by pressing the Play/Pause button, but it won't unlock. When it awakes, it remembers everything — including its combination.

Don't bother to call Apple to see whether the company can unlock your iPod or iPhone for you. If you can't attach it to the proper computer or enter the correct combination, your only recourse is to restore the iPod or iPhone to its factory conditions.

To set a combination lock for your iPhone or iPod touch, follow these steps:

1. **Choose Settings⇨General⇨Passcode Lock from the Home menu.**

   The Set Passcode display appears.

2. **Enter a four-number passcode by touching numbers in the calculator-style keypad.**

   If you change your mind, touch the Cancel button to cancel the operation.

3. **Enter the same passcode number again to confirm the passcode.**

   After entering the passcode again, the Passcode Lock menu appears with the Turn Passcode Off, Change Passcode, and Require Passcode options.

4. **Select the Passcode option you want to use.**

   You can turn the passcode off, change it, or set the Require Passcode option to Immediately, After 1 minute, or after several minutes.

5. **When done, touch General to return to the General menu.**

To set a combination lock for your iPod classic or iPod nano, follow these steps:

1. **Choose Extras⇨Screen Lock.**

   The Screen Lock icon appears with your combination lock set to zeros.

2. **Select the first number of the combination by scrolling the click wheel.**

   While you scroll with your iPod, the first digit of the combination changes. You can also press the Previous/Rewind or Next/Fast-Forward button to scroll through numbers.

3. **Press the Select button to pick a number.**

   This sets your choice for the first number and moves on to the next number of the combination.

4. **Scroll to select each number of the combination and then press the Select button to set the number.**

   Repeat this step for each number of the combination. When you pick the last number, the message `Confirm Combination` appears. Repeat Steps 2 and 3 for each number of the combination to confirm it. When you finish confirming the combination, the Lock and Reset options appear.

5. **Choose Lock or Reset.**

   Select Lock to lock the iPod, or Reset to reset the combination to zeros and return to Step 2. To unlock the iPod after locking it, press any button and then repeat Steps 2 and 3 to enter each number of the combination.

Don't forget this combination! Use a four-digit number that is easy to commit to memory.

To unlock a locked iPod or iPhone, you must do one of the following:

- ✔ **Enter the same combination.** After correctly entering the combination, the iPod unlocks and returns to the last viewed screen.

- ✔ **Attach the iPod or iPhone to the computer you used to synchronize it with iTunes.** When you disconnect it after synchronizing with iTunes, the iPod or iPhone is no longer locked.

- ✔ **Restore your iPod or iPhone to its original factory settings.** As I describe in Chapter 20, this erases everything in the process. This is, of course, a measure of last resort.

To set the combination lock on fifth-generation iPods and some older models, follow these steps:

1. **Choose Extras⇨Screen Lock.**

   The Screen Lock menu appears.

2. **From the Screen Lock menu that appears, choose Set Combination.**

   The Enter New Code display appears.

3. **Select the first number of the combination by scrolling the click wheel.**

   While you scroll with your iPod, the first digit of the combination changes in the Enter New Code display. You can also press the Previous/Rewind or Next/Fast-Forward button to scroll through numbers.

4. **Press the Select button to confirm.**

   This confirms your choice for the first number and moves on to the next number of the combination.

5. **Scroll to select each number of the combination and then press the Select button to confirm.**

   Repeat this step for each number of the combination. When you confirm the last digit, the iPod displays the Screen Lock menu.

To lock your fifth-generation iPod with this combination, follow these steps:

1. **(Optional) Start playing music before locking the iPod.**

2. **Choose Extras⇨Screen Lock⇨Turn Screen Lock On.**

   The iPod displays this message:

   ```
   If you forget the code, connect iPod to your computer
   to unlock it.
   ```

   Underneath the message are the Lock and Cancel choices.

3. **Choose Lock.**

When it's locked, an Enter Code display appears on your iPod even while music is playing. A key in the upper-right corner indicates that your iPod is locked.

To change the combination lock for a fifth-generation iPod, choose Extras⇨Screen Lock⇨Change Combination. The Enter Old Code display appears for you to enter the original combination. After entering it correctly, the Enter New Code display appears, and you can enter a new combination.

If you frequently turn your Screen Lock on and off, you might want to add it to your iPod main menu for fast access. To learn how to customize your menu, visit this book's companion Web site.

Chapter 19

Synchronizing Personal Info with Your iPod or iPhone

1 chose an iPod classic for music and videos, but I also find it useful while traveling for viewing the personal information — contacts, appointments, and events — that I manage on my computer. The same is true for the iPod nano I carry into the gym. iPod classic, nano, and older models offer *one-way* synchronization from computer to iPod.

An iPod touch or iPhone lets me go one step further and send and receive e-mail (as I describe in Chapter 16) and use my Safari browser bookmarks (as I show in Chapter 15). I can also add personal info directly to my iPod touch or iPhone, and synchronize that information back with my computer, which is *two-way* synchronization.

You manage your contacts, calendars, e-mail, and Web bookmarks on your computer. If you're a Mac user, you have it easy: You can use the free iCal and Address Book applications to manage your calendars and contacts, the free Mail program to manage e-mail, and the free Safari Web browser to manage your bookmarks. All these applications are provided with Mac OS X. If you're a Windows user, you can choose between Microsoft Outlook (and its accompanying Address Book) and Outlook Express to manage calendars, contacts, and e-mail, and you can use Microsoft Internet Explorer to manage bookmarks.

You use iTunes to synchronize your iPod classic, iPod nano, iPod touch, or iPhone with calendars and contacts on your computer. If you also signed up for Apple's MobileMe service (formerly the .Mac service, now www.me.com), you can automatically keep your iPod touch or iPhone synchronized along with several computers, all at once, with the latest e-mail, bookmarks, calendar entries, and contacts. MobileMe stores all your e-mail, contacts, and calendars on a Web server. You can then keep your iPod touch or iPhone synchronized to your computer wirelessly, from anywhere, without having to connect the device to your computer. Your iPod touch or iPhone can receive pushed data over a Wi-Fi connection as long as the device is awake (the screen is on, or it is connected to your computer or to a power adapter). Changes you make to contacts and calendars at me.com are updated on your device in seconds, and vice versa.

You probably already know how to manage your calendar activities and your contacts on your computer. In fact, you're probably knee-deep in electronic contacts, and your electronic calendars look like they were drawn up in the West Wing. If not, visit the tips section of the author's Web site (`www.tonybove.com`) for tips on using MobileMe, on adding and editing contacts and calendar information on your Mac (with Address Book and iCal) or Windows computer (with Outlook), and on saving and exporting industry-standard calendar and contact files that you can then add to your iPod. I also explain how to use third-party utilities to manage personal information on your iPod.

Synchronizing Contacts and Calendars

To synchronize your iPod or iPhone with contacts and calendars using iTunes, follow these steps:

1. **Connect your iPod classic (or older model), iPod nano, iPod touch, or iPhone to your computer.**

   iTunes launches automatically (if it isn't running already and you haven't changed the sync preferences for the device as described in Chapter 11).

2. **Select the iPod or iPhone name in the Devices section of the iTunes Source pane.**

   If iTunes launched automatically, the iPod or iPhone should already be selected; if it isn't, select it. The iPod or iPhone Summary page appears to the right of the Source pane.

3. **Click the Contacts tab for an iPod classic or iPod nano (or older model), or click the Info tab for an iPod touch or iPhone.**

   The Contacts and Calendars synchronization options page appears for an iPod classic, nano, or older model, as shown in Figure 19-1. The Info page appears for an iPod touch or iPhone, as shown in Figure 19-2, offering not only the MobileMe setup button and Contacts and Calendars sections, but also, if you scroll the page, Mail Accounts, Web Browser information, and Advanced sync options.

Figure 19-1:
Set an iPod nano (or iPod classic or older models) to synchronize with a group of contacts and calendars.

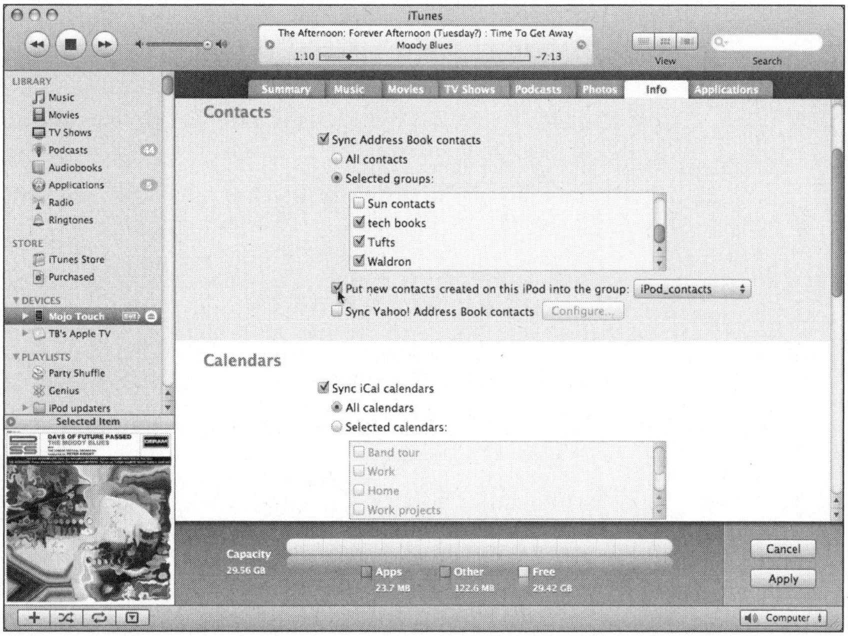

Figure 19-2:
Set an iPod touch (or iPhone) to synchronize all contacts and calendars with iTunes.

4. **Select the option to synchronize contacts.**

   On a Mac: Select the Sync Address Book Contacts check box (refer to Figure 19-1 for an iPod classic, nano, or older model; or see Figure 19-2 for an iPod touch or iPhone). For color-display iPods, you can also select the option to Include Contacts' Photos (these are copied automatically with the iPod touch or iPhone).

   The iPod touch or iPhone Info page also lets you sync with Yahoo! Address Book contacts. If you sync with Yahoo! Address Book, you need to click Configure once to enter your login information.

   On a Windows PC: Select the Sync Contents From option and choose Windows Address Book or Microsoft Outlook from the drop-down menu.

5. **Select the All Contacts option. (Alternatively, select the Selected Groups option and choose which groups to synchronize.)**

   You can synchronize all contacts (as in Figure 19-2) or just selected groups of contacts (such as the iPod_contacts group, as shown in Figure 19-1). To choose groups, select the check box next to each group in the list; scroll the list to see more groups.

   iTunes automatically keeps your contacts synchronized if you make changes on your computer or on your iPod touch or iPhone.

6. **To synchronize calendars, scroll the page and select the Sync iCal Calendars option (Mac) or the Sync Calendars from Microsoft Outlook option (Windows PC).**

7. **Select the All Calendars option. (Alternatively, if you're using iCal with Mac OS X, select the Selected Calendars option and choose the calendars to synchronize.)**

   You can synchronize all calendars, but not selected calendars, with Microsoft Outlook in Windows. (The selected option is grayed out.) With iCal on Mac OS X, you can synchronize all calendars or just those you select. To choose specific calendars, select the check box next to each calendar in the list.

   The iPod touch and iPhone also provide the Do Not Sync Events Older Than *xx* Days option, in which you can set the *xx* number of days.

8. **Select the calendar to use for new events entered into your iPod touch or iPhone (Mac OS X only).**

   If you're using Mac OS X and iCal, you should set the calendar to use for new events you create on your iPod touch or iPhone. Choose a calendar name in the Put New Events Into the Calendar option. When you create a new event on your iPod touch or iPhone (as I describe in Chapter 16) and sync it back to your computer, the new event will appear in this calendar. This affects only new events — events you modify on your iPod touch or iPhone retain their calendar information from before.

Because you can't select individual calendars with Outlook in Windows, this option is grayed out — all events you create on iPod touch or iPhone synchronize with the Outlook main calendar.

9. **Click Apply to apply the changes. (Alternatively, click Cancel to cancel the changes.)**

   iTunes starts to synchronize your iPod or iPhone. Wait until it finishes synchronization before ejecting and disconnecting your iPod or iPhone. The iTunes status pane (at the top) displays the message Sync is Complete.

10. **After iTunes finishes synchronizing, eject the iPod or iPhone by clicking the Eject button next to its name in the Source pane, and then disconnect your iPod or iPhone.**

   Remember to wait for the OK to disconnect message or the iPod or iPhone main menu before disconnecting your iPod or iPhone.

After setting the synchronization options, every time you connect your iPod or iPhone, iTunes automatically synchronizes your device with your calendars and contacts unless you change these options or sync options described in Chapter 11.

If you select a calendar or a group of contacts to be synchronized and later want to remove that particular calendar or group of contacts, deselect the calendar (see the preceding Step 7) or the group (see the preceding Step 5) and then click Apply to resynchronize. iTunes synchronizes only the group of contacts and calendars selected, removing from an iPod or iPhone any that aren't selected.

If you sign up for MobileMe, you can use the service to synchronize your contacts, calendars, and bookmarks by *pushing* them to your computer and to your iPod touch or iPhone, so that the information arrives immediately on your iPod touch or iPhone without having to connect the device to your computer. For example, if you add a contact to the address book on your computer, the new contact is automatically pushed to iPod touch or iPhone as well as to any other computer or device configured with the service.

To learn more about using MobileMe to synchronize contacts and calendars, visit the tips section of the author's Web site (www.tonybove.com).

After you synchronize and otherwise finish using your iPod or iPhone with your computer, be sure to eject the device. If you forget this, the device might not properly close its flash drive or hard drive and become unresponsive, and you might need to reset it.

Managing E-Mail Accounts on Your iPod touch or iPhone

Your iPod touch or iPhone can send and receive e-mail (as I describe in Chapter 16). You use iTunes to synchronize your iPod touch or iPhone with e-mail accounts on your computer.

iTunes can synchronize accounts in Mail and Microsoft Entourage on a Mac running OS X, or in Microsoft Outlook 2003 or 2007 and Outlook Express on a PC running Windows. Your iPod touch or iPhone can use the Exchange ActiveSync protocol to sync e-mail, calendars, and contacts with Microsoft Exchange Server 2003 Service Pack 2 or Exchange Server 2007 Service Pack 1. For many e-mail accounts, the settings automatically appear.

MobileMe, Microsoft Exchange, and Yahoo! Mail e-mail accounts *push* e-mail messages to your computer and your iPod touch or iPhone so that they arrive immediately, automatically. Other types of accounts *fetch* e-mail from the server — you must first select the account in Mail before your iPhone or iPod touch retrieves the e-mail.

To learn how you can use MobileMe to keep your iPod touch or iPhone synchronized with personal information including e-mail messages, visit the tips section of the author's Web site (www.tonybove.com).

If you chose automatic syncing during the iPod touch or iPhone setup (as I describe in Chapter 2), your e-mail accounts should already be set up on your iPod touch or iPhone. If not, you can set iTunes to sync your e-mail accounts automatically, or you can manually set up your e-mail accounts directly on your iPod touch or iPhone. You can also make changes to an e-mail account's settings directly on your iPod touch or iPhone — changes you make are *not* copied to your computer, so you can use different settings on your iPod touch or iPhone without affecting your computer's e-mail.

Need help setting up e-mail accounts on your iPod touch? Try Apple's online Mail Setup Assistant (www.apple.com/support/ipodtouch/mailhelper), which provides step-by-step instructions based on your specific e-mail address.

Synchronizing e-mail accounts automatically

Synchronizing an e-mail account to your iPod touch or iPhone copies *only* the e-mail account setup information; the messages are retrieved by the iPod touch or iPhone over the Internet. Whether the messages in your inbox appear on your iPhone or iPod touch *and* on your computer depends on the type of e-mail account you have and how you've configured it.

To synchronize your iPod touch or iPhone with your e-mail accounts, follow these steps:

1. **Connect your iPod touch or iPhone to your computer.**

   iTunes launches automatically (if it isn't running already).

2. **Select the iPod touch or iPhone name in the Devices section of the iTunes Source pane.**

   If iTunes launched automatically, the iPod touch or iPhone should already be selected; if it isn't, select it. The iPod touch or iPhone summary page appears to the right of the Source pane.

3. **Click the Info tab.**

   The Info page appears for an iPod touch or iPhone. Scroll the page to see Mail Accounts, as shown in Figure 19-3.

4. **Select the Sync Selected Mail Accounts option (Mac), or choose Outlook or Outlook Express from the pop-up menu for the Sync Selected Mail Accounts From option (Windows PC).**

Figure 19-3:
Set an iPod touch (or iPhone) to synchronize with e-mail accounts.

5. **Choose e-mail accounts to sync.**

   To choose accounts, select the check box next to each account in the list; scroll the list to see more e-mail accounts.

6. **Click Sync to finish.**

   You may have to click Apply first if you've made other changes. (Alternatively, click Cancel to cancel the changes.)

   iTunes starts to synchronize your iPod or iPhone. Wait until it finishes synchronization before ejecting and disconnecting your iPod or iPhone. The iTunes status pane (at the top) displays the message Sync is Complete.

iTunes also offers Advanced options at the bottom of the Info page (refer to Figure 19-3) for synchronizing your iPod touch or iPhone from scratch to replace all contacts, calendars, mail accounts, or bookmarks. You can choose which ones to replace by selecting the check box next to each option. iTunes replaces the information once, during the next sync operation. After that operation, these Advanced options are automatically turned off.

Setting up and deleting e-mail accounts manually

You can also enter an e-mail account's settings directly into your iPod touch or iPhone using the on-screen keyboard, without affecting any settings you may already have on your computer for that account. Follow these steps:

1. **Choose Settings⇨Mail, Contacts, Calendars from the Home menu.**

   The Mail, Contacts, Calendars settings screen appears with the Accounts section at the top.

2. **Touch Add Account at the end of the list of accounts in the Accounts section.**

3. **Choose your e-mail account type from the list of account types: Microsoft Exchange, MobileMe, Gmail, Yahoo! Mail, AOL, or Other.**

4. **Enter your account information: name, e-mail address, password, and optional description.**

   Enter information by tapping next to a field's name (such as Name or Address) to display the on-screen keyboard. Use the keyboard to enter the information, and tap Return to move on to the next field.

5. **Touch Save in the upper-right corner to save the account information, or Cancel in the upper-left corner to cancel.**

   For Microsoft Exchange, MobileMe, Gmail, Yahoo! Mail, or AOL: Your iPod touch or iPhone verifies the account, and then lists the account in the Accounts section of the Mail, Contacts, Calendars settings screen.

   For Other: Your iPod touch or iPhone searches for the account on the Internet and displays the New Account settings screen. Tap IMAP (Internet Message Access Protocol) or POP (Post Office Protocol) depending on the type of e-mail account — ask your e-mail service provider if you don't know. Then enter or edit the existing account information (also get this information from your service provider if you don't know):

   - Your e-mail address

   - The host name for your incoming mail server (for example, `mail.example.com`) along with your username and password for incoming mail

   - The host name for your outgoing mail server (for example, `smtp.example.com`) along with your username and password for outgoing mail

   If you touch Cancel, you return to the list of account types (Step 3). Touch Mail in the upper-left corner to return to the Mail, Contacts, Calendars settings screen.

   If the account can't be verified, the message Cannot Get Mail appears, indicating that the username or password is incorrect. Tap OK, and try Steps 4 and 5 again (or touch Cancel to cancel).

To delete an e-mail account from your iPod touch or iPhone, choose Settings⇨Mail, Contacts, Calendars from the Home menu; tap an account in the Accounts section; and then scroll down and tap Delete Account. Deleting an e-mail account from iPod touch or iPhone doesn't delete it from your computer.

Changing e-mail account settings manually

To turn off e-mail accounts or change account settings, choose Settings⇨Mail, Contacts, Calendars from from your iPod touch or iPhone Home menu, and then touch an account in the Accounts section to see that account's settings screen.

Changes you make to accounts are *not* transferred back to your computer when you synchronize, so it's safe to make changes without affecting e-mail account settings on your computer.

The settings are different depending on the type of e-mail account (POP or IMAP) you're using. To adjust e-mail server settings, touch Host Name, User Name, or Password under Incoming Mail Server or Outgoing Mail Server. Ask your network administrator or Internet service provider for the correct settings.

You can turn the account off (without deleting it) by choosing an account and touching the On button next to Account at the top of the screen (touch it again to turn the account back on). After turning an account off, Mail stops checking e-mail or sending e-mail with that account and doesn't display it in the list of accounts until you turn it back on.

Mail offers advanced settings for POP and IMAP accounts as well as for MobileMe, AOL, and other popular accounts. For POP accounts, touch the account in the Accounts section of the Mail, Contacts, Calendars settings screen, and then touch Advanced at the bottom of the account's settings screen to change the following advanced settings:

- ✔ **Use security (SSL) and password settings:** Ask your network administrator or Internet service provider about whether your e-mail account uses SSL; if it does, turn on SSL by touching the Off button so that it changes to On.

- ✔ **Authentication:** Ask your network administrator or Internet service provider about whether your e-mail account requires authentication and which type of authentication; if it does, touch Authentication and choose the method required — MD5 Challenge-Response, NTLM, HTTP MD5 Digest, or Password. (It is beyond the scope of this book to explain all these options — ask your network administrator or Internet service provider.)

- ✔ **Delete from server:** Decide when deleted messages should be removed permanently from your iPod touch or iPhone. Your options are Never, Seven Days, or When Removed from Inbox.

- ✔ **Server Port:** Set your server port, which must be provided by your network administrator or Internet service provider.

For IMAP, MobileMe, AOL, and other popular accounts, touch the account in the Accounts section of the Mail, Contacts, Calendars settings, and then touch Account Info to change the e-mail account's Name, Address, Password, Description, and Outgoing Mail Server. Touch Advanced in the Account Info screen to change the following advanced settings:

✔ **Mailbox Behaviors:** In the Mailbox Behaviors section of the Advanced settings screen, choose

- Drafts Mailbox to set whether drafts are stored on your iPod touch or iPhone, or remotely on your e-mail server. If you store drafts on your iPod touch or iPhone, you can view and edit them even without connecting to the Internet.

- Sent Mailbox to set whether sent messages are stored on your iPod touch or iPhone, or remotely on your e-mail server.

- Deleted Mailbox to set whether deleted messages are immediately trashed or saved remotely on your e-mail server.

✔ **Deleted Messages:** Decide when deleted messages should be removed permanently from your iPod touch or iPhone. Touch Remove and then choose a time. Your options are Never or After One Day, After One Week, or After One Month.

✔ **Incoming Settings:** You can turn SSL on or off and set the Authentication method (as described previously in this section). You can also set an IMAP Path Prefix and change your server port. It is beyond the scope of this book to explain these settings, so ask your network administrator or Internet service provider to help you.

Synchronizing Web Bookmarks with Your iPod touch or iPhone

Don't go on a Web hunt without your bookmarks! You can use iTunes to synchronize your bookmarks — from Safari on a Mac, or from Safari or Microsoft Internet Explorer on a Windows PC — with the Safari Web browser in your iPod touch or iPhone. Follow these steps:

1. **Connect your iPod touch or iPhone to your computer.**

   iTunes launches automatically (if it isn't running already or you haven't changed its sync preferences as described in Chapter 11).

2. **Select the iPod touch or iPhone name in the Devices section of the iTunes Source pane.**

   If iTunes launched automatically, the iPod touch or iPhone should already be selected; if it isn't, select it. The iPod touch or iPhone summary page appears to the right of the Source pane.

3. **Click the Info tab.**

   The Info page appears for an iPod touch or iPhone. Scroll the page to see Web Browser options (refer to Figure 19-3).

4. **Select the option to Sync Bookmarks.**

   On a Mac running OS X, the option is Sync Safari Bookmarks; on a Windows PC, iTunes selects Internet Explorer or Safari for this option, depending on which one is your default browser.

5. **Click Sync to finish.**

   You may have to click Apply first if you've made other changes. (Alternatively, click Cancel to cancel the changes.)

   iTunes starts to synchronize your iPod or iPhone. Wait until it finishes synchronization before ejecting and disconnecting your iPod or iPhone. The iTunes status pane (at the top) displays the message Sync Is Complete.

To learn how you can use MobileMe to keep your iPod touch or iPhone synchronized with your bookmarks, visit the tips section of the author's Web site (www.tonybove.com).

Chapter 20

Updating and Troubleshooting

· ·

In This Chapter

▶ Troubleshooting iPod and iPhone problems

▶ Resetting your iPod, iPhone, or Apple TV

▶ Updating iPod, iPhone, or Apple TV software

▶ Restoring iPod touch, iPhone, or Apple TV settings

▶ Restoring an iPod, iPhone, or Apple TV to its factory condition

· ·

*T*his chapter describes some of the problems that you might encounter with your iPod (iPod classic, iPod nano, iPod touch, or older-model iPod) or iPhone, and how to fix them. If your iPod or iPhone fails to turn on or your computer fails to recognize it, you can most likely find a solution here or directions on how to find more information.

This chapter also covers updating the firmware and software on your iPod or iPhone, and restoring your iPod or iPhone to its factory default condition. (*Firmware* is software encoded in hardware.) Restoring a device is a drastic measure that erases any music or information on the device, but it usually solves the problem if nothing else does.

Taking Your First Troubleshooting Steps

Problems can arise with electronics and software that can prevent an iPod or iPhone from turning on at all or from turning on properly with all its content and playlists. You can also have problems in the connection between your iPod or iPhone and your computer.

Checking the Hold switch

If your iPod classic, nano, or older iPod model refuses to turn on, check the position of the Hold switch — on the top of an iPod classic or older model, or on the bottom next to the dock connection on the iPod nano. The Hold switch locks the iPod buttons so that you don't accidentally activate them. Slide the Hold switch away from the headphone connection, hiding the orange layer, to unlock the buttons. (If you see the orange layer underneath one end of the Hold switch, the switch is still in the locked position.)

The "hold" switch for an iPod shuffle is actually the on-off switch, located on top next to the word OFF. Slide this switch away from OFF to turn on your iPod shuffle.

Rather than a hold button, iPod touch and iPhone models display the message Slide to unlock — slide your finger across this message to unlock your iPod touch or iPhone.

Checking the power

Got power? The battery might not be charged enough. If the battery is too low for normal operation, the iPod or iPhone refuses to turn on. Instead, a low battery screen appears for a short while, and then if no power arrives to save the iPod or iPhone, the icon disappears altogether. At that point, your only choice is to connect the iPod or iPhone to an AC power source, wait for a moment, and then turn the power on by pushing any button on an iPod classic, nano, shuffle, or older iPod model, or by pushing the Home button on the iPod touch or iPhone.

If your source of AC power is your computer, make sure that the computer is on and not set to go to sleep. The Battery icon in the upper right of the display indicates whether the iPod or iPhone battery is full or recharging. For more information about maintaining a healthy battery, see Chapter 1.

If your current-model iPod shuffle doesn't turn on or respond, recharge its battery by first connecting it to its dock and then connecting the dock to the AC power adapter or the USB connection on your computer. First-generation iPod shuffle models connect directly to the USB connection on your computer.

Resetting an iPod classic, iPod nano, or older iPod

This operation resets the operating system of an iPod and restarts the system (similar to resetting the operating system of a computer). It does *not* restore the iPod to its original factory conditions, nor does it wipe anything out — your content and iPod settings remain intact. Sometimes when your iPod gets confused or refuses to turn on, you can fix it by resetting its operating system.

For iPod classic and nano models, fifth-generation video iPods, fourth-generation iPods, iPod mini, and color-display iPods, follow these steps:

1. **(Optional) Connect the iPod to a power outlet by using the AC power adapter.**

   You can reset your iPod without connecting it to power if it has enough juice in its battery. However, if you have access to power, it makes sense to use it because the reset operation uses power.

2. **Toggle the Hold switch.**

   Push the Hold switch to hold (lock) and then set it back to unlock.

3. **Press the Menu and Select buttons simultaneously and hold for at least six seconds or until the Apple logo appears; then release the buttons when you see the Apple logo.**

   The appearance of the Apple logo signals that your iPod is resetting itself, so you no longer have to hold down the buttons.

Release the Menu and Select buttons as soon as you see the Apple logo. If you continue to press the buttons after the logo appears, the iPod displays the low battery icon, and you must connect it to a power source before using it again.

For first-, second-, and third-generation iPod models, follow these steps:

1. **(Optional) Connect the iPod to a power outlet by using the AC power adapter.**

2. **Toggle the Hold switch.**

   Push the Hold switch to hold (lock) and then set it back to unlock.

3. **Press the Menu and Play/Pause buttons simultaneously and hold for at least five seconds until the Apple logo appears; then release the buttons when you see the Apple logo.**

   The appearance of the Apple logo signals that your iPod is resetting itself, so you no longer have to hold down the buttons.

After resetting, everything should be back to normal, including your music and data files.

You can get more information, updated troubleshooting instructions, and links to the iPod repair site by visiting the Apple support site for the iPod (www.apple.com/support/ipod).

Resetting an iPod shuffle

To reset an iPod shuffle, first disconnect it from your computer (if you haven't already done so) and then switch the On/Off switch to the Off position. Wait five seconds and then switch the On/Off switch back to the On position.

To reset the first-generation iPod shuffle, first disconnect it from your computer (if you haven't already done so) and then switch the slider on the back to the Off position. The green stripe under the switch should not be visible. Wait five seconds and then switch the slider back to the Shuffle Songs or Play in Order position.

Resetting an iPod touch or iPhone

You probably won't be too surprised to discover that, on the off chance your iPod touch or iPhone gets confused or refuses to turn on, you can fix it by resetting it and restarting the system — just like all the other iPods out there. This does *not* restore the iPod touch or iPhone to its original factory conditions, nor does it erase anything — your content and settings remain intact.

What's different about the iPod touch and iPhone is the fact that they actually run applications. If your iPod touch or iPhone freezes while running an application (such as Mail or Safari), press and hold the Home button below the screen for at least six seconds, until the application quits. If the iPod touch or iPhone still doesn't respond, turn it off by pressing the Sleep/Wake (On/Off) button on the top, and then press the same button again to turn it back on.

If that doesn't work, press and hold the Sleep/Wake button on the top for a few seconds until a red slider appears on the screen that says "slide to power off," and then slide the slider with your finger. The iPod touch or iPhone powers down. Then press and hold the Sleep/Wake button until the Apple logo appears. The iPod touch or iPhone starts up again.

Finally, if none of these options works, reset the iPod touch or iPhone by pressing and holding the Sleep/Wake button and the Home button at the same time for at least ten seconds, until the Apple logo appears.

After resetting, everything should be back to normal, including your music and data files.

You can get more information, updated troubleshooting instructions, and links to the iPhone repair site by visiting the Apple support site for the iPhone (www.apple.com/support/iphone).

Draining the battery

Certain types of battery-powered devices sometimes run into problems if the battery hasn't drained in a while. In rare cases, an iPod or iPhone might go dark. Try resetting the iPod or iPhone first. If the device still doesn't work, disconnect it from any power source and leave it disconnected for approximately 24 hours. After this period, connect it to power and reset.

If you left the iPod or iPhone in the cold, let it warm up to room temperature before waking it from sleep. Otherwise, the battery may not function properly and a low-battery icon might appear (if the device wakes at all). If the iPod or iPhone doesn't wake from sleep after warming up, reset the device as I describe in the preceding section. Try to keep your iPod or iPhone at room temperature — generally near 68° Fahrenheit (F)/20° Celsius (C). However, you can use the iPod or iPhone anywhere between 50–95° F (10–35° C).

Updating Your iPod, iPhone, or Apple TV

You should always keep your iPod, iPhone, and Apple TV updated with new versions of the software that controls the device. iTunes automatically checks for updates of this software and lets you update your devices without affecting the music or data stored on them.

If you use MusicMatch Jukebox rather than iTunes on your Windows PC, skip this section and see the tips section of the author's Web site (www.toney bove.com).

Make sure that you use the newest version of iTunes. To check for the availability of an updated version for Windows, choose Help⇨Check for iTunes Updates.

If you use a Mac and you enabled the Software Update option in your System Preferences, Apple automatically informs you of updates to your Apple software for the Mac, including iTunes, iCal, and Address Book. All you need to do is select which updates to download and then click the Install button to download them. iTunes includes updates for all generations of iPods and can detect which iPod model you have.

When you turn on your iPod or iPhone, built-in startup diagnostic software checks the device's software for problems and attempts to repair the software if necessary. If the iPod or iPhone finds an issue while it's on, it automatically uses internal diagnostics to repair any damage. You might see a disk scan icon on your iPod or iPhone screen after turning it on, indicating that a problem was fixed. If you see this indicator, update your iPod or iPhone software with iTunes.

Checking the software version

To determine which version of iPod software is installed on your iPod classic, nano, or older iPod, choose Settings⇨About from the iPod main menu. (With first- and second-generation iPods, choose Settings⇨Info.) Similarly, on an iPod touch or iPhone, choose Settings⇨General⇨About. Next to the word Version is information that describes the software version installed.

You can also determine the software version on your iPod or iPhone by using iTunes. Connect the iPod or iPhone to your computer and select the iPod or iPhone in the iTunes Source pane (in the Devices section). The device's summary page appears to the right of the Source pane, and the software version appears next to the Software Version heading at the top of the page.

Updating with newer software

iTunes tells you whether your iPod or iPhone has the newest software installed. Connect the iPod or iPhone to your computer and select it in the iTunes Source pane (in the Devices section). The iPod or iPhone summary page appears to the right of the Source pane, and the Version section of the page tells you whether your iPod or iPhone software is up to date and when iTunes will check for new software. (See Figure 20-1.) You can check for new software at any time by clicking the Check for Update button on the Summary page.

Some iPod models need to be disconnected from the computer temporarily and connected to a power source to finish the process of updating the software. Follow the instructions to disconnect your iPod and connect it to an AC power adapter, if required.

Updating an Apple TV

Apple TV can access the Internet through your wireless or Ethernet network, so the device can automatically check whether new software is available. Apple TV checks the Apple update server on a weekly schedule. When Apple TV detects an update, it downloads the update automatically and displays on your TV the message "An update is available for your Apple TV, do you want to install it now?" Apple TV then displays on your TV two choices: Update Now, or in case you're a procrastinator, Update Later. Choose either option using your Apple Remote.

You don't have to wait for Apple TV to check for an update. You can update Apple TV at any time by choosing Settings⇨General⇨Update Software from the Apple TV main menu using your Apple Remote. To check the software version running in Apple TV, choose Settings⇨General⇨About.

Restoring Your iPod, iPhone, or Apple TV

You can restore any iPod, iPhone, or Apple TV to its original "factory" condition. This operation erases the storage (flash memory in an iPod touch, iPhone, iPod nano, or iPod shuffle; or hard drive in an iPod classic or Apple TV) and returns the device to its factory settings. If you intend to change the computer you're using for synchronizing your iPod or iPhone, you have to restore the device, especially if you're switching from a Mac to a PC as your synchronizing computer.

To replace content that was erased by the restore operation, synchronize your iPod or iPhone from your computer's iTunes library, as I describe in Chapter 11.

Be sure that you back up any important data that you keep stored on an iPod classic, nano, shuffle, or older iPod model enabled as a hard drive. To learn how to enable these devices as hard drives, visit this book's companion Web site.

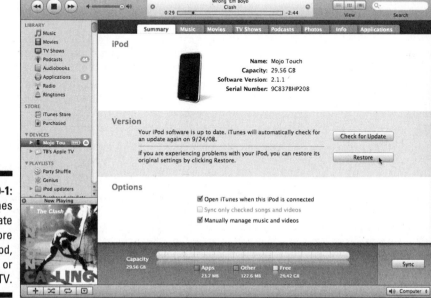

Figure 20-1:
Use iTunes to update or restore your iPod, iPhone, or Apple TV.

Restoring previous iPod touch, iPhone, or Apple TV settings

iTunes provides protection and backs up your iPod touch, iPhone, or Apple TV settings so that you can restore them. iTunes automatically copies from your iPod touch, iPhone, and Apple TV any notes, contact favorites, sound settings, and other preferences when you sync the device to your computer. You can then restore this information if you get a new iPod touch, iPhone, or Apple TV, or if you need to restore the device to factory conditions, and want to use these preferences with the new or restored device.

You can also restore settings from your computer after resetting the settings for an iPod touch or iPhone — not resetting the operating system, as described in "Resetting an iPod touch or iPhone" in this chapter, but resetting your custom settings such as Wi-Fi networks, your Home menu layout, your on-screen keyboard dictionary entries, and your Auto-Lock and Brightness settings. You may want to reset the settings on an iPod touch or iPhone if you're having trouble connecting to a Wi-Fi network. To reset the settings in your iPod touch or iPhone, choose Settings⇨General⇨Reset. You can then choose Reset All Settings, Erase All Content and Settings, Reset Keyboard Dictionary, Reset Network Settings, or Reset Home Screen Layout. When you reset network settings, your list of previously used networks is removed, and Wi-Fi is turned off, disconnecting you from the network. Your Wi-Fi setting and Ask to Join Networks option remains on, so your iPod touch or iPhone may connect to Wi-Fi again (or try to).

To learn more about customizing your iPod touch or iPhone Home menu and resetting your custom settings, visit this book's companion Web site.

You can also restore settings from your computer after resetting the settings for an Apple TV. To reset the settings in your Apple TV, choose Settings⇨General⇨Reset Settings. You can then choose Reset Settings to reset your preferences without changing network configuration or syncing settings.

To restore your settings, connect your new, restored, or reset iPod touch or iPhone to the same computer you used before. For Apple TV, unplug Apple TV from the power outlet, wait 30 seconds, and plug Apple TV back in. iTunes should open automatically (if not, open iTunes). Follow the on-screen instructions to restore your settings.

To delete the backed-up settings for your iPod touch, iPhone, or Apple TV, open iTunes and choose iTunes⇨Preferences (on a Mac) or Edit⇨Preferences (on a Windows PC). Click the Syncing tab; select the iPod touch, iPhone, or Apple TV in the Syncing window; and click Remove Backup. You don't need to connect your iPod touch or iPhone.

Restoring to factory conditions

Restoring an iPod, iPhone, or Apple TV erases its storage and returns the device to its factory settings. To restore an iPod or iPhone, follow these steps for both the Mac and Windows versions of iTunes:

1. **Connect the iPod or iPhone to your computer.**

   iTunes opens automatically.

2. **Select the iPod or iPhone in the Devices section of the Source pane, and click the Summary tab (Settings tab for an iPod shuffle) if it is not already selected.**

   The device's Summary (or Settings) page appears to the right of the Source pane.

3. **Click the Restore button.**

   An alert dialog appears to confirm that you want to restore the device.

4. **Click the Restore button again to confirm the restore operation.**

   A progress bar appears, indicating the progress of the restore operation.

5. **For some iPod models, follow the instructions to disconnect your iPod and connect it to an AC power adapter, if required.**

   You might need to disconnect an iPod temporarily and connect it to an AC power adapter after the restore operation and during the process of updating the software. If you see a message asking you to disconnect the iPod, follow the instructions displayed with the message. You might also need to reconnect the iPod to the computer after this process.

   iTunes notifies you when the restore is finished.

6. **Synchronize your iPod or iPhone with content from your iTunes library.**

   Synchronize your iPod or iPhone with the content in your library, or manually manage your content, as I describe in Chapter 11.

7. **When you finish synchronizing the iPod or iPhone with content and data, eject the device by clicking the Eject button next to its name in the Source pane.**

To restore your Apple TV, press and hold both Menu and Menu down/scroll (-) on the Apple Remote for six seconds or until the status light blinks amber. Then use your Apple Remote to choose a language on the Apple TV, and then choose Factory Restore. You can also restore your Apple TV by using your Apple Remote to choose Settings⇨General⇨Reset Settings from the main menu and then choosing Factory Restore.

Part V
The Part of Tens

The 5th Wave
By Rich Tennant

"The sensor in my running shoe is transmitting information and encouragements to my iPod. Right now, Lance Armstrong is encouraging me to stop running like a girl."

In this part . . .

In this part, you find two chapters chock-full of information.

- ✔ Chapter 21 offers ten common iPod and iPhone problems and their solutions, including how to synchronize your device when your library is too large.

- ✔ Chapter 22 provides 11 tips on using the equalizer to fine-tune the sound, and how to set the volume to the right level

Chapter 21

Ten Problems and Solutions

● ●

In This Chapter

▶ Waking up your iPod or iPhone

▶ Keeping your battery juiced

▶ Restoring your iPod or iPhone to factory condition

▶ Helping your computer recognize your iPod or iPhone

● ●

*U*nfortunately, humans — as well as the machines that they make — are not perfect. Even though I think that the iPod and the iPhone come as close to perfection as possible, at some point, your iPod or iPhone isn't going to work like you expect it to. When that happens, you can turn to this chapter. Here I show you how to fix the most common problems.

How Do I Get My iPod or iPhone to Wake Up?

If your iPod or iPhone doesn't turn on, don't panic — at least not yet. Try the following suggestions to get your iPod or iPhone to respond:

- ✔ **For iPod classic, nano, and all older models (before the sixth generation), check the Hold switch position on top of the iPod.** The Hold switch locks the iPod buttons so you don't accidentally activate them. Slide the Hold switch away from the headphone connection, hiding the orange layer, to unlock the buttons. (There is no hold button on current iPod shuffle models; check the Off switch and slide it to the on position.)

- ✔ **For iPod touch and iPhone models, press the Home button or the Sleep/Wake (On/Off) button on the top.**

✔ **See whether the iPod or iPhone has enough juice.** Is the battery charged? Connect the iPod or iPhone to a power source and see whether it works.

✔ **Reset your iPod or iPhone if it still doesn't turn on.** See Chapter 20 for resetting instructions.

If your iPod shuffle doesn't turn on or respond, recharge its battery by connecting it to the USB connection on your computer. If the iPod shuffle status light blinks orange when you press a button, the buttons are disabled. Press and hold the Play/Pause button for at least three seconds or until the status light blinks green.

How Do I Get My Battery to Last Longer?

You can do a lot to keep your battery going longer (much to the envy of your friends), including the following:

✔ **Press the Play/Pause button to pause (stop) playback.** Don't just turn off your car or home stereo or remove your headphones because if you don't also pause playback, your iPod or iPhone continues playing until the playlist or album ends. When playback is paused, the power-save feature automatically turns off an iPod after two minutes of inactivity. (You have to turn off an iPhone or iPod touch manually.)

✔ **Turn off the iPod or iPhone when you're not using it.** Rather than waiting for for the power-save feature to turn off the iPod, turn it off yourself to save battery time. For iPod classic, nano, and all older models (pre-sixth generation), press and hold the Play/Pause button to turn it off. You can put the iPhone or iPod touch into standby "sleep" mode (in which the display is off and power slows to a tiny trickle) by pressing the Sleep/Wake (On/Off) button on the top. You can turn the iPhone or iPod touch completely off by pressing the Sleep/Wake (On/Off) button again. Note that starting up an iPhone or iPod touch takes quite a bit of power — you should do that while it's plugged into AC power or your computer.

✔ **Turn off backlighting or turn down brightness.** If you don't need to use backlighting to see your display on an iPod classic, iPod nano, or older model, turn it off because it drains battery power if the iPod isn't plugged into a power source. Turn down the brightness on an iPod touch or iPhone by choosing Settings➪Brightness and dragging the brightness slider to the left.

✔ **Turn off Wi-Fi (iPhone or iPod touch).** Turn off Wi-Fi (choose Settings➪ Wi-Fi and touch the On button to turn it off) when you're not browsing the Internet. Also, check e-mail less frequently (see Chapter 16 for details).

✔ **Turn off Bluetooth (iPhone).** On an iPhone, turn off Bluetooth (choose Settings➪General➪Bluetooth and touch the On button to turn it off) if you're not using a Bluetooth device.

✔ **Set the Hold switch to the locked position when you're not using your iPod classic or iPod nano (or older model).** Keep the controls locked so that they don't accidentally get turned on when you're not using your iPod.

How Do I Keep My Scroll Wheel or Touch Display from Going Crazy?

Occasionally, an iPhone or iPod touch display or an iPod scroll wheel stops working properly. If the scroll wheel doesn't scroll or the touch display is no longer sensitive (or is *too* sensitive, reacting crazily), try resetting the iPod or iPhone, as described in Chapter 20. ***Remember:*** Resetting the iPod or iPhone doesn't change its contents. After resetting, the iPod or iPhone should work properly.

Second- and third-generation iPods use a nonmoving scroll wheel that works like a *trackpad* (also sometimes called a *touchpad*) of a laptop computer. The trackpad-style scroll wheel is far better than the first-generation moving wheel, which could be hampered by sand or dirt and had moving parts that could be damaged. However, it has problems of its own: It goes crazy sometimes, and it can be very sensitive (not necessarily to criticism, but to the touch of your finger).

The trackpad-style scroll wheel translates the electrical charge from your finger into movement on the iPod display. If you accidentally use more than one finger, the scroll wheel might misread the signal and skip over selections or go backward while scrolling forward, and so on. ***Maintenance tip:*** If the scroll wheel has excessive moisture on it from humidity or a wet hand, wipe the wheel with a soft, dry cloth.

Don't use pencil erasers, pen caps, or other types of pointers to scroll the scroll wheel. They won't work with trackpad-style scroll wheels, and using them might damage other types of scroll wheels. Also, don't scroll with fingers sporting rings or a hand with a heavy bracelet or similar jewelry because the metals can throw off the sensors in the scroll wheel.

How Do I Get My Computer to Recognize My iPod or iPhone?

If you can't get your computer to recognize your iPod or iPhone, make sure that your iPod or iPhone is securely connected to your computer's USB connection (or FireWire connection in older models), and that it is the *only* device using that connection. If you use a hub to share devices, try not using the hub to see whether it works without the hub.

If you're using MusicMatch Jukebox, go to the tips section of the author's Web site (www.tonybove.com) for more troubleshooting tips.

Also, make sure that your USB or FireWire cable is in good condition for connecting to your computer. For older-model iPods that work with either FireWire or USB, try one type of connection or the other; if one connection type works but not the other, the problem is probably not in your iPod. Try connecting your iPod to another computer by using the same type of connection to see whether the same problem occurs. (Your computer might be to blame.)

If the same type of connection (FireWire or USB) to the other computer works, the problem is most likely your computer's connection or software. If the same type of connection doesn't work, the problem is most likely your cable or connection. You can try a new cable to see whether that works or try the same type of connection with a different computer. Even if these suggestions seem obvious, doing them in the correct order can help you diagnose the problem.

What Are These Strange Icons on My iPod?

If you see an icon of a circle with a diagonal line across it, you should also see the words Do not disconnect. Don't do anything until the iPod finishes its update and displays the main menu or the OK to disconnect message. If this symbol stays on for a very, very long time (like, 20 minutes), try resetting the iPod, as described in Chapter 20.

Other strange icons might appear. When you turn on your iPod, built-in diagnostic software checks the iPod. If the iPod finds a problem when it's turned on, it automatically uses internal diagnostics to check for and repair any damage. You might see a disk folder icon on your iPod screen after turning it on, indicating that a problem was fixed. If this happens, restore your iPod to its factory condition (see Chapter 20) and reload content into it.

If the iPod displays any other strange icon, such as a backward Apple logo, a disk icon with a flashing question mark, or the dreaded disk-with-magnifying glass icon, the device might need to be repaired. If you get the "sad iPod" icon (with a frown and asterisks for eyes) or the folder icon with an exclamation point, try the troubleshooting steps in Chapter 20. If nothing seems to work, the iPod probably needs to be repaired. You can arrange for repair by visiting the Apple support site for the iPod (`www.apple.com/support/ipod`).

How Do I Restore My iPod or iPhone to Its Factory Condition?

Restoring an iPod or iPhone erases its storage and returns the device to its factory condition. You can use iTunes to restore your iPod or iPhone, as I describe in Chapter 20. When finished, resynchronize your content and personal information back to your iPod or iPhone using iTunes.

How Do I Update My iPod or iPhone Software?

To determine which software version is installed on your iPod classic or nano models, press the Menu button until you see the iPod main menu. Then choose Settings⇨About; in earlier versions, choose Settings⇨Info. Look at the version number that describes the software version installed on your iPod.

To see which version of the software you are using in your iPhone or iPod touch, choose Settings⇨General⇨About, and the version number appears next to the Version heading.

You can use iTunes to automatically check which software version you're using and to update or restore your iPod or iPhone (see Chapter 20).

How Do I Synchronize My iPod or iPhone When My Library Is Larger Than Its Capacity?

If you have less space on your iPod or iPhone than content in your iTunes library, you can synchronize selected content only, or you can manually manage music and videos on your iPod or iPhone. You can also select specific photo albums or videos, or select specific playlists, rather than copying everything.

When you synchronize by playlist, you can create playlists exclusively for your iPod or iPhone. You can also limit a smart playlist to a certain size: for example, 3.7GB (for a 4GB iPod nano).

By combining the features of smart playlists (Chapter 10) and synchronizing by playlist (Chapter 11), you can control how much of your iTunes library content is copied to and deleted from your iPod or iPhone.

You can even create multiple iTunes libraries — including sub-libraries, based on your complete library — that you can set up so you can automatically synchronize different iPods. To learn how, visit this book's companion Web site.

You can also keep your iPod or iPhone synchronized to a subset of your library based on ratings. iTunes creates a new playlist specially designed for updating your iPod or iPhone automatically — a smart playlist named "*your iPod/iPhone name* Selection." iTunes decides which songs and albums to include in this playlist by using the ratings that you can set for each song in the iTunes song information, as I describe in Chapter 9.

How Do I Cross-Fade Music Playback with My iPod or iPhone?

You can fade the ending of one song into the beginning of the next one to slightly overlap songs, just like a radio DJ, when you use iTunes — see Chapter 6. The *cross-fade setting* is the amount of time between the end of the fade-out from the first song and the start of the fade-in to the second song.

To cross-fade songs on your iPod nano or iPod classic, choose Settings➪ Playback➪Audio Crossfade and select On.

You can also cross-fade songs when playing your iPod or iPhone through iTunes on your computer. To do this, you must first use iTunes to set the iPod or iPhone to manually manage content, as I describe in Chapter 11. If you're playing songs on an iPod or iPhone that's connected to your computer and also playing songs from your iTunes library (or even on a second iPod or iPhone, both connected to your computer), your songs cross-fade automatically if you set the Crossfade Playback option.

To change the Crossfade Playback option in iTunes, choose iTunes⇨ Preferences (Mac) or Edit⇨Preferences (Windows) and then click the Playback tab. You can then increase or decrease the amount of the cross-fade. See Chapter 6 for details.

For complete instructions on how to play your iPod or iPhone songs through iTunes on your computer, visit this book's companion Web site.

How Do I Decrease Distortion or Set a Lower Volume?

iPod and iPhone models have a tiny but powerful amplifier to deliver audio signals through the headphone connection. The amplifier has a frequency response of 20 hertz (Hz) to 20 kilohertz (kHz), which provides distortion-free music at the lowest or highest pitches, but the amplifier might cause distortion — and possibly ear drum damage — at maximum volume depending on the recorded material.

For optimal sound quality, set the iPod or iPhone volume to no more than three-quarters of the maximum volume and adjust your listening volume by using the volume control or equivalent on your car stereo or portable speaker system. (If no volume control exists, you have no choice but to control the volume from the iPod or iPhone.) By lowering the iPod or iPhone from maximum volume, you give your ears a break and also prevent over-amplification, which can cause distortion and reduce audio quality. See Chapter 14 for details on how to set the iPod or iPhone volume limit and adjust the iPod or iPhone volume.

Chapter 22

Eleven Tips for the Equalizer

· ·

In This Chapter

▶ Adjusting the equalizer on your home stereo

▶ Taking advantage of the iPod equalizer preset

▶ Getting rid of unwanted noise

· ·

*Y*ou play your iPod or iPhone in many environments, but the song that sounds like music to your ears in your car might sound like screeching hyenas when you're on a plane. In this chapter, I show you how to fix most sound problems that occur with iPods and iPhones. Soon, you'll be cruising to the beat all the time — no matter where you are.

To select an iPod equalizer preset with sixth-generation or older-model iPods, choose Settings⇨EQ from the main menu to display a list of presets. With the iPod touch, choose Settings from the home menu, and choose EQ to display a list of presets. With the iPhone, choose Settings from the home menu, choose iPod from the Settings menu, and then choose EQ to display a list of presets. You can then scroll the list of presets and select one. The equalizer is set to Off until you select one of the presets. For more information about using the iTunes and iPod equalizers, see Chapter 13.

Setting the Volume to the Right Level

Before using the equalizer in an iPod or iPhone to refine the sound, make sure the volume of the iPod or iPhone is set to no more than about half or three-quarters of its max so you don't introduce distortion. (See Chapter 14 for details on how to set the volume limit and also adjust volume.) Then set your speaker system or home stereo volume before trying to refine the sound with equalizers.

Adjusting Another Equalizer

When you have the iPod or iPhone connected to another system with an equalizer, try adjusting *that* equalizer first:

- **Home stereo system:** Refine the sound with your home stereo equalizer because that can be set precisely for the listening environment and might offer more flexibility.

- **Car stereos:** The same rule applies as with your home stereo: Adjust the car stereo equalizer when you begin to listen to music on your iPod or iPhone — before adjusting your iPod or iPhone equalizer.

Setting Booster Presets

When playing music with your iPod or iPhone through a home stereo or speakers (without a built-in equalizer) in a heavily draped and furnished room, try using the Treble Booster equalizer preset or create your own equalizer preset that raises the frequencies above 1 kilohertz (kHz). Boosting these higher frequencies makes the music sound naturally alive.

To learn how to create your own equalizer presets, see this book's companion Web site.

Reducing High Frequencies

When using your iPod or iPhone to play music through a home stereo (without a built-in equalizer) in a room with smooth, hard walls and concrete floors, you might want to use the Treble Reducer equalizer preset, which reduces the high frequencies to make the sound less brittle.

Increasing Low Frequencies

If you use high-quality, acoustic-suspension compact speakers, you might need to add a boost to the low frequencies (bass) with the Bass Booster equalizer preset so that you can boogie with the beat a little better. The Small Speakers equalizer preset also boosts the low frequencies and lowers the high frequencies to give you a fuller sound.

Setting Presets for Trucks and SUVs

I have used an iPod in different types of cars, such as a sedan and a four-wheel-drive truck. Trucks need more bass and treble, and the Rock equalizer preset sounds good for most of the music that I listen to. I also recommend using the Bass Booster equalizer preset when using an iPod or iPhone in a truck if the Rock preset doesn't boost the bass enough. In a sedan, an iPod or iPhone sounds fine to me without any equalizer adjustment.

Setting Presets When You're Eight Miles High

When using your iPod or iPhone on an airplane where jet noise is a factor, try using the Bass Booster equalizer preset to hear the lower frequencies in your headphones and compensate for the deficiencies of headphones in loud environments. You might want to use the Classical equalizer preset, which boosts both the high and low frequencies for extra treble and bass. Try the Bose QuietComfort 3 Acoustic Noise Canceling headphones (www.bose.com) for plane travel — they work better than all others I've tried, but they're pricey at about $350. You can still pick up the Bose QuietComfort 2 (previous model) from Amazon.com for $299, which is just as good. While there are many "noise canceling" headphones on the market, you have to try them first in a noisy environment to see whether they work to your satisfaction.

If you're in an unpressurized environment at or above 10,000 feet — such as on a mountain peak — don't try to use an iPod classic or older model iPod. Leave it turned off. Like many laptops, these models use hard drives that can fail if operated at altitudes above 10,000 feet. The drive heads float above the recording surface on a small cushion of air produced by the spinning platters. If the air is too thin to create this cushion, the heads may contact the surface, possibly even damaging it.

Reducing Tape Noise and Scratch Sounds

To reduce the hiss of an old recording or the scratchy sound of songs recorded from a record, reduce the highest frequencies with the Treble Reducer equalizer preset.

Reducing Turntable Rumble and Hum

To reduce the low-frequency rumble you sometimes hear in songs recorded from a turntable as well as that humming sound (when unwanted noise from the turntable's power supply bleeds into the recording), choose the Bass Reducer equalizer preset.

Reducing Off-Frequency Harshness and Nasal Vocals

To reduce a particularly nasal vocal sound reminiscent of Donald Duck (caused by off-frequency recording of the song source, making the song more harsh-sounding), try using the R&B equalizer preset, which reduces the midrange frequencies while boosting all the other frequencies.

Cranking Up the Volume to Eleven

If you want that larger-than-life sound, use the Loudness preset and then jack up the Preamp slider to the max, turn your stereo all the way up, and put your fingers in your ears to protect them. Then consult the DVD *This Is Spinal Tap* or the Spinal Tap fan site at http://spinaltapfan.com.

Index

BUSINESS, CAREERS & PERSONAL FINANCE

0-7645-9847-3

0-7645-2431-3

Also available:
- Business Plans Kit For Dummies
  0-7645-9794-9
- Economics For Dummies
  0-7645-5726-2
- Grant Writing For Dummies
  0-7645-8416-2
- Home Buying For Dummies
  0-7645-5331-3
- Managing For Dummies
  0-7645-1771-6
- Marketing For Dummies
  0-7645-5600-2

- Personal Finance For Dummies
  0-7645-2590-5*
- Resumes For Dummies
  0-7645-5471-9
- Selling For Dummies
  0-7645-5363-1
- Six Sigma For Dummies
  0-7645-6798-5
- Small Business Kit For Dummies
  0-7645-5984-2
- Starting an eBay Business For Dummies
  0-7645-6924-4
- Your Dream Career For Dummies
  0-7645-9795-7

HOME & BUSINESS COMPUTER BASICS

0-470-05432-8

0-471-75421-8

Also available:
- Cleaning Windows Vista For Dummies
  0-471-78293-9
- Excel 2007 For Dummies
  0-470-03737-7
- Mac OS X Tiger For Dummies
  0-7645-7675-5
- MacBook For Dummies
  0-470-04859-X
- Macs For Dummies
  0-470-04849-2
- Office 2007 For Dummies
  0-470-00923-3

- Outlook 2007 For Dummies
  0-470-03830-6
- PCs For Dummies
  0-7645-8958-X
- Salesforce.com For Dummies
  0-470-04893-X
- Upgrading & Fixing Laptops For Dummies
  0-7645-8959-8
- Word 2007 For Dummies
  0-470-03658-3
- Quicken 2007 For Dummies
  0-470-04600-7

FOOD, HOME, GARDEN, HOBBIES, MUSIC & PETS

0-7645-8404-9

0-7645-9904-6

Also available:
- Candy Making For Dummies
  0-7645-9734-5
- Card Games For Dummies
  0-7645-9910-0
- Crocheting For Dummies
  0-7645-4151-X
- Dog Training For Dummies
  0-7645-8418-9
- Healthy Carb Cookbook For Dummies
  0-7645-8476-6
- Home Maintenance For Dummies
  0-7645-5215-5

- Horses For Dummies
  0-7645-9797-3
- Jewelry Making & Beading For Dummies
  0-7645-2571-9
- Orchids For Dummies
  0-7645-6759-4
- Puppies For Dummies
  0-7645-5255-4
- Rock Guitar For Dummies
  0-7645-5356-9
- Sewing For Dummies
  0-7645-6847-7
- Singing For Dummies
  0-7645-2475-5

INTERNET & DIGITAL MEDIA

0-470-04529-9

0-470-04894-8

Also available:
- Blogging For Dummies
  0-471-77084-1
- Digital Photography For Dummies
  0-7645-9802-3
- Digital Photography All-in-One Desk Reference For Dummies
  0-470-03743-1
- Digital SLR Cameras and Photography For Dummies
  0-7645-9803-1
- eBay Business All-in-One Desk Reference For Dummies
  0-7645-8438-3
- HDTV For Dummies
  0-470-09673-X

- Home Entertainment PCs For Dummies
  0-470-05523-5
- MySpace For Dummies
  0-470-09529-6
- Search Engine Optimization For Dummies
  0-471-97998-8
- Skype For Dummies
  0-470-04891-3
- The Internet For Dummies
  0-7645-8996-2
- Wiring Your Digital Home For Dummies
  0-471-91830-X

* Separate Canadian edition also available
† Separate U.K. edition also available

Available wherever books are sold. For more information or to order direct: U.S. customers visit www.dummies.com or call 1-877-762-2974.
U.K. customers visit www.wileyeurope.com or call 0800 243407. Canadian customers visit www.wiley.ca or call 1-800-567-4797.

SPORTS, FITNESS, PARENTING, RELIGION & SPIRITUALITY

0-471-76871-5

0-7645-7841-3

Also available:
- Catholicism For Dummies
  0-7645-5391-7
- Exercise Balls For Dummies
  0-7645-5623-1
- Fitness For Dummies
  0-7645-7851-0
- Football For Dummies
  0-7645-3936-1
- Judaism For Dummies
  0-7645-5299-6
- Potty Training For Dummies
  0-7645-5417-4
- Buddhism For Dummies
  0-7645-5359-3

- Pregnancy For Dummies
  0-7645-4483-7 †
- Ten Minute Tone-Ups For Dummies
  0-7645-7207-5
- NASCAR For Dummies
  0-7645-7681-X
- Religion For Dummies
  0-7645-5264-3
- Soccer For Dummies
  0-7645-5229-5
- Women in the Bible For Dummies
  0-7645-8475-8

TRAVEL

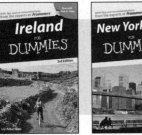

0-7645-7749-2

0-7645-6945-7

Also available:
- Alaska For Dummies
  0-7645-7746-8
- Cruise Vacations For Dummies
  0-7645-6941-4
- England For Dummies
  0-7645-4276-1
- Europe For Dummies
  0-7645-7529-5
- Germany For Dummies
  0-7645-7823-5
- Hawaii For Dummies
  0-7645-7402-7

- Italy For Dummies
  0-7645-7386-1
- Las Vegas For Dummies
  0-7645-7382-9
- London For Dummies
  0-7645-4277-X
- Paris For Dummies
  0-7645-7630-5
- RV Vacations For Dummies
  0-7645-4442-X
- Walt Disney World & Orlando
  For Dummies
  0-7645-9660-8

GRAPHICS, DESIGN & WEB DEVELOPMENT

0-7645-8815-X

0-7645-9571-7

Also available:
- 3D Game Animation For Dummies
  0-7645-8789-7
- AutoCAD 2006 For Dummies
  0-7645-8925-3
- Building a Web Site For Dummies
  0-7645-7144-3
- Creating Web Pages For Dummies
  0-470-08030-2
- Creating Web Pages All-in-One Desk
  Reference For Dummies
  0-7645-4345-8
- Dreamweaver 8 For Dummies
  0-7645-9649-7

- InDesign CS2 For Dummies
  0-7645-9572-5
- Macromedia Flash 8 For Dummies
  0-7645-9691-8
- Photoshop CS2 and Digital
  Photography For Dummies
  0-7645-9580-6
- Photoshop Elements 4 For Dummies
  0-471-77483-9
- Syndicating Web Sites with RSS Feed
  For Dummies
  0-7645-8848-6
- Yahoo! SiteBuilder For Dummies
  0-7645-9800-7

NETWORKING, SECURITY, PROGRAMMING & DATABASES

0-7645-7728-X

0-471-74940-0

Also available:
- Access 2007 For Dummies
  0-470-04612-0
- ASP.NET 2 For Dummies
  0-7645-7907-X
- C# 2005 For Dummies
  0-7645-9704-3
- Hacking For Dummies
  0-470-05235-X
- Hacking Wireless Networks
  For Dummies
  0-7645-9730-2
- Java For Dummies
  0-470-08716-1

- Microsoft SQL Server 2005 For Dummi
  0-7645-7755-7
- Networking All-in-One Desk Referen
  For Dummies
  0-7645-9939-9
- Preventing Identity Theft For Dummie
  0-7645-7336-5
- Telecom For Dummies
  0-471-77085-X
- Visual Studio 2005 All-in-One Desk
  Reference For Dummies
  0-7645-9775-2
- XML For Dummies
  0-7645-8845-1